OHIO FAMILIES
A Bibliography of Books About Ohio Families
by Donald M. Hehir

HERITAGE BOOKS, INC.

Other Heritage Books from
Donald M. Hehir:

*Georgia Families: A Bibliographic Listing of
Books About Georgia Families*

*Kentucky Families: A Bibliographic Listing of
Books About Kentucky Families*

Published 1993 by

HERITAGE BOOKS, INC.
1540-E Pointer Ridge Place,
Bowie, Maryland 20716
(301) 390-7709

ISBN 1-55613-895-4

A Complete Catalog Listing Hundreds of Titles
on Genealogy, History, and Americana
Available Free on Request

TABLE OF CONTENTS

ACKNOWLEDGEMENTS

Particular thanks are due to Karen Ackermann at Heritage Books for her very helpful advice on putting together this and previous works and to Donald Odell Virdin for his always helpful suggestions and encouragement.

INTRODUCTION

The works in this bibliography, covering over 1800 family names, deal with families who have some connection to Ohio. A separate section lists family histories and genealogies on microfilm at the Library of Congress as of mid-1992. A brief introduction to that section of this book may be found on page 333.

By far the largest portion of the works covered in this book can be found at the Library of Congress in Washington, D.C., the National Genealogical Society (NGS) Library Arlington, Virginia, or in the Daughters of the American Revolution (DAR) Library in Washington, D.C.

Also included are a significant number of books from more than 15 historical association and public libraries from Massachusetts to California, including the New York Public Library, the Allen County Public Library (Fort Wayne, Indiana), and the San Francisco Public Library.

The reader should remember that no work of this kind can ever be complete. Many family histories are privately printed and never make their way into large collections. Similarly, many newer works will not have been published, or cataloged, in time for inclusion in this book. It is neither possible, nor practicable, to review individual bibliographies and family histories. For this reason, family names included here may, or may not, be primarily or exclusively associated with Ohio and some works, published in Ohio and included here, may occasionally refer to non-Ohio families, with the only reference to the State being the fact that the bibliography or history was published there. They have been included in order to cast as wide a net as practicable to include all possible references to families with some association with Ohio. By the same token, there may be other published material on Ohio families in works relating to other areas of the country, but they are not included here, because there was no way to identify a relationship to Ohio. Many of the books cited here include references to other states and countries.

This work follows primarily the Library of Congress system for cataloging names, so, for example, a work on "Cline" might be shown under the Library of Congress Family Name Index of "Kline" even when "Kline" is not mentioned in the title or the description of the book.

Similarly, since different libraries catalog publications with slightly differing classification systems, family names may have different spellings, depending on the system being used. As a result, there are listings in this book, which may in some cases be duplicative of other listings, since it was not always possible to determine if references were to the same book, to different editions, or to different books.

In compiling the bibliographies and family histories listed, I have attempted to err on the side of including, rather than excluding, works with similar titles and publication dates where the possibility exists that the books are, at least, different editions of the same work. The Cross-Reference Index will show the page location in this book of all families mentioned in the descriptions in the original source documents.

Among the various sources , the use of the terms "pages" and "leaves" is not always consistent from library to library, so that the same book in different libraries may be shown as having "n" leaves, or "n" pages. Similarly, different catalogers may use different styles to indicate pagination, e. g. 47 pages in one source may appear as 2, 1, 44 pages in a different source, yet both are indicating a total of 47 pages. This adds to the problem of determining whether different catalogers were reporting on the same, or different, editions, of the same book. In the interests of simplicity, I have shortened some lengthy pagination descriptions so that, for example, a pagination description of 5p., 1., 145, (1)p,, 1 l., is generally rendered here as 5, 145, 1p.

Another area, which may present difficulty to the reader, occurs when catalogers indicate the pagination as, for example, 160 [i.e.326]p. Usually this means that there are 160 numbered pages with data on one side only, with the added possibility of additional blank pages and some sheets numbered on both sides. In such cases, the bracketed figure generally indicates the total number of pages in the volume. This, fortunately, does not often occur.

Where different library catalogers have used different descriptions for the same work, the more detailed description has generally been followed, and in some cases, differing descriptions have been combined to provide the user with as much information possible about the content of an individual work.

FORMAT: The description of bibliographies and family histories contained in this volume generally follows the format indicated below:

FAMILY NAME -- Author (Compiler or Editor). *Title. Subtitle.* Place of Publication, Date of Publication. Number of pages or leaves. Additional Descriptive Material, if any. [Source abbreviation. Library catalog or page number in that source for the referenced work may also be given, e. g. L600 shows that the genealogy is listed as item 600 in <u>Genealogies in the Library of Congress</u>].

Note that in the Section dealing with Histories and Genealogies on Microfilm at the Library of Congress, the last item will be the catalog number for the Microfilm which contains the book, chart, or other document cited.

ABBREVIATIONS FOR SOURCES

Each source cited and its abbreviations used in this work are as follows:

A   –   Appendices to KAMINKOW, Marion J. Genealogies In The Library of Congress. Baltimore, Maryland, 1972.

C   –   KAMINKOW, Marion J. Genealogies In The Library of Congress, Second Supplement 1976 – 1986. Baltimore, Maryland, 1987.

D   –   MICHAELS, Carolyn Leopold and Kathryn S. Scott. DAR Library Catalog, Volume One, Second Revised Edition, Family Histories and Genealogies. Washington, DC, 1983.

DC   –   GRUNDSET, Eric B. & Bebe METZ. DAR Library Catalog, Volume Three Centennial Supplement: Acquisitions 1985-1991. Washington, DC, 1992.

DS   –   MICHAELS, Carolyn Leopold and Kathryn S. SCOTT. DAR Library Catalog, Volume One – Supplement – Family Histories and Genealogies. Washington, DC, 1984.

G   –   GENEALOGIES Cataloged in the Library of Congress Since 1986. Washington, DC, 1992.

L   –   KAMINKOW, Marion J. Genealogies In The Library of Congress. Baltimore, 1972. 2. v. A-L and M-Z.

NG   –   National Genealogical Society Library Book List, 5th Edition. Arlington, Virginia, 1988.

NGS   –   National Genealogical Society Library Book List, 5th Edition Supplement. Arlington, Virginia, 1989.

S   - KAMINKOW, Marion J. Genealogies In The Library of Congress Supplement 1972-76. Baltimore, 1976.

VV   - VIRDIN, Donald O. Virginia Genealogies and Family Histories. Bowie, Maryland, Heritage Books, Inc., 1990.

VP   - VIRDIN, Donald O. Pennsylvania Genealogies and Family Histories. Bowie, Maryland, Heritage Books, Inc., 1992.

X   - KAMINKOW, Marion J. A Complement To Genealogies In The Library of Congress. Baltimore, 1981.

XA   - Appendix to KAMINKOW, Marion J. A Complement To Genealogies In The Library of Congress. Baltimore, Maryland, 1981.

In the above sources the numbers following the entry in the text refer to the number assigned to the entry in the source publication and not to a page number:

A - C - G - S - D - DC - DS - L

In other sources, the number refers to the page number where the genealogy or family history is located in that source, e. g. NG123 shows that the genealogy is located on page 123 of the National Genealogical Society Library Book List.

NG - NGS - VP - VV - X - XA

While most citations are to specific library collections, the Virdin Virginia (VV) and Pennsylvania (VP) genealogies are not contained in any specific library. Library collections for entries followed solely by [VV] or [VP] may be in some of the other library collections cited, but the user is advised to consult other libraries and historical and genealogical societies in the states concerned. All other source references are to libraries and genealogical societies located in the Metropolitan Washington, DC area, except those marked "X-_____ or XA-_____".

Note that the entries for the Complement to the Genealogies in the Library of Congress, "X" and "XA", are for genealogies and family histories not in the Library of Congress at the time "A Complement... " was written and many are not in the Library of Congress collection to this date. The coding, at the end of each entry, will indicate if any particular "X" or "XA" entry is also shown as being in the Library of Congress collection. The X is followed, by the initials of the Library, or Libraries, where the genealogy or family history is located, e.g.

[X-FW] Allen County Public Library, Fort Wayne, Indiana

[X-NY/SL] New York Public Library and St. Louis Public Library.

Library Designators used with the "X" (and "XA") entries are:

AH   Alaska Historical Society

BA   Boston Athenaeum

CH   Cincinnati Historical Society

DP   Denver Public Library

FW   Allen County Public Library, Fort Wayne, Indiana

GF   Genealogical Forum of Portland, Oregon

IG   Idaho Historical Genealogical Library, Boise

KY   Kansas State Historical Society, Topeka

LA   Los Angeles Public Library

LI	Long Island Historical Society, Brooklyn, N. Y.
MH	Minnesota Historical Society, St. Paul
NJ	Gloucester County Historical Society, Woodbury, N. J.
NY	New York Public Library
OH	Ohio Historical Society, Columbus
OL	The State Library of Ohio, Columbus
OS	Oregon State Library, Salem
PH	The Historical Society of Pennsylvania, Philadelphia
PP	Library Association of Portland, Oregon
SF	San Francisco Public Library
SP	Seattle Public Library
SL	St. Louis Public Library
SU	Sutro Branch of the California State Library, San Francisco
SW	Spokane Washington, Public Library
WR	Western Reserve Historical Society, Cleveland, Ohio

GLOSSARY

?   -   Indicates a doubt by the compiler of this work as to the accuracy of the material shown in the original source; Also, indicates a conflict in the data shown in different sources when referring apparently to an identical work.

!   -   Indicates a doubt by the compiler of the source document as to the accuracy of the material shown in the referenced work.

c.   -   Circa. (Also, ca.)

ed.   -   Edition.

enl.   -   Enlarged,

l.   -   Leaf (Leaves).

NAS   -   No Author or Compiler shown in the source listing.

NP   -   No Place of Publication indicated.

n.d.   -   No Date of Publication indicated.

numb.   -   Numbered.

p.   -   Page(s).

pni   -   Pagination Not Indicated

rep.   -   Reprint.

rev.   -   Revised, Revision.

sic   _   Used to indicate that the previous word or phrase has been copied precisely from the original source even though apparently misspelled or incorrect.

unp.   -   Unpaged.

v.   -   Volume or Volumes.

ABBOTT -- Abbott, Asa Appleton. *A Pioneer Family of the West.* Cleveland, OH, Evangelical Press, 1926. 4, 81p. [L15; D4].

ABBOTT -- Abbott, Jeanne. *Genealogy and Family Memorial of James S. Abbott.* Columbus, OH, 1905. 31p. [X1-LI].

ABBOTT -- Abbott, Lyndon Ewing. *Genealogy of Lyndon Ewing Abbott, Including Whittecar and Pierce Families.* Dayton, OH, 1985. 100 leaves. NGS gives 106p. 1. Abbott family. 2. Whittecar family. 3. Pierce family. 4. Abbott, Lyndon Ewing, 1910-   -Family. [G1; NGS2].

ABBOTT -- Abbott, Lyndon Ewing. *Genealogy of Lyndon Ewing Abbott (maternal side): Laughlin, Ewing, Fleming, Brinkerhoff, Houghtelin, and Other Families.* Dayton, OH, 1986. unp. [NGS2].

ABEL -- Stock, Harold Thompson. *Florence Abel Stock (Mrs. Arthur James Stock I) and Her Ancestry.* Cleveland, OH, Hampton Corp., 1986. xii, 242p., 12p. of plates. 1. Abell family. 2. Stock, Florence Abel, 1875-1966-Family. G lists under ABELL. [G2; NGS2].

ABELL -- Armstrong, Richard M. *Abel Family History: The Descendants of George Abel, A German Immigrant Who Settled in Loudoun County, Virginia.* Decorah, IA, Anundsen Pub. Co., 1987. 289p. 1. Abel family. 2. Abel, George, 1754-1835-Family. 3. Ohio-Genealogy. [G1].

ABELL -- Woodruff, Howard W., Mrs. *John Wagner and His Twelve Children of Harrison County, Ohio and Surrounding Counties, 1776-1984: Related Families: Abel, Barnhouse, Bentz, Bricker, Feltenberger, Heisler, Hosterman, Smith, Steffy, Winnings.*

Independence, MO, A.L.W. Woodruff, 1984.
102p. C and DC list under WAGNER. 1. Wagner
family. 2. Wagner, John-Family. 3. Abell
family. 4. Barnhouse family. 5. Ohio-
Genealogy. [G2; C727; DC3787].

ABER -- NAS. *Aber Quarterly V. 1 - ;
Winter, 1971.* Columbus, OH, Aber Amily
Association of America. FW has 4 volumes.
[X3-FW/OH].

ACHOR -- Achor, Robert L. *Notes and
Materials on the Achor Family of Western Ohio;
Including Richoux and Borne Families of
Louisiana; Worz, Smithson, and Hickey Families
of Ohio.* Miami, FL, 1970. iv, 51p. 1. Achor
family. 2. Bourne family. 3. Hickey family.
4. Smithson family. 5. Ohio-Genealogy. 6.
Louisiana-Genealogy. [G2].

ACHOR -- Achor, Robert L. *Notes and
Materials on the Achor Family of Western Ohio;
Including Richoux and Borne Families of
Louisiana; Worz, Smithson, and Hickey Families
of Ohio.* Miami, FL, 1988. iv, 51, 69p.
"Including 1986-87 supplement" - Cover. 1.
Achor family. 2. Bourne family. 3. Hickey
family. 4. Smithson family. 5. Ohio-
Genealogy. 6. Louisiana-Genealogy. [G2].

ACKER -- Acker, George H. *Descendants of
Peter Acker and His Wife Jane Sutherland.*
Cleveland, OH, Acker, 1966. 75 leaves.
[D23; X3-FW].

ADAMS -- Crum, Lola Adams and LeAnn E.
(Herron) Brandon. *Adams - Kimbrel Family: A
Century in Kansas.* Dodge City, KS, L. Crum,
Akron, OH, L. E. Brandon, 1986. 191p. 1.
Adams family. 2. Kimbrel family. 3. Kansas-
Genealogy. [G3].

ADAMS -- Adams, Enid Eleanor Smith.
*Ancestors and Descendants of Jeremiah Adams,
1794-1883, of Salisbury, Connecticut, Sullivan
County, New York, Harbor Creek, Pennsylvania
and Vermillion, Ohio, Including Known*

Descendants of His Brother and Sisters; 7th in Descent from Henry Adams of Braintree, MA., Most of Whom Went to Michigan. Victor, Idaho: Ancestor Hunters, 1974. xvi, 716p. [NG14; D41; VP1].

ADAMS -- Plumb, Charles Sumner. *Seth Adams, a Pioneer Ohio Shepherd. (In Ohio Archaeological and Historical Quarterly.)* Columbus, OH, 1934. Vol. XLIII, p.1-34. [L113].

AIKEN -- Cozad, Ralph E. *Annals of the Robert Aiken Family.* Cleveland, OH, Cozad, 1984. 18, 1 pages. [D83].

AKKER -- Achor, Robert L. *Notes and Materials on the Acher Family of South Western Ohio; Including Richoux and Bourne Families of Louisiana; Worz, Smithson, and Hickey Families of Ohio.* Miami, FL, 1970. iv, 51p. [S27].

ALCORN -- Alcorn, Nellie W. *Eli Greenville Alcorn, 2nd Branch of the Kentucky Alcorns.* Columbus, OH, American Text Book,1958. 44p. [X9-FW].

ALDEN -- Alden, Frank Wesley. *John Alden of Ashfield, Mass. and Chautauqua County, New York.* Delaware, OH, Alden, 1909. 84p., plates. [L188: D114].

ALDRIDGE -- Arledge, Tacy A. *History and Descendants of Isaac Arledge.* New Holland, OH, Arledge, 1981. v, 107 leaves. [C8].

ALEXANDER -- Alexander, Robert J. *Four Alexander Families of Wayne County, Ohio.* New Brunswick, NJ, Mega-Ton Publishers, 1975. 234p., 6 leaves of plates, [S41].

ALEXANDER -- Hannum, William H. *The Alexanders of Central Ohio...* Columbus, OH, The Inskeep Prtg. Co. cop. 1929. 24p. [X11-DP/FW/LA/NY].

ALEXANDER -- Powers, Robert B. *A Record of My Maternal Ancestors.* Delaware, OH, Powers, 1966, 1967. 366p. [D152].

ALKIRE -- Phillips, W. Louise & Alkirie, Robert L. *The Alkire Family of Franklin County, Ohio (with roots in WV/VA).* Columbus, OH, W. L. Phillips, R. L. Alkire, 1987. 1 v. NGS shows no volume indication, publisher nor place of publication. 1. Alkire family. 2. Ohio-Genealogy. [G8; NGS2].

ALLEBACH -- Conrad, Mabel A. *Allebach Genealogy, 1719-1953.* Troy, OH, 1953. 34, 1 pages. [X13-PH].

ALLEN -- Allen, Asa W. *Genealogy of the Allen and Witter Families.* Salem, OH, Luther W. Smith, 1872. 251p. [L242; D165].

ALLEN -- Baldwin, Alma H. *Genealogy of the Allen Family from Shenandoah County, Virginia to Ohio, Indiana, Wisconsin, Iowa and Kansas.* 108p. [X15-KH; VV2].

ALLEN -- Begley, Jackson Allen. *A History and Genealogical Record of the Allens, Begleys, and Mays of Kentucky.* Cincinnati, OH, Begley, 1949. 137p. [L292; D181].

ALLEN -- Duty, Allene Beaumont. *The Allen Family: Fourteen generations: The Descendants and Ancestors of Diarca Allen, 1761-1850, of Lebanon, New Hampshire.* Cleveland, OH, 1973. 198p. [S47; NGS2].

ALLEN -- Duty, Allene Beaumont. *The Allen Family: Fourteen generations.* Cleveland, OH, Duty, 1973. 170 leaves. [D184].

ALLGYER -- Baumgartner, Ruth E. (A.) *Of Our Years.* Cleveland, OH, Baumgartner Print., 1971. 29p. [X16-FW].

ALLISON -- Stover, Frances Copeland. *The Benjamin Allison Family from Orange County,*

New York to Gallia County, Ohio. NP, Stover, 1972. xxxxiv(sic), 132p. [D212].

ALSPACH -- Alspach, Clifford F. *The Alspach Family 1738-1967.* Akron, OH, Alspach, 1966. 5, 165p. [D222].

ALSPACH -- Alspach, Clifford. *The Alspach Family 1738-1967; Henry Alspach, 1773-1825, His Forefathers, His Sons and Daughters and Their Descendants.* Akron, OH, 1967. 165p. [X18-NY/FW].

ALTAFFER -- Altaffer, Maurice W. *The Altaffer Family; a Short Chronicle of the Altaffer Family of Virginia and Ohio.* London: Favil Press, 1968. 42p. [L329; VV3].

AMER -- Erzen, Ellen Amer. *AMER, a Family History.* Rocky River, OH, E. A. Erzen, 1988. 135 leaves. 1. Amer family. 2. German-Genealogy. 3. Ohio-Genealogy. [G11].

AMOS -- Amos, Sara McFadden. *Our Amos Family.* Cambridge, OH, Robert W. Amos, 1982. 140p. [DS16].

ANDERSON -- NAS. *Anderson - Overton; A Continuation of Anderson Family Records, Published in 1936, and The Early Descendants of Wm. Overton & Elizabeth Waters of Virginia, and Allied Families, published 1938, by W. P.Anderson.* Cincinnati, OH, The Gibson and Perin Co., 1945. 2, 376p. [L390; VV4].

ANDERSON -- Anderson, Annie W. *Anderson, Longworth, and Howell (Families).* Cincinnati, OH, 1965. pages not numbered. [X21-FW].

ANDERSON -- Anderson, Robert M. *Family Chart of the Andersons of Kent and Ohio.* NP, 1902. 1 Genealogical Chart. [X20-FW/OH].

ANDERSON -- Anderson, W. B. and Luke S. Murdock. *Andersons. This Chart is Prepared* *for Alexander F. Anderson of Cincinnati, Ohio, from the Chart of Edward Lowell Anderson, Prepared in 1912 by William Clayton Torrence from the Scattered Records Available in the Virginias; Amplified from the "Anderson Family Records".* Cincinnati: Gibson-Perrin Co., 1936. Genealogical Table. [L386; VV3].

ANDERSON -- Anderson, W. P. *Anderson Family Records.* Cincinnati, OH, Anderson, 1936. 174p. [L385: D260].

ANDERSON -- Anderson, W. P. *Anderson Family Records.* Cincinnati, OH, Press of W. Schaefer, 1956. 174p. [X21-PP].

ANDERSON -- Fellers, Forest S. *John Wesley Anderson Family, Roney Corners, Wood Co., Ohio.* NP, 1964. 77 leaves. [D269].

ANDERSON -- Lockert, Mildred Anderson. *The Thomas James Anderson Family of Mars, Pennsylvania.* Chagrin Falls, OH, M. A. Lockert, 1984. iii, 47p. [C15].

ANDERSON -- Sallee, Elsie Cox. *The History and Genealogy of the Joshua Anderson-Elizabeth Brearley Anderson Family, with Their Descendants and Related Families.* Springfield, OH, Lagonda Chapter, D.A.R., 1967. 10, 92, ix leaves. [D278; X21-CH/FW].

ANDERSON -- Williamson, Ralph. *Stevenson and Anderson Families of New Jersey, Ohio, Indiana, and Kansas.* Trenton, NJ, Parker Print., 1976. ix, 170p. [X22-FW].

ANDREW -- Andrew, James H. *Historical and Biographical Sketch of One Branch of the Andrew Family, from 1750 -1904.* Cedarville, OH, 1904. 60p. FW lists as ANDREWS. [X23-LI; X23-FW].

ANDREWS -- Andrews, Alfred S. *Andrews, Clapp, Stokes, Wright, Van Cleve Genealogies.* Cleveland, OH, Author, 1970 or 1971. 1 vol.

(various pagings). In pocket: The Wright Bros. by C. H. Gibbs-Smith. [X24-FW/IG/NY/OH/PH].

ANDREWS -- Andrews, Alfred S. *Andrews, Clapp, Stokes, Wright, Van Cleve Genealogies. Rev. ed.* Ft. Lauderdale, FL, Andrews, 1975. 641 p., 2 leaves of plates. [X24-DP/FW/GF/LA/MH/NY/OH].

ANDREWS -- Andrews, Frank H. *William Andrews of Hartford, Conn. and His Descendants in the Direct Line of Asa Andrews of Hartland Conn. and Hartford, Ohio:* Chester Andrews and Descendants. *Rev.* Wells Andrews and Descendants, Nelson Andrews and Descendants, Sherman and Schuyler Andrews. Washington, IL, Tazewell County Reporter, 1938. 69p. X libraries give underscored title. 1. Andrews family. 2. Andrews, William, ca. 1595-1659-Family. [G14; X23-FW/LA/NY].

ANDREWS -- Andrews, Thomas Sheldon. *Ira Andrews & Ann Hopkinson Their Ancestry and Genealogy. Also a Treatise on Marriage and Divorce, and the Laws of Psychol and Constitutional Hereditary Transmission.* Toledo, OH, Blade Printing and Paper Co., 1879. vi, 437p. D gives underscored part of title. [L409; D292].

ANDREWS -- Frandsen, Florence R. *The Frandsen Family of Erie County, Ohio:* Related and Collateral lines, Andrews, Asmus, Fox, Fox - Hess, Fox - Strong, Galloway, Hollister, Lamb, Lemunyon, Reeder. Harbor City, CA, F. R. Frandsen, 1989. v, 334p., 27 leaves of plates. D gives underscored title; no place of publication, 334p. and 20 leaves. 1. Frandsen family. 2. Andrews family. 3. Asmus family. 4. Fox family. 5. Ohio-Genealogy. [G14; DC1321].

ANDREWS -- Read, Helen Hunt. *Descendants of John and Benjamin Andrews: Sons of the Immigrants John and Mary.* Toledo, OH, H. H. Read, Priv. Print., 1982. 18 leaves, 1 leaf of plates. [C16].

ANGEL -- Gruber, Walter Wilbert. *Genealogy of Charles Angel, Sr.* New Philadelphia, OH, Acme Printing Co., 1948. 152p. [D301].

ANNETTE -- Hasson, Ethel (W.). *Annette Family.* Centerburg, OH, 1943. 3 leaves. [X25-OH].

ANSHUTZ -- Anschutz, Philip J. *Sketches of the Anschutz Family, Pennsylvania.* Cincinnati, OH, 1895. 15p. [X25-FW].

ANTISELL -- Wyman, Mary Elizabeth Tisdel. *The Genealogy of the Descendants of Lawrence and Mary Antisell of Norwich and Willington, Conn.* Painesville, OH, Wyman (Columbus, Ohio, Champlain Printing Co.) 1908. 335p. [L470: D325].

ANTL -- Gardiner, Duncan B. *The Antl and Schuerger Families of Metzenseifen.* Lakewood, OH, Family Historian, 1989. 152p., 27p. of plates. 1. Antl family. 2. Scherger family. 3. Germany-Genealogy. 4. Ohio-Genealogy. [G16].

ARCHER -- Archer, Martin B. *Genealogical History of the Archer family, From the Time of the Settlement of James Archer 1st, to the Fifth Generation, 1803-1919.* Columbus, OH, 1919. 100p. [NG16].

ARCHER -- Archer, M. B. *Genealogical History of the Archer Family, from the Settlement of James Archer 1st, to the Fifth generation.* Columbus, OH, F. J. Heer Printing Co., 1919. 50 leaves. [D339].

ARCHER -- Archer, M. B. *Index of Personal Names "Genealogical History of the Archer Family" 1803-1919,... published by the F. J. Heer Printing Co.,* Columbus, OH, 1919. Arlington, VA, Archer, 1976. 77 l. [C19].

ARNOLD -- Rich, Florence E. *John Arnold (Descendants).* Cincinnati, OH, 1941. 5p. [X29-OH].

ARNOLD -- Regan, M. O. *Ancestry and Descendants of John Chambers Arnold and Mary Elizabeth (Shepherd) Arnold.* Wilmington, OH, Author, 1964. 36p. -- *Batten Addition and Corrections.* 1966. 16p. [X29-FW].

ARTHUR -- Fisher, M. Jane Free and Richard P. Arter. *The Arter / Arthur Family of Fountain Valley.* Galion, OH, M.J.F. Fisher, Press printers, 1979. 239p., 1 leaf of plates [C21].

ASMUS -- Frandsen, Florence R. [G22]. See above: ANDREWS. [G14].

ATHEY -- Athey, C. E. *Genealogy of the Athey Family in America 1642-1932.* Marietta, OH,

Athey, 1932. 95p. Index comp. by Altha T. Coons, 1939, bound separately. Index by Altha T. Cooms, 1939, bound separately. [D397].

ATHEY -- Bauer, Fern I. *History of the John and Frances Rue Athey (Athy) Family.* Springfield, OH, Bauer, 1980. 176p. [DC130].

ATKINSON -- Jones, Norman, et al. *Descendants of Samuel Howard and Hannah Rice Atkinson.* Wooster, OH, Atkinson Print., 1972. 34 leaves. [X33-FW].

AUER -- Klein, Stanley S. *Auer Family Tree.* Cincinnati, OH, 1966, 36p. [X35-FW].

AUGENSTEIN -- Biedel, Helan Clark. *Family Records of Mathaeus Augenstein, Buergermeister, Nussbaum Germany, Matthew Augenstein, American Citizen, Washington, Co., Ohio 1812-1897, and Summary of the Augenstein Family Reunion Minutes, 1926-1975.* Zenith, WA, Biedel, 1975. 7, 56 leaves. [D415].

AUKLAND -- Aukland, Willis R. *Some Descendants of Thomas Aukland, 1822-1890 and William Aukland, 1818-1851.* Columbus, OH, 1968. 42p. [X35-FW].

AULD -- Auld, David Walton. *The House of Samuel Auld of Sadsbury -- 4th rev.* Saratoga, CA, Auld, 1980. Genealogical Table originally published as the Family of Auld of White Deer, Deersville & Steubenville, 1975. [C24].

AVERELL -- Avery, Clara A. *The Averell - Averill - Avery Family.* Cleveland, OH, Avery (Evangelical Publ. House), 1914, Vol. I 592p., vol. II 593-1095p. [L651].

AVERELL -- Avery, Clara A. *The Averell - Averill - Avery Family.* Cleveland, OH, Avery (Evangelical Publ. House), 192_. Vol. I 592p, vol. II 593-1095p. [D435].

AVERY -- NAS. *Averys of Groton... A Biographical Sketch of Elroy M. Avery, Reprinted from the History of the City of Cleveland...* NP, 1888. 8, 423-426p. [X36-FW/MH/NY].

AVERY -- Avery, Elroy McKendree. *The Groton Avery Clan.* Cleveland, OH, Elroy Avery, 1912. 2 v. Revision of: The Averys of Groton by Homer De Lois Sweet, 1894. [D436].

AVERY -- Avery, E. M. *Avery Notes and Queries. Qtrly. about History of Groton Averys. no. 1-18; Feb 1898-May 1902.* Cleveland, OH, 1898-1902. 246p. DAR has 1-4, typed copies of nos. 4-18. [L657; NG17; D440].

AYRES -- Ayres, Thomas D. *Ayres Genealogy, Some of the Descendants of Capt. John Ayres of Brookfield, Massachusetts.* Mentor, OH, 1972. 20 leaves. [S100].

AYRES -- Ayres, Thomas D. *Ayres Genealogy, Some of the Descendants of Capt. John Ayres of Brookfield, Massachusetts. 2d ed.* Mentor, OH, 1973. 22, 3 leaves. [S101].

AYRES -- Ayres, Thomas D. *Ayres Genealogy, Some of the Descendants of Capt. John Ayres of Brookfield, Massachusetts. 3d ed.* Mentor, OH, 1976. 42 leaves. [S102].

B

BACKHOUSE -- Backus, William W. *A Genealogical Memoir of the Backus family, with the Private Journal of James Backus, together with His Correspondence Bearing on the First Settlement of Ohio, at Marietta,in 1788. Also, Papers and Correspondence of Elijah Backus, Showing theCharacter and Spirit of the Time During the Revolutionary Period. In two parts: Part I. Genealogical, including Journal of James Backus, and Poems by Miss Sarah Backus. Part II. Historical, Containing Sketches of the First Settlements of Connecticut and Ohio, with Miscellaneous Papers of Historic Interest.* Norwich, Conn., Press of The Bulletin Co., 1889. 385, iv p. [L712].

BACKUS -- Thomas, Edwin Backus. *Backus Manuscript. Tracing Descendants of William Backus, Senior from Saybrook, CT, 1637 to Toledo, Ohio, 1928.* Naples, FL, 1976. pni. [NG17].

BACON -- Vincent, Eli B. *Bacons in Washington County, Ohio and in Makaska County, Iowa.* Marietta, OH, Vincent, 1931. 28p. [X40-FW].

BADGLEY -- Derringer, Joyce Burt. *Genealogy and History of Anthony Badgley.* Alexandria, OH, J. B. Derringer, 1986, 1982. iv, 64 leaves. 1. Badgley family. 2. Badgley, Anthony, fl. 1692-1715-Family. 3. New Jersey-Genealogy. [G28].

BAILEY -- Bailey, David. *Bailey. A Record of the Descendants of John and Hannah Bailey.* New Vienna, OH, 1879. 24p. [X42-FW/LI].

BAILEY -- Bailey, Marshal P. *Bailey Genealogy.* Salem, OH, 1963. 20p. [X43-MH].

BAILEY -- Bailey, Samuel Wayne. *Genealogy of a Bailey Family.* Dayton, OH, Bailey, 1978. 1 v. (various pagings). [C29].

BAILEY -- Dewey, J. Ernest. *Bailey (Bayley) Family Record.* Toledo, OH, n.d. 8, 2p. [X43-WR].

BAIR -- Bair, Harold R. *Some Bair Facts.* Columbus, OH, n.d. 2 vols. [X44-IG/OH].

BAIRD -- Macquin, Hazelle Baird. *The Baird - Brown Family of Mcarthur, Ohio and Their Descendants in Illinois, Michigan and Elsewhere.* NP, Macquin, 1972. iii, 96, 7 l. [D518].

BAKER -- Baker, Edward T. *A Genealogy of Eber and Lydia Smith Baker of Marion , Ohio and Their Descendants.* (Chariton, IA, L. A. Copeland, 1910). 13p. [X44-LI/NY].

BAKER -- Baker, Edwin R. *Ancestry of the Four Children of Oliver Banker and Mary Ellen Rice, Who Came to St. Paul, Minn. in 1885 from Ohio.* St. Paul, MN, 1904. [X44-MH].

BAKER -- Cummings, Joann Schoeppner. *Ancestors and Descendants of Isaac and Jane (Owens) Baker Who Lived Mostly in Monroe, Noble, and Washington County [sic], Ohio.* Marietta, OH, J. S. Cummings, ND, 1985. 180p. [DC159].

BALCH -- Towne, Jeanette C. *Genealogy of Charles & Electra (Covey) Balch, Le Roy Township, Lake County, Ohio.* Painesville, OH, Towne, 1979, 45 l, 3 l. of plates. [C32].

BALDRIDGE -- Shepard, Clarence E. *A Small Twig From The Baldridge Tree: The Descendants of William Baldridge of Russell County, Virginia.* Dayton, OH, C. E. Shepard, 1984. 24, 535, 155, 108p. 1. Baldridge family. 2. Baldridge, William, ca.1770-ca.1825-Family. 3. Kentucky-Genealogy. [G31; C32].

BALDWIN -- Baldwin, Charles Candee. *The Baldwin Genealogy from 1500-1881.* Cleveland, Oh., The Leader Printing Co., 1881. 974p. [L822; NG18].

BALDWIN -- Baldwin, Charles Candee. *The Baldwin Genealogy From 1500.* South Plainfield, N. J., Printed privately by R. M. Baldwin Co., 1967. 84 1. Revision of C.C. Baldwin's The Baldwin Genealogy, from 1500-1881, with extension to 1867, by Robert Mark Baldwin, Jr. [L856].

BALDWIN -- Baldwin, C. C. *The Baldwin Genealogy Supplement.* Cleveland, Ohio, Cleveland Leader Print. 1889. 975-1373p. [L824].

BALDWIN -- Baldwin, Evelyn B. *Notes to "The Baldwin Genealogy... by C. C. Baldwin"... Supplementing the Data on p.780-784 ... of the Baldwin Genealogy.* Washington, DC, 1925. 12p. [X47-FW].

BALDWIN -- Baldwin, Evelyn B. *Baldwin Family Working Papers.* Washington, DC, 1927. 2 vols. [X47-FW].

BALDWIN -- Lynbarger, Donald F. *The Family of Cornelius Baldwin; Notes Gathered From Many Sources.* Cleveland, OH, 1965. 14 1. [L853].

BALES -- Clark, Louise Sheerman. *The Sheerman Family in America, Australia, and England, and Allied Families: Bales, Ramey, West, and Yocom.* Springfield, OH, L. S. Clark, 1984. xiii, 62p. 1. Sherman family. 2. Bales family. 3. Ramey family. 4. Ohio-Genealogy. [G32].

BALL -- Gans, Emmett William. *A Pennsylvania Pioneer: Biographical Sketch, with Report of the Executive Committee of the Ball Estate Association.* Mansfield, OH, R. J. Kuhl, Printer, 1900. 3, 704p. [L868; D563; VP12].

BALL -- Harms, Grace Powell. *James Ball and Colvin Powell Connections: Descendants of James Ball of Maryland, Ohio, and Indiana, and of Colvin and Barbara Ellen Powell of Ohio and Iowa.* Baltimore, MD, Gateway Press, Savannah, GA, 1983. viii, 115p. [C33].

BALL -- Hess, Juanita W. *The Descendants of William Ball of Hope.* Columbus, OH, 1976. 8 leaves. [X48-OH].

BALLINGER -- Harvey, Lanse B. (signed). *The Ballinger Family from 1660 to 1900 Including Seven Generations...* Kenton OH, 1929. 32p. Also includes Haines family. [L907].

BALSLEY -- Bryan, Kathryn A. Polsley. *Genealogy of the Baltzly, Balsey, Polsley Family with Variations of the Name, also a Sketch of Major William Haymond.* Columbus, OH, The F. J. Heer Printing Company, 1939. xx, 380p. [L915].

BALTZER -- Singer, Dorothy. *Statistical Data Pertaining to the Ancestry and Posterity of Balzer, Schatzel, Hoss, Schaefer Families. - Rev.* Springfield, OH, D. Singer, 1982. 186 leaves. [C34].

BALTZLY -- Bryan, Katherine A. Polsely. *Genealogy of the Baltzly - Balsley - Polsley Family.* Columbus, OH, F. J. Heer, 1939. xx, 380p. [D589].

BANCROFT -- Bancroft, Constance Marie. *The Bancroft Tree: 350 Years in America, 1632-1982.* Alliance, OH, Williamsburg Press, 1983. iii, 116p. 1. Bancroft family. [G32].

BANCROFT -- Bancroft-Fant, Mrs. L. *Ethan Bancroft's Ancestory and Descendants.* "Old Northwest" Genealogical Quarterly, Columbus, OH, 1907. V. 10, P. 67-75. [L919].

BANCROFT -- Bancroft-Fant, Luella. *Ethan Bancroft's Ancestory and Descendents (!) thru Lyman Munson Bancroft.* NP, 1932. 8p. [L921].

BANCROFT -- Bancroft-Fant, Luella. *Ethan Bancroft's Ancestory and Descendents (!) More Recent Data and Material on Several Allied Families Has Been Added Here to the Article Published in the 1907 Number of the Old*

Northwest Genealogical Quarterly. NP, 19 p.
[L922].

BANKS -- Richardson, Hope S. *The Heart's
Turning: A Narrative History of the Banks
Family in 19th Century Ohio.* Columbus, OH,
DaySpring Publications, 1988. vii, 76p. 1.
Banks family. 2. Ohio-Genealogy. [G33].

BANNISTER -- Jonasson, Mildred King. *Isaac
King (ca. 1779-1851) of Worcester County,
Maryland, Ross County, Ohio, and Hancock
County, Indiana: Including Allied Families of
Banister, Carr, Dennis, De Shazo, Drury,
Fesler, Frazier, Hasten, Lamb, Lewis, Miller,
Pollock, Vassar, Wachtel, and Others. 1st ed.*
Santa Maria, CA, M.K. Jonasson, 1987. xxiii,
385p. 1. King family. 2. King, Isaac, ca.
1779-1851-Family. 3. Bannister family. 4.
Carr family. NGS lists under KING.
[G33; NGS8].

BARB -- NAS. *Barb Family of Germany, New
Jersey, Shenandoah County, Va., and Ohio.* NP,
1973. 5 leaves. [X51-OH].

BAREKMAN -- Barekman, June B. *Some Bible
Records on a Family Named Barackman,
Barickman, Barkman, Barrackman, Barrickman,
Bergman; from Germany to the Colonies: Va., W.
Va., Ind., Penna., Ky., Ill., Md., and Ohio.*
Chicago, IL, 1967. 19 leaves.
[X52-FW/NY/PH; VV10].

BAREKMAN -- Barekman, June B. *Barrickman -
Barrackman of Crawford County, Pennsylvania.*
Chicago, IL, Genealogical Services &
Publications, 1974. 37, vi p. Records of the
Barkman - Barrackman - Barrickman - Barackman
family from Crawford County, Pennsylvania to
Ohio - Kansas - Nebraska. [S139].

BARGER -- Barger, G. J. P. *Family tree of
William James Barger Born in 1826 in Pike
Co., Ohio (and) Margaret Ann Boggs Born 1833
in Jackson, Co. Ohio. Charted on a Time Scale
by His Grandson, G. J. P. Barger.* Washington,
DC, 1959. 1 v. [L995].

BARGER -- Barger, G. J. P. *Time Scale Chart of Family Tree.* NP, [L996].

BARKER -- Newhall, Barker. *The Barker Family of Plymouth Colony and County.* Cleveland, OH, F. W. Roberts Co., 1947. 102p. [L1007; D632].

BARNES -- NAS. *History of the Descendants of the Families of Ira Barnes, Haram Barnes, Richard Wadsworth, and Levi Prentice of Mustcash Ohio from 1817-1913.* Payne, OH, 1913. 48p. [X54-FW].

BARNES -- Conquer, Belle Barnes. *Barnes and Allied Families of Pennsylvania and Ohio.* Franklin, PA, 1977. [VP13].

BARNES -- Rev. Barnes, Geo. N. *Barnes Genealogies, Including a Collection of Ancestoral, Genealogical and Family Records and Biographical Sketches of Barnes People Collected and Compiled from Authentic Sources by Rev. Geo. N. Barnes.* Conneaut, OH, The Rieg and Smith Printing Co. 1903. v, 221p. [L1029; D650].

BARNES -- Whipple, Florence Julia S. *The Saga of George Newton Barnes.* Conneaut, OH, 1965. 21p. [NG18; X55-FW].

BARNETT -- Martin, J. R. *Our Family Ties; Descendants of John and Thomas Barnett of Virginia-Ohio-Missouri-Iowa.* NP, 1957. 20, ii p. [X55-FW; VV11].

BARNHOUSE -- Woodruff, Howard W., Mrs. [G35]. See above: ABELL. [G2].

BARNS -- Barnes, John Albert. *A History of John Barns and His Descendants.* Greenville, OH, Barnes, Barnes 1927. 81, 7 leaves. [D675].

BARR -- Barr, Mary. *Memoir of Mary Barr (with Genealogy).* Cincinnati, OH, 1863. 10p. [X56-LI].

BARR -- Barr, M. Nathaniel. *Bar, Barr, Barnat, Bernat Heritage: The Family Tree.* Hamilton, OH, American Printing & Lithographing Co., 1985. 199 leaves, 2 1. of plates. 1. Barr family. 2. Bernat family. 3. Polish-Genealogy. [G36].

BARR -- Barr, Wallace. *The Strode - Barr Descendancy.* Amanda, OH, W. Barr, 1988. i, 74p. 1. Stroud family. 2. Barr family. [G36].

BARR -- Barr, William B. *History of the Barr Family Beginning with Great Grandfather Robert Barr, and Mary Wills; Their Descendants Down to the Latest Child.* Hamilton, Ohio, Press of Brown & Whitaker, 1901. 216p. D gives underscored part of title; also Hoboken, NJ, Barr... [L1070; D682].

BARR -- Miller, Dwight, P. *Historical Notes, the Barr - Brisbin - Brown - McTeer - Miller - Moorehead - Osborn Families. Related Thompson Records also included.* Columbus, OH, Miller, 1964. 99, xvii p. [D685].

BARRACKMAN -- Barekman, June B. *The Barrackman - Barkman - Barekman Family of Knox County, Ohio.* Chicago, IL, Barekman, 1961. 1 v. (various foliations). Bound with Barrickman Families of Franklin, Ripley and Marion Counties, Ohio / Researched by Vivian Barrickman Shoemaker; Published by June B. Barekman, 1962 -- The Genealogy of the Jacob Barrickman Family of Pennsylvania, Kentucky to Franklin, Ripley and Marion Counties, Indiana / by Vivian Barrickman Shoemaker; Edited and Additional Research done by June B. Barekman and Hank Jones, 1967. [D687].

BARRACKMAN -- Barekman, June B. *The Barrackman - Barrickman Families of West Virginia.* Chicago, Barekman, 196_. 76, 25 leaves. (5 v. bound together). Some Bible Records on a Family Named Barackman, Barekman, Barickman, Barkman, Barrackman, Barrickman, Bergmann, from Indiana, Illinois, Kentucky,

Ohio / by June B. Barekman, 1967? -- The
Genealogy of Michael Barrickman Family Group
of Fredrick (sic) County Maryland and His Sons
and Grandsons of Pennsylvania, Ohio, Indiana,
Illinois, Iowa, and All Points West and
Northwest / by June B. Barekman, 1968 --
Barrickman - Barrackman of Crawford County,
Pennsylvania / June B. Barekman, 1974.
[D688].

BARRICKMAN -- Lent, Roberta Lee and June B.
Barekman. *Genealogy of the Michael Barrickman
Family Group of Frederick County, Maryland;
and His Sons and Grandsons of Pennsylvania,
Ohio, Indiana...* Chicago, IL, Authors, 1968.
37p. [X57-FW/IG/PH; VP13].

BARRICKMAN -- Barekman, June B. *Barrickman
-Barrackman of Crawford County, Penn.; Records
of the Barkeman - Barrackman - Barrickman -
Barackman Family... Who Moved to Ohio, Kan.
and Neb.* Chicago, IL, Genealogical Services,
1974. 37, 6p. [X57-FW; VP14].

BARRON -- Barron, William P., Jr. *The Barron
Family of Pulaski County, Kentucky, 1798-1975.*
Niles, OH, Family Heritage Publications, 1982.
130p. in various parings. [C39].

BARRON -- Barron, William P., Jr. *The Barron
Family in America, 1635-1883: From Talbot
County, Maryland to All Points West; With
Notes on Related Families, Boyd, Carlton,
Jackson, McBee, McKenzie, Phelps, Vaught,
Whitaker, Walker, Walters.* Fostoria, OH,
Family Heritage Publications, 1984. 671p.
[C39].

BARTENFELD -- Hamel, C. C. *Bartenfeld
Family of Lorain, Oh.* Vertical File in
Library of Congress. [L1099].

BARTHOLOW -- Heller, Ethel Bartholow. *The
Bartholow Family in America.* Tallmadge, OH,
E. M. B. Heller, 1980. __v. C gives:
Contents: V. 1 The story of Michael Barron of
Carroll County, Maryland, His Ancestors and
Descendants and Allied Families. [C40; D709].

BARTON -- French, Ellen Cochran. *Barton & Hummel Family Histories' (sic) Early Pioneers to Pennsylvania, to Tuscarawas Co., Ohio, to Henry County, Iowa.* Fairfield, IA, Tribune Print Co., 1967. [VP14].

BASINGER -- Samsel, Edna F. *Descendants of Christian D. Basinger; A Brief Historical Sketch of Six Generations, 1818-1955.* Columbus Grove, OH, Author, 1955. 56p. [X60-FW].

BASSETT -- McClure, Grace. *The Bassett Women.* Athens, OH, Swallow Press/Ohio University Press, 1985. xvi, 229p. 9 pages of plates. [C41].

BASYE -- Lucas, Ernest Garrett. *From Paris to Springfield. -- The Slave Connection: Basye, Basey.* Springfield, OH, E. G. Lucas, 1983. xxiii, 222p., 1 folded leaf of plates. [C42].

BATCHELDER -- Sterner, Pauline L. *The Ancestry of the Families in Hancock County, Ohio, of Alge, Beck, Schaller, Sterner, and Weitz, and Batcheldor, Clark, Cole, and Lilly in Nelson County, Kentucky.* Findlay, OH, Sterner, 1976. x, 51p. 1. Sterner family. 2. Beck family. 3. Batchelder family. 4. Hancock County(Ohio)- Genealogy. 5. Nelson County(Ky)-Genealogy. C lists under STERNER. D and FW list under BECK. [G39; C666; D866; X70-FW].

BATES -- Bates, Edward C. *The Family of Daniel Bates of Hanover, New Jersey, Cincinnati and Sandusky.* Lakewood, OH, 1949. 7 numb. leaves. [X62-MH/SL].

BATES -- Cunningham, Mildred Bates. *Some Bates from Connecticut, New York, Ohio, and Beyond.* Kalamazoo, MI, 1983. 175p. [C42; NG19].

BATTELL -- Battelle, Lillian S. *Battelle Genealogical Record.* Cincinnati, Press of R. Clark & Co., 1889. 20p. [L1184].

BATTELL -- Hammett, Lillian Battelle. *Battelle Genealogical Record.* NP, 1932. vi, 80 numb. leaves. [L1185].

BATTLE -- Battelle, Lucy Catherine. *A History of the Battelle Family in England.* Columbus, OH, Battelle Press, 1985. ix, 970p. ltd. ed. 100 copies. [C43].

BATZ -- Hamel, Claude Charles. *The Batz - Baats family in America, which Descended from the Ancient French Nobility and which, in France, Produced the Branches of D'Armanthieu, D'Artagnan, De Castelmore, De Duisse, De Mirepoix, and De Trenquellon.* Amherst, Ohio, 1951. 49 leaves. [L1194].

BAUER -- Weiss, Lister O. and Edna M. (Fetzer). *A History and Genealogy of Hans Bauer and His Descendants.* Akron, OH, Mr. & Mrs. Lister Weiss, et al, 1952. 126p. [L1198; D776].

BAUER -- Weiss, Lister O., and Edna M. *Supplement to the Hans Bauer family history, 1952 -1967.* Orrville, OH, 1967. 45 leaves. [L1198].

BAUERSACHS -- Bowersox, Dorothy LeVier. *The Genealogical History of the Bauersachs Family in America, 1665-1988: Johann Line.* Des Plaines, IL, Bauersachs Genealogical Society, 1988. 1 v. (loose-leaf). 1. Bauersachs family. 2. Bauersachs, Johann, b. 1665-Family. 3. Bowersox family. 4. Ohio-Genealogy. [G40].

BAUERSACHS -- Kelly, Beverly Jean. *Jacob Bowersox, Father of Seventeen Children.* Findlay, OH, B.J. Kelly, 1985. 41, 11 leaves, 1 leaf of plates. 1. Bowersox family. 2. Bowersox, Jacob, 1809-1899-Family. 3. Ohio-Genealogy. 4. Bauersachs family. [G41].

BAUGHMAN -- NAS. *Descendants of Christian and Elizabeth Baughman in America.* Columbus, OH, Baughman Association Historical Committee,

(Suburban Printing), 1970.   317p.
[S161; D781].

BAUMES -- Baumes, Ogden. *Our Baumes Family.*
Cincinnati, OH, Gaumer Pub., 1955, 59p.
[X64-FW].

BAUMGARDNER -- Beatty, Winnifred. *The Baumgardner Family.* Urbana, OH, Gaumer Pub.
Co., 1944. 48p.   [D788].

BAUSSER -- NAS. *The Bausser - Bowser Family of Basil, Switzerland, Pennsylvania, and Perry County, Ohio.* NP, 1973. 16 l. [X64-OH; VP15].

BAXTER -- Lynch, Edith & Palette, Anna May. *Baxter Genealogy.* Masbury, OH, Offensend, 1965. 5, 20p. [DC226].

BAXTER -- Turner, Ronald R. *Descendants of Thomas and Esther Baxter.* Cleveland, OH, R. R. Turner, 1982. x, 60p. [C44].

BEACH -- Pabst, Anna C. Smith. *The John Beach and John Wade Families.* Delaware, OH, Pabst, 1960. 227 leaves.   D gives 227, 12 leaves. [L1244; NG19; D814].

BEAL -- Lowe, Blanch Beal. *William Beal, Bucks County, Pa.* Newark, OH, Lowe 1961. xvii, 134p. [D819].

BEAN -- Lochary, Clara Eleanor Henry. *An Appendage to the Bean Family, Hardy County Virginia Line, now West Virginia.* comp. by Josephine Bean Wilson (1917) and Concerning the Archibald Bean Family.   Pomery, OH, Lochary, 1973. 63 leaves. [D837].

BEAN -- Wilson, Josephine Bean. *The Bean Family Hardy County, Virginia Line, now West Virginia.* Athens, OH, Wilson, 1917. 14, 1p. [D842; VV14].

BEANE -- Beane, Wilbur Edward. *The Beane Family.* Columbus, OH, Beane, 1955.   59p. [D844].

BEARD -- Asterino, Virginia Beard. *A Beard Mosaic; David Beard and His Descendants.* Also *Taylor, Neal, Clark, Odum Fam.* Urbana, OH, Asterino, 1973. xx, 371p. D gives underscored title. [NG20; D846].

BEARD -- Beard, John and Glenneta B. Schott. *The Beard Family Geneology (!) The Beard Family from Virginia to Ohio and West.* Dublin, OH, 1975. 1 vol. (various pagings). [X68-OH].

BEARSE -- Meadows, Fanny L. (S.) *Genealogical Record of Austin Bearse (or Bearce) of Barnstable, Cape Cod Mass... 1638-1933; A Record of His Descendants Under Six Different Spellings of the Name...* Cleveland, OH, Author, 1933. 390, 100 leaves. [X68-FW].

BEATTY -- Beatty, Charles Clinton. *Record of the Family of Charles Beatty, Who Emigrated from Ireland to America in 1729.* Steubenville, OH, Press of W. R. Allison, 1873. 120p. [X68-LI/PH].

BEATTY -- Beatty, Charles Clinton. *Record of the Family of Charles Beatty, Whom (sic) Emigrated from Ireland to America in 1729.* Ann Arbor, MI, University Microfilms International, 1979. 120p. 2 leaves of plates. Reprint of 1873 ed. published by the Press of W. R. Allison, Steubenville, Ohio. [C46].

BEAUMAN -- Fairchild, Mary C. Doll. *Memoirs of Colonel Sebastion Beauman and His Descendants with Selections from His Correspondence.* Franklin, OH, Editor Pub. Co. 1900. 3, 137p. Narrative of Some Events in the Lives of Her Maternal Ancestors and Her Own Early Life by Mrs. Eliza Susan (Morton) Quincy, p. 41-119. Life of Rev. Geo. J. L. Doll p.120-137. [L1292].

BEAUMONT -- Duty, Allene Beaumont. *The Beaumont Family, Ancestors and Descendants of*

George Henry Beaumont of Cleveland, Ohio,
U.S.A. and London, England: His Beaumont
Ancestry in London, Hertfordshire,
Bedfordshire, England. Cleveland, OH,
Xerox Reproduction Center, 1980. viii, 198p.
D gives underscored tiled; viii, 198, 8p.
[C46; D858].

BECK -- Beck, W. M. *Beck Family in America.*
Bucyrus, OH, J.W. Hopley, n.d. 37p. [X70-FW].

BECK -- Conover, Charlotte Reeve. *A History*
of the Beck Family together with a
Genealogical Record of the Alleynes and the
Chases from whom they are Descended. Dayton,
OH, Conover, 1907. 3, 255p. D gives
underscored part of title. [L1308; D865].

BECK -- Sterner, Pauline Louisa Beck. [G44].
See above: BATCHELDER. [G39; D866; X70-FW].

BEEBE -- Brown, Sarah. *Bezaleel Beebe.* Mt.
Vernon, OH, 1973. 3 leaves. [X72-OH].

BEEM -- Beem, Nelson. *A History of the*
Michael Beem Family. Loudonville, OH, Beem,
1936. 96p. [L1350; D890].

BEEM -- Beem, Nelson. *Descendants of Michael*
Beem, Sr. and His Wife Elizabeth (Green)
Beem. Loudonville, OH, Author, 1965. 3 vols.
[X72-FW].

BEEMAN -- Fowler, Fred E. *A Short Sketch of*
Some of the Descendants of William Beeman,
1820-1904 and His Wife, Electa Jones Beeman,
1826-1911. Tyrrell, OH, The Compiler, 1937.
62p. WR has 1940 edition, 68p. [X72-OH].

BEESON -- Beeson, Elmer Garfield. *Beeson*
Family History. Dayton, OH, J. J. Scruby,
Print Co., 1952. 124p. [L1359].

BELDEN -- Bailey, Zelma (Belden). *The*
Beldens, Ohio Branch. Washington, DC, 1949.
40p. [L1371].
        -- *Supplement [Belding] The Family*

Records Up-dated to 1977. NP. 1977. 35p. 3 leaves of plates. G lists as BELDING. 1. Belding family. 2. Ohio-Genealogy. [G46; C50].

BELL -- Clark, Arthur H. Jr. *The Bell Family with roots in Northern Ohio. With Narrative of William Bell (1813-1891) and Excepts from the Diaries of Beecher Bell (1814-1915) and a Bit of Genealogy of Allied Families of Cleveland, Webber, Baldwin, Sykes, and Underhill.* Glendale, CA, A. H. Clark, 1981, 103p. [C50].

BELL -- Evans, John James. *The Bell - Hays Families in Greene County, Pennsylvania and Knox County, Ohio, 1750-1987.* Athens, OH, J.J. Evans, 1987. ii, 519p. 1. Bell family. 2. Hays family. 3. Greene County(Pa.)-Genealogy. 4. Knox County(Oh.)-Genealogy. [G46].

BELLINGER -- Ballinger, Dwight Gail. *Ballinger - Pope Family History: Antecedents and Descendants of Louis Warner Ballinger and Pearl Elizabeth Pope Ballinger.* Cincinnati, OH, D.G. Ballinger, 1987. 100 leaves. 1. Bellinger family. 2. Pope family. 3. Ballinger, Louis Warner, 1890-1972-Family. [G47].

BELVILLE -- Taylor, Paul Belville. *Jean Bellville, the Hugenot: His Descendants.* Kettering, OH, Belville Family Association, 1973. xxii, 610p. FW shows under BELLEVILLE. [S193; X75-FW].

BENADUM -- Benadum, Malcolm K. *The Benadum, Benedum, Bennethum Family.* Columbus, OH, Benadum, 1935. 137 l. [L1422; D938].

BENNETT -- Bennett, R. *A Partial Explanation of the Devices in Arms of the Bennett and Burch Families (with) References to the Pedigrees of Each.* Cincinnati, OH, 1869. Broadside. [X77-LI].

BENNETT -- Bennett, Uriah P. *Centennial Family Re-Union of the Descendants of Joshua*

Bennett (b. 1788) Held 1888, Frazesysburg, Ohio. Lee's Summitt, MO, 1888. 26p. [X78-LI].

BENNETT -- Bennett, Stanley O. *The Bennett Family and Related Lines.* Bradenton, FL, Genie Plus, 1986. vii, 300p. 1. Bennett family. 2. Ohio-Genealogy. [G49].

BENNETT -- Smith, Shirley K. *The Bennett - McVicker Family History: The Ancestors and Descendants of Abraham Bennett and His Wife, Jane Cairns, and John McVicker and His Wife Agnes Watson, in Scotland, Pennsylvania, Ohio, Iowa and Other Locations: Covering 300 Years from 1687-1987.* Decorah, IA, Anundsen Pub. Co., 1987. vi, 216, 3p. 1. Bennett family. 2. McVicker Family. 3. Bennett, Abraham, 1834-1886-Family. 4. McVicker, John, 1830-1900-Family. 5. Scotland-Genealogy. 6. Great Britain-Genealogy. 7. Iowa Genealogy. [G49].

BENTLEY -- Brinkerhoff, General Roeliff. *The Bentley Family with Genealogical Records of Ohio Bentleys and Known as the Tribe of Benjamin.* Mansfield, OH, Brinkerhoff, 1897. 20p. D gives 20 leaves. [L1482; D983].

BENTON -- Houser, Madeline Benton. *The Ropes of the Past.* Bethel, OH, Houser, 1976. 179p. [C54].

BENUA -- Benua, Albert Ray. *The Benua History.* Columbus, OH, 1962. 1 v. [L1496a].

BERNAT -- Barr, M. Nathaniel. [G52]. See above: BARR. [G36].

BERRY -- Agricola, David V. *The Berry Family of Lawrence Co., Ky. - 1st ed. -* Lakewood, OH, Agricola, 1978. vi, 64p. 1. Berry family. 2. Lawrence County(Ky.)-Genealogy. [G52].

BERRY -- McCallion, Frances Virginia Dresser. *William Berry.* Wickliffe, OH, McCallion, n.d. 128p. [DC293].

BERRY -- Morris, Barbare Jean McCallion. *William Berry.* Willoughby, OH, Morris, n.d. 161 leaves. [DC294].

BEST -- Best, Nolan Rice. *History of Peter and Mary Best and Their Family. Read before a Reunion of Their Descendants, Held near the Old Homestead in Hilliar Township, Knox County, Ohio on the Centenary of the birth of Peter Best, May 13th, 1897.* NP, Pub. by Direction of the Family, 1897. 15p. [L1535].

BEST -- Bloomquist, C. Ross. *A Best Genealogy.* Binghampton, NY, Bloomquist, 1970. 112 leaves. Bound with a McLeod Genealogy: The Descendants of John McLeod, Immigrant to Central Ohio in 1818 by C. R. Bloomquist, 1969. [D1016].

BICHSEL -- Miller, Betty A. and Oscar R. *Bixel Family History: Descendants of Abraham Bixel and Magdalena Shumacher, 1843-1984.* Berlin, OH, B.A. and O.R. Miller, 1984. 94p. 1. Bixel family. 2. Bichsel family. 3. Bixel, Abraham, 1843-1931-Family. 4. Ohio-Genealogy. [G55].

BIDDLE -- Seaman, Vashti, K. *Family Record of Andrew Biddle, Wife, Christina Cover and 3 Grandsons of Fulton, Co., Ohio.* NP, 1967. 70 leaves. [D1052].

BIGGLER -- Burns, Norman. *The Bigler Family; Descendants of Mark Bigler who Immigrated to America in 1733.* Bradford, OH, 1960. 138p. [L1591].

BIGGS -- Schieltz, Ruth C. *1695-1988: Diller & Biggs and Collateral Families: Biggs, Doll, Fortman, Hartnagel, Homan, Kroger, May, Meyer, Renn, Wiegel, Wellman, Willhoff, Zumbihl.* Versailles, OH, R.C.W. Schieltz, 1988. 318p. 1. Diller family. 2. Biggs family. 3. Germany-Genealogy. 4. Ohio-Genealogy. [G56].

BILL -- Cobb, John L. *Some Ancestors and Descendants of Edward 4 Bill and of Oliver 5*

Bill. Cleveland Heights, OH, Cobb, 1978. 42p., 2 p. of plates. [C61; NG21; D1069].

BINGMAN -- Adams, Ann Newby. *A Branch of the Bingman Family.* Daytona Beach, FL, A.N. Adams, 1985. 21, 3 leaves, 4 leaves of plates. 1. Bingman family. 2. Ohio-Genealogy. 3. Illinois-Genealogy. [G57].

BINKLEY -- Binkley, Jonathan A. *The Binkley Family: Bloyer, Cheeseman, Cromwell, Morgan, Ritenour, Roland, Shaffer, Whisler.* Toledo, OH, J. A. Binkley, 1984. 108p. [C62].

BIRD -- Finley, Rex Bird. *Thomas Bird of Holmes County, Ohio and His Descendants.* Wichita, KS, Advanced Data Reproduction, 1987- . _ v. [DC314].

BISHOP -- NAS. *Bishop Family. Former Residents of Fauquier and Loudon Counties, Virginia, Clark County, Ohio and Elkhart County, Indiana.* NP, n.d. 1 leaf. [X91-OH; VV16].

BISHOP -- Scott, Stanley Richmond. *Family History of John Bishop of Whitburn, Scotland, Robert Hamilton Bishop of Oxford, Ohio, Ebenezer Bishop of McDonough County, Illinois; John Scott of Ireland.* Ann Arbor, MI (D gives: Topeka, KS, Scott, Cambridge, MA, Montgomery) 1951. 148p. [NG21; D1099].

BISSELL -- Bissell, Walter L. *The Family of Martin and Betsey Bissell of Windsor, Ct., and Rootstown, O.* Cleveland, OH, Bissell, 1943. 40p. [D1100].

BIXEL -- Miller, Betty A. [G58]. See above: BICHSEL. [G55].

BLACK -- Black, Howard C. *William Black and His Descendants...of Augusta County, Va., and Clark County, Kentucky.* Cincinnati, OH, 1973. [X93-FW; VV16].

BLACK -- Black, J. G. *Historical Sketch of Samuel and Margaret Black, John and Elizabeth*

Oliver, and Their Families. Wooster, OH, 1903. 20p. [L1652].

BLACK -- Hughes, Raymond Finley. *William Black and His Descendants.* Cincinnati, OH, Hughes, 1973. iii, 143p. [D1116].

BLACK -- Jones, David Tracy. *Pioner Blacks in Adams County, Ohio.* Wabash, Ind., F. H. DeCamp Print. Co., 1963. 13 1. [L1658].

BLACK -- Moulinier, M. E. B. *Genealogy - Memoirs.* Cincinnati, OH, Author, 1955, 169p. Contains also Haviland Genealogy. [X93-FW].

BLACKMORE -- Mallett, Manley W. *Mallett - Blackmore Connection with Notes on Trowbridge.* Columbus, OH, n.d. Various pagings. [X94-FW].

BLAINE -- Blaine, John Ewing. *The Blaine Family; James Blaine, Emigrant, and His Children, Ephraim, Alexander, William, Eleanor...* Cincinnati, OH, The Ebbert & Richardson Co., 1920. 4, 99, 9p. [L1679].

BLANCHARD -- Hunt, Jonathan. *History of the Blanchard Family from 1636 to the Present Time.* Reedtown, OH, 1898. 9p., 11 leaves. [X96-LI].

BLEVINS -- Doup, Mary. *Hampton-Blevins Family History, 1989. Rev. 1990.* __, OH, 1990. 1 v. (unpaged). 1. Hampton family. 2. Blevins family. [G62].

BLINN -- Blinn, Jane. *Blinn Family Data.* Perrysburg, OH, 1966. 50 leaves. [X98-OH].

BLISS -- Scott, Martha Louise. *Zadock Bliss (1788-1853) Keziah Haskins Bliss (1786-1851) Historical and Genealogical Records of Their Descendants to 1951.* Cleveland, 1951. 139p. [L1749].

BLOCH -- Gustafson, Leona L. *Glustave and Emilie Bloch: Early Homesteaders in Gosper*

County, Nebraska. Dayton, OH, 1988. 19p. [NGS3].

BLODGETT -- Mallett, Manley W. *Blodgett - Firman - Eastwood - Brown Connection.* Toledo, OH, 1976. 14p. vi, 3 leaves. [X99-FW].

BLUBAUGH -- Blubaugh, Homer Dennis. *The Blubaugh Families in America.* Westerville, OH, Blubaugh, 1983, ii, 514, 15p. [C68].

BLUE -- Blu, Elmer F. *The Descendants of John Blue of Lancaster Co., Pa., South Carolina, Fleming Co., Kentucky, Ohio, Illinois and Indiana.* NP, 1944. 20, 2 leaves. [D1230].

BLUE -- Blue, William Henry. *Descendants of John Blaw (d.1757 Somerset, Co., NJ).* Columbus, OH, National Blue Family Association, 1984. ii, 311p. 1. Blue family. 2. Blaw, John, d.1757-Family. [G63; C68].

BLUE -- Blue, William Henry. *Descendants of John Blaw (Blue), (d. 1757 Somerset, Co., NJ). - 3rd. ed.* Columbus, OH, National Blue Family Association, 1986. ii, 610p. 1. Blue family. 2. Blaw, John, d.1757-Family. [G63].

BLUE -- Blue, William Henry. *Descendants of John Blaw (Blue), (d. 1757 Somerset, Co., NJ). - 4th. ed.* Mt. Victory, OH, National Blue Family Association, 1990. iv, 1116p. 1. Blue family. 2. Blaw, John, d.1757-Family. [G63].

BLUE -- Haney, Alice Blue. *John Blew (Blue) of Hampton County, Virginia and Some of His Descendants.* Columbus, OH, Haney, 1967. VIII i.e. I, 42 leaves. [D1232; VV18].

BLUM -- Martin, Clara Blume. *Record of Andrew Frederick Blum & Sarah Kline Blum.* Logan, OH, Ohio DAR, 1972. 126 leaves. [D1236].

BOGARDUS -- Bogardus, William Brower. *Anneke Jans-Boggardus and Adam Brouwer:*

Research and Bibliography. Wilmington, OH, Bogardus, 1989. vi, 46p. [DC356].

BOHNING -- Bohning, H. H. *Bohning Family History, Centennial Anniversary, 1843-1916-1943.* Cleveland, OH, 1943. 16p. [X103-FW].

BOIES -- Boies, Robert Brice. *Genealogy of the Boies Family of Pennsylvania and Adjoining Counties in Eastern Ohio and James Boies of Milton, Massachusetts.* McAllen, TX, R. B. Boies, 1986. 141p. [NGS3; DC].

BOLEN -- O'Connor, William G. *Dozens of Cousins.* Trotwood, OH, W.G. O'Connor, 1986. v, 351p. 1. O'Connor family. 2. Bolen family. [G65].

BOLLES -- Steed, Mildred Hoyes. *Ancestry of Demaris Bolles and Descendants of Demaris Bolles and John Mason.* Painesville, OH, Steed, 1968. 48 l. [D1269].

BONE -- Conklin, Carrie Bone. *The Bone Family; an Historical Sketch delivered at The Second Reunion of the Bone Family at Lebanon, Ohio, August 1, 1901.* Lebanon, OH, 1901. 8p. [L1865].

BONHAM -- Bonham, Samuel Jeremiah. *The Bonham Family.* Niles, Ohio, Bonham, 1955. 101 l. D gives: 12, 101 leaves. [L1867; D1296].

BONNELL -- Bonnell, George. *Genealogical Material Relating to the Bonnell Family.* Cincinnati, OH, 1970. 14 l. [X107-CH].

BONNER -- Sale, Walter. *The Bonner Graveyard, History, Drawings, Illustrations, and Some Genalogical Information...* Columbus, OH, Author, 1958. 15 leaves. [X107-CH].

BOOHER -- Booher, Emma R. *Rich Hill, Westmoreland County, Virginia, 1740, to Rich Hill, Noble County, Ohio, 1880.* NP, 1976. 167p. [X108-OH; VV20].

BOONE -- Norris, Madelene Jones. *History of the Artis, Boone, Charlton, Jones, Reynolds, and White Families.* Trotwood, OH, M.J. Norris, 1986. 169p. 1. Boone family. 2. Jones family. 3. Charlton family. 4. Afro-American-Genealogy. [G69].

BOOSINGER -- Taylor, Dorothy Russ. *The Boosinger Family of Ohio.* Alexandria, VA, Taylor, 1980. 221p. [D1331].

BORST -- Garlet, Charles B. *The George and John Borst Families of Ross County, Ohio.* Rockville, MD, Garlet, 198_. 9 1. [C76].

BOUCHER -- Burkhardt, Franklin A. *The Boucher Family (Bowsher, Bauscher, Bausher, Bousher) Comprising a Genealogy of the Branches of Strawn, Harpster, Tedrow, Cryder, Reichelderfer, Critchfield, Stahl, Straw, Brant and Other Families. Descendants of Daniel Boucher of Albany Township, Berks County, Pa. Notes of other Boucher Families. Henry Boucher descendants (Indiana, Pa.) a Brief History of the Ohio Reunions of Kindred Families.* New York, NY, Press of F. E. Burkhardt, 1917. 2, 402p. [L1969; VP25].

BOUIC -- Bouic, Margaret E. M. *Genealogy of the Bouic Family.* Ostrander, OH, 1976. Pagination not shown. [X113-FW].

BOURN -- Dykes, Hannah S. B. *History of Richard Bourne and Some of His Descendants.* Wareham, MA, Dykes, Cleveland OH, Benjamin F. Bourne, 1919. v, 227p. D lists under BOURNE. [L1979; D1380].

BOURNE -- Achor, Robert L. [G75]. See above: ACHOR. 1970. [G2]

BOURNE -- Achor, Robert L. [G75]. See above: ACHOR. 1988. [G2]

BOWEN -- NAS. *Bowen and Hutchfield Families of Carnarvon County, Wales and Ohio.* NP, 1973. 8 leaves. [X115-OH].

BOWER -- Bower, Raymond E. *John Bower and His Descendants.* Chillicothe, OH, 1941. 16p. [X115-MH/NY/OH].

BOWER -- Bower, Ambrose M. *A Directory of the Bower (Bowers) and Swickard Families.* Lebanon, OH, Bower (Brown Pub. Co.), 1935. 64p. [L2022; D1397].

BOWER -- Quayle, Myrna Stanley. *John Paul Bower: His Ancestors and Descendants, 1670-1984.* North Royalton, OH, Quayle, 1985. 692p. [DC396].

BOWERS -- Bowers, Floy. *The Bauer, Bower, Bowers Family.* unk., OH, F. Bowers, 1981. 101p. [C69].

BOWERS -- Casari, Robert B. *A Brief History of the Bowers Family of Ross County, Ohio. - Rev.* Chillicothe, OH, R. B. Casari, 1982. 1 v. various foliations. [C79].

BOWERS -- Waugh, Patricia Lee Russ. *A Waugh Family History: John of Litchfield, Connecticut, Milo and Elizabeth (Kious) of Ohio and Indiana: Allied Lines of Bowers, Bucher, Hamilton, Hopkins, Kious, Minor & Ward.* Kansas City, KS, P. L. Russ Waugh. 1986. 535p. 1. Waugh family. 2. Waugh, John, 1687-1781-Family. 3. Waugh, Milo, 1804-1859-Family. 4. Bowers family. 5. Bucher family. [G77].

BOWERSOX -- Bowersox, Dorothy LeVier. [G77]. See above: BAUERSACHS. [G40].

BOWERSOX -- Kelly, Beverly Jean. [G78]. See above: BAUERSACHS. [G40].

BOWLER -- Bowler, Noadiah Potter. *Record of the Descendants of Charles Bowler, England-1740-America, Who Settled in Newport, Rhode Island.* Cleveland, OH, Forman-Bassett-Hatch Co., 1905. 247, 3, xlvi p. [L2029; NG23; D1406].

BOWSER -- Rendt, Gloria Woods. *The Family History of Jeremiah and Caroline (Williams) Bowser.* Youngstown, OH, Franciscan Fathers, Catholic Pub. Co., 1977. ii leaves, 136p. Contains the Bowser family history by A. B. Bowser. 1. Bowser family. 2. Williams family. [G79].

BOYCE -- Boies, Robert B. *Genealogy of the Boies Family of Pennsylvania and Adjoining Counties in Eastern Ohio & James Boies of Milton, Mass. - 1st. ed.* McAllen, TX, R. B. Boies, Sr., 1986. iv, a-i, 141p. 1. Boyce family. 2. Boies, James, ca.1700-1796-Family. [G79].

BOYD -- NAS. *Proceedings of the First (-Seventh) Boyd Reunion (Convention)...1881-92.* Boyd Association, Historical Committee, Youngstown, OH, Youngstown Publishing Company, 1882-1894. 7 v. in 1. (Titles vary). [L2055].

BOYDSTUN -- Weaver, Gustine Nancy (Courson). *The Boydstun Family.* Cincinnati, OH, Powell & White, 1927. 145p. [L2076; NG23; D1449].

BOYER -- Spenny, Lorin L. *Descendants of Henry Boyer Jr., and Leah Weimer Boyer of Perry County, Ohio.* Dayton, OH, Spenny, 1980. 95 leaves. [C81].

BRADFORD -- Pethtel, Rheba I. *The Pethtel Way.* Columbus, OH, Pinsky Pub. Co., 1986-v.<1 >. 1. Pethtel family. 2. Bradford family. [G81].

BRADFORD -- Sisson, E. P. W. Ed. *Reminiscenses of the Bradford and Waters Families.* Marietta, OH, J. Mueller, 1885. 16p. [X120-FW].

BRADLEY -- Bradley, Alva. *Ancestors and Descendants of Morris A. Bradley.* Cleveland, OH, Priv. Print., 1948. xi, 169p. Two hundred copies printed. [L2139].

BRADLEY -- Ensworth, Sarah Isabelle Bradley. *The Bradleys and Allied Families of South Carolina.* *Also Wilson Family.* Medina, OH, Ensworth Printing Co., 1969. 428p. A & D gives underscored title. [A76; NG24; D1491].

BRADLEY -- Nezbeth, Linda B. *The Byrd Family of Franklin County, Virginia with Bradley, Dillon, and Perdue Lines.* Baltimore, MD, Gateway Press, Warren OH, 1986. xii, 115p. 1. Byrd family. 2. Bradley family. 3. Dillon family. 4. Virginia-Genealogy. [G82].

BRADLEY -- Robertson, Kate B. *Bradley Genealogy.* Columbus, OH, n.d. 1 vol. [X121-OH].

BRANCH -- Paulson, A. E. Branch. *History of the Leading Branch Families in America, 1638-1904.* Ashtabula, OH, Paulson, 1904, 50p. (p. 41-46 blank). [L2171].

BRANCH -- Paulson, A. E. Branch. *History of the Descendants of Peter Branch, 1638-1914.* Visalia, CA, L. C. Branch, (Ashtabula, OH, Ashtabula Printing Co.), 1914. 48, 15p. [L2174; D1522].

BRANDT -- Fellers, F. W. *Brandt Family of the Early Days.* Walhonding, OH, 1965. 9p. [X122-FW].

BRANTHAVER -- Branthoover, W. R. *Branthaver, Branthoover, Brunthaver Genealogy.* Fairport Harbor, OH, Branthoover, 1968. 251p. FW lists under BRANTHOOVER. [D1535; X123-FW].

BRANTHOOVER -- NAS. *Adam Branthoover Family Association Publications... 1916, 1917.* Freemont, OH, 1916-1917. 2 parts in 1. [X123-FW].

BRANTHOOVER -- Branthoover, W. R. *Branthaver, Branthoover, Brunthaver Genealogy, 1748-1970, Additions and Corrections.* Fairport Harbor, OH, 1970. 54p. [X123-FW].

BRANTHOOVER -- Branthoover, W. R. *The Brandhofer, Brauneler, Brenneiser Family from Eastern to Western Pennsylvania.* Fairport Harbor, OH, W. R. Branthoover, 1980. 100p. 1. Branthoover family. 2. Browneller family. 3. Brenneisen family. 4. Pennsylvania-Genealogy. [G84].

BRAYTON -- NAS. *The Francis Brayton Genealogy.* Cleveland, OH, 1976. 21 leaves. [XA1069-WR].

BRAYTON -- Hills, Rev. A. M. *Life and Labors of Mrs. Mary A. Woodbridge...* with an introduction by Lady Henry Somerset, Joseph Cook, John G. Woolsey and Others. Ravenna, OH, F. W. Woodbridge, 1895. 2, 401p. "Genealogy of the Brayton and Mitchell Families". p397-401. [L2203].

BRENEMAN -- Breneman, Charles D. *A History of the Descendants of Abraham Breneman.* Elida, OH, Breneman, 1939. xv, 566p. [D1554].

BRENNEISEN -- Branthoover, W. R. [G86]. See above: BRANTHOOVER, [G84].

BRENNEMAN -- Breneman, Charles D. *A History of the Descendants of Abraham Breneman, Born in Lancaster County, Pennsylvania, December 3, 1774, and Settled Near Edom, Rockingham County, Virginia, in 1770, or soon after, and a Complete Genealogical Register with Biographies of Many of His Descendants, from the Earliest Available Records to the Present Time, Giving Dates in Three Centuries.* Elida, OH, 1939. [VV23: VP29].

BRENT -- Crawford, Andrew. *Family Lineage of Brent, Crawford, Curd & Perkins for C.A.R., D.A.R., S.A.R., and Colonial Dames of the XVII Century to Hugh Brent, 1620-1671, Nicholas Perkins, 1614-1656, Edward Curd, ? -1742.* Fairborn, OH, A. Crawford, 1988. iv, 85

leaves. 1. Brent family. 2. Crawford family.
3. Curd family. 4. Perkins family. 5. Brent,
Hugh, ca.1620-1671-Family. 6. Perkins,
Nicholas, 1614-1656-Family. 7. Curd, Edward
d.1742-Family. [G86].

BRENTLINGER -- Brentlinger, Ellsworth, et
al. *Genealogy and Biography of the Brentlinger
Family, 1927.* Dayton, OH, Press of the
Groneweg Printing Co., 1927. 168p.
[L2234].

BRETZ -- Bretz, J. Harlen. *An Incomplete
Genealogy of the Family of John Bretz of
Fairfield, Co. Ohio, With a Partial History of
One Line of Descent in This Family.* Chicago,
IL, 1949. 65 leaves. [L2241; NG24].

BREWER -- Scholz, L. E. L. B. *Family
History of Peter Brewer Family, 1777-1970.*
Dayton, OH, 31p. [X126-FW].

BREWSTER -- Brewster, Carl M. *A Genealogy
of the Eight Brewster Cousins of Northern Ohio
and Their Descendants.* Ann Arbor, MI, Edwards
Brothers, 1937. xiii, 55p. Limited edition:
200 copies. [L2249; D1568].

BRICKER -- Bailey, Marshal P. *The Bricker
Genealogy.* Salem, OH, 1962. 23p.
[X127-MH].

BRICKER -- Gardner, Frank W. *Bricker and
Allied Families King - Timmons, Madison
County, Ohio.* Columbus, OH, 1939. 1 vol
(various pagings). Xerox copy of material in
the Zook papers: data from court, military,
census, pension, and official records.
[X127-Library not given].

BRIDGE -- Herman, Berthenia Davis. *A
Genealogy of the Davis, Kimbrough, Flewellen,
Bridges, McArthur, Henry, Butler, Wimberly,
and Lang (Lange) Families.* London, OH, B.
D. Herman, 1988. 83p. 1. Davis family. 2.
Kimbrough family. 3. Bridge family. 4.
Afro-American Genealogy. [G88].

BRIDGE -- Karrer, Annie May Hurd. *The Bridge Family of New Jersey, Ohio, and Wisconsin.* Port Republic, MD, Karrer, 1956. 39 leaves. [D1581; X127-FW].

BRIGGS -- Briggs, Samuel. *A Partial Record of the Descendants of Walter Briggs of Westchester, N.Y.* to which is added *Some Account of His Ancestry, Collateral Branches, etc.* Cleveland, OH, Fairbanks, Briggs & Co., 1878. 50, 1p. D gives underscored part of title. [L2261; D1591].

BRIGGS -- Briggs, Sam. *The Archives of the Briggs Family.* Cleveland, OH, T.C. Schenck & Co., 1880. xiv, 264, 1p. [L2262].

BRIGHAM -- Gibson, Nancy Brigham. *A Brigham Family History: Descendants of Thomas Brigham, the Immigrant of The Massachusetts Bay Colony, in Fulton, Ohio.* Rancho Palos Verdes, CA, N.B. Gibson, 1987. 199 leaves. [DC456].

BRIGHT -- Huffman, Hazel Wise. *Looking Back: A Family History and Genealogy of and by Hazel Wise Huffman, Related Families: Bright, Buckingham, Cole, Egbert, Jaqua, Jenkins, McCrea, Nicewanner, Opp, Webster, Weldon, Wise, Wisely.* __, Ohio. H, W, Huffman, 1985. ix, 107p. 1. Wise family. 2. Bright family. 3. Buckingham family. 4. Pennsylvania-Genealogy. 5. Ohio-Genealogy. C lists under WISE. [G88; C761].

BRINEY -- Hudson, Roland V. *My Wife's Ascendants: The Briney and the McCracken Families and Colleteral Lines.* Tiffin, OH, 1973. 139 leaves. [S318].

BRINKERHOFF -- Brinkerhoff, Col. Henry R. *Family History of James Brinkerhoff, 1746.* NP, n.d. 179p. "See also family history of Joris Dickinson Brinkerhoff". [X128-OH].

BRINKERHOFF -- Brinkerhoff, Roeliff. *Genealogy Justified: A Paper on the Brinkerhoff Family... Reprinted From the Ohio*

38

Liberal....1884). NP, n.d., pagination not shown. [X128-FW/OH].

BRINTON -- Harry, Robert Jesse. *The Ancestors and Descendants of Hugh Harry and Elizabeth Brinton.* Northfield, OH, R. J.Harry, 1987. vi, 593p, 16 p. of plates. Two hundred copies printed. 1. Harrell family. 2. Brinton family. 3. Harry, Hugh, d.1708-Family. 4. Brinton, Elizabeth, b. 1665-Family. [G89].

BRISTOW -- Bristow, Wesley O. and Sarah Cherry Bristow. *Family Roster.* Princeton, MO, 1930. 64p. Bel Air, MD, A.M. Bristow, 1971. 1 v. (unpaged). [A88].

BROMFIELD -- *Bromfield Family (Louis Bromfield).* In the Ohio Genealogical Society's Report, May 1962. In Vertical File at the Library of Congress. [L2325].

BROSIUS -- NAS. *Minutes of the Brosius Genealogical Society... 1883.* Alliance, OH, Garrison, 1883. 3p. [X132-FW/PH].

BROUGHTON -- Phillips, Vernon S. *Amos Broughton, 1743-1837 of Hoosic, Rensselaer County, NY and Some of His Descendants. The Puritan Manuscripts.* Columbus, OH, 1932. 1p. 8 numb. leaves. [L2400].

BROWN -- Brown, James C. *Brown and Comly Families Genealogy; Memorial to Asa Brown and Hannah Comly-Brown.* Newark, OH, Am. Tribune, 1912. 123p. [X134-FW/LA].

BROWN -- Brown, John E. *John Brown and Mary Ann Longstreth, Who Lived Happily Together for more than Fifty Years; Also, Some Notes Concerning the Brown and Longstreth Families.* Columbus, OH, 1926. 32p. [X134-LI/MH/NY].

BROWN -- Brown, John E. *A Supplement to John Brown and His Wife Mary Ann Longstreth. More about Their Forebears and Collateral Lines and Data as to Their Children and Childrens'*

Children. Columbus, OH, 1956. 36p.
[X135-MH/SU].

BROWN -- Brown, Larry E. *Pike County Ohio, One Families (sic) Crossroads.* Fairborn, OH, 1987. 203p. [NGS4].

BROWN -- Krulce, Ruth. *The George Brown Family That Settled in Lawrence Township, Marion County, Indiana: Allied Line, Reuben, Martin, Huntington Township, Brown County, Ohio, Oxford Township, Butler County, Ohio.* Lawrence, IN, C.M. Stewart, 1987. 70 1, 1 leaf of plates. 1. Brown family. 2. Brown, George, ca.1777-ca.1844-Family. 3. Martin family. 4. Martin, Reuben, 1842-1928-Family. 5. Indiana-Genealogy. 6. Ohio-Genealogy. [G99].

BROWN -- Ravenscroft, Ruth Thayer. *Family of Abraham Brown, His Descendants of New Jersey and Ohio.* NP, 1959. vii, 87, 1 1. [D1727].

BROWN -- Sayre, Mortimer Freeman. *Brown and Sayre Ancestory.* Annapolis, MD, H.S. Sayre, (Columbus, Ohio: Spahr & Glenn), 1971. 132p. X gives: "Limited ed." [D1728; X137-FW/NY].

BROWN -- Smith, Mary W. *The Browns of Nottingham, Penna. and Related Families.* Canton, OH, 1969. 1 vol. (various pagings). [X137-FW/PH; VP32].

BROWN -- Wing, George Clary. *Early Years on the Western Reserve, with Extracts of Letters of Ephraim Brown and Family, 1805-1845.* Cleveland, OH, Arthur H. Clark Co., Printer, 1916. 142p. [L2448].

BROWNELL -- Brownell, Elijah Ellsworth. *Brownell Family.* Dayton, OH, Author, n.d. 32 pages. [X138-FW/IG].

BROWNELL -- Brownell, Elijah Ellsworth. *Brownell Family Miscellaney.* Dayton, OH, Author, 1952. 77 leaves. [X138-SP].

40

BROWNELL -- Brownell, Elijah Ellsworth. *Brownell Scrapbook.* Dayton, OH, Brownell, 1943-1956. 1. v. (various pagings). [D1743].

BROWNELLER -- Branthoover, W. R. [G101]. See above: BRANTHOOVER. [G84].

BROWNLEE -- NAS. *The Brownlee Manuscripts of Trumbull County, Ohio.* NP, Ohio DAR, G.R.C., 1961. 65p., 287 leaves. [D1750].

BRUBACHER -- Brubacher, Aden H. *Records of the Ancestors and Descendants of Jacob Sherk Brubacher and His Brother Daniel Sherk Brubacher... Deacons in the Mennonite Church... in Juniata County, Pa. ... in Stark and Wayne Counties, Ohio.* Elmira, ONT., 1974. 150P. [X139-FW; VP32].

BRUBAKER -- Brubaker, Joan B. *Brubaker Genealogy.* West Alexandria, OH, 1970. 34 leaves. [X139-FW/OH].

BRUCE -- Bruce, Mrs. Wm. *Some Intermarriages of Some Old Springfield, Ohio Families.* Springfield, OH, 1967. Genealogical Table. [S348].

BRUMBAUGH -- Brumbaugh, Eral D. *Von Brumbaugh, from 1728-1970.* Greenville, OH, Quality Pr., 1970. 20p. [X139-FW].

BRUMFIELD -- Brumfield, Ray C. *Brumfield Family Letters, 1817-1880. Ohio, Indiana, Illinois and Iowa.* Ridgeville, IN, n.d. 109p. [X140-FW].

BRUNING -- Schott, Glenneta. *Guillaim Heinrich Frederick Bruning of Newstadt, Germany, and Descendants, Ancestor of Agatha Bruning, Wife of Phillip Schott and Wm. M. Schmidt Family of Weisberger...* Dublin, OH, 1975. 7, 6p. [X140-OH].

BRUSH -- NAS. *A Concise Genealogy of Isaac Elbert Brush & Delia Williams Phillips His Wife and Their Descendants.* Cleveland, OH,

Priv. Print., 1932. 2 v. in 1.
[XA1069-FW/NY].

BRYAN -- Baldwin, C. C. *Alexander Bryan of Milford, Connecticut His Ancestors and Descendants.* Cleveland, OH, Leader Printing Co., 1889. 27p. [L2543].

BRYAN -- Bryan, Lindsay D. M. *Morgan Bryan and His Descendants.* Dayton, OH, Author, n.d. 72p. [X141-FW].

BRYANT -- Braiden, Clara Vaile. *Bryant Family History: Ancestors and Descendants of David Bryant (1756) of Springfield, N.J., Washington, Pa., Knox County, Ohio, and Wolf Lake, Nobel Co., Ind.* Chicago, IL, Priv. Print. 1913. xiv, 258p. [L2548].

BRYANT -- Forbes, Elizabeth Bryan. *The John Bryan Family.* - *Rev. ed.* Spirit Lake, IA, E.B. Forbes, 1985- . 1 v. (loose-leaf). 1. Bryant family. Bryan, John, 1777-1848-Family. 3. Ohio-Genealogy. [G103].

BUCHANAN -- Buchanan, Belle C. *First Annual Reunion of the Descendants of Col. George Buchanan.* 1st- 1892- Piqua, OH, Correspondent Press, 1893. 55p. L gives underscored title.
[L2571; D1797; X141-LI/MH/OL].

BUCHANAN -- Buchanan, Jim. *The Buchanans of Ohio.* Bowie, MD, Heritage Book, 1987. 169, 1p. 1. Buchanan family. 2. Ohio-Genealogy. [G103; NGS4].

BUCHER -- Waugh, Patricia Lee Russ. [G104]. See above: BOWERS. [G77].

BUCKINGHAM -- Buchingham, James & Tilton, Mary J. *The Ancestors of Ebenezer Buckingham, Who was Born in 1748, and of His Descendants.* Chicago, IL, R. R. Donnelley & Sons Company, Printers, 1892. 256p. [L2587].

BUCKINGHAM -- Huffman, Hazel Wise. [G104]. See above: BRIGHT. [G88; C761].

BUHRER -- Knull, Paul. *Descendants of Andrew D. (1840-1920) and Verena Sigg (1838-1939) Buhrer, Swiss Immigrants Who Came to America in 1871 and Settled Near Archbold, Ohio.* NP, 1971. 8p. [X144-FW].

BUKEY -- Bukey, N. J. *History of the Bukey Family, 1750-1945.* Cincinnati, OH, 1945. 30 leaves. [X144-FW].

BULL -- Swisher, Bob. *The Bulls: An Ohio Valley Family.* Richmond, VA, 1978. 20 leaves. 1. Bull family. 2. Ohio River Valley-Genealogy. [G105].

BUNKER -- Moran, Edward C. *Bunker Genealogy. Revised by Ward Bunker.* Troy, OH, Bunker Family Association of America, 1971 - 1 vol. (loose-leaf). [X146-NY].

BURGNER -- Burgner, Joseph. *History and Genealogy of the Bergner Family in the United States of America, as descended from Peter Burgner, a Swiss Emigrant of 1734.* Oberlin, OH, Oberlin News Press, 1890. vi, 172p. [L2680; D1899].

BURGNER -- Burgner, W. C. *Burgner (Burgener) Genealogy.* Lima, OH, 1946. Unpaged. [X148-FW].

BURKHOLDER -- Burkholder, Albert N. *The Swiss Origin of the Burkholder Family of America.* Troy, OH, 49 leaves. Originally published Harrisburg, PA, 1939. 1. Burkholder family. 2. Switzerland-Genealogy. 3. Mennonites-Genealogy. [G107].

BURNER -- Dowling, Heidi L. *The Berner Bridge: The Story of John and Margaret Berner and Their Eight Children.* Colfax, WA, H.L. Dowling, 1988. 90p. 1. Burner family. 2. Berner, John, 1844-1908-Family. 3. Berner, Margaret, 1846-1916-Family. 4. Ohio-Genealogy. [G108].

BURNS -- Parsons, Walter A. *A Record of the Families of Burns - Calvin Who Came From*

Pennsylvania and Other Points into the Western Reserve and Some Emigrating to Other States. East Cleveland, OH, 1929. 1 vol. (various pagings). [XA1069-WR].

BURR -- NAS. *Peter Burr of Berkeley County, Va., and Warren and Clinton Counties, O.* Muncie, IN, 1975. 27 leaves. [X150-FW; VV28].

BURROUGHS -- Burroughs, L. A. *Genealogy of the Burroughs Family.* Garrettsville, OH, The Pierce Printing Co., 1894. 24p. [L2730].

BURROWS -- Burrows, Raymond Earl. *Robert Burrows and Descendants.* Cleveland, OH, Burrows, 1975. 2 v. (1815 p). [S373; D1946].

BURT -- Ohio DAR G.R.C. *The Burt, Goddard and Hatch Family Histories.* NP, 1969. 148 l. [D1951].

BURWELL -- NAS. *Proceedings of the Burwell Family Picnic, Burwell's Farm, Milford, Connecticut, August 18, 1870.* Cleveland, OH, G. S. Newcomb & Co. Printers, 1870. 26 l. [L2746; NG26].

BUSH -- Bush, Eunice Donna Hornby. *Ter Bush, T Bush & Bush Family and Allied Families of New York and Ohio.* NP, 1948. 96 leaves. [D1966].

BUSHNELL -- Knight, George Wells. *Asa Smith Bushnell, Governor of Ohio.* Reprinted from "Old Northwest" Genealogical Quarterly for July, 1904. Columbus, OH, Press of Spahr & Glenn, 1904. 13p. [L2753].

BUTLER -- Heron, Mary. *The Butlers.* Mt. Vernon, OH, 1973. 7 leaves. [X154-OH].

BUTLER -- Ravenscroft, Ruth Thayer. *Proof of Descent of Saranne Butler Geer from Reverend Samuel Stone through the Butler Family of Connecticut, Ohio and Pennsylvania.* NP, 1956. 1 vol. (various pagings). D gives: no date/pagination. [D1991; X153-PH; VP37].

BUTLER -- Swainson, Bernice Lewis. *The Ancestors and Descendants of Joseph Butler, Revolutionary Soldier Buried in Ohio.* Piedmont, CA, Swainson, (Massillon, OH, Fair) 1968. 25 leaves. [D1992].

BUTT -- Richardson, W. V. *The Blood Line of Thomas Butt of the Revolutionary War and the Blood Line of Archibold Butt of the War of 1812: A History of Two Blood Related Branches of the Butt(s) Family in the Early Days of Maryland, Va. (now W. Va.), Ohio, Illinois, Iowa, Missouri, and Kansas.* Wichita, KS, Richardson, 1978. Various Pagings. [C105].

BUTTERS -- Butters, George. *The Genealogical Registry of the Butters Family... Including the Descendants of William Butter, of Woburn, Mass., 1665 and the Families of New York, Pennsylvania, West Virginia, Ohio, Iowa and Others Bearing the Name, Who Settled in America.* Chicago, D. Oliphant, Printer, 1896. VP lists under BUTLER. [VV29; VP36].

BUTTERWORTH -- NAS. *Reminiscences of Henry Thomas Butterworth and Nancy Irvin Wales, His Wife, with Some Account of Their Golden Wedding, 1880.* Lebanon, OH, Lebanon Gazette, Print., 1886. 121p. [X154-FW/LI].

BUTTERWORTH -- Butterworth, Eli. *Genealogy of Some of the following Families and Kinsfolks: Butterworth, Moorman, Smith, Irvin, Munger, Coffman, Jordan, Scott.* Marion, OH, R. I. Butterworth, 1968. 89-184, 20p. [X154-FW].

BUTTERWORTH -- Butterworth, Russel I. *Butterworth Genealogy Appendix.* Marion, OH, 1968. 20 leaves. Supplements the Butteworth Genealogy, pub. by Eli Butterworth about 1938. [X154-OH].

BYERS -- Byers, Janet McCulloch. *A History of the Byers Family.* Middleport, OH, Quality Print Shop, 1969. 72p. [L2809; D2006].

BYRD -- Finley, Rex Bird. *Thomas Bird of Holmes County, Ohio and His Descendants.* Wichita, KS, Advanced Data Reproductions. v. <1 >. 1. Byrd family. 2. Bird, Thomas, ca. 1765-1835-Family. [G113].

BYRD -- Harton, Marilyn K. Bird. *Byrds and Sonners of Shenandoah Valley, Virginia and Their Migration to Wells County, Indiana.* Worthington, OH, M. K. B. Harton, 1983. i v. in various foliations. [C107; VV30].

BYRD -- Nezbeth, Linda B. [G113]. See above: BRADLEY. [G82].

C

CAHILL -- Dougall, Richardson. *The Cahills of Cincinnati, including...* Portland, OR, Dougall, 1990. xvi, 306p. [DC567].

CAHOON -- Cahoon, Ida M. *History of the Cahoon Family, with Especial Reference to Joseph Cahoon, First Settler of Dover, Ohio and His Descendants.* Cleveland, OH, Press of W. A. Robertson, 1910. 47p. [XA1069-NY/OH].

CAINE -- Caine, Albert H. *John H. Caine and His Family.* Cincinnati, OH, 189_. 9 port., 3 plates. [X158-NY].

CALDER -- Currie, Barbara Calder. *Olney, 350 Years in America: A Detailed Study of William and Charlotte (Tanner) Olney and Their Twelve Children as Pioneers in Iowa and the Pacific Northwest: Olney, French, (Calder), Brown, Moore Connections in Oregon and Washington before 1900.* Fairborn, OH, B. C. Currie, 1986. 1 v. (unpaged). 1. Olney family. 2. Olney, William, 1792-1853-Family. 3. Olney, Charlotte, 1795-1845-Family. 4. French family. 5. Calder family. 6. Iowa-Genealogy. 7. Northwest, Pacific-Genealogy. [G114].

CALEF -- Walker, Richar Bordeaux. *Cutting Stevens Calef and His Wife Martha Howard Paine: Their Ancestors and Descendants.* Kettering, OH, R.B. Walker, 1989. vi, 85p. 1. Calef family, 2. Payne family. 3. Calef, Cutting Stevens, 1796-1844-Family. 4. Paine, Martha Howard, 1801-1844-Family. [G115].

CALKINS -- Calkins, Jerome R. *The History and Genealogy of a Branch of the Calkins Family.* Toledo, OH, 1967. 79, 14 leaves. [X159-SP].

CALLAND -- Cory, Mary Bell. *The Calland Family.* Dayton, OH, Doan & Cook, 1964. 205p. [D2061].

CALLAWAY -- Calaway. Merle L. *The Descendants of the "Connecticut Calaways" and Family Album, Illustrated Photos, and Charts.* Conneaut, OH, Calaway, 1976. 287p. [X160-FW].

CAMP -- Byrd, Helen Norris. *Family History of Norman Etheredge Manning.* Napoleon, Oh, Gibbs Pub. Co., 1985. 1 v. (various foliations). One Geneal. Table on 2 folded leaves in pocket. 1. Manning family 2. Manning, Norman Etheredge, 1930- - Family. 3. Etheridge family. 4. Camp family. 5. Murray family. [G117].

CAMPBELL -- Downing, Ruth C. T. *Campbell, Evans, Hosler, & Thomas Family Trees of Ohio.* Circleville, OH, 1973. 47p. [X163-OH].

CAMPBELL -- Temple, Sarah E. *Our Campbell Ancestors, 1742-1937. Tradition and History of the Family of Five Campbell Brothers and Sisters; John, James Douglas, Hester, Mary and Samuel: Including What is Known of Them in New Jersey, York County, Pennsylvania, Union County, South Carolina and in Ohio. A Genealogy of the Known Descendants of John Campbell through His Son James, and Samuel Campbell through His Son Ralph, also Brief Ancestral Notes on Families Connected by Marriage with the Foregoing; viz. Parnell,*

Clark, Spray, Wilson, Haskett, Mendenhall, and Underhill. Burbank, CA, I. Deach, Jr., 1939. 225p. [L2955; VP39].

CANDEE -- Baldwin, Charles Candee. *The Candee Genealogy.* Cleveland, OH, Leader Printing Co., 1882. 240p. [D2120].

CANFIELD -- Adams, Florence Gossard. *The Genealogical Records of the Jared Canfield Family.* Bowling Green, OH, Wood County Chapter of the Ohio Genealogical Society, 1987. iv, 44 leaves. 1. Canfield family. 2. Canfield, Jared, 1789-1870-Family. [G118].

CANFIELD -- Canfield, D. R. *Four Families in the Black Swamp.* Perrysburg, OH, Author, 1949. 133p. [X164-FW].

CANTER -- Canter, James Allison. *Family Records: The Descendants of John and Barbara Canter.* Englewood, OH, J. A. Canter, 1985. 315 leaves. [C112].

CARBAUGH -- Cunningham, Ruth Coward. <u>*Arthur Cunningham, about 1755-1829, Pennsylvania, Maryland, Virginia, and Ohio and Some of His Descendants:*</u> *John Carbaugh, William Harrelson, Jesse Wells, and Some of Their Descendants.* Bountiful, UT, Family History Publishers, 1990. vii, 133p. G gives as 1 v. (various pagings). 1. Cunningham family. 2. Cunningham, Arthur, ca.1755-1829-Family. 3. Carbaugh family. 4. Carbaugh, John, 1794-1871-Family. 5. Harrell family. 6. Harrelson, William, 1807-1877-Family. 7. Wells family. 8. Wells, Jesse, b. ca.1780-Family. D giveshas underscored title. [G120; D910].

CAREY -- Haines, Ruth. *Plumstead to Clear Creek, a History of the Family of Samuel Carey who Married Rachel Doane.* Waynesville, OH, Haines, 1969. 158 l. [D2144; X165-FW/PH].

CAREY -- Toennies, Dorothy Carey, et al. *Branches of the John Carey Family of Buck's County, Pennsylvania to Virginia, Ohio and on*

West. NP, Toennies & Matthews, 1969. 199 leaves. FW has supplement 1970 and corrs. 1971. [D2145; X165-FW/NY; VP40].

CARL -- Schneider, Donald R. *Descendants of Samuel and and Catherina Carl.* Beloit, OH, D.R. Schneider, 1984. 343p. 1. Carl family. 2. Carl, Samuel, ca.1794-1840-Family. [G120].

CARLE -- Carle, Roscoe. *American Ancestors of Roscoe Carle & Dottie (Hale) Carle and Their Children, Stanton Carle, and Constance Carle of Fostoria, Ohio with the Carle, Egbert, Williams; Hales, Post, & Eastlick Connections and Notes on the Family Names and Probable Origins and Migrations in Northern European Countries.* Fostoria, OH, The Times Press, 1933. 20, 3p. [L3009].

CARLILE -- James, Larry A. *The Carlile and Davison Families of Trumbull County, Ohio.* NP, 1987. 8 leaves. [DC603].

CARNEY -- Kearney, Michael John. *Midwest Families: A Genealogical and Historical Compendium of Several Families from Ireland, Germany, Switzerland and Belgium Who Settled in Iowa, Ohio and Missouri in the Middle of the Nineteenth Century.* Park Ridge, IL, Kearney, 1979. Various pages and leaves of plates. [C115].

CARPENTER -- Lloyd, Emma Rouse. *Carpenter Family of Kentucky.* NP, n.d. Pages not shown. (Available for Consultation at the Lloyd Library 309 West Court Street, Cincinnati, 2?, Ohio). [L3028].

CARPENTER -- Clark, Will C. *A Circular Relating to the Genealogy of the Carpenter Families in America.* Cincinnati, OH, 1879. 7p. [L3031].

CARR -- Carr, Louise Jeannette (Baltzly) & Charles E. *The Passing Shadows of the Carr Clan, Pioneers of Jefferson, Stark,*

*Tuscarawas, and Wayne Counties, Ohio, 1658-
1976.* Beach City, OH, Carr & Carr, 1976.
141p. D gives underscored part of title.
[NG28; D2181].

CARR -- Jonasson, Mildred King. [G122]. See
above: BANNISTER. [G33; NGS8].

CARREL -- Hudson, Roland V. *My Carrel
Ascendants.* Tiffin, OH, 1972. 1 vol. (unp.)
[X168-OH].

CARRIGAN -- Peoples, William L. *Genealogy
of the Corrigan Families.* Westlake, OH, W.L.
Peoples, 1988. 116 leaves. 1. Carrigan
family. 2. Ohio-Genealogy. [G123].

CARROLL -- Corcoran, Freda Carroll. *Carroll
Genealogy.* Circleville, OH, F.C. Corcoran,
1986. 13, 17p., 21 pages of plates. 1.
Carroll family. 2. Ohio-Genealogy. [G123].

CARRUTHERS -- Jennings, Elizabeth Robison.
*Robison Family History: Ancestors and
Descendants of Clarence Hall Robison (1873-
1952) (Including Crothers, Lamme, Baines, and
Mitchell Lines).* Berkeley, CA, 1983 [i.e.
1985]. iv, 84 leaves, 14 leaves of plates.
1. Robinson family. 2. Robison, Clarence
Hall, 1873-1952-Family. 3. Carruthers family.
4. Lamm family. 5. Ohio-Genealogy. [G124].

CARTER -- NAS. *Genealogy of William R.
Carter of Pennsylvania of Loudoun Co., Va., of
Preble County, Ohio and Clinton, Co., Ind.*
South Bend, IN, n.d. Includes genealogy of
allied families of Byers, Richards, Jury,
Thomas, Douglas, Hughes, McCullough, and
Smiley. [S423; VV33].

CARTER -- Carter, F. R. Nicholas. *Genealogy
of William R. Carter of the State of
Pennsylvania, of Loudon Co., Virginia, of
Preble Co., Ohio, and Clinton Co., Ind.* South
Bend, IN, Carter, 1974. 1 v. (various
foliations). [D2207; VV33; VP41].

CARTER -- Carter, James Grafton. *Wigton - Carter Family, 1066-1974, and Related Families Crooks, Fawcett, Gates, Horner, Lisle, Porter, Tharp, Wallace.* Columbus, OH, Carter, 1975. 308 leaves. [S429; X171-FW].

CARTER -- Carter, Marion A. *Carter Family.* Columbus, OH, Carter, 1957. iii, 48 leaves. [D2210].

CARTER -- White, Franklin H. *Newton and Howe, Hale and Carter. The Ancestors and Descendants of James Newton and Esther Hale of Hubbardston and Greenfield, Massachusetts.* Wyoming, OH, White House Enterprises, 1989. v, 179p. 1. Newton family. 2. Howe family. 3. Newton, James, 1801-1891-Family. 4. Newton, Esther Hale, 1799-1885-Family. 5. Hale family. 6. Carter family. 7. Massachusetts-Genealogy. [G125].

CARVER -- Carver, Minnie. *History of Salmon Carver (1790-1874) His Ancestry and Descendants.* Willoughby, OH, 1930. 59, 6 leaves. [X171-FW].

CARVIN -- Carvin, Joseph Franklin. *William Carvin, Sr., ? to 1762. A Virginia Pioneer and His Descendants.* Columbus, OH, J. F. Carvin, 1983. iv, 93 leaves. [C119].

CARY -- Cary, S. F. *Cary Memorials.* Cincinnati, OH, Cary, (J. J. Farrell & Co., printers, 1874. 264, xiii p. [L3128; D2238].

CASE -- Amner, Mary Case. *The Cases of Greenville, Ohio and Allied Families.* Kent, OH, M. C. Amner, 1983. 52 l. [C120].

CASE -- Case, Samuel R. *The Case Family History.* Bowling Green, OH, 1897. 113p. [X172-FW].

CASE -- Cleveland, James D. ... *A Biographical Sketch of the Founder of Case School of Applied Science and His Kinsmen.*

Cleveland, OH, Short & Forman, 1891. 1, 219-254p. (Tract (V.3.) No. 79 Western Reserve Historical Society... [L3150].

CASTOR -- Caster, Leland L. et al. *John Caster senior (1754-1823), Noah Castor (1764-1829), Arnold Carter (Before 1765 - ca 1825.) and Descendants.* Richmond, TX, Castor Family Association of America, 1985. iii, 93 1. 2 leaves of plates. Title Page: Some Caster/Castor Genealogies from Western Pennsylvania and Ohio. [C120].

CATLIN -- Baldwin, C. C. *Catlin.* Cleveland, OH, The Cleveland Leader Printing Company, 1882. 1, 141-147p. From the author's Candee Genealogy, Cleveland, 1882. [L3178].

CATON -- Hagen, Louis William. *The Caton Family, Descendants of John Caton (1757-1831) Revolutionary Soldier of New York and Ohio.* Rochester, NY, Hagen, 1976, 1969. 52 leaves. [D2272].

CAVE -- De View, Donna Harper. *Benjamin Cave, 1760-1842.* Knoxville, TN, 1960. 8 leaves. "Written to Supplement A Cave Genealogy Compiled and Privately Printed... in 1949 by Byron L. Cave of Lancaster, Ohio. Genealogy of the Cave family." [L3185].

CAVEN -- Hill, Leonard Uzal. *The Genealogical Record of George and Elizabeth Caven, Immigrants From Ireland and Pioneer Settlers in Springcreek Township, Miami County.* Piqua, OH, 1949. 45 1. [L3186].

CAWOOD -- Cawood, Richard L. *Who is this Fellow Cawood. (sic).* E. Liverpool, OH, 1962. 133p. [X174-FW].

CHABOT -- Titus, Frank H. *Peter Chabot and His Descendants.* Portsmouth, OH, 1906. 24p. [L3208].

CHACE -- Case, C. V. *Genealogical Record of the Chace and Hathaway Families from 1630-*

1900. Ashtabula, OH, Case, 1900. 38, 3p. [D2288].

CHALFANT -- Hott, Richard and Kathryn. *Higgins Ancestors.* Adelphi, MD, R. D. Hott, 1985. x, 228p. 1. Higgins family. 2. Chalfant family. 3. Cobbum family. 4. Pennsylvania-Genealogy. 5. Ohio-Genealogy. 6. Indiana-Genealogy. [G131].

CHAMBERS -- Carvin, Joseph Franklin. *Genealogy of the Family of Cyrenius Whiten Chambers.* Columbus, OH, J. F. and M. Carvin, 1983. ii, 67 leaves. [C123].

CHAMBERS -- Garrard, Lewis H. *Memoir of Charlotte Chambers.* Philadelphia, PA, Garrard, 1856. vii, 2 1, LX, 135p. 'Consists (principally) of letters written by Mrs. Chambers, while living near Cincinnati, from 1797-1821. These... also give an account of the Ludlow Family, including a narratives of Israel Ludlow's Connection with Mathias Denman and Robert Patterson, in the Proprietorship of the Law on which Cincinnati now stands'. P.G. Thompson Bibliography of Ohio, 1880. p.129-130. [L3237].

CHANCE -- Chance, Hilda. *Chance of Ohio, Virginia, North Carolina, Georgia, Texas, Tennessee, Kentucky, Delaware, Maryland, Pennsylvania, Michigan, California, Indiana, New Jersey.* Liberty, PA, 1970. 19 leaves. [A122; VV36].
-- *Supplement to Chance of Ohio, Virginia, etc.* Liberty, PA, 1970. [VV36].

CHANDLER -- Read, Helen Hunt. *William and Annis Chandler's Descendants. Including Information on the Families of Abbot, Bellows, Brown, Mason, Pearl, Sabin, Wright and Others.* Toledo, OH, H. H. Read, 1983. ii, 136 leaves. [C123].

CHAPMAN -- Chapman, Emilas Ravaud. *Chapman Genealogy, Being the Descendents(!) of John Chapman, The First Settlor of Stonington,*

Conn. Who Married Sarah Brown, Down the Generations from 1610-1931... Akron, Oh, Chapman, n.d. 2p. 19 numb. leaves. [L3294].

CHAPMAN -- Hamilton, Harriett R. *Chapman (Family)*. Toledo, OH, 1911. 45p. [X179-FW].

CHAPMAN -- Machir, Violette S. *Some Chapman, Jolly, Rayburn, and Smith Families in W. Va. & Ohio*. Middleport, OH, Quality Print Shop, 1965. 152p. [D2357; X179-FW/MH; VV36].

CHARLTON -- Norris, Madalene Jones. [G133]. See above: BOONE. [G69].

CHASE -- Case, C. V. *Genealogical Record of the Chace and Hathaway Families from 1630-1900*. Ashtabula, OH, The Wilson-Clark Co., Printers, 1900. 38, 4p. [L3320].

CHATFIELD -- Chatfield, Harry E. *Two Brothers and Friends: A Chatfield History & Genealogy*. Security, CO, Chatfield Western Publications, 1988-<1990 >. v. <1-4 >. Contents: v. 1. Thomas Chatfield lineage. -v. 2. Early English genealogy. George Chatfield lineage, part I. -v. 3. George Chatfield lineage, part II. -v. 4. Chatfields of Colorado, Illinois, Iowa, Ohio & Maichigan (sic). Revised vols. I, II, & III. 1. Chatfield genealogy. 2. Ohio-Genealogy. [G134].

CHAUMETTE -- Close, Virgil D. *The First Four Generations Descended from Pierre De la Chaumette (Peter DeLashmutt): With References to other De la Chaumette Lines in America: Delashmitt, Delashmet, Lashmet, Shumate*. Newark, OH, V. D. Close, 1984. vi, 26 leaves. NG lists as DeLaCHAUMETTE; DC as: DeLASHMUTT. [C126; NG29; DC981].

CHERRY -- Cherry, Marjorie Loomis.... *Early Fireland Families. Vol 1. The Cherry Tree*. Sandusky, OH, 1941. 165 leaves typewritten and pasted. [X183-GF].

CHERRY -- Sieferman, Lucile M. *Some "Twigs" of the Jesse Cherry Branch of the Cherry Tree (Hancock Co., O.) and Allied Families of William Long and Thomas Cole (Fairfield, Co., Ohio.)* Urbana, IL, 1964. 51 leaves. [X183-OH/SP].

CHERRY -- Sieferman, Lucile M. *Jesse Cherry Family, Allied Families of Long & Cole with Additional Records on the Cherry, Ramsey, Ingold and Longworth - Longwith Families of N.J., Ohio and Va.* Washington, DC, Sieferman & Baer, 1965. 162 leaves. [D2392; VV37].

CHEW -- Chew, Dorothy Clendenin. *John Chewe, Some Descendants in Virginia, Maryland and Ohio.* Dalton, GA, D.C. Chew, 1982. 26 leaves. [C127; VV37].

CHRISTY -- Bowman, Deanna Holcomb. *Christy and Other Fairfield County, Ohio Families, 1790-1985.* Rev. Colorado Springs, CO, Bowman, 1987. 74, 21 leaves. 1. Christie family. 2. Ohio-Genealogy. G lists under CHRISTIE. [G138; DC710].

CHRYSLER -- Raymond, Edith Madeline Replogle. *A Crisler Genealogy: Descendants of Aaron and Susannah (Baker) Crisler of Preble County, Ohio.* Pullman, WA, M.R. Raymond, 1986. xx, 137p. 1. Chrysler family. 2. Crisler, Aaron, 1775-1852-Family. [G139].

CHURCH -- Smith, Edward Church. *Ancestors and Descendants of Uriah Church, junior of Middlefield, Mass.* Lakewood, Ohio, 1946. 31 leaves. [X187-NY].

CHURCH -- Smith, Edward C. *Maternal Ancestry of Edward Charles Smith.* Lakewood, OH, Author, 1958. 139 leaves. [X187-FW].

CHURCHILL -- Chamberlain, Ernest Barrett. *The Churchills of Oberlin.* Oberlin, OH, Oberlin Improvement and Development Organization, 1965. 112p. [DC713].

CHURCHILL -- Phillips, W. Louis. *The Descendants of Selden Churchill (14 Dec. 1783-1866) of Chathem, CT and Richfield, NY, and His Wives (1st) Mary Duel and (2nd) Lucretia Clements.* Logan, OH, W. L. Phillips, 1900. 1 v. (unpaged). 1. Churchill family. 2. Churchill, Selden, 1783-1866-Family. 3. New York (State)-Genealogy. [G139].

CLABAUGH -- Hublinger, Alice Basler. *The Henry J. Clabaugh and Susarn Barnhiser Family and Descendants.* Barberton, OH, A. B. Hublinger, 1979. 107p. [C132].

CLARDY -- Crider, Lorraine L. *Four Family Bible Records; Clardy, Barnes, (James) Vannatta, (Christopher C.) Vannatta.* Lakewood, OH, 1959. 1 Vol. various pagings. [X188-NY].

CLARK -- NAS. *Genealogy of the Clark and Forward Families (from 1668).* Cleveland, OH, 1860. 12p. [X188-FW].

CLARK -- Clark, Everett J. *Clark Family. History of John Clark and His Descendants, 1650-1970.* Dayton, OH, 1970. 4 leaves. [X191-OH].

CLARK -- Clark, Faith. *A Clark - Fogle Family History: Descendants and Ancestors of Alexander Bierce Clark and Faith Fogle Clark of Canton, Ohio.* Mitchellville, MD, The Author, 1990. 72p. 1. Clark family. 2. Vogel family. 3. Clark, Alexander Bierce, 1874-1929-Family. 4. Clark, Faith Fogle, 1873-1959-Family. 5. Ohio-Genealogy. [G141; DC720].

CLARK -- Clark-Mullikin, Katharine. *Chronicles of the Clark Family. Collected June 27, 1882.* Cincinnati, OH, 1887. 123p. [X189-LI].

CLARK -- Clarke, William P. *History of the Patrick Clarke and Catherine Wade Clarke Lines.* Toledo, OH, W. Toledo Pub. Co., 1946. 138p. [X190-FW/LA].

CLARK -- Dennis, Katharine G. *Family Records of George Clark, Zebadiah Farnham and Benjamin Durkee, with Their Descendants.* Norwalk, OH, 1928. 52p. [X189-FW/LA].

CLARK -- Fowler, Fred E. *Short Sketches of Some of the Descendants of Doctor William A. Clark of Cherry Valley, Ashtabula County, Ohio, Who Died Oct. 11, 1865, aged 81 Years.* NP, 1937. 14p. [XA1070-WR].

CLARK -- Gray, L. W. *Gemealogy of the Clark Family of America, Descended from Major Stephen Clark of Kittery Maine.* Toldeo, OH, Blade Print., 1889. 165p. [X189-FW].

CLARK -- Johnson, Carol Clark. *A Genealogical History of the Clark and Worth Families and other Puritan Settlers in the Massachusetts Bay Colony.* Cygnet, OH, Clark, 1970. xxiii, 550p. [A131; D2494].

CLARK -- Marshall, D. P. *Clark, Harlan, Marshall, McComas, McKeand, and Other Families of West Virginia and Ohio.* NP, 1945. 51 leaves. [D2496].

CLARKE -- King, Nellie Clarke. *Some New England Families, Clarke - Kellogg, Vol. II.* Cleveland, OH, King (J. B. Savage Co., Printers), 1922. 207p. [D2520].

CLABOUGH -- Hubbinger, Alice Bosler. *The Henry J. Clabaugh and Susan Barnhiser Family and Descendants.* Barberton, OH, A. B. Hubbinger, 1979. 107p. [C132].

CLAYPOOLE -- Claypoole, Edward A. *Sketch of Norton Fravel Claypoole...* Chicago, IL, or Nashport, OH, Claypoole, 1892. 4p. [X192-FW/PH].

CLAYTON -- Klaiber, Teresa Lynn Martin. *Clayton Connections: A Researcher's Guide to New Jersey Clayton Ancestors.* New Concord, OH, T. L. M. Klaiber, 1984. 79p. [C136].

CLAYTON -- Vitz, A. C. *Clayton Family Story.* Wyoming, OH, 1976. 17p. [X193-FW].

CLEGG -- Clegg, Blain L. *Cleggs of the Upper Ohio Valley: A Family Genealogy.* Largo, FL, B.L. Clegg, 1990. v, 377p., 1 leaf of plates. 1. Clegg family. 2. Ohio River Valley-Genealogy. [G144].

CLEVELAND -- Cleveland, Edmund Jones & Horace Gillette Cleveland. *The Genealogy of the Cleveland and Cleaveland Families. An Attempt to Trace, in Both Male and Female Lines, the Posterity of Moses Cleveland... (and) of Alexander Cleveland... with numerous Biographical Sketches; and containing Ancestries of Many of the Husbands and Wives; Also a Bibliography of the Cleveland Family and a Genealogical Account of Edward Winn of Woburn, and Other Winn Families.* Hartford, CT, Case, Lockwood & Brainerd Company, 1899. 3 v. [L3588].

CLEVELAND -- Williams, W. W. *An Account of the Lineage of General Moses Cleveland, of Caterbury (Windham County) Conn., The Founder of the City of Cleveland, Ohio. Also a Sketch of His Life from the Jan (1885) number of the Magazine of Western History by the Hon. Harvey Rice.* Cleveland, OH, Williams, 1885. 14p. [L3586].

CLIFTON -- Wright, Nell M. *Our Clifton Ancestors and Their Descendants.* Chillicothe, OH, N. M. Wright, 1982. vi, 103p. [C137].

CLINE -- Fisher, Jane. *The Cline's.* Galion, OH, Jane & Rus Fisher, 1976. 46, 7p. [D2567].

CLINGAN -- Mansperger, Martin Matheny. *Clingan and Springer Families.* Columbus, OH, Mansperger, 1961. rev. 1962. 48 leaves. [D2568].

CLOPPER -- Clopper, Edward Nicholas. *An American Family; Its Ups and Downs Through*

Eight Generations in New Amsterdam, New York, Pennsylvania, Maryland, Ohio and Texas from 1650-1880. Cincinnati, OH, Cloper, 1950. xiii, 624p. D gives underscored title: VP gives: Author unknown. [L3607; D2571; VP46].

CLOUSER -- Flinn, Richard D. *The Clouser and Cripps Families of Ross County, Ohio.* Hillsboro, Ohio, R. D. Flinn, 1987. liv, 510p. 1. Clouser family. 2. Crisp family. [G145; DC757].

CLOYES -- Obetz, Genevieve M. *Cloyes and Dagwell Family Genealogies.* Columbus, OH, 1972. 1 vol. (unpaged). [X196-OH].

COALE -- Coale, Willis Branson. *The Coale Family: Nine Generations. Also Cole Family.* Cleveland Heights, OH, 1972. 2 v. [NG31].

COALE -- Coale, Willis Branson. *The Coale Family: Nine Generations.* Cleveland Heights, OH, Coale, 1976. 2 v. Vol 2 issued separately in 1971 under title: Map of nine Coale generations. [C140; X197-FW/NY].

COATES -- Snow, Jane Elliott. *Family History. Coates, Wilcox, and Teachout Families.* Cleveland, OH, W. M. Bayne Printing House, 1901. 5, 120p. [L3630; D2592].

COBB -- Cobb, John L. *The Descendants of the Marriage of Solomon & Hannah (Wells) Cobb of Cambridge, Washington, Co., N.Y.* Cleveland, OH, Cobb, 1966. 14, iv, 2 leaves. [D2595].

COBB -- Cobb, Philip L. *A History of the Cobb Family.* Cleveland, OH, Cobb, 1907-1923. 215p. Pts. I-III (Barnstable family) bound together, Pt. IV Boston family, bound separately. Pt. IV Supplement, Soloman & Hannah Cobb, bound separately. L indicates 4 v.; omits reference to supplement. [L3633; D2597].

COBB -- Cobb, Philip Lothrop. *The Descendants of the Marriage of Solomon & Hannah (Wells) Cobb of Cambridge, Washington*

Co., NY. Cleveland, OH, 1966. 14, lv leaves, 2p. NG omits pagination. [L3633; NG31].

COBBUM -- Hott, Richard. [G146]. See above: CHALFANT. [G131].

COBERLY -- Arthaud, John Bradley. *The George Coberly (1788-1855) and Mary Ann Mathews (1813-1901) Family of Ohio and Livingston County, Missouri with Allied Families of Dain, Garr, Melton, Phillips, and Walling, and the William Coberly (1776-1833) Family.* Columbia, MO. 1984. 133 leaves. [NG31].

COBERLY -- Arthaud, John Bradley. *The George Coberly and Mary Ann Mathews (1813-1901) Family of Ohio and Livingston County, Missouri with Allied Families of Dain, Garr, Melton, Phillips, and Walling, and the William Coberly (1776-1833) Family.* NP, 1984. vii, 134 leaves. [DC767].

COBERLY -- Arthaud, John Bradley. *A Coberley, Coberly, Cuberly Genealogy 1690-1985: The Descendants of James Stell Coberly (1723-c1800).* Columbia, MO, J. B. Arthaud, 1985. 668p. [DC768].

COBLENTZ -- Striker, Kenneth W. *The Coblentz Family in America, 1743 - 1982. suppl.* Dayton, OH, 1986. 20p. [NG31].

COCHRAN -- Haughton, Ida Cochran. *Chronicles of the Cochrans; Being a Series of Historical Events and Narratives in which Members of This Family have Played a Prominent Part.* Columbus, OH, Stoneman Press, 1915. 148p. Part 1. Scottish History. Pt. 2. Pioneer History. Part 3. Miscellaneous History. D gives underscored part of title and "See also: Volume second, 1925." {See just below}. L does not indicate number of volumes. [L3647; D2603; X198-NY/PH].

COCHRAN -- Haughton, Ida Cochran. *Chronicles of the Cochrans.* Columbus, OH, F. J. Heer Printing, 1925. 186p. [D2604].

COE -- Coe, Daniel B. & Eunice A. Lloyd. *Record of the Coe Family and Descendants From 1596 to 1856 (Daniel Coe) From 1856 to 1885 (Eunice Lloyd)*. Cincinnati, OH, Standard Pub. Co., 1885. 16p. " Record of the Coe family and descendants from 1596-1858" first published in 1856 by Daniel Benton Coe. [L3672].

COFFIN -- Coffin, Addison. *Life and Travels of Addison Coffin*. Cleveland, OH, W. G. Hubbard, 1897. 570p. [X199-FW].

COFFIN -- Coffin, Louis (1962). *Supplement to the Coffin Family, 1962*. Cincinnati, OH, 1966, 40p. [X199-NY/PH].

COFFIN -- Lukins, C. M. *Tristram Coffin Family*. Alliance, OH, n.d. Pages unnumbered. [X199-FW].

COFFINBERRY -- Scott, Beatrice Berman. *Genealogy of the Coffinberry Family. Descendants of George Lewis Coffinberry, 1760-1851, Revolutionary War Soldier, and H i s Wife, Elizabeth (Little) Coffinberry. Also Related Families : Coffenberry, Gilkison, Keasey, Platt.* Cleveland, OH, F. A. Myers, 1952. 64p. [L3693].

COLE -- Cole, Frank T. *The Early Genealogies of the Cole Family in America, Including Coles and Cowles, with Some Account of the Descendants of James Cole by (sic) Hartford, Connecticut, 1635-1652, and of Thomas Cole, of Salem, Massachusetts, 1649-1672.* Columbus, OH, Cole (Printed by Hann & Adair), 1887. 4, xxxii, 307, 6p. D gives xxxii, 308p. [L3737; D2662].

COLEMAN -- Cofrode, Caroline Coleman. *A Coleman Family History: Descendants of Charles Coleman, born 1763, Kent County, Maryland, including Ancestors and Descendants of Frank Matthias Coleman.* North Canton, OH, R.F. Coleman, 1985 or 1986. A-W, 19p., 1 folded

leaf of plates. 1. Coleman family. 2.
Coleman, Charles, 1763-1827-Family. [G149].

COLLINS -- Collins, Clarence Lyman. *Collins
Memorial.* Cleveland, OH, 1959. 297p.
[L3816].

COLLINS -- Siegel, Ernestine. *The Family of
William J. Collins, Jr., of Lycoming Co., Pa.
and Defiance Co., Ohio.* Rev. Tampa, FL, E.
Siegel, 1970. A-D, 42 leaves. [X203-NY].

COLSTON -- Colston, Edward. *Correspondence,
Genealogy, Bills, Receipts, Memorials,
Diaries, etc. of the Colston and Stevenson
Families.* Cincinnati, OH, 1810-1969. 4
boxes. [X204-CH].

COLT -- Colt, Thomas Clyde. *Memories of the
19th Century. With a Genealogy of the Colts
in the United States of America appended.*
Dayton, OH, T. C. Colt, Jr., 1979. 119 pages.
2 leaves of plates. [C143].

COMPTON -- Compton, Justin S. *Genealogical
Data Concerning Compton, McClellan, Boyd,
Probasco Families.* Dayton, OH, J. S. Compton,
1963. 121 leaves. [X205-CH/FW/NY].

CONNER -- Conner, E. Margaret Masters &
Robert Monroe Conner. *Conner and Masters,
Pioneer Families of Guernsey County, Ohio;
From Pioneers to the Twentieth Century.*
Cambridge, OH, 1963. 170p. [L3897].

CONNOLLY -- Manley, Nancy L. C. *James C.
Connolly: Parents and Descendants, 1805-1974.*
Alvordton, OH, 1974. vi, 186p. [X208-FW/NY].

CONRAD -- NAS. *The Lineage of Jacob Conrad
Who Came from Switzerland in 1823 and Settled
in Louisville, O.* NP, 1964. 39p. [X208-FW].

CONRAD -- Conrad, S. E. *Conrad Family Tree
from 1750-1910.* Wooster, OH, 1910. 38p.
[X208-FW].

CONRAD -- Graber, Martha E. *Joseph Conrad Family.* Canton, OH, Standard Print, 1937. 18p. [X208-FW].

CONWAY -- Conway, Patrick Joe. *The Conway Clan of Doona, Ballycroy, County Mayo, Ireland.* Cleveland, OH, P. J. Conway, 1988. 47 leaves. 1. Conway family. 2. Ireland-Genealogy. [G154].

COOK -- Cook, Bill J. *The Cook Family Genealogical Records and Their Family Connections.* Glendale, OH, Greenwood Cottage Press, 1971. 1 v. unpaged. [S545].

COOK -- Kirtland, Jared P. *Family History: Genealogy of the Cooke Family; An Interesting Glimpse of Early New England Life.* Cleveland, OH, Foreman-Bassett-Hatch, 1875. 26p. Continued by Mrs. Josiah Barber, p. 22-26, Cleveland, OH, 1897. [X209-FW].

COOLIDGE -- Crawford, Frederick Coolidge. *One Branch of the Coolidge Family, 1427-1963.* Cleveland, OH, Crawford, 1964. vi, 85, 6p. L gives vi, 85p. [L3964; D2814].

COOLIDGE -- Winslow, Grace Davenport. *My First Day and My Last Day with Grandma Coolidge.* Cleveland, OH, Lezius-Hiles Co., 1967. 54p. [L3965].

COOMBS -- Coombs, William Carey. *The Story of Anthony Coombs and His Descendants.* Amelia, Oh, Coombs, 1913. vii, 219p. [D2817].

COPE -- Cope, Walter A. *Darlington Cope and His Descendants, 1815-1967.* Columbus, OH, Cope, 1967. G gives 1968. 27p. 1. Cope family. [G156; D2838; X212-FW/NY/PH].

COPELAND -- Broward, Charles S. *The Ancestors and Descendants of Earl Percy Copeland and Olive Princess Henrietta Norton of Marietta, Ohio, and Rochester, Indiana.* NP, 1965. 30 leaves. Includes ... pg. 18-

22... Ancestors and Descendants of Josiah Snell Copeland and Katharine Guild of Easton Mass... [A143].

COPELAND -- Copeland, Elijah. *The Ascendants and Descendants of Josiah Snell Copeland and Katharine Guild.* Marion, OH, 1883. 36p. [X212-FW/LI].

CORBETT -- Corbett, Clyde Henry. *Genealogy of the Descendants of Robert Corbett.* Canton, OH, Canton Print. Co., 194_?, 50p. [A144].
-- NAS. *Supplement to the Genealogy of a Northern Ohio Corbett Family, Since May, 1947.* Cover Title: Genealogy of the descendants of Robert Corbett. Canton, OH, Canton Print. Co., 1970. 11p. [A144].

CORBETT -- Corbett, Clyde Henry. *Genealogy of the Descendants of Robert Corbett.* Canton, OH, Canton Print. Co., 1959, 50p. [X213-NY].

CORNELL -- NAS. *Cornell Cousins.* Fenton, MI, Hilton, OH, Dexter, Cornell, Family Association of America. 1974-?. __ v. DAR Library v. 1, no. 1 (Nov. 1970)- v. iv, no. 2. (July 1974). [D2877].

CORNELL -- Day, Jesse H. *The Descendants of Brownell Cornell.* Athens, OH, J.H. Day, 1987. viii, 82p., 9p. of plates. 1. Cornell family. 2. Cornell, Brownell, 1800-1877-Family. [G159].

CORSON -- Corson, Orville. *Three Hundred Years with the Corson Families in America Including the Staten Island-Pennsylvania Corsons, the Sussex County, New Jersey Corsons, the Coursons of Dufriesshire, Scotland, the Coursons of Amwell Township, Hunterdown County, New Jersey, the New England Corson families, the Canadian Corson family.* Middletown, OH, Corson, 1939. 2 v. [D2891].

COTTER -- Dromey, John H. *Cotter Kin: A Brief History of James Cotter (ca. 1799-1877)* *from County Kerry, Ireland through Pennsylvania and Ohio to the State of Iowa, His Wife, Mary (Conley) Cotter (ca. 1810-1850), and Some of Their Descendants.* J. H. Baring, MO, J. H. Dromey, 1984. 64p. [C152; VP51].

COTTNER -- McElwain, Mrs. Edgar. *Some Descendants of Jacob and Susannah Cook Cottner.* Lafayette, Oh, McElwain, 1965. 109, 7 leaves. [D2911].

COULSON -- Coulson, J. H. *Lineages of the Coulsons...* Canal Dover, OH, 1902. pni. [X217-CH].

COURTRIGHT -- Courtright, Dudley, Vattier. *History of the Van Kortryks of Courtrights, Allied Families Staudt / Vattier, Moore.* Columbus, OH, F. J. Heer Printing Co., 1924. 105p. [L4118; D2934].

COWAN -- Sellers, Julia E. *A Genealogy of James Cowan, Sr. and His Descendants.* Lebanon, Oh, Bell Press, 1919. 43, 1p. [L4132; D2950].

COWGILL -- Cowgill, Chester A. *Cowgill Genealogy.* Middletown, OH, 1973. 14 leaves. [X218-FW].

COWING -- Ritchie, Kathryn E. *Estes Howe Cowing, of Wyoming Ohio. His Family and Descendants.* Chicago, IL, Author, 1967-68. 93p. [X219-CH/FW].

COX -- Cox, Harold E. *Family Tree of Jesse Cox.* Columbus, OH, n.d. Folded Genealogical Table. [X221-OH].

COX -- Speck, Grace Croy. <u>*Genealogy of the Cox Families of Virginia and Ohio, 1755-1955.*</u> Concord, OH, Speck, 1955. 39p. D and VV give underscored title. [D2979; X220-NY; VV45].

COX -- Staats, Mary H. *Genealogy of the Samuel and Elizabeth Cox Family of Virginia* *and Ohio.* Ann Arbor, MI, Braun Brumfield, 1975. 214, xxxxi(sic) p. [D2980; VV46].

CRABB -- Crabs, John. *Biography of Henry Crabs and His Wife Anna George.* Mineral Ridge, OH, 1959. 54p., 5 leaves. Typed from record written in 1883. [X220-FW].

CRAIG -- Craig, Winchell McKendree. *The Craig Family; Genealogical and Historical Notes About the Craigs of America, Fayette County, Ohio, United States, (and) Canada.* Rochester, MN, 1956. 149p. [L4181].

CRAMER -- Cramer, Clarence E. *The Family of John Helfer Cramer (Revolutionary War Pension W-2762) with Historical Background...* Chicago, IL, 1944. pni., Presented at John Cramer family re-union, Bascom, OH, August, 23, 1943. [L4188].

CRANZ -- Johnson, Arthur C. Sr. *The Cranz Family.* Columbus, OH, Author, 1931. 68p. [X221-CH/OS].

CRATER -- Crater, Doyle M. *Descendants of Jacob Greter of Montgomery County, Pennsylvania.* Norwood, OH, 1938. 23 numb. leaves. [L4206].

CRATER -- Crater, Doyle M. *Descendants of Moritz Crater, 1703-1772,* Lakewood, OH, 1939. 1 vol. (loose-leaf). [L4207].

CRATER -- Crater, Doyle M. *Descendants of Jacob Crater.* Norwood, OH, 1945. 1p., 35 numbered leaves. [L4208].

CRAWFORD -- Bradshaw, J. D. *The Family of Michael Curren & Sarah Crawford of Columbiana County, Ohio: Being a Compilation of the Ancestors and Descendants of Michael Curren (1810-1858) and Sarah Crawford (1813-1886) and Allied Families.* Richmond, VA, Dietz Press, 1989. xix, 387p. 1. Curren family. 2. Curren, Michael, 1810-1858-Family. 3.

Crawford, Sarah, 1813-1886-Family. 4.
Crawford family. 5. Ohio-Genealogy.
[G164; DC913].

CRAWFORD -- Crawford, Andrew J. *Crawford &*
Allied Families (Brent, Curd, Dungan,
Kindrick, Perkins, Etc.) 1540-1971. Fairborn,
OH, 1971, 189p. [NG33; X224-FW].

CRAWFORD -- Crawford, Andrew J. [G164].
See above: BRENT. [G86].

CRAWFORD -- Crawford, George F. *History &*
Family Tree of the Crawford Family.
Greenville, OH, 1937. 5 leaves, 8 numb.
leaves. [L4218].

CRAWFORD -- Crawford, H. M. *Crawfords of*
Adams County, Ohio. Poughkeepsie, NY, 1976.
142p. [X224-FW].

CRAWFORD -- Crawford, Hammond. *Brief Sketch*
of the Crawfords, Pathfinders in America, and
Especially Abel Jones Crawford. Mantua, OH,
Crawford, 1949. 15 leaves. [X224-NY].

CRAWFORD -- Crawford, H. Marjorie.
Crawfords of Adams County, Ohio.
Poughkeepsie, NY, Crawford, 1943. iv, 97,
13p. [L4222; D3038].

CRAWFORD -- Emahiser, Grace U. *From the*
River Clyde to the Tymochtee and Col. William
Crawford. Fostoria, OH, 1969. 307p.
[L4225; NG33].

CRAWFORD -- Foster, Harriett McIntire.
James Crawford, Revolutionary War Soldier. A
Refugee From Nova Scotia. A Pioneer Settler
in Ohio. In Old Northwest Genealogical
Quarterly, Columbus, OH, 1911. v. 14, p. 135-
149. [L4212].

CRAWFORD -- Lones, Lela Lillian. *Crawfords*
of Columbiana County, Ohio, and Benjamin
Williams. Perry, IA. L.L. Lones, 1989. c-h,

87p. 1. Crawford family. 2. Williams family. 3. Williams, Benjamin, 1753-1823-Family. 4. Ohio-Genealogy. 5. Pennsylvania-Genealogy. [G164].

CRAYTOR -- Crayton, Doyle M. *Genealogy of the Cratar, Crater, and Craytor Families of New York and Ohio.* Lakewood, OH, 1933. 68 leaves. [X224-NY].

CREEL -- NAS. *Creel Family Quarterly. Vol 1, no. 1-3/4; Jan - July/Oct, 1976.* Akron, OH, 1 vol. [X224-FW/NY].

CREEL -- NAS. *Creel Family Quarterly.* Akron, OH, The Family. 1976- . _v. Check DAR Shelflist for Library Holdings. [DC879].

CRESAP -- Towt, Mrs. Clara E. Brasee. *The Colonel Thomas Cresap Genealogical Chart.* Columbus, OH, 1932. The Cresap Society. 2 Genealogical Tables. [L4231].

CRESAP -- Holladay, Mrs. S. W. & Lieut. James C. Cresap. *Original 'Circle' Chart of Lieut. James C. Cresap, U.S.N. dated 1894...* Columbus, OH, Cresap Society, 1932. Geneal. Table. [L4232].

CRESAP -- Pinkerton, Mary Beam. *On the Trail of Thomas Cresap: A Trip to Yorkshire, England.* Columbus, OH, Published by the Cresap Soc., 1932. 18p. [X225-PH].

CRESAP -- Wroth, Lawrence C. *The Story of Thomas Cresap, a Maryland Pioneer, Read before the Maryland Historical Soc.* Columbus, OH, Cresap Soc., 1928. 44p. [X225-FW].

CRESWELL -- Storemont, James Creswell. *The Creswell Notebook: A Family History. American Ancestory and Descendants of Samuel Creswell (1820-1912) of Greene County, OH., Who Married Eliza Jane (Huffman).* Lake Alfred, FL, Creswell Family. 1979. xvi, 175p. [C158; NG33].

CREW -- NAS. *The Crews of Richmond (Jefferson County, Ohio).* NP, 1934. 9 leaves. [X226-OH].

CREW -- Baker, Alice C. *Story of My Children's Grandparents (pt. 3); Edwin Baker (1836-1912) a Boy of Cape Cod... Martha A. Thomas (1841-1921) Green Mts. of Vt., Henry Crew (1859-1953) an Ohio Lad... Helen C. Coale (1859-1941)... of Old Baltimore.* Chevy Chase, MD, 1926. 155p. Part 1 - 2 wanting. [X225-FW].

CREW -- Bedell, L. Frank. *A Genealogy of the Crew and Ellyson Families.* Barnesville, OH,.. Friend Boarding School, 1969. 1 vol. (irregular paging). [X225-FW/NY].

CRISP -- Flinn, Richard D. [G165]. See above: CLOUSER. [G145].

CRISLER -- Raymond, Madeline Replogle. *A Crisler Genealogy: Descendants of Aaron and Susannah Baker Crisler of Preble County, Ohio.* Pullman, WA?, M. R. Raymond, 1986. 137p. [DC882].

CRISPIN -- Crispin, Rev. William Frost. *A Biographical & Historical Sketch of Captain William Crispin of the British Navy, Together with Portraits and Sketches of Many of His Descendants and of the Representatives of Some Families of English Crispins; Also an Historical Research Regarding the Remote Ancestry of English & American Crispins, and a Tracing of the Name, from 361 B.C. to the Present, Including Genealogies of the Crispin Families and Some Related Families, The Penns, the Holmes, the Masons to Which is added a Section on Genealogy and Ancestry.* Akron, OH, The Commercial Printing Co., 1901. 144p. [L4254].

CROCKETT -- Crockett, Harrison. *Robert Crockett Family of Ohio.* Mishawaka, IN, Author, 1968. 306, ix p. [X227-FW].

CROCKETT -- Hill, Dorothy V. *The Crockett, Davidson (Davison), Graham, Montgomery, Stockton and Allied Families of Virginia, Kentucky and Missouri, also the Taylor - Hill and March - Cureton Families of Virginia - Ohio - New England - Alabama - California.* NP, 1969. 108 leaves. [D3078; VV47].

CROSBY -- NAS. *Crosby Genealogy (in part), (Descendants of Samuel Crosby, Jr. and Louissa (Phillips) Crosby).* NP, DAR, OH, 1942. 10, 2, 9p. [X229-FW].

CROSS -- Cross, Roselle Theodore... <u>My Childrens' Ancestors</u>; *Data Concerning about Four Hundred New England Ancestors of the Childrean of Roselle Theodore Cross and His Wife Emma Asenath (Bridgeman) Cross; Also Names of Many Ancestors in England, and Descendants of Mr. and Mrs. Cross's (sic) (grandparents,) Theodore and Susannah (Jackson) Cross, Samuel and Lois (Temple) Murdock, Noah and Asenath (Judd) Bridgman, Jacob and Lydia (Slack) Daggett; with an indtoructory essay on genealogy, and an appendix of miscellaneoies.* Twinsburg, OH, (Columbus, OH, The Champlin Press) 1913. 212p., plates. NG & D give: underscored part of title; D gives: Twinsburg, OH... [L4308; NG34; D3099].

CROUSE -- Carroll, Phyllis Bicknell. *Krouse - Krauss Genealogy: The Antecedents and Descendants of Georg & Katherine (Bernhardt) Krauss of Auerbach in Hessen-Darmstadt Who Immigrated to Findlay, Ohio, 1845.* Baltimore, MD, Gateway, 1986. 152p. 1. Krause family. 2. Crouse family. 3. Krauss, Georg, 1824-1879-Family. 4. Ohio-Genealogy. [G167].

CROUSE -- Crouse, John H. *History of the Crouse Family of Pennsylvania and Ohio.* Chicago, IL, A. C. Pr., 1932. 107p. [X230-FW].

CROWELL -- Crowell, H. *Crowel History: or 'Footprints on the sands of time.'* OH, 1899;

55p. *Supplement*, Dayton, OH, 1904. 64p. [L4322].

CRUM -- Lybarger, Donald Fisher. *The Crum Family, Notes Concerning the Descendants of Anthony Crum Sr. of Frederick County, Virginia.* Cleveland, OH, Lybarger, 1963. 71 leaves. D gives underscored title. [L4334; D3120; VV48].

CRYDER -- Crider, Lorraine L. *Abraham Cryder, Ohio Pioneer.* NP, 1961. 27 leaves. [D3127].

CULBERTSON -- Culbertson, Lewis Rogers. *Genealogy of the Culbertson and Culberson Families...* Zanesville, OH, The Courier Company, Printers, Publishers and Binders. 1893. vii, 336p. [L4345].

CULBERTSON -- Culbertson, Lewis Rogers. *Supplement to the Culbertson Genealogies.* Cincinnati, OH, The Cincinnati Lancet-clinic, 1896. 38p. [L4345].

CULBERTSON -- Culbertson, Lewis Rogers. *Genealogy of the Culbertson and Culberson Families. Rev.* Zanesville, OH, The Courier Co., Printers, 1923. 2p, iv-vii, 478p. N gives 478p. [L4346; NG34].

CUMMER -- Cummer, Wellington W. *Cummer Memoranda: A Record of the Progenitors and Descendants of Jacob Cummer, A Canadian Pioneer.* Cleveland, OH, O. S. Hubbell, 1911. 11, 222p. [X232-FW/LI/PH].

CUMMER -- Duty, Allene Beaumont. *Data Relating to Descendants of John Cummer and Sarah Lockman Smith.* Cleveland, OH, Lorraine Belfry Harper, 1972. 35 leaves. Bound with: Duty family: Descendants of Ebenezer Duty of Ohio. Compiled by Allene Beaumont Duty. 88 leaves. [DS169].

CUMMING -- Burrel Edith L. *Genealogy and History of These Families, William Cumming,*

Dorsey, Black, Weisel (Wisel). Findlay, OH, Burrell, 1967. 46 leaves. [D3139].

CUNNINGHAM -- Cunningham, Ruth Coward. [G169]. See above: CARBAUGH. [G120; DC910].

CUNNINGHAM -- Cunningham, Mark H., Jr. *A Genealogy and Brief History of One Branch of the Cunningham's - 1st ed.* Findlay, Ohio, M.H. Donaldson, Jr., 1991. 206p. 1. Cunningham family. 2. Ohio-Genealogy. [G169].

CURREN -- Bradshaw, J. Douglas. [G170]. See above: CRAWFORD. [G164; DC913].

CURRIER -- Currier, Edwin M. *Address of Historical Sketch Delivered at Currier Family Reunion. Toledo, Ohio, October 3, 1910.* Lowell, MA, Courier-Citizen Co., 1913. 19p. [L4386].

CURRY -- NAS. *The Curry and Robinson Families of Union County, Ohio.* NP, 1916. 10p. [X233-OH].

CURRY -- Hall, William C. *The Leonard Curry Genealogy: Being a History of Leonard Curry and His Wife, Penelope Bryan, Both Born in Green Co., Ohio and Their Descendants.* Nevada, IA, Hall, 1980. v leaves, 123p. 2 leaves of plates. [C163].

CURTIS -- Preston, Luara Guthrie (Curtis). *The Curtis Family. A Record of the Descendants of Deodatus Curtis of Braintree, Massachusetts.* Marietta, OH, 1945. 168p. [L4402].

CUSHMAN -- Burt, Alvah Walford. *Cushman Genealogy and General History Including the Descendants of the Fayette County, Pennsylvania, and Monongalia County, Virginia, Families.* Cincinnati, OH, A.W. Burt, 1942. 432p. [L4420; D3193; VV49].

72

CUSICK -- Komar, Linda Gail. *John Cusick of Jefferson and Harrison Counties, Ohio; Early 1800's and His Descendants.* St. Petersburg, FL, Genealogy Pub. Service; Fairfax, VA, 1990. viii, 204p. 1. Cusick family. 2. Cusick, John, 1787-ca. 1861-Family. [G170].

CUTLER -- Blazier, George J. *The Cutler Collection of Letters and Documents, 1748-1925; Letters and Other Memorabilia of Manasseh Cutler, 1742-1823, Ephraim Cutler, 1767-1853, William Parker Cutler, 1812-1889, Julius Perkins Cutler, 1814-1904, and Their Relatives and Associates.* Gathered and Preserved by Mary Dawes Beach, Cataloged by Mary Louis Otto. Marietta, OH, Marietta College, 1963. vii, 102p. [L4441].

D

DALLAS -- Dallas, Zella Rogers. *Families of Dallas, Lourens, Rogers, and Some of Their Relatives.* __, OH, Z.R Dallas and E.R. Lourens, Enon, OH, 1984. 5 v. (xix, 4019p.). Vol. 5. Index. 1. Dallas family. 2. Lourens family. 3. Rogers family. [G172].

DALTON -- Ceasor, Ebraska Dalton. *My Family.* Cleveland, OH, E.D. Ceasor, 1988. 91, 28p. 1. Dalton family. 2. Ceasor, Ebraska Dalton, 1920- -Family. 3. Afro-American-Genealogy. [G173].

DAMM -- Pascoe, Patty Dahm. *Christ and Anna, Descendants of Anton Bach, Jacob Damm, John Hartman, George Kremer, and John Yocum. Including Local History and Memorabilia of Sandusky, Ohio and Surrounding Areas.* Baltimore, MD, Gateway Press, 1980. xiii, 443p. [C168].

DANA -- Burrage, Florence Dale. *The Danas and the Dana Farm, Belpre, Ohio. Together with a Brief Account of the Family and Farm of*

Benjamin Dana of the Cedars, Beverly, Ohio. NP, 1941. 142 numb laeves. [L4502].

DANIELS -- Walker, Elizabeth Porcher. *The Daniels of Pomeroy, Ohio.* Manchester, CT, E. P. Walker, 1983. 34p. [C169].

DARNALL -- Perkings, Lawrence U. *Darnall Genealogy... Henry Lewis Darnall of Holmes County, Ohio.* Berkeley, CA, 1950. 9 leaves. [X240-SU].

DARROW -- Keller, D. P. *Darrow: Notes Regarding the Darrow Family in New York, Ohio and Missouri.* Des Moines, IA, 1964. 19p. [X241-FW].

DAVENPORT -- Davenport, D. G. A. *Davenport Family Record; Being the Pedigress and Descendants of Darius and Cyrus Davenport ca. 1820-1865.* Cincinnati, OH, Author, 1895. 25p. [X242-FW].

DAVENPORT -- Davenport, Darius. G. A. *Davenport Family Record.* Cincinnati, OH, John Scott Darius, 1969. Unpaged. [X242-CH/FW].

DAVENPORT -- Davenport, Dr. John Scott. *The Davenports of Randolph County, North Carolina. An Interim Report.* Cincinnati, OH, 1971. 11 leaves. [X242-GF].

DAVID -- David, Bruce William. *The David Family Scrapbook.* Cleveland Heights, OH, David, 1958. 99p. Contents - v. 1. Ancestors in the American Revolution, 1640-1958. [L4574; D3293].

DAVID -- David, Bruce William. *The David Family Scrapbook.* Cleveland Heights, OH, David, 19__, __v. DAR Library has v. 4 & 5 (1961/1964) bound together. [D3294].

DAVID -- David, Bruce William. *The David Family Scrapbook.* Cleveland Heights, OH, David, (1959, ca.1958-64), 3 vols. NY has vols. 1, 4 & 5. [X242-NY].

DAVIDSON -- Harbarugh, Elizabeth Davidson. *The Davidson Genealogy*. Ironton, OH, Harbaugh, 1948. x, 482p. [L4585; D3299].

DAVIDSON -- Smith, Berniece C. *A Davidson - Stewart Genealogy of Wood County, Ohio: A Two-Family History*. Bowling Green, OH, B.C. Smith, 1988. 225p. 1. Davidson family. 2. Stuart family. 3. Ohio-Genealogy. [G176].

DAVIS -- Biedel, Helen Clark. *Washington County, Ohio, Death Records of the Davis Families*. NP, 1949. 6 l. Bound with: Davis records, Washington County, Ohio - early gateway to the West by Helen C. Biedel. [D3307].

DAVIS -- Biedel, Helen Clark. *Davis Records: Washington County, Ohio,...* Tacoma, WA, Author, 1955. 43p. [X244-SU].

DAVIS -- Davis, Francis Y. *Genealogy of the Ancestry and Descendants of Captain Francis Davis, Founder of Davisville, New Hampshire, and Some of the Posterity of His Brother Gideon Davis: with Record and Many Accounts of Francis Davis, the Emigrant from Wales to America...* Dayton, OH, The Otterbein Press, 1910. 202p. [L4605].

DAVIS -- Davis, J. O. *Davis Family History*. Pleasant Hills, OH, Author, 1935. 30p. [X244-FW].

DAVIS -- Davis, W. E. *The Davis Family: Joseph, Ellenor (Lewis), Mathias, Richard, etc.* Glendale, OH, W.E. Davis. 1985. 1 v. (various foliations). 1. Davis family. 2. Kentucky Genealogy. 3. Davis, Joseph, b. ca.1770-Family. [G177].

DAVIS -- Heck, Arch Oliver. *Descendants of Hezekiah Davis I, A Settlor in Northe (sic) eastern Tennessee in the Latter Part of the 1700's*. Columbus, OH, 1965. 4 v. (xii, 467p). [L4643].

DAVIS -- Herman, Berthenia Davis. [G177]. See above: BRIDGE. [G88].

DAVIS -- Johnson, Joanne Cherry. *Rev. John Hampton Davis of Highland County, Ohio: His Family and Ancestors, Descendants.* Chillicothe, OH, J. C. Johnson, 1983. vi, 91p. [C172].

DAVIS -- Nicholson, Susie Davis. *Davis. The Settlers of Salem, West Virginia, Their Ascendants and Some of Their Descendants.* Strasburg, OH, Gordon Printing, 1975. ix, 308p. [S639; D3347].

DAVIS -- Nicholson, Susie Davis. *Davis: "the Settlers of Salem, West Virginia" (Their Ancestors and Some of Their Descendants).* Strasburg, OH, Gordon Print, 1979. [VV53].

DAVISON -- Atkin, Angelo F. *Family History.* Bowling Green, OH, Atkin, 1936. 29p. [D3360].

DAVISSON -- Davisson, Richard L. *Life of Josiah Davisson, II ... 1743 ... 1825; An Address Delivered ... in Monroe Township, Preble Co., Ohio.* NP, 1916. 14p. [X246-FW].

DAY -- Andrews, Adele. *Ancestors and Descendants of Giles and Hannah Cutler Day.* Norwalk, OH, 1940. various pagings. [X247-FW].

DAY -- Day, George E. *A Genealogical Register of the Descendants in the Male Line of Robert Day of Hartford, Conn., Who Died in the Year 1648.* 2nd ed. Northampton Printed by J. & L Metcalf, 1848. With a Supplement Giving Descendants of Captain John Day, number 194, Who Moved to Sheffield, Ohio in 1816. Oberlin, OH, Press of the News Printing Company, 1913. 163p. [L4675].

DAY -- Fisher, Miriam M. *Day Family Genealogy. Rev. ed.* Cincinnati, OH, 1956. Unpaged. [X247-CH].

DAY -- McGivney, Vivian and Mrs. Ken (Vivian) Nogle. *Third Supplement to the Descendants of Robert Day of Hartford, Connecticut and Captain John Day, Number 194, of Sheffield, Ohio and Alfred Day of Mondovi, Wisconsin, 1978 ed.* Hartford, KY, McDowell Publications, 1978. Includes reprint of portions of: A genealogical register of the descendants in the male line of Robert Day / G. E. Day, 2d ed. Northampton, OH?, printed by J. & L. Metcalf. 1858. [C174].

DAY -- Rowe, Stanley M. *The Journals of Thomas Davis Day.* Cincinnati, OH, Rowe, 1990. 87p. [DC974].

DAY -- Smith, Loire Perkins. *Our "Days" of Noble County, Ohio. Their American Ancestry and Descendants.* Akron, OH, 1967. 1 v. (various pagings). [L4686].

DAYTON -- Ogden, Evelyn L. *Jonathan Dayton, 1760-1824.* Dayton, OH, (Elizabeth, NJ) 1941. 6 leaves. [X247-NY].

DEAN -- Cooper, Marion Deane. *Descendants of John Dean Who Came From England to Dedham, Mass., with Related Families.* Cleveland Heights, OH, 1951. 1 v. (various pagings). [L4719].

DEAN -- Cooper, Marion Deane. *Descendants of John Dean (1650-1727) of Dedham, Mass.* Cleveland Heights, OH, 1957. iii, 217p. X gives 127p.? [NG36; D3405; X248-FW/MH].

DEAN -- Cooper, Marion D. *Descendants of John Dean (1650-1727) of Dedham, Mass. with Additions.* Cleveland Heights, OH, 1957. 2 vols. [XA1070-WR].

DEAN -- Daen, B. S. *Corrections and Additions to A History of the William Dane Family.* Cleveland, OH, 1904. 2p. [X248-LI].

DEAN -- Dean, B. S. & J. E. *A History of the William Dean Family of Cornwall, Conn. and*

Cleveland, Ohio. *Containing the Direct Descent From Thomas Dean of Concord, Mass, Together with a Complete Genealogy of William Dean's Descendants.* Cleveland, OH, Press of the F. W. Roberts Co., 1903. 69p. [L4714].

DEANE -- White, Louie, Dean. *Deane and Allied Family Records of Cogan, Hammond, Haskell, Hathaway, Oliver, Putnam, Reed, Sisson, Waldo, White, Williams.* Brunswick, OH, Laura V. Cheek, 1977. 150 leaves. [D3415].

DEANE -- White, Louie, Dean. *Deane and Allied Family Records of Cogan, Hammond, Haskell...* Brunswick, OH, L. V. Cheek, 1977. 154 p. [DC984].

DeBROSSE -- Goubeaux, Leo C. *The Story of the DeBrosse Family: Vernois-le-Fol, Doubs, France, 1776-1833; Russia, Ohio, U.S.A, 1833-1986.* Cincinnati, OH, F. M. DeBrosse, 1986. vii, 131p. D gives underscored title. [G182; DC988].

DeCAMP -- DeCamp, Crane. *Record of the Decendants of Ezekiel and Mary Baker DeCamp of Butler County, Ohio.* Cincinnati, OH, DeCamp, 1976. 275p. in various pagings. [C176].

DeCAMP -- DeCamp, Crane. *Record of the Descendants of Ezekiel and Mary Baker De Camp of Butler County, Ohio.* Cincinnati, OH, DeCamp, 1976. 3p. 16 leaves including double genealogical chart. [X250-CH/FW/NY].

DeCAMP -- De Camp, James M. *Record of the Descendants of Ezekiel and Mary Baker DeCamp, of Butler County, Ohio.* Cincinnati, OH, Western Methodist Book Concern, 1896. 177p. [L4735].

DECKER -- Decker, Daniel Leroy. *The Decker Family History.* Kent, OH, Decker, 1978. 68 leaves. [C176].

DEHART -- DeHart, Dora. *A History of Jacob and Mary (Day) Dehart*. Middletown, OH, D. DeHart, 1983. 80p. [C177].

DeHAVEN -- Dyke, Mrs. Decrel. *DeHaven and Related Families*. Marysville, OH, n.d. 27 plus leaves. [X251-GF].

DELANEY -- Eskew, John Daniel. *The Laney Family of Henry County, Georgia*. West Chester, OH, J.D. Eskew, 1990. viii, 63p. 1. Delaney family. 2. Georgia-Genealogy. [G184].

DELL -- NAS. *The Descendants of Frederick Dell & Charles Dell*. Middletown, OH, Dell, Rockey & Wolford, 1990. ii, 77 leaves, 1 leaf of plates. 1. Dell family. 2. Dell, Frederick, 19th century-Family. 3. Dell, Charles, 19th century-Family. 4. Ohio-Genealogy. [G184].

DEMING -- King, Isaac F. *Genealogical Leaflet of the David Deming Family*. Colombus, OH, 1892. 6p. [X253-OH].

DEMING -- Deming, Moses. *Autobiography of Moses Deming, 1777-1868 of Liverpool, Medina County, Ohio in 1810*. Copied from his original manuscript by Doris Wolcott Strong. NP, 1938. 107p. [DC1006].

DEMING -- Strong, Doris Wolcott. *The Ancestors and Descendants of Moses Deming, 1777-1868, One of the First Group of Settlers in 1811 to Liverpool (Now Valley City) Medina County, Ohio, in the "Connecticut Western Reserve"*. Washington, DC, 1941. 1, 2, 12 numb. leaves. [L4798].

DEMUTH -- Battershell, C. F. *The Demuth Family and the Moravian Church*. New Philadelphia, OH, Battershell, 1931. 52p. [D3488].

DEMUTH -- Mueller, Th. *Genealogy of the Demuth Family, Begining About 1650*.

Gnadenhutten, OH, W. R. Van Vleck, 19___. 1
leaf. [L4803].

DENHAM -- Fisher, Edward M. *The George and
Elizabeth Denman Family History.* Columbus,
OH, E. M. Fisher, 1981. 1 v. various pagings.
Priv. Printing of 84 copies. [C179].

DENHAM -- Snyder, Betty Pond. *Denman -
Frisinger and Allied Families: Early Ohio
Pioneers.* Baltimore, MD, Gateway, 1987. x,
299p. 1. Denham family. 2. Frisinger family.
3. Ohio-Genealogy. [G185].

DENISON -- Kimmons, Georgia Denison.
*Descendants of Elihu II and Hester Conklin
Denison.* Bowling Green, OH, Kimmons, 1938.
25 leaves. [D3497].

DENLINGER -- Denlinger, Carl E. *A
Genealogical Study of the Denlinger Family.
Compiled in 1969 and updated in 1975.*
Maunaee, OH, Denlinger, 1975. v, 127p.
[X254-PH].

DENLINGER -- McNeely, Elsie D. *John
Denlinger Family Tree (1809-1958).* Arcanium,
OH, n.d. 101p. [X254-FW].

DENNIS -- Young, Elaine Dennis. *Some
Descendants of Robert Dennis of Portsmouth,
Rhode Island.* Norwalk, OH, Young, 1957.
viii, 64p. [L4822; D3501].

DENMAN -- Snyder, Betty Pond. *Denman -
Frisinger and Allied Families, Early Ohio
Pioneers.* Baltimore, MD, 1987. 299p.
[NGS5].

DERBY -- Derby, Samuel Carroll. *Darby -
Derby. John Darby of Marblehead, Mass., and
His Descendants. Five Generations.* Columbus,
OH, 1909. 7 p. [L4848].

DERR -- Abbott, Lyndon Ewing. *Genealogy of
Mildred née Schaeffer Abbott.* Columbus, OH,
Chatham Communications, 1984. 1 v. (various

pagings). 1. Shaffer family. 2. Abbott, Mildred Schaefer, 1910- -Family. 3. Derr family. 4. Wolpers family. 5. Kemp family. [G186].

DERTHICK -- Goodpasture, Robert Abraham. *James Derthick of Shalersville, Ohio.* *His Family and Some Records.* 3rd rev. - Final. Georgetown, CA, 1974. pt. 1. NG gives underscored title. [NG36; X256-FW/LA/NY].

DeSTEIGER -- Singer, John. *Family Trees: "Emperor Charlemagne" Year 742 A.D. to "DeSteiger" and Descendants.* Springfield, OH, Singer, 1983. 143 leaves. [C181].

DEVORE -- Schweitzer, Dorothea F. *DeVore - Bracy Descendants, 1812-1961.* Leipsic, OH, 1961. 27 leaves. Record of George Washington De Vore and Mary June (Bracy) De Vore and their descendants. [X258-FW].

DEWEESE -- LaMunyan, Phillip E. Mrs. *The Dewees Family: Genealogical Data, Biographical Facts amd Historical Information.* Bowling Green, OH, Wood County Chapter, Ohio Genealogical Society, 1985. 294 [i.e. 166p., 4 leaves of plates. Reprint. Originally published: Norristown, Pa.: W. H. Roberts, 1905. 1. Deweese family. 2. Pennsylbania-Genealogy. [G188].

DICK -- Duquid, Lee S. *The George Dick Descendants from Germany.* Fort Wayne, IN, L. S. Duguid, 1985. ii, 150 leaves. 1. Dick family. 2. Dick, George, ca.1765-1835-Family. 3. Bavaria (Germany)-Genealogy. 4. Ohio-Genealogy. [G189].

DICKINSON -- Dickinson, Marguerite S. *Descendants of Captain John and Elizabeth Howland Dickinson of Oyster Bay, Long Island.* Millersburg, OH, 1968. 32 leaves. [A183].

DICKINSON -- Maddox, William H. *Dickinson Family Reunion.* Wauseon, OH, 1930. 11 leaves. [X260-PH].

DICKINSON -- Maddox, William Hedrick. *Joseph Dickinson and Family; Some of His Ancestors and Descendants.* Wauseon, OH, Maddox, 1944. 3p., 137 leaves. D gives underscored title and 137 leaves. [D3583; X260-FW/OH/PH].

DIEFENBACH -- Diefenbach, Mrs. Joseph C., Translator. *John Baltaser Diefenbach and His Descendants.* Akron, OH, 1940. 57 leaves. [L4944].

DIGGES -- Whitesides, Lawson Ewing. *Early Digges Family Progenitors and Some Descendants Fron Kent in Old England to the New World, America.* Glendale, OH, L. E. Whitesides, 1984. 50 leaves. [DC1042].

DIGGS -- Diggs, William S. *Digges - Diggs Family.* Cincinnati, OH, 1907. 67p. [X261-FW].

DIKE -- NAS. *Genealogy of the Dike Family.* Columbus, OH, n.d. Mercury Letter Service. 411p. [X262-FW].

DIKE -- Burkhart, Nellie K. Thurston. *Genealogy of the Dike and Torrance Families from 1623 and 1701.* Columbus, OH, Mercury Letter Service, 1959. 9, 54 leaves. X gives 54 leaves. [D3605; X262-FW].

DILGARD -- Hublinger, Alice Basler. *Descendants of Paulus Dilgard, Jacob Dilgard I, Jacob Dilgard II, Jacob Dilgard III.* Barberton, OH, A. B. Hublinger, 1987. 250p. 1. Dilgard family. 2. Ohio-Genealogy. [G191].

DILLER -- Diller, Eunice C. *John and Elizabeth (Zimmerly) Diller and Their Descendants.* Wooster, OH, 1970. 49p. [X262-FW/OH].

DILLER -- Schieltz, Ruth C. Wagner. [G191]. See above: BIGGS. [G56].

DILLMAN -- Baer, Mabel Van Dyke. *Dillman Family Research, Pennsylvania, Ohio, and Indiana, including Revolutionary War Pension of Andrew Dillman with Dillman Deeds of Claremont County, Ohio, 1800's.* NP, 1964-1965. 82 leaves. [D3617; VP60]

DILLON -- Dillon, Paul Eugene. *The Dillon Family of Early Buck County, Pennsylvania to Their N.E. Ohio Descendants, 1731-1988.* Columbus, OH, P.E. Dillon, 1988. 137p. 1. Dillon family. 2. Pennsylvania-Genealogy. 3. Ohio-Genealogy. [G191].

DILLON -- Nezbeth, Linda B. [G191]. See above: BRADLEY. [G82].

DISHER -- Rose, Verna. *Christian Disher Family, 1765-1983.* Waterville, OH, Community Printing & Advertising, 1984. 149 leaves, 4 leaves of plates. 1. Disher family. 2. Disher, Christian, 1797-1878-Family. [G192].

DOBBINS -- Landis, Carolynn Butler. *The Ancestors & Descendants of Benjamin Dobbins and Mary Ann Sanderson of Fayette County, Ohio.* NP, 1985. 76p. [DC1058].

DODD -- NAS. *Our Dodd Family, Ancestors and Descendants of James Dodd, b. England 1830 to d. Ohio, USA, 1902.* Dayton, OH, 1971. 36p. [S702].

DODD -- Dodd, Bethuel Lewis. *Ancestors and Descendants of Lewis Dodd and Elizabeth Baldwin Dodd...* Cleveland, OH, C. C. Baldwin, 1889. viii, 11p. [L5025].

DODGE -- Dodge, Martin, A. M. *Memorial of Joseph Dodge by His Son. Presented to the 36th Annual Reunion of the Canfield Family, June 26, 1915.* Cleveland, OH, 1915, 22p. [L5043].

DOLBEER -- Dolbeer, Martin L. *An Account of the Dolbeer Family, Ohio Branch.* Greenville, PA, 1971. 100 leaves. [X266-LA/OH].

DOLL -- Shaver, Mathias Evelyn. *Michael Genealogy: The Family of John and Charlotte (Doll) Michael and Related Families.* Harrison, OH, E.M. Shaver, 1989- v. <1-14 >. Contents: -1 John N. Michael Genealogy; Cornelius Michael; Rhuana Elizabeth Michael -2 George Peter Michael -3 John Henry Michael; Jacob Albert Michael -4 Mary Ann Michael Main -5 Wesley Michael; Enos Ezra Michael; Andrew Michael -6 Doll genealogy; Rauch; 2 Smith genealogies -7 Mathias -8 Andrew Michael research gleanings -9 A Michael family supplement-Winterroth-Michael children -10 Stoeffel Christopher Michael of W. V. & Mrs. Phebe Johnston Craig families -11 Jacob Michael of Virginia & Michael W. V.; Rocky Gap group, 3 Michael families -12 Andrew Michael family -13 Michael Ancestors. -14 2 Smith/Michael genealogies of Maryland, West Virginia & Virginia. 1. Michael family. 2. Michael, John N., 1804-1884-Family. 3. Doll family. 4. Michael Charlotte Doll, 1804-1867-Family. 5. Mathias family. [G195].

DOMINY -- Dominy, Newton, J. *Genealogical History of the Dominy's (sic) Family at East Hampton, Long Island, New York, Beekmantown, Clifton County, New York, Darby Township, Madison County, Ohio, Washington Township, Franklin County, Ohio and Its Allied Families. Dated - ... 1926.* Dublin, OH, N. J. Dominy, 1956. x, 260p. [X266-NY/OH].

DONAHUE -- Lubinski, Tom. *Donoghue - Poole: A Family History of the Leeds County, Ontario Residents: John Donoghue, 1796-1866 and Frances Poole, 1800-1891, and Their Descendants* - 2nd ed. Dayton, OH, T. Lubinski, 1987. 153p. in various pagings. 1. Donahue family. 2. Donoghue, John, 1796-1855-Family. 3. Poole family. 4. Ontario-Genealogy. 5. Canada-Genealogy. [G195].

DONALDSON -- Donaldson, Wayne. *The Donaldson Line: From Donaldson, Nicodemus, Lefever, Simpson, Ashbaugh, Jones, 1730-1981: Maryland, Pennsylvania, Ohio, Wisconsin.* Ann

Arbor, MI, Donaldson, 198_. 80 leaves.
[C189; VP61].

DONALDSON -- Longley, Elizabeth Donaldson.
William Mills Donaldson and Forbears, a
Compilation of Genealogical Facts and Family
Traditions... Cincinnati, OH, The Ebbert &
Richardson Co., 1922. 143p. X gives author
as Donaldson, William H. [D3682; X267-CH/FW].

DONALDSON -- McKitrick, May Donaldson. *A*
Genealogical Record of One Branch of the
Donaldson Family in America, Descendants of
Moses Donaldson, Who Lived in Huntington
County, Penn., in 1770. Columbus, OH, F. J.
Heer Printing Co., 1916. 332p.
[L5070: D3683; VP61].

DONNER -- Donner, Henry F. and Harold L.
The Descendants of Friedrich and Friedericka
Donner. Cleveland Heights, OH, H. F. Donner,
1980. 4, 43, 12 1. 6 plates of leaves.
[C189].

DOOLITTLE -- Doolittle, William Frederick.
The Doolittle Family in America. Cleveland,
OH, Doolittle, (Press of National Printing
Co.), 1901-1908. 7 pts. in 2. [L5081; D3691].

DOOLITTLE -- Doolittle, William Frederick.
The Doolittle Family in America. Cleveland,
OH, Press of National Printing Co., 1901-1967.
8 v. (1350p). [A194].
                -- *Index.* by Leonard H. Doolittle.
NP, 1970. 17p. [A194].

DOTY -- VanSant, Mrs. Effie E.   ...*Doty*
Family History and Genealogy. Findlay, OH,
Kistler's Printing Shop, 1935. 104p.
[L5107].

DOUGHERTY -- NAS. *A Cross-Reference for*
the Names Daugherty - Daughery and Variant
Spellings in the Index to the Federal
Census... 1820, 1830, 1840 *for...* Ohio.
Seattle, WA, 1973. various pagings.
[X269-SP].

DOUGHERTY -- McKitrick, James R. *The Monroe County Dougherty Clan: The Known Descendants of Daniel, Patrick, and Stephen Dougherty.* __, OH, J. R. McKitrick, 1989. 325p. 1. Dougherty family. 2. Ohio-Genealogy. [G197].

DOUGHTON -- Doughten, Thomas Edson. *A Monography Study of Joseph Doughton (... 1771-...1832(, the Progenitor of the N.C. Branch of the Family.* Toledo, OH, Bryan, OH, Century Pr., 1973. 30p. [NG38; X269-FW].

DOUGHTON -- Doughten, Thomas Edson. *Brief Glory; The Story of Orrin Gilbert Doughton (14 March 1835 - 17 Dec 1902) of Williams County, Ohio.* NP, 1979. 42p. [NG38].

DOUGLAS -- Hasson, Ethel W. *Douglas.* Centerburg, OH, 4 leaves. [X270-OH].

DOUTHIT -- Douthit, Ruth Long. *Here Come the Douthits: Coast To Coast Across Two Generations - 1st ed.* Columbus, OH, 1983. vii, 396p. [C191; NG38].

DOWLER -- Lybarger, Donald F. *The Story of the Dowler - Hartshorne, Fisher - Lybarger Families.* Cleveland, OH, Lybarger, 1938. 63 leaves. A gives: 1938, (i.e. 1962). [A198; D3724].

DOWNEY -- Price, Norma Adams. *The Family of James and Mary Killin Downey of Xenia, Ohio, and Atlanta, Illinois.* Tempe, AZ, N.A. Price & P.A. Adams, 1986. 53p. 1. Downey family. 2. Downey, James, 1783-1859-Family. 3. Ohio Genealogy. 4. Illinois-Genealogy. [G199].

DOWNS -- McCarthy, George Gilbert. *The Downs Family of Virginia, Ohio & Indiana.* Baltimore, MD, Gateway Press, 1982. xiii, 197p. [C192; DS195].

DOZER -- Dozer, David D. *Chronological Record of the Dozer Family from August 31,*

1805 to July, 1924. Zanesville, OH, Danker Printing Co., 1924. 54p. [L5163].

DRAIS -- Drais, Lenora M. *Tracing the Drais Family.* Findlay, OH, Drais, 1970. 100 l. [D3738].

DREISBACH -- Ellis, Carolyn B. *Dreisbach Families. Collection in Three Parts.* Findlay, OH, 1939. 64 leaves. (Various pagings). [X273-MH].

DREISBACH -- May, Richard Holman. *A Supplement to the Abraham Holman Family of Ross County, Ohio (Including the Dreisbach and Eyestone Lines): A Genealogy Originally Compiled by Richard Holman May and Published by the Godfrey Memorial Library, Middletown, Conn. in 1959.* Mill Valley, CA, May, 1979. 39p. 1. Hollerman family. 2. Dreisbach family. 3. Eyestone family. [G200].

DREISBACH -- Smith, Charles A. *Dreisbach Families of Pennsylvania and Ohio. Martin Dreisbach Descendants Pennsylvania to Fairfield-Pickaway Counties, Ohio, 1717- 1925.* Findlay, OH, 1933. 55p. [X273-OH; VP62].

DRESSER -- Dresser, Mrs. Jasper Marion. *Dresser Genealogy. 1638-1913.* Buffalo, Cleveland, (etc.) Mrs. Solomon Robert Dresser, The Matthews-Northrup Works. 1913. 20 l. [L5192].

DREYER -- Dreyer, George Charles. *Dreyer Genealogy: Descendants of Henning Dryer (1679-1746) of Flegessen, Germany.* North Bend, OH, Dryer, 1984. 149, 9, 4p. [C193].

DROSTE -- Price, Vergie Farley. *Hune - Drost.* Columbus, OH, Pfeifer Print. Co., 1982. iv, 275p. 1. Hohn family. 2. Droste family. 3. Ohio-Genealogy. [G201].

DRUSHEL -- Drushel, Raymond W. *The Drushel Descendants of John Drushel and Katharine Mowry Drushel, 1749-1949.* Akron, OH, Elyria,

OH, Drushel, 1950. 113 leaves.
[S728; X275-FW/NY].

DUGAN -- Donaldson, Mrs. Richard A. IV.
*Dugan Memorials and Genealogy. An Account of
Joseph and Deborah (Norman) Dugan of Ohio and
Their Descendants with a Brief Sketch of Some
of the Descendant Families in Other States,
Whose Family Relationships Have Not As Yet
Been Established.* Denville, NJ, L. Colletta,
1964. xxiv, 147p. [L5251].

DUMMERMUTH -- Rabatin, Martha. *A
Dummermuth Family History.* Canton, OH, 1982.
52p. [NG38].

DUNAHAY -- Dunahay, Lowell V. *"Kith-Kin" of
Samuel Burdine Dunahay and Angel Carrothers: A
Short History and Genealogy of This Scotch-
Irish Family and Showing Migration of Our
Ancestors from Ireland to Pennsylvania and
Ohio and on the 110th Anniversary of Their
Marriage.* Lima, OH, L. V. Dunahay, 1981. iv,
29p. [C197].

DUNLEVY -- Kelly, Gwendolyn Dunlevy. *A
Genealogical History of the Dunlevy Family;
Don-Levi, Donlevy, Dunleavy, Dunlavey,
Dunlevey, etc.* Columbus, OH, The Evans
Printing Company. 1901. 45, xi, 47-335p., 5
leaves, 32p. D gives 335, 43p. and notes:
"Poor condition. Inquire at desk"
[L5313; DC1124].

DUNSMOOR -- Gard, Nellie Ataline. *Ancestors
and Descendants of Phineas and Polly (Gage)
Dunsmoor.* Marietta, OH, Richardson Print.
Corp., 1971. xv, 453p. [S750; D3853].

DURAND -- Durand, Celia C. <u>Genealogy of the
Durand Family</u>; *A Record of the Descendants of
Francis Joseph Durand together with
Biographical Notes and Some Family Letters.*
Oberlin, OH, Durand, 1925. 136p. D gives
underscored title. [A204; D3862].

DURHAM -- NAS. *History of One Branch of the
Durham Family Since Their First Settlement in*

America, a. d. 1722. New Richmond, OH, 1883. 143 leaves. [X282-FW].

DURHAM -- NAS. *Family Record, 1699-1964 of that Branch of the Durham Family Descended from Samuel Durham (1699 - 1772) of Durham, England, Which Settled in Clermont and Hamilton Counties, Ohio, Which Includes entries for Members of the Allgair, Andres, Axline, Ayres, Barrow, Brown, Burdsal, Gwaltney, Hill, Langdon, Lathrop, Lloyd, Marriott, Merriles, Morgan, Ong, Rothenhoefer, Shumard, Stites, and Webb Families. Also Included is a Short History of the Durham Family.* New Richmond, OH, 1883. 129p. in 1 box. [X282-OH].

DURST -- Durst, Ross Compton. *The Durst Family History, 1738-1957.* Cuyahoga Falls, OH, Durst, 1957. 13p. X give 13 numb. leaves. [D3875; X282-MH].

DURST -- Durst, R. C. *Descendants of Casper Durst and Related Families.* Cuyahoga Falls, OH, 1966. 60p. [X282-FW].

DURYEE -- Duryee, Harold T. <u>The Charles Duryee Family</u>: *The Descendants of Charles Duryee, Son of Joost, of Bushwick, Long Island, New York. With Collateral Families of Schenck, Woodward, Moore, Fish, Leverich, Morse, Bosworth, Dean, Brooks, and Howe.* Canfield, OH, Duryee, 1955. 111, 20p. D gives 131p.; underscored part of title. [L5357; D3878].

DUTY -- Duty, Allene Beaumont. *Duty Family: The Descendants of Ebenezer Duty of Ohio.* Cleveland, OH, 1972. 97 l. [S755; NGS5].

DWAN -- Schubert, Leland W. *An Incomplete History of the Family of Helen and John Dwan, 1862-1945.* Shaker Heights, OH, The Corinthian Press, 1973. x, 77p. [X283-MH].

DWIGHT -- Dwight, Charles Harrison and Virginia Moore Burke Dwight. *Some Hugenot and*

Related Families: A Brief Account of the Lines of Descent of Coulter, Moore, Gayneau, Loveday, Wilson, Frazer, Dwight, and Schneider, Who Emigrated from Frances and the British Isles to America up to 1816. Cincinnati, OH, Dwight, 1975. 36p. [S756].

E

EARHART -- Ansen, Cornelia E. *Some Lateral Branches of the Peter Earhart Family of Penna. Ohio and Indiana.* Muncie, IN, 1975. Various pagings. [X285-FW; VP64].

EARP -- Earp, Charles Albert. *The Joshua Earp Family of Maryland, Kentucky and Ohio.* NP, The Author, 1990. 6 leaves. [DC1140].

EASTMAN -- Higgins, Marie Washburn. *The Eastman - Washburn Book: The Ancestry and Posterity of Hannah Eastman Washburn.* Akron, OH, Higgins, 1928. 43, 1p. D gives 43p. and underscored part of title. [L5422; D3928].

EBERT -- Anderson, Russell H. *Ebert, Ebbert; The Descendants of Matthew Ebert.* Cleveland, OH, 1950. 37p. [X287-FW/PH].

EBY -- Minnick, Effie Eugenia (Eby). *Descendants of Christian Eby (6), 1777-1859, and His Wife, Susannah McDonald Eby, 1781-1866.* Greenville, OH, 1951. 266p. [L5444].

EDWARDS -- Edwards, William H. *Timothy and Rhoda Ogden Edwards of Stockbridge Mass. and Their Descendants, a Genealogy.* Cincinnati, OH, Robert Clarke Co., 1903. 167p. [D4001].

EDWARDS -- Hublinger, Alice Basler. *The William Edwards Family of Coventry, England - Who Came to America in 1863.* Barberton, OH, A.B. Hublinger, 1987. 223p. 1. Edwards family. 2. Edwards, William, 1819-1895-Family. 3. Great Britain-Genealogy. [G209].

EDWARDS -- McGee, Barbara. *Rufus Edwards Family and Other Edwardses of the Connecticut Western Reserve of Ohio.* NP, McGee, 1978. iv, 211p. [D4005].

ELAM -- Elam, Harvey W. *The Elam Family, With Special Reference to Josiah Elam and His Descendants.* Xenia, OH, Elam, 1933. 200p. [L5543; D4029].

ELCHERT -- Koop, Myra C. Studer. *Ancestors and Descendants of Johannes Kölble: A History of the Elchert's (sic), Kelble's (sic), and Kelbley's (sic).* Plano, TX, M.C.S. Koop, 1988. 624p. 1. Kelbley family. 2. Kölble, Johannes, 1778-1860-Family. 3. Elchert family. 4. Ohio-Genealogy. [G210].

ELDER -- Elder, Thomas A. *Genealogy of David Elder and Margery Stewart.* Wooster, OH, Elder, 1905. 52p. [L5545; D4031].

ELDER -- Hull, Lillian E. Elder. The *Historical Record of the Elder Family; A Publication Devoted to the Historical Records of the Elder Family in America.* Mansfield, OH, Hull, Richmond Print., 1945. 76p. D gives underscored title. [D4032; X293-FW/MH].

ELIOT -- Rochelle, Herschel B. *The Elliotts of Stark and Logan Counties, Ohio.* Battle Creek, MI, 1949. Gene. Table. [L5576].

ELIOT -- Warren, Saretta, Elliott. *Ancestry and Stories of an Elliott Family. Its Genealogy Traced from Earliest Settlements of America: Families of Foote, Van Patten, Elliott, Jackson: Haworth, Lamb, and Harvey Families (sic).* Wilmington, OH, Warren, 1974. Leaves A-J, 152, 5p. FW lists as ELLIOTT. [S785; X295-FW].

ELLENWOOD -- Ellenwood, Willard White. *History of the Ellenwood - Wharton and 20 Allied Families 1620-1968, Needham, Sheed, Doty, Potter, Chamberlain, Irvine, Weir, Smith, Sanor, Wilkenson, Soule, Devol, Fleck,*

Cowell, Henderson, Delano, Oakes, Bent, Freeman, Atherton. New Carlisle, OH, Ellenwood, 1969. xxi, A-H, 932p. L lists as ELLINWOOD. D gives 930p. and underscored part of title. [L5599; NG40; D4047].

ELLENWOOD -- Gard, Nellie Ataline. *Our Ellenwood Clan.* Marietta, OH, Gard, 1980. xiv, 575 p. [D4048].

ELLINGER -- Smith, Ned Burton. *The Ellinger and Heiser Families, 1748-1938.* Youngstown, OH, 1938. 3 leaves. [L5597].

ELLIOTT -- Elliott, Edwin Ebenezer. *Daniel Elliott, Patriot and His Descendants.* Middletown, OH, Pierson, 1969. 1 v. (various foliations). [D4055].

ELLIOTT -- Elliott, Edwin Ebenezer. *Daniel Elliott, Patriot and His Descendants, 1769-1930.* 2nd edition. Middletown, OH, Clye E. Pierson, 1969. 1 v. [DC1171].

ELLIS -- Emerson, Ann-Jannette. *James & Mary Veatch Ellis: Their Sons & Other Descendants.* Santa Monica, CA, R.C. Emerson Co., 1985. xv, 703p. 1. Ellis family. 2. Ellis, James, b.1717-Family. 3. Veitch family. 4. Ohio-Genealogy. [G212].

ELLIS -- Ellis, Frank Rogers. *Descendants of Rowland Ellis and Sallie Abrams of Massachusetts.* Cincinnati, OH, 1893. 6 numb. leaves. [L5604 & L5607].

ELLIS -- Foos, Katharine S. *The Ellis Family.* Dayton, OH, U.B. Pub. House, 1900. viii, 128p. [L5606; D4071].

ELLIS -- Miller, Milo H. *A History and Genealogy of the John Ellis Family, 1797-1935.* Bedford, OH, Miller Printing Co., 1936. xxxiii, 165p. [L5613; D4078].

ELLIS -- Willis, Francis O. *Millwood, A Family Tree; A Partial History of the*

*Descendants of John Ellis of Rehoboth, Mass.,
Mainly Comprising His Grandson, Benjamin
Ellis, Jr., of Millwood, O., and His
Descendants. Allied Names: Ellis, Ingallis,
Ballou.* Swampscott, MA, 1909. 103p.
[L5608].

ELLISON -- Ellison, F. Vernon. *Arthur
Ellison of Adams County, Ohio and Some of His
Descendants and Relatives.* Middletown, OH,
Ellison, 1979. 101p. [C209].

ELLSWORTH -- NAS. *The John Ellsworth
Family Records. Washington, Township, Clermont
County, Ohio.* NP, n.d. 4p. [X297-FW] .

ELLYSON -- Bedell, L. Frank. *Dr. Robert and
Elizabeth Ellyson.* Barnesville, OH, The
Fiduciary Trustees of Friends Boarding School,
1969. 1 v. (various pagings). A gives: Cover
title: A genealogy of the Crew and Ellyson
families. [A214; D4087].

ELY -- Ely, Heman. <u>Records of the
Descendants of Nathaniel Ely</u>, *the Emigrant,
Who Settled First in Newton, now Cambridge,
Mass. Was One of the First Settlers of
Hartford, also of Norwalk Conn., and a
Resident of Springfield, Mass., From 1659
until His Death in 1675.* Cleveland, OH, Short
and Forman, Printers & Stationers, 1885. ix,
515p. D gives underscored title.
[L5640; D4096].

EMAHISER -- Emahiser, George Clifton.
Lineage of Clifton Burr Emahiser Family.
Fostoria, OH, 1977. 19 1. [NG40].

EMERICH -- Haines, Kenneth D. *Emerich
Family: By the Name of Emerich, Emerick,
Emyerich, Emrich, and Emrick.* Dayton, OH,
Haines, 1963. 158 leaves. [S791; D4101].

EMERICK -- Haines, Kenneth D. *By The Name
of Emerich, Emerick, Emmerich, Emrich, and
Emrick.* Dayton, OH, 1973. 158p. [X298-FW].

EMERSON -- Emerson, Ellen Tucker. *The Letters of Ellen Tucker Emerson, Edited by E. W. Gregg.* Kent. OH, Kent State University Press, 1982. 2 v. [C210].

EMMITT -- Corrigan, M. J.... *Life and Reminiscenses of Hon. James Emmitt as Revised by Himself.* Chillocothe, OH, Peerless Printing and Mfg. Co., 1888. 624p. [X299-FW].

EMRICH -- Emrich, Oran S. *Descendants of John Emrich, Pennsylvania and Ohio, 1769-1864.* Oxon Hill, Md, Emrich, 1980. 123, 21 leaves. [C212; VP66].

EMRICH -- Emrich, Oran S. *Descendants of Andreas Emmerich of Lancaster County, Pennsylvania.* Dayton, OH, Ohio Connection, 1987. 325p. "New Revised". 1. Emrich family. 2. Emmerich, Andreas, 1681-1769- Family. [G214].

ENDICOTT -- Jones, Ralph E. *The Endicott Family, Descended From Gov. John Endecott, Mass. Bay, Boston, 1628.* Warren, OH, 1935. 5 numb. leaves. [L5672].

ENDSLEY -- Endsley, John Darrel. *The Endsley Family in the New World.* Paulding, OH, Endsley, 1976. 206p. [D4127; X299-FW/PH].

ENGLAND -- NAS. *Family Records of Rev. James J. and Sarah Rousch England and Descendants Delaware County, OH.* NP, Illinois DAR, G.R.C. 1986. 73 leaves. [DC1194].

ENGLE -- Engle, Winfield S. H. *The Melchor Engle Family..., History and Genealogy, 1730-1940.* Lima, OH, Engle, 1940. 243, 1 leaf, 245-500p. D gives 500p. and underscored title. [L5683; D4132].

ENSCH -- Hamel, Claude Charles. *Genealogy of the Ensch Family in the Grand Duchy of*

Luxemburg. Showing Marriage into the Baatz Family of the Country. Amherst, OH, 1948. 4 leaves. [L5688].

ERWIN - Brandt, Frank E. B. *Erwin Family Record, Compiled from Old Bibles in the Possession of F. E. Brandt; Births, Deaths, and Marriages.* Hamilton, OH, Republ. Print., 1895. 8p. [X302-FW].

ESTADT -- Cummings, Joann Schoeppner. *Ancestors and Descendants of Frank and Rachel (Ebert) Estadt Who Lived in Noble County, Ohio in 1861.* Marietta, OH, Comservco, 1980. 100p. [DS222].

ESTERLY -- Keyser, I. N. *Genealogical Tables: Descendants of Michael and Catherine Esterly.* Columbiana, OH, The Michael Esterly Memorial Assoc. 1929. Pagination not indicated. [X304-OH].

ESTERLY -- Keyser, Isaac N. *Esterly Family; Descendants of Michael (1762-1843).* Urbana, OH, M. A. Keyser, 1937. 2 parts in 1 vol. (24, 36p.). [X304-FW].

ETHERIDGE -- Byrd, Helen Norris. [G218]. See above: CAMP. [G117].

EVANS -- NAS. *Bible Records From Missouri, Ohio, Nebraska to Idaho.* NP, Alaska DAR, G.R.C. 1983. 31 leaves. [DS224].

EVANS -- Evans, Owen David and Annie Jackson Evans. *The Evans - Jackson Genealogy; The Jones and Evans Families of Portage County and Mahoning County, Ohio. and the Jackson and Somers Families of Portsmouth, New Hampshire and Buffalo, N. Y.* NP, 1954. 69 leaves. [L5764].

EVERETT -- Strong, Elmer E. *Gilman Everett of East Springfield, Erie County, Penna. and His Descendants.* Cincinnati, OH, 1962. 62p. [X306-FW].

EWIN -- Euans, Clifton Clark. *A Record of the Descendants of John Ewin (Ewins) of Burlington County, N.J. and His Grandson Moses Euans of Logan Co., Ohio.* Erie, PA, Euans: Cook, 1962. 166 leaves. X lists under EWAN. [D4202; X306-FW/NY/SP].

EWING -- NAS. *Memorial of Thomas Ewing of Ohio.* New York, NY, 1873. 289p. [NG41].

EWING -- Abbott, Lyndon Ewing. *Genealogy of Lyndon Ewing Abbott (maternal line): Laughlin, Ewing, Fleming, Brinkerhoff, Houghtelin, and Other Families.* Dayton, OH, E. E. Abbott, 1986. 64 leaves (some folded). 1. Laughlin family. 2. Ewing family. 3. Fleming family. [G219].

EYESTONE -- May, Richard Holman. [G220]. See above: DREISBACH. [G200].

EZEKIEL -- Ezekiel, Henry C. *Genalogicl Record, 1892?, of the Ezekial Family of Philadelphia, Pennsylvania; Richmond, Virginia, and Cincinnati, Ohio.* NP, n.d. 73p. on 53 leaves. Pages 35 and 36 missing. [X308-CH; VV63].

F

FAGIN -- NAS. *Descendants of Patrick Fagin.* Fagin Family Association, 1st ed. Felicity, OH, 1967. 100 leaves. [L5817].

FAIRBANKS -- Fairbanks, Charles H. *Fairbanks Family Records.* Cleveland, OH, A. W. Fairbanks, Printer, 1886. 30p. [L5823].

FARBER -- Weaver, Samuel Edwin. *Farber Families of an Early Ohio Pioneer Who Settled Sandy Creek Valley, Tuscarawas County, Ohio in 1806.* Denver, CO, R. H. Dodge, 1978. 47 leaves. [C219].

FARMER -- Farmer, Walter I. *In America Since 1607: the Hollingsworth, Farmer, and Judkins Families, Their Ancestors, Descendants and Many Related Families.* Baltimore, MD, Gateway, Cincinnati, OH, W. I. Farmer, 1987. xi, 304p. 1. Hollingsworth family. 2. Farmer family. 3. Judd family. [G222].

FARMER -- Painter, Lydia Ethel Farmer. *(The) Memoirs of James and Meribah Farmer.* Cleveland, OH, The Whitworth Bros. Co. printing, 1900. 4, 128p. [X311-FW].

FARVER -- Farver, Warner. E. *A History of the Descendants of Christian and Susannah Farver, 1752-1955.* Baltic, OH, X gives Millersburg, OH, Farver, 1955. 205p. [D4281; X313-FW/NY/SP].

FARRINGTON -- Rochelle, Herschel B. *Farrington and Kirk Family: Ancestors and Descendants of Abraham Farrington (1765-1845) of New Jersey and Ohio and Wife Deborah Kirk (1781-1829) of Chester Co., Pennsylvania.* Hillsborough, NC, Rochelle, 1983. v, 361p. [C220; NG41].

FAULKNER -- Faulconer, James Gayle. *The Faulconer Family: A History.* Troy, OH, Faulconer, 1980. 19 leaves. [C221].

FAULKNER -- Faulconer, James Gayle. *Thomas Faulconer and His Descendants.* Baltimore, MD, Gateway Press, Troy, OH, 1984. 198p. [C221].

FAWCETT -- Fawcett, Thomas Hayes. *The Fawcett Family of Frederick County, Virginia.* Chesterland, OH, Katherine Fawcett Kneal, 1973. v. 71,4 l. Originally Published in 1936. [D4299].

FAY -- Fay, Orlin P. *Fay Genealogy.* Cleveland, OH, J. B. Savage, 1898. 420 leaves. [D4302].

FAY -- Johnson, George Henry. *One Branch of the Fay Family Tree; An Account of the*

Ancestors and Descendants of William and Elizabeth Fay of Westboror, Mass., and Marietta, Ohio. Columbus, OH, Champlin Press, 1913. 130p. D gives underscored part of title and 130 leaves. [L5926; D4303].

FEATHERINGILL -- Waterfield, Marjorie F. *History of the Featheringill, Bogart, Fruchey, Holmes, and Metcalf Families.* Maumee, OH, 1976. 64p. [X315-FW].

FECHER -- Fecher, Constantine John. *The Ancestral Tree: A Biographical Sketch: Leaves, Limbs, and Trunk.* Dayton, OH, University of Ddayton Press, 1978. xi, 312p. [C223].

FEE -- Fee, William I. *Bringing The Sheaves.* Cincinnati, OH, Cranston & Curts, 1896. iv, 663p. [D4307].

FEE -- McGroarty, Wm. B. *Fee Family in Maryland, Pennsylvania, Kentucky & Ohio, 1703-1944.* Alexandria, VA, 1944. 20p. [X315-FW; VP71].

FELLERS -- NAS. *Enos Fellers Family; Background and Posterity.* Walhonding, OH, 1965. 69, 14p. [X315-FW].

FELLERS -- Fellers, Forrest S. *Enos Fellers Family; Background and Posterity.* Walhonding, OH, 1960. 68, 4 leaves. [X315-LA/NY].

FELLERS -- Fellers, Forrest S. *Enos Fellers Family.* Walhonding, OH, 1963, 68 leaves. [NG42].

FENDRICK -- Schopfer, Alton L. *Genealogy, The Fehndrich (Fendrick) Family in Switzerland and Ohio.* Santa Barbara, CA, A. L. Schopfer, 1984. 112p. [C224].

FENTON -- Brown, Willis B. *Family History of Jeremiah Fenton (1764-1841) of Adams County, Ohio and His Descendants.* Des Moines, IA, 1910. xiii, 199, 7p. [L5968].

FERGUSON -- Raudabaugh, James E. *Ancestors and Descendants of Alfarata Ferguson and Samuel H. Raudabaugh.* Ottawa, OH, Raudabaugh, 1982. 118p. [C225].

FERNER -- Ferner, O. A. *Ferner - Farner - Furner Families.* Alliance, OH, Ferner, 1941. 29p. [D4352].

FERNOW -- Fearnow, Edgar C. *The Fernow Family (also Spelled Ferneat, Ferno, Fearnow) Written for the Fearnow Family Reunion and 170th Anniversary of the Birth of John Fernow, (1760-1825), Who Settled near Bath, Va., (now Berkeley Springs, West Virginia), in 1784, and Emigrated to Ohio in 1814.* Capital Heights, MD, 1930. 65 leaves. [L5988; VV65].

FERRIS -- NAS. *Ferris Family in America.* NP, 197_. 54p. [X318-FW].

FERRIS -- Scofield, Harriet. *A Genealogy of the Ferris Family.* Cleveland, OH, Scofield, 1953. 72, xiv leaves. [D4359].

FERSON -- Pierce, Doris Whittier. *Family of James Ferson, Jr. and Mary (McNeill) Ferson.* Sunbury, OH, Pierce, 1975. 138 leaves. [D4360].

FESMIRE -- Khalid, Alice Ann Fesmire. *Fesmire, A Family History and Genealogy: Martin Fesmire and His Descendants in North Carolina and Tennessee with Branches in Indiana, Ohio, Mississippi, Texas, and Oklahoma.* Baton Rouge, LA, Land and Land Printers, 1982. 218p. [C226].

FESSLER -- Fessler, William T. *Fessler Ancestories (sic): Foreign Origins and Family Summaries and Briefs in Pennsylvania: Also Briefs in California, Illinois, Indiana, Iowa, Kansas, Kentucky, North Carolina, Missouri, Ohio, Virginia: Plus Hundreds of Other Surnames.* Haddonfield, NJ, Fessler, 1980. 124p. [C226; VV65].

FETZER -- Fetzer, John E. *One Man's Family; A History and Genealogy of the Fetzer Family.* Ann Arbor, MI, Ann Arbor Press, 1964. xviii, 212p. [L6009].

FIELD -- Mattoon, Winford Lecky. *The Descendants of Israel Field.* Columbus, OH, 1926. 3 leaves. [L6027].

FIELDING -- Knittel, Nina Fielding. *A Century in America with Descendants of the Henry and Charlotte (Aland) Feilding () Family, 1881-1981.* North Jackson, OH, Knittel, 1983. 84p. 1p. of plates. [C227].

FIELDS -- Dawson, Elsie F. Fields. *Notes on the Field and Congeneric Families of Ohio and Indiana, 1800-1982.* Winter Park, FL, Ray Fields Dawson, 1982. 74p. [DC1246].

FIKE -- Feick, Anita Gundloch. *Building America: A History of the Family Feick (Feik, Fike).* Baltimore, MD, Gateway Press, Sandusky, OH, 1983. C-E, 489p. 5 pages of leaves. [C228].

FINCKEL -- Finckel, George M. *The Finckel Family from 1719-1921.* Columbus, OH, n.d. 86 leaves. [X320-OH].

FINFROCK -- Wilcox, Charles Finfrock. *Johannes Fünfrock: A Genealogy in Alsace-Lorraine and America.* -1st ed. Troy, OH, C.F. Wilcox, 1986. xxiv, 327p. 1. Finfrock family. 2. Fünfrock, Johannes, ca. 1535- ca. 1600-Family. 3. Alsace-Lorraine (Germany)-Genealogy. 4. Germany-Genealogy. NG lists as FUNFROCK. [G228; NG44].

FINLEY -- Finley, James B. *Autobiography of Rev. James B. Finley.* Cincinnati, OH, Finley, 1853. 454p. [D4391].

FINLEY -- Stout, Herald F. *The Clan Finley, A Condensed Geneaology of the Finley Family at*

Home and Abroad. Dover, OH, Stout, The Eagle Press, 1940. 2, xiii, 143, 10p. [L6053]

FINLEY -- Stout, Herald F. *The Clan Finley, A Condensed Genealogy of the Finley Family at Home and Abroad.* Dover, OH, Stout, The Eagle Press, 1956. 2 v. bound together. X gives 176p. & 2nd ed. revised and corrected. D gives underscored title. [D4395; X320-FW/MH/SU].

FINNELL -- Finnell, Arthur Louis. *Thomas Finnell of Coshocton County, Ohio and Some Allied Families, Wolfe, Barnes, Roos, Andrew.* Tyler, MN, 1967. 2 v. in 1. [NG42].

FINTON -- Finton, Ken. *The Finton Family in America.* Greenville, OH, Finton, 1966. 80, 3 leaves. [D4399].

FISCHER -- Hamel, Claude Charles. *Genealogy of a Branch of the Fischer Family from Germany, Which Settled in Vermilion Township, Erie Co., Ohio.* Amherst, OH, 1949. 5 leaves. [L6059].

FISCHER -- Hamel, Claude Charles. *Genealogy of a Branch of the Fischer Family from Germany, Which Settled in Vermilion Township, Erie Co., Ohio.* Elyira, OH, 1960. 9 leaves. [L6060].

FISH -- NAS. *Genealogy of One Line of the Fish Families Whose Ancestors Settled in the State of Connecticut about 1651, or Possibly Earlier. Fish, Morgan, and Avery, 1637-1941.* Cleveland, OH, 1941. 2, 33 numb. leaves. [L6067].

FISH -- Fish, Margaret Ruth. *Thomas Fish of Pennsylvania, Ohio, Illinois; Family Outline.* Vincennes, IN, 1965. 37, 10 l. [L6070].

FISH -- Fish, Margaret Ruth. *Thomas Fish of Pennsylvania, Ohio, Illinois; Family Outline.* Vincennes, IN, Fish, 1970. 66 leaves. [D4402; VP72].

FISH -- Wise, L. G. *Genealogy of the Descendants of Ebenezer Fish.* Cleveland, OH, 1931. 8p., 14 leaves. [X321-FW].

FISHER -- Fisher, Thelma. *Fisher Family History.* Wilmington, OH, Cox Printing Co., 1978. A-Z, 2, 87p. Cover Title: Atkinson - Fisher english quaker emigrants with William Penn. [C229].

FISHER -- Leslie, R. P. F. *Families of Fisher, Durnell, Littler, Zimmerman; and Records of Fairview Friends Meeting.* Wilmington, OH, Clinton County Hist. Soc., 1960. Various pagings. [X322-FW].

FISHER -- Lybarger, Donald F. *Notes Concerning the Fisher Family of Fishing Creek Valley, Newberry and Fairview Townships, York County, Pennsylvania.* Cleveland, OH, Lybarger, 1966. 31p. [L6094; D4423; VP73].

FISHER -- Maingi, Sharon Ochs. *The Descendants of Johannes Fischer.* Dayton, OH, Daymont Print Co., 1990. 224p. 1. Fisher family. 2. Fischer, Johannes, 1819-1912-Family. 3. Germany-Genealogy. 4. Ohio-Genealogy. [G230].

FISHER -- Potts, Genevieve. *Genealogy of the Michael Fisher Family of Ohio.* NP, n.d. 9p. [X322-OH].

FISHER -- Thomas, Alfred A. *Some Family Genealogies; Being Certain Data of the Forefathers, Written for His Son, Thomas Head Thomas.* Dayton, OH, Thomas, 1908. 26p. Pt. I Fisher ancestry. - Pt. II, Head, ancestry. [L6082; D4429].

FITCH -- Fitch, John G. *Genealogy of the Fitch Family in North America.* Olmstead, OH, Samuel Barker, Printer, 1886. 115p. [D4436: X323-FW/LI/NY].

FITKIN -- Fitken, Glenn Ludgate. *Descendants of Will Fitkins, Leckhampstead,*

Buckinghamshire, England, 1563. Toledo, OH, Fitkin, 1977. iv, 39p. 1 fold. leaf. of plates. [C230].

FLAGG -- Flagge, D. W. *Flagg Ancestry, 1637-1957.* Dayton, OH, Author, 1957. 84p. [X325-FW].

FLATH -- Singer, Dorothy. *Flath and Schmid (Smith) Genealogies with "ancestral charts from Germany": Peter Flath Married Elizabeth Gelsenliter and Elisabeth Flath, 1934 [i.e.1834]-1889 Married Romuald Schmid, 1824-1892: Ancestors, Descendants, Siblings.* Springfield, OH, D.B. Singer, 1989. 233 leaves. 1. Flath family. 2. Flath, Peter, 1834-1910-Family. 3. Schmid, Romuald, 1824-1892-Family. 4. Schmidt family. 5. Smith family. 6. Germany-Genealogy. 7. Ohio-Genealogy. [G231].

FLEMING -- Abbott, Lyndon Ewing. [G232]. See above: EWING. [G219].

FLEMING -- Shuck, Larry G. *Shucks, Fleshmans, Sydenstrickers & Other Families.* Baltimore, MD, Gateway Press, Cincinnati, OH, L. G. Shuck, 1986. iv, 446p., 1 leaf of plates. 1. Schuck family. 2. Fleshman family. 3. Seidensticker. [G232].

FLICKINGER -- Flickinger, Edward. *History of the Flickinger Family.* Galion, OH, Edward Flickinger, 1902. 39p. [D4485].

FLORA -- Flora, Joel Cephas. *A Genealogy and History of Desecendants of Jacob Flora Senior of Franklin County, Virginia.* Dayton, OH, J.C. Flora, 1951. 375p. L lists under FLORY [L6183; D4495].

FLORY -- Dowling, Hannah F. B. *Supplement to Flory, Flora, Fleury Family History. by Walter Q. Bunderman, Reading, 1948.* Dayton, OH, 16p., 7 leaves. [X327-FW].
  -- Marchinkowski, John P. *Another Supplement.* NP, 1973. 156p. [X327-FW].

FLORY -- Dowling, Hannah F. B. *Michael Flory and Hannah Wogoman Genealogy*. Dayton, OH, Author, 1964. 16p. [X327-CH].

FLOYD -- Floyd, Marjorie Dodd. *Descendants of Col. Mathew Floyd, Loyalist of South Carolina and His Son Abraham Floyd*. Dayton, OH, Mrs. C. E. Floyd, 1980. 93 leaves, 2 leaves of plates. [C232].

FLUETSCH -- Howe, Helen Cooper. *The Family Tree of Nicholas Fluetsch*. Cincinnati, OH, Howe, 1978. 120p. [C233].

FOBES -- NAS. *The Descendants of Nathan and Rebecca Fobes of Wayne Township, Ohio*. No Title Page, NP, n.d. 95p. [X327-FW/LI].

FOLLETT -- Ward, Harry Parker. *A Brief Sketch of the Life of Persis Follett Parker. Together with a Few Notes of Family History*. Columbus, OH, The Champion Printing Co., 1893. 43p. [L6201].

FOLLETT -- Ward, Harry Parker. <u>The Follett - Dewey - Fassett - Safford Ancestory of Captain Martin Dewey Follett (1765-1831)</u> and *His Wife Persis Fassett (1765-1849)*. Columbus, OH, Champlin Printing Co., 1896. 245p. L gives 277p. DC gives underscored title. [L6202; D4530; DC1281].

FOLSOM -- Folsom, Seward G. *Searching for Great Grandfather*. Lima, OH, 1941. 13p. [X329-OH].

FONTAINE -- La Fontaine, Leo S. *The Story of the La Fontaine Family of Vance, Belgium, and Seneca County, Ohio, USA with the Nye, the Warnimont and Allied Families*. Charlotte Harbor, FL, L.S. LaFontaine, 1986. xviii, 478p. 1. Fontaine family. 2. Nye family. 3. Warnimont family. 4. Belgium-Genealogy. 5. Ohio-Genealogy. [G234].

FOOS -- Bailey, Rosalie F. *The Foos Family of Pennsylvania and Ohio, with Appendix on*

Griffith families of Eastern Pennsylvania. Philadelphia, PA, The Genealogical Society of Eastern Pennsylvania, 1951. [VP75]

FOOT -- King, Mrs. James A. (Nellie Clark). *Some New England Families...* Cleveland, OH, J. B. Savage Co., 1922. 2 v. v. 1. Foote - Bingham -- v. 2. Clarke - Kellogg. [L6224].

FOOTE -- King, Nellie Clarke. *Some New England Families.* Cleveland, OH, J. B. Savage Co., 1922. 206p. [D4543].

FOREAKER -- Fedorchak, Catharine Foreaker. *Fore(a)ker Family of Guernsey County, Ohio; James Fouracre, 1775-1849.* Gary, IN, C. F. Fedorchek (sic), 1957. 53 leaves. X gives: various pagings. [NG43; X331-NY].

FORAKER -- Fedorchak, Catharine Foreaker. *Fore(a)ker Family of Guernsey County, Ohio.* Gary, IN, Fedorchak, 1957, 1960. 53 leaves. L gives: 1 v. (various pagings). D gives: "Indexes: Bound with Foraker Findings, 1960". (1957 version may be some as work immediately above.) [L6226; D4544].

FORAKER -- Fedorchak, Catharine Foreaker. *Foreaker Findings; A Compilation of Records Pertaining to the Name of Foraker, Foreaker, Fouraker, Foreacre, and Fouracre.* Gary, IN, Author, 1960. 62p. X gives: companion to previous volume. NY and SL have 1958 (sic) edition. 1 vol. [NG43; X329-FW/MH/NY/SL].

FORBES -- Duty, Allene Beaumont. *The Forbes Family.* Cleveland, OH, Duty, 1972. 79 leaves. [D4545].

FORBES -- Duty, Allene Beaumont. *The Forbes Family: The Descendants of Deacon Daniel Forbes of St. Lawrence County, New York (1789/90-1877).* Cleveland, OH, Duty, 1972. 86 leaves. [S883].

FORCUM -- Forcum, James Ralph, Jr. *One Forcum Family, 1760-1976. -- 1980 Up-date --.*

Hamilton, OH, Forcum, 1980, 32 leaves. [C235].

FORD -- Eastwood, Elizabeth Cobb Stewart. *The Descendants of Andrew Ford of Weymouth, Massachusetts.* Cleveland, OH, Eastwood, 1968. 3 parts. [DC1288].

FORD -- Eastwood, Elizabeth Cobb Stewart. *The Descendants of Andrew Ford of Weymouth, Massachusetts.* Cleveland, OH, Eastwood, 1982. 155p. [DS242].

FORD -- Stewart, Elizabeth Cobb. *The Fords of Cummington Hill, a Chapter of Family History.* Cleveland, OH, Stewart, 1959. 23 leaves. [L6250; NG43; D4562].

FOREMAN -- Forman, William P. *Records of the Descendants of John Foreman.* Cleveland, OH, Short & Foreman, Printers and Stationers. 1885. 29p. [D4566].

FORMAN -- Dandridge, Anne Spottswood. *The Forman Genealogy. Decendants of Robert Forman of Kent Co., Maryland, Who Died in 1719-1720; Also Descendants of Robert Forman of Long Island, New York, Who Died in 1671. The Forman Family of Monmouth, Co., New Jersey: Together with Notices of Other Families of the Name of Forman.* Cleveland, OH, Forman-Bassett-Hatch Co., 1903. 151p. D gives 149p. and underscored title. [L6262; D4572].

FORMAN -- Forman, Charles. *Three Revolutionary Soldiers: David Forman (1745-1797); Jonathan Forman (1755-1809); Thomas Marsh Forman (1758-1845).* Cleveland, OH, The Forman-Bassett-Hatch Co., 1902. 28p. [L6261; NG43].

FORMAN -- Forman, William P. *Records of the Descendants of John Foreman Who Settled in Monmouth County, New Jersey, about the Year A.D. 1685.* Cleveland, OH, Stewart, 1959. 29p. [L6260].

106

FORNEY -- Forney, Howard G. *The Descendants of Johann Adam Forney, 1557-1963*. Warren, OH, 1965. 236p. [X331-FW/NY]

FORSYTH -- Forsythe, Glenn Luther. *The Pioneer Forsythes of Fayette County, Pennsylvania and Their Descendants: Nine Generations of the Descendants of Thomas and Nancy (Parker) Forsythe*. Toledo, OH, Forsythe, 1982. vii 1., 263p, 5 pages of plates. [C235].

FORTNEY -- NAS. *The Fortineux - Fortinet Family: Fortney, Fortna, Fordney, Furtney in America*. by Fortney-Fortna Genealogy Family, Inc. -- Marceline, MO, Walsworth Pub., Coolville, OH, Evajean Fortney McKnight, 1989. xiv, 600p. 1. Fortney family. [G236].

FOSTER -- Dawson, Wayne E. *The History and Ancestry of Rev. John Foster, 1735-1800: His Family, His Life, His Ancestry, Ross County, Ohio*. Clayton, CA, W.E. Dawson, 1984. vii, 255p. [C236].

FOSTER -- Dowling, Hannah (Foster). *My Foster Family, 1603-1969, Mass., New York, New Jersey to Ohio*. Dayton, OH, 1969. 26 leaves. [L6320].

FOSTER -- Foster, Joseph. *Colonel Joseph Foster, His Children and Grandchildren*. Cleveland, OH, 1947. 400p. [NG43].

FOSTER -- Foster, Nancy B. *Genealogical and Biographical Record of Frank Foster and Alice Firbank Foster*. Cincinnati, OH, N.B. Foster, 1990. xi, 403p., 12 leaves of plates. 1. Foster, Frank, 1860-1914. 2. Foster, Alice Firbank, 1862-1933. 3. Missionaries-Nigeria-Biography. 4. Missionaries-England-Biography. 5. Clergy-United States-Biography. 6. Foster family. [G236].

FOURNEY -- Farney, Howard G. *Descendants of John Adams Forney, 1557-1963*. Warren, OH, 1964. 236p. [X333-FW]. See also above: FORNEY. [X331-FW/NY].

FOWLER -- Fowler, Charles Evans. *The Fowler Family of Maryland and Ohio, Probably from New Jersey and New England; One Thousand Years of the Fowlers.* New York, 1937. 1 v. (various pagings). [L6342].

FOWLER -- Fowler, Fred Irwin. *Short Sketch of Some of the Descendants of John L. Fowler, 1795-1856 and Jane Freer, 1792-1868, His Wife of Geauga County, Ohio, and Some Others.* 2nd ed. Brookfield, OH, 1950. 1 v. various pagings. [L6345].

FOWLER -- Goss, Paul H. *Some Fowler Descendents of Northumberland, Columbia and Lycoming Counties, Penna. and Trumbull, Mohoning and Portage Counties, Ohio.* NP, n.d. 1 volume of highly varied material. [X334-OH].

FOWLER -- Howell, Clara Hortense (Fowler) and Machir, Violette, S. *Fowlers and Kindred Families of Meigs and Mason Conties.* Middleport, OH, Quality Print Shop, 1964. 92p. NG gives 91p. [NG43; D4618; X334-FW/NY/PH].

FOWLER -- Smith, Edward C. *Maternal Ancestry of Edward Fowler Smith, Naperville, Illinois.* Lakewood, OH, 1958. i, 35 leaves. [X334-NY].

FOX -- Coffman, Dorothy Yoder. *The Johan Heinrich Fuchs/Fox and Johan Nicholaus König/King Families: Beginning 1749 in York County, Pennsylvani, to Ohio, 1804, through Five Generations.* Malvern, PA, D.Y. Coffman, 1988. v, 79p. 1. Fox Family. 2. Koenig family. 3. Fox, Henry-Family. 4. König, Johan Nicholaus-Family. 5. King family. 6. Pennsylvania-Genealogy. 7 Ohio-Genealogy. [G238].

FOX -- Frandsen, Florence R. [G238]. See above: ANDREWS. [G14].

FRAME -- Ellis, Kathryn Young. *Inez Frame Patterson (1882-1951), Her Ancestors, Family and Descendants.* Dayton, OH, Ellis, 1985.

133p. 1. Frame family. 2. Patterson family.
3. Patterson, Inez Frame, 1882-1951-Family.
[G238; DC1317].

FRANCIS -- Redman, Mahlon L. *A History of
the Francis Family, 1763-1923.* Newark, OH,
Thomas & Schneider, 1923. 34, 2p. D gives
underscored title. [NG43; D4648].

FRANDSEN -- Frandsen, Florence R. [G239].
See above: ANDREWS. [G14; DC1321].

FRANKENSTEIN -- Coyle, William. *The
Frankstein Family in Springfield.*
Springfield, OH, Clark County, Historical Soc.
1967. 33p. [X337-CH/NY/PH].

FRAZER -- Frazer, Margaret Gruse. *Frazers -
Baptists - Beatitudes; Descendants of James
George Frazer (1799-1878) of Campbell County,
Virginia and Highland County, Ohio.* Vandalia,
OH, Dayton, OH, Shelton, 1972. 24p. D gives
22p. and underscored part of title. VV lists
under FRASER. [S912; D4668; VV70].

FRAZER -- Franzer, Margaret Gruse & Shelton,
Elva F. *Frazers, Baptists, Beatitudes;
Descendants of James George Frazer (1799-1878)
of Campbell County, Virginia and Highland
County, Ohio.* Vandalia, OH, 1972. 24p.
[NG43].

FRAZIER -- Shipps, Blanche Frazier. *The
Cornelius Samuel Frazier and Ella Amoretta
Palmer Family History.* Delaware, OH, Shipps,
19__, 35 leaves. X gives no date.
[D4674; X338-OH].

FREEBURN -- Freeburn, Dwight. *Retracing our
Footprints of the Freeburn Family in America.*
Berea, OH, D. and E. Freeburn, 1986. 275
leaves. Rev. ed. of: Footprints of the
Freeburn Family in America. 1982. 1.
Freeburn family. [G241].

FREED -- Van Fossán, Jean. *Caldwell - Freed
Families.* Lisbon, OH, Author, 1960. 7p.
[X339-FW].

FREEMAN -- Freeman, Raymond B. *A History of Samuel Freeman of Miami County, Ohio, and His Descendants.* Western Springs, IL, 1955 - __Vols. SU has parts 1, 2, and 3. [X339-SU].

FREEMAN -- Freeman, Raymond B. *A History of Samuel Freeman of Miami County, Ohio, and His Descendants.* NP, 1970. 162, 16 l. [S919].

FREEMAN -- Steen, Moses D. A. *The Freeman Family, a Genalogical and Historical Record of One Hundred and Sixty Years.* Cincinnati, OH, 1900. 77p. [X339-FW/LI].

FREIBARGER -- Brumley, Wilma J. *Ludwig Freiberger / Freibarger, wife Mary and Their Children.* West Union, OH, 1987. 235p. [NGS5].

FRENCH -- Currie, Barbara Calder. [G241]. See above: CALDER. [G114].

FREY -- Hosteller, Susan B. F. *Descendants of Samuel D. Frey.* Plain City, OH, 1955. 49p. [X340-FW].

FREY -- Ryerse, Phyllis B. *Frey Genealogy.* Upper Sandusky, OH, 1963. 39 leaves. [X341-OH].

FRIEDRICH -- Richardson, John E. *The Friederich Family in America.* Cincinnati, OH, Author, 1930. 22p. [X341-CH/FW].

FRIEND -- Friend, Lester D. *The Friend Family; Vital Statistics.* Warren, OH, 1965. 2 Vols. [X341-FW/NY/OL].

FRIEND -- Friend, Lester D. *The Friend Family Statistics.* Warren, OH, 1969. 1 Vol. [X341-FW].

FRINK -- Hamel, Claude Charles. *Genealogy of a Bramch of the Frink Family from New York Who Were Among the Early Settlers of Lorain County, Ohio.* Amherst, OH, 1948. 4 leaves. [L6474].

FRISBIE -- Frisbie, Nora G. *The Frisbie Family in Ohio.* NP, n.d. 89p. [X342-OH].

FRISCH -- Hamel, Claude Charles. *Genealogy of the Descendants of Nicholas and Margareta (Baatz) Frisch of Holler, Canton of Echternach, Grand Duchy of Luxemburg.* Amherst, OH, 1951. 6 leaves. [L6477].

FRISINGER -- Snyder, Betty Pond. [G242]. See above: DENHAM. [G185].

FRITTS -- Fritte, Gregory A. *The Fritts (Fritz) Family Heritage.* Toledo, OH, Fritts (Becker Impressions), 1979. _ v. [D4712].

FRITZINGER -- Hott, Kathryn. *Goldner Ancestors.* Adelphi, MD, K. and R. Hott, 1983. xiii, 193p., 13p. of plates. 1. Goldner family. 2. Herter family. 3. Fritzinger family. 4. Pennsylvania-Genealogy. 5. Ohio-Genealogy. 5. Indiana-Genealogy. [G242].

FROLICH -- Hamel, Claude Charles. *Genealogy of a Branch of the Frolich Family Which Emigrated from Hesse-Cassel (Now the Province of Hesse-Nassau) Germany to America in 1855.* Amherst, OH, 1948. 11 leaves. [L6481].

FROST -- NAS. *Frost Family.* Canton, OH, Caxton Pr., 1923. 46p. [X343-FW].

FRUTH -- Fruth, Glenn J. *A History of the Melchoir Fruth Family: From 1833-1964.* Rev. by Alvin R. Furth. Carey, OH, 1964. 100p. [L6496].

FRY -- Frye, George Walter. *Colonel Joshua Fry of Virginia and Some of His Descendants and Allied Families.* Cincinnati, OH, Frye, 1966. 59, 531, 54, 91p. [D4728; VV71].

FULLER -- Butler, Jean Fuller. *A History of the Fuller Family and Other Collateral Lines.* 2nd edition. Ironton, OH, J.F. Butler, 1989. 277p. DC shows 278p. 1. Fuller family. [G245; DC1357].

FULLER -- Butler, Jean Fuller. *Old European Progenitors and Mayflower Ancestors of the A.T.F. and Mary Swain Fuller Family.* Ironton, OH, J. F. Butler, 1990. 331p. 1. Fuller family. 2. Fuller, Alphonso T.F., 1792-1857- Family. 3. Swain Family. 4. Fuller, Mary Swain, 1800-1883-Family. 5 Mayflower (ship). [G245].

FULTON -- NAS. *Genealogy of Two Generations of the Fulton Family in Ohio.* NP, 1929. 4p. Also additional data relative to the Fulton family. NP, 1930. 3p. Photocopy, 1964. 4 sheets. [X345-PH].

FULTON -- Clay, Roy U. *A History of the Fulton Family of Providence, MD and Harrison County, OH.* Boiling Springs, PA, R.U. Clay, 1981. A-B leaves, 86, 19p. 1. Fulton family. 2. Rowland family. 3. Maryland-Genealogy. 4. Ohio-Genealogy. [G245].

FULTON -- Kovacs, Gayle L. *Handshue, Fulton, Wolf Family Tree.* Fairborn, OH, G.L. Kovacs, 1987. 1 v. (various pagings). 1. Handshue family. 2. Fulton family. 3. Wolfe family. [G246].

FULTON -- Moore, E. D. *Leaves from the Fulton Family Tree.* New Philadelphia, OH, 1930. 92 leaves. [X345-FW].

FULTON -- Moore, E. D. *William Fulton - Our Ancestor.* New Philadelphia, OH, 1932. 2 leaves. [X345-PH].

FUNK -- Strock, Richard M. and Robert F. *Some Strock, Harbaugh, Funk, and Reynolds Families of Washington and Frederick Counties, Maryland, and Franklin County, Pennsylvania: Includes Some Descendants in Colorado, Illinois, Kansas, Michigan, Missouri, Ohio, Texas, etc. Organized around the Direct and Colateral Lineage of the Authors (brothers) with Direct Lineage Extending Back to the Immigrants.* Cincinnati, OH, R.M. Strock, 1988. 29, 15 leaves. 1. Strock family. 2.

Harbaugh family. 3. Funk family. 4. Reynolds family. [G246].

FURNAS -- Furnas, Tanzy R. *Genealogy of the Furnas Family*. Dayton, OH, Furnas Bros. 1897. 22p. [X347-FW/PH].

FUSON -- Ferguson, Sylvia C. Fuson. *The Virginia - Ohio Fusons: A Genealogical History of the Virginai - Ohio Branch of the Fuson Family in America*. Oxford, OH, The Oxford Press, 1939. 4, 224p. [L6550; VV71].

FUSON -- Ferguson, Sylvia Celicia Fuson. *The Virginia -Ohio Fusons*. -- *Rev*. Evansville, IN, Unigraphic, 1979. 753p. VV gives title as in original immediately above. [C245; D4773; VV72].

G

GABRIEL -- Johnson, Christina G. *William Gabriel and His Descendants*. Marysville, OH, 1976. 1 vol. Unpaged. [X349-OH].

GADDY -- Irwin, Ruth Beckley. *A Springer Family History: Some Descendants of Dennis Springer and Ann Prickett, Including Family Histories for Prickett, Gaddis, McIntire, Shepherd, Van Meter, Boyles, Bellatti, and Girton*. Columbus, OH, R.B. Irwin,Decorah, Iowa: Anundsen Pub. Co., 1987. xi, 122p. 1. Springer family. 2. Springer, Dennis 1712-ca. 1760-Family. 3. Prickett family. 4. Gaddy family. [G247].

GAGE -- Smith, Myron Alphonso. *Genealogical History of the Gage Family*. Columbus, OH, Smith, 1944. 120 leaves. [D4789].

GAGE -- Smith, Myron Alphonso. *Genealogical History of the Gage Family, Particularly of the American Descendants of Baron John Gage of England*. Columbus, OH, 1969. 120p. [X349-FW/SP].

GAGE -- Gage, Norris Lancaster. ...*Gage Genealogy.* Ashtabula, OH, 1889. 16p. "From the Granite Monthly, November, 1882. [L6558].

GAILLARD -- Gaillard, William. *The History and Pedigree of the House of Gaillard or Gaylord in France, England, and the United States...* Cincinnati, OH, William and W. H. Gaillard, 1872. 2, 64, 6p. [L6577]. -- *Another Issue.* Cincinnati, Published by the Author and W. H. Gaillard (1872). (Same pagination). [L6577].

GAILLARD -- Gaillard, William. *The History and Pedigree of the House of Gaillard or Gaylord in France, England, and the United States...* NP, 1969. 85p. [S947].

GALBREATH -- Galbreath, Joseph W. *Galbreath; The Descendants of Alexander of Campbelltown, Scotland and York, Pa., 1784-1930, also Some Notes on the Galbreaths of England and Scotland.* Warren, OH, 1930. [VP79].

GALLOWAY -- Galloway, Erin Lynn. *From Scotland to Pennsylvania and Beyond: The Family of Enoch Galloway, Sr.* Salesville, OH, E.L. Galloway and B.L. Smith, 1987. xxii, 600 leaves. 1. Galloway family. 2. Galloway, Enoch, 1798-1864-Family. [G248].

GALLOWAY -- Kendall, George W. & William A. Galloway (both of Xenia, OH). *Genealogy of the Descendants of George Galloway and Rebekah Junkin, 1700-1925, in the United States of America.* Evanston, IL, C. E. Galloway, 1926. 53p. [L6599].

GAMBLE -- Martin, William Gamble. *The Gamble Family of Butler Township, Knox County, Ohio.* Bucyrus, OH, 1962. 2 Parts. Section 1. Chart. - Section 2. Narrative. [L6614].

GARBER -- Garber, Clark M. *The Garber Historical and Genealogical Record; A Publication Devoted to the History and*

Genealogy of the Garber Family in America. V. 1. n. 1 - __. Mansfield, OH, The Richland Printing Company. 1937. v. FW has Vol. 1. no. 1-3, Vol 2. no. 1, Vol. 3 no. 1-2. [L6622; X353-FW].

GARD -- Baer, Frank L. *Gard Families of New Jersey, Pennsylvania, West Virginia, and Ohio.* NP, 1963. 34 leaves. [D4823; VP79].

GARDNER -- NAS. *John Gardner.* Mt. Gilead, OH, 1911. 1 leaf (Geneal. Table). [X353-OH].

GARDNER -- Amrhein, Mary Sackett. *Reuben Condit Gardner, John Corliss George, and John Roloson Families of Delaware County, Ohio.* Delaware, OH, Amrhein, 1969. 67 leaves. [D4830].

GARDNER -- Gardner, Charles F. *The Gardners of Perry Township, Tuscarawas County, Ohio.* New Philadelphia, OH, Gardner, 1984. iiii(sic), 7p, 107 pages of plates. 1. Gardner family. 2. Perry(Tuscarawas County, Ohio)-Genealogy. [G250; C249].

GARR -- Garr, John Calhoun. *Genealogy of the Descendants of John Gar, or more particulary of His Son, Andreas Gaar.* Cincinnati, OH, J.C. Gaar, 1894. xvi, 607, 1p. D gives xiii, 3, 720p. [L6669; D4862].

GARRETSON -- *The Garretson News.* Vega, TX, Lima, OH, Garretson Society, 1942-. _v. Library Holdings Vol. ii, no.2 (June, 1954). FW has 15 vols. Irregular Oct 1941-Apr 1959 Quarterly 1972. Publication suspended May, 1959 to Oct., 1971? L gives no dates. [L6672; DC1388; X355-FW/NY].

GARTON -- Dickson, Lura M. *Ancestry and Descendants of David Garton of New Jersey and Ohio.* Montezuma, IA, Dickson, 1952. 67 l. [S966; D4882].

GARTRELL -- Haines, Randall A. *The Gartrell - Gatrell Ancestry of Colonial Maryland.*

Cincinnati, OH, R.A. Haines, 1989. v, 141 leaves. 1. Gartrell family. 2. Maryland-Genealogy. [G251].

GASTEIER -- Gastier, Eric J. *History of the Gasteier Family in the United States - 1986 ed. - 3rd ed.* Milan, OH, 1986. 1 v. (looseleaf). 1. Gastier family. [G252].

GATCH -- NAS. *Descendants of Godfrey Gatch of Baltimore County, Maryland, and Others of the Surname with Material on Early Methodist History in Maryland, Virginia, and Ohio. 1st ed.* Baldwin City, KS, 1972. xi, 505p. *-- 2d ed., with Supplement...* 1973, xiv, 522, 7p. [S967].

GATES -- Bellatti, Margaret Bomlin. *My Gates Ancestry: Ancestry of Samuel Gates (1785- -1841) of Bridgton, Maine, Waterford, Ohio, and Greene County, Illinois and Descendants of His Daughter Phebe Gates Strawn of Jacksonville, Illinois.* Jacksonville, IL, M. T. Belatti, 1979. 70p. [C251].

GEDNEY -- Tatum, V. H. *The Gedney Story: History, Legend, and Fact Concerning This Family Since About 920 A.D. Genealogy of One Branch of Gidney from 1603 in England, New England and Ohio Beginning with John Gidney.* Cincinnati, OH, Assur-Flint Printing Co., 1965, 1964, 16p. [L6711].

GEIGER -- Geiger, John D. *Family Record of the Descendants of John G. Geiger, 1822-1886 and Mary Lugibihl, 1825-1899. Ed. 2.* Mt. Vernon, OH, 1970. 106p. [X359-FW].

GENNING -- Saxbe, William Bart. *Johann Genning (1818-1898) and His Descendants: A Toledo Family.* Baltimore, MD, Gateway, 1988. xi, 285p. [DC1400].

GENSON -- Genson, Chloe Roderick and Charles Wilson Genson. *A History and Genealogy of the Samuiel Cox Genson Family: His Ancestors and Descendants.* Baltimore, MD, Gateway Press,

Bowling Green, OH, 1983, iii, 261p.
[C254].

GEORGE -- Spraley, Evelyn George.
*Descendants of John Nicholas Georges and Mary
Catherine Hallotte, 1790-1986.* Greenville,
OH, E.G. Spraley, 1987, 66p. 1. George
family. 2. Georges, John Nicholas, 1790-1869-
Family. 3. Ohio-Genealogy. [G255].

GEORGIA -- Brooks, Elmore L. *A Genealogical
Record of the Georgia Family in America; Being
the Children and Descendants of William and
Sarah (Cable) Georgia and the Children and
Descendants of Elijah Burr (1st) and Keziah
(Stewart) Georgia... First Two Men of This
Name to Come to America.* Cleveland, OH, 1921.
D gives 1924 and underscored part of title.
314p. Contents: -Book one, relates to the
family and descendants of Miles and Sally
(North) Georgia. - Book two, relates toe
thos(sic) of Elijah Burr (2nd) and Keziah
(Tense) Georgia. These two men were the sons
of William Georgia, one of the first two
brothers to come to America. -Book three,
which(sic) relates to the children and
descendants of Elijah Burr (1st) and Keziah
(Stewart) Georgia. This was the other first
brother to come to America.
[L6740; D4937].

GERBER -- Gerber, Elias P. *Historical
Sketches of Seven Generations.* Kidron, OH,
Gerber, 1938. 263p. [D4938].

GERBERICH -- Garvick, Kenneth Ryan. *The
Gerberich Descendants From York, Pennsylvania.*
Columbus, OH, 1987. 17p. [NG45].

GEREN -- Geren, Roy S. *Geren Families of
Ohio.* Celina, OH, 1975. A-F, 21p.
[X360-FW].

GERRARD -- Brien, L. D. M. *Gerrard Family
of Southern Ohio.* Dayton, OH, Author, 19__.
67p., 42 leaves. [X360-FW].

GERARD -- Garrard. Herbert L. *Garrard Family Histories (Gerrard, Gerard, Garard) when Living in West Virginia, Pennsylvania, Ohio and Indiana, 1720-1980. Also Some McCormick Records.* Noblesville, IN, Garrard, 1980. 10 leaves. 1. Gerard family. 2. McCormick family. [G255].

GERVAIS -- Jarvis, Ruth R. *The Ancestry and Children of Israel Jarvis and His Wife, Regina M. Beaudry: with the Names of Their Children...* Findlay, OH, Jarvis, 1976. 38 leaves. [X361-MH].

GETTER -- Smith, Carl T. *The Getter Family, Being the Record of John Getter, (1777-1844) and Mary M. Lambert (1782-1824) His Wife and Their Descendants of Jefferson Township, Montgomery County, Ohio.* Dayton, OH, 1942. 11 leaves. [X361-NY].

GETTY -- Gettys, Robert Clay. *Gettys Family in America: Sketches of History, Local, Genealogical, and Biographical: McClellandtown, Waynesburg, Pennsylvania, and Mansfield, Ohio.* Belfast, Northern Ireland, R. C. Gettys, 1986. 145p. in various pagings, 17p. of plates. 1. Gettys family. [G255; NGS6].

GHOLSON -- Gholson, Edwin. *Notes on the Genealogy of the Gholson Family.* Cincinnati, OH, Cincinnati Law Library Assoc., 195_. 62p. [X361-CH.FW].

GHORMLEY -- Ghormley, Carmen. P. D. *The Ghormley Story.* Greenfield, OH, Greenfield Printing and Publishing Company, 1970. xiv, 192p. [S982; D4955; X361-NY].

GIBBS -- Herbruch, Wendell. *Notes Upon the Ancestry of the Gibbs Family of Canton.* Canton, OH, 1944. 133 numb. leaves, 3 l. [L6779].

GIBSON -- Gibson, William T. *Capt. James Gibson and Anne Belle, His Wife and Their*

Descendants, Pioneers of Youngstown, OH. NP, 189_. 52p. [L6780].

GIBSON -- McNellis, Edna M. *The Family Past and Present of Alvin Roy and Grace Emery Gibson.* Barberton, OH, McNellis, 1983. 14 leaves (12 & 13 missing). [DC1412].

GIBSON -- Miskimens, Dorothea. *Data on Some of the Gibson Families of Guernsey County, Ohio.* Sylmar, CA, D. Miskimens, 198_. 20 leaves. 1. Gibson family. 2. Guernsey County (Ohio)-Genealogy. [G257].

GIDDINGS -- NAS. *History of the Giddings Family.* Lindenville, OH, S. J. Mann, printers. 1892. 12p. [X363-OH].

GIFFIN -- Alban, William Rowland Mrs. *The Descendantsof Alexander Giffen and His Wife Mary (Hinkle) Giffen.* Galena, OH, W.R. Alban, 479p. Errata Slip laid in. 1. Giffen family. 2. Giffen Alexander, 1798-1879-Family. 3. Giffen, Mary, 1799-1891-Family. 4. Ohio-Genealogy. [G257].

GIFFEN -- Giffin, J. W. *Giffen. Genealogic Family History of the Descendants of Robert Giffen and Mary Bane Giffen Settlers at Big Spring, Pa. in 1777, Removed to Wheeling, Va., 1787.* Cleveland, OH, Central Publishing House, 1927. 174p. D gives underscored title. [D4974; X363-LI/NY; VP81].

GILLASPIE -- Weinberg, Lettie Marie Gillaspie. *The Generations.* N. Canton, OH, Weinberg, 1985. 1 v. (various pagings). [DC1419].

GILBERT -- NAS. *Gilbert - Barber Families.* Darrowville, OH, School Publishing. Co., 1903. Unpaged. [X364-FW].

GILBERT -- Davis, W. E. *The Gilbert Family: Garvis, Aquilla, Benjamin, etc.* Glendale, OH, W.E. Davis, 1985. 1 v. (various foliations). 1. Gilbert family. 2. Gilbert, Garvis, 1680-1739-Family. [G258].

GILBERT -- Gilbert, A. A. *Gilberts of Bel Pre, Ohio, Their Ancestors and Descendants... New England Ancestors of Dr. George Nye Gilbert and His Wife Lucy Eaton Putnam... with Lineages of the Early Ohio Families of Howe, Loring, Nye, Putnam, Stone, and Waldo; Suppl. of other descendants of Jonathan Gilbert.* Chicago, IL, 1935, 13 leaves. [X364-FW]

GILBERT -- Walton, William H. *...The Captivity and Sufferings of Benjamin Gilbert and His Family, 1780-83, Reprinted From Original of 1784, with Introduction and Notes by Frank H. Severance.* Cleveland, OH, The Burrows Brothers Company, 1904. 204p. [L6800].

GILLET -- Ross, Julius. *Our Pilgrim's Progress: The Gillets of Conn., Ohio, Missouri, Iowa and Wisconsin.* Beloit, WI, Press Printing, 1988. 2 v. Contents: v. 1. The Gillets of Conn, Ohio, Missouri, Iowa, and Wisconsin. - v. 2. The Rozsas, Ross, and Somodis of Hungary and Wisconsin. DC gives 226p. 1. Gillette family. 2. Connecticut-Genealogy. G lists as GILLETTE. [G259; DC1420].

GILLETT -- Thomas, Wilma Gillet. *The Joseph Gillett / Gillet / Gillette Family of Connecticut, Ohio and Kansas.* Chicago, IL, Adams Press, 1970. vi, 135p. [A257; X366-NY].

GILLILAND -- Gilliland, Lyle Willis. *Willis and Gilliland Families of Hanover County, Virginia, Rutherford County, North Carolina, Pendleton County, South Carolina, Brown County, Ohio, Putnam County, Illinois, Douglas County, Oregon.* Eugene OR, Paul A. Grant, 1979. 16 l, 2 leaves of plates. [C259; VV75].

GILLILAND -- Wilson, Betty. *The Gilliland Family: (States Included) Highland Co., Ohio, Clinton Co., Ohio, Indiana, Illinois, North Carolina.* Indianapolis, IN, Wilson, 1978 or

1979. 44 leaves in various foliations, 1 plate of leaves. [C259].

GILMOR -- Gilmor, Elizabeth. *William Gilmor -- Sarah Hannah, 1778; Arthur Scott, Jr. -- Ann Hamilton, 1788; The Union of Four Families in the Marriage of William Gilmor and Agnes Scott in 1820.* Wooster, OH, Gilmor, 1932. 238p. L lists as GILMORE. D gives underscored title. [L6860; D5016].

GILMORE -- Gilmore, Allen J. *Mr. Allen J. Gilmores Family.* Chagrin Falls, OH, 1938. 8 leaves. [X367-OH]

GILMORE -- Hamel, C. C. *Gilmore.* Amherst, OH, n.d. 8 leaves. [X367-OH].

GILMORE -- Hamel, C. C. *Extracts from: History of Goffstown (N. H.) 1733-1920 by George P. Hadley.* Amherst, OH, n.d. 5 leaves. [X367-OH].

GILMORE -- Hamel, C. C. *Gilmore Death Dates.* Amherst, OH, n.d. 3 l. [X367-OH].

GILMORE -- Hamel, C. C. *Gilmore Marriages.* Amherst, OH, n.d. 6 leaves. [X367-OH].

GILMORE -- Hamel, C. C. *Gilmore Birth Dates.* Amherst, OH, n.d. 4 leaves. [X367-OH].

GILMORE -- Hamel, C. C. *Gilmore - Massachusetts Line.* Amherst, OH, n.d. 13 leaves. Extracted from genealogical and personal memoirs relating to the families of the State of Massachusetts, by W. R. Cutter, 1910. [X367-OH].

GILMORE -- Hamel, C. C. *Gilmore (Massachusetts Line).* Amherst, OH, n.d. 17 leaves. Copied from Gilmore Ancestry by Pascal B. Gilmore, 1925. [X367-OH].

GILMORE -- Hamel, Claude Charles. *Genealogy of the Lorain, Lorain County, Ohio Branch of* *the Gilmour – Gilmore Family New Hampshire Line.* Amherst, OH, 1948. 74 l. [L6862].

GILMORE -- Hamel, Claude Charles. *Genealogy of the Lorain, Lorain County, Ohio Branch of the Gilmour – Gilmore Family New Hampshire Line. Rev. ed.* Amherst, OH, Author, 1954. 73 leaves. [X367-SL].

GILMORE -- Hamel, Claude Charles. *Genealogy of the Geauga County, Ohio Branch of the Gilmour – Gilmore Family New Hampshire Line.* Rev. Elyria, OH, 1960. 56 l. [L6865].

GILMOUR -- Hamel, Claude Charles. *Genealogy of the Lorain, Lorain County, Ohio Branch of the Gilmour – Gilmore Family, New Hampshire Line.* NP, 1950-1962. v. [D5023].

GIRTY -- Butterfield, Consul W. *History of the Girtys: Being a Concise Account of the Girty Brothers...* Cincinnati, OH, Robert Clarke, 1890. 425p. [X369-SU].
      -- Reprint of Above. Columbus, OH, Longs College Book Co., 1950. 426p. [X369-SU].

GLANCY -- Smith, Walter Burges. *The James Glancy Genealogy, 1765-1986: James (1765-1828) of Pennsylvania and, by 1828, of Knox County, Ohio, and His Descendants.* Washington, DC, 1986. 493p. [NGS6].

GLANDER -- Glander, Herman C. *An Historical Sketch of the Glander Family in Connection with Some Historical Facts of Their Land of Origin...Together with a Register of Names of the Descendants and Members of the Glander Family in America from 1832-1916.* West Alexandria, Ohio, Glander, 1916. 5, 155p. D gives underscored part of title and;, with: A Register of the names of the Glander family in America from 1832-1916 by Grace A. Mayo. [L6893; D5046].

GLASCOCK -- Glassco, Lawrence A. *The Glascock (Glasscock) – Glassco Saga.* Niles,

OH, Glassco, 1974.   xx,   189p.
[S997; NG46; D5047].

GLASGOW -- Faris, David. *The Glasgow Family of Adams County, Ohio: A Genealogy of the Descendants of Robert Glasgow (1749-1839) and His Wife Rosanna of Bush Creek, Adams County, Ohio.* Baltimore, MD, Gateway, 1990. 493p., 12 leaves of plates. 1. Glasgow family. 2. Glasgow, Robert, 1749-1839-Family. 3. Middle West-Genealogy. [G261].

GLEASON -- Andrews, Adele. *The Ancestors and Descendants of Elijah Gleason and His First Wife, Cynthia Johnson, and His Second Wife, Betsey Davis.* Norwalk, OH, Andrews, 1960. 115 l. [L6904; D5058].

GLEASON -- Gleason, Walter Tolman. *The Gleason Family of (Greendale) Worcester, Massachusetts.* Cincinnati, OH, Stratford Press, 1961. 21, iv p. [D5060; X370-FW/MH/NY].

GOETZ -- Goetz, Louis G. *From This Staff, a Family History.* Cleveland Heights, OH, Author, 1966. 210p. Also Davison. [X372-CH].

GOLDNER -- Hott, Kathryn. [G264]. See above: FRITZINGER. [G242].

GOLDSBOROUGH -- Hovemeyer, Eric E. *The Goldsberry Register. 1st ed.* Cincinnati, OH, Havemeyer, 1980. ii, 41 l. [C264].

GOOD -- Geake, Gold C. *Good Family of Van Wert County, Ohio.* NP, n.d. 35p. [X374-FW].

GOODALL -- Allerton, Earl Wayne. *The Family Notes of Earl Wayne Allerton on Goodall - Jencks and Allied Families.* Cleveland Heights, OH, L. M. Miller, 1984. 219 leaves. [C266; NG46].

GOODING -- Pabst, Anna C. S. *George B. Gooding, 1797-1856, Innkeeper, Farmer of*

Dighton, Mass. & Delaware County, Ohio.
Delaware, OH, A. C. S. Pabst. 1968. 34
leaves. [X374-NY].

GOODNER -- Lacey, Hubert Wesley. *The*
Goodner Family, A Genealogical History with a
Brief History of the Family of Jacob Daniel
Scherrer and Notes on Other Allied Families.
Dayton, OH, Lacey, 1960. xii, 511p. D gives
underscored title and 511p.
[L6978; D5122].

GOODPASTURE -- Goodpasture, Robert Abraham.
Early Goodpaster (Goodpasture) Families in
America. Sunnyvale, CA, 1972- 1 v. 5 parts.
Pt. 1. Virginia, Tennessee, Kentucky, Ohio 1st
ed; rev. - Pt. 2 Kentucky, Ohio, Indiana,
Illinois, Iowa Records... [S1022].

GORDON -- Gordon, Bruce. *The Gordon*
Genealogies: Robert Bruce, and Ann Gordon
Families. Fairborn, OH, Bruce, 1990. 120,
A1-A11p. [DC1462].

GORDON -- Gordon, Frank S. *The Gordons of*
Pitlurg and the Descendants of Thomas Gordon,
Who Came to America in 1684 and Settled in
Perth Amboy, New Jersey. Columbus, O H ,
College Book Company, 1941. 127p., 3 leaves.
[L7057].

GORHAM -- King, Helen Hester. *Some*
Descendants of Captain John Gorham of Plymouth
Colony in New York State and The Western
Reserve. Cleveland, OH, Walker Printing
Service, 1955. xliv, 55p. D gives 55p.
[L7073; D5156].

GOSS -- Heuss, Lois Ione Hotchkiss.
Frederick Goss of Rowan County, North
Carolina, and His Descendants. Akron, OH,
1968. xii, 616p. NG gives 617p.
[L7083; NG47].

GOTT -- Gott Family Members. *The Gott*
Family. Akron, OH, 1928. 2-22 numb leaves.
[L7089].

GOTT -- Gott, Philip Porter. *An Ohio Gott Family, Ancestors and Descendants. The First Gotts in America.* Pittsburgh, PA, M. J. Moshier, 1940. 4p. [L7090].

GOTT -- Gott, Philip Porter. *Ancestors & Descendants of an Ohio Gott Family 1628-1972. Fourteen Generations of Gotts in the United States Begining with the Immigrant Ancestor Charles Gott.* Fort Lauderdale, FL, P. P. Gott, 1972. xiii, 171p. [S1030; NG47; D5170].

GOULD -- Caine, Albert H. *George Parker Gould and His Family.* Cincinnati, OH, 1902. 13p. [XA1071-LI/MH/NY].

GRAESSLE -- *History of the Graessle - Gracely Family.* Lima, OH, The Lisle Press, 1941. 42p. [L7120].

GRABER -- Graber, Peter. *History of the Graber and Stall Families.* Canton, OH, 1917. 28p. [X380-FW].

GRAHAM -- Graham. Albert B. *Graham Genealogy, 1759-1946.* Columbus, OH, 1950. 19p. [X381-OH].

GRAHAM -- Graham. Bernice. *Graham Descendants of William and Dinah Ann (Wilson) Graham.* Marietta, OH, Graham, 1967. xii, 386p. [D5193].

GRAHAM -- Graham, David. *A Short History of the Graham Family, Reynoldsburg, Oh., 1879.* Columbus, OH, Graham Family Association, 1931. 2, 19p. [L7134].

GRATZ -- Moore, Catherine B. *Gratz - Rogers Family.* Columbus, OH, 1969. 36 leaves. [X383-FW/OH].

GRAY -- May, Richard Holman. *George Gray Genealogy; of Marion County, Ohio.* Mill Valley, CA, 1973. 30 leaves. [S1047; NG47].

GRAYDONS -- Ratliff, Lucy Graydon. *The Graydons of Cincinnati, 1850-1984.*

Cincinnati, OH, L. G. Ratliff, 1984. 137p.
DC gives 137, 8p. G lists under GRAYDON. 1.
Graydon family. 2. Ohio-Genealogy. 3.
Northern Ireland-Genealogy.
[G271; NGS6; DC1484].

GREATHOUSE -- Nelson, Alice (Winters)
Greathouse. *Greathouse Family; A History.*
Chillicothe, OH, L. Greathouse, 1949. 23 1.
[L7216].

GREEN -- Greene, Maxon F. *The Ancestry and
Descendants of Paris Green of Alfred, Allegany
County, N. Y.* Delaware, OH, 1927. 40p.
[X385-OH].

GREEN -- Heiss, Willard C., Ed. *Notes on the
Green Family of Clinton County, Ohio.*
Indianapolis, IN, Author, 1968. 67p.
[X385-OH].

GREENLEAF -- Ford, Mrs. Horatio. *Ancestors
and Descendants of Almira Louisa Greenleaf.*
South Euclid, OH, 1929. 2p. 2 Genealogical
Tables. [L7265].

GREER -- Gerlach, Elmer K. *Greer, George &
Elizabeth and Descendants.* McConnelsville,
OH, E. & K. Gerlach, 1990. 1 v. (various
pagings). 1. Greer family. 2. Greer, George-
Family. 3. Ohio-Genealogy. [G273].

GREGG -- Ogden, John D. L. *George and Sarah
Gregg, Pioneer Settlers of Noble County, Ohio.*
Alexandria, VA, Ogden, 1986. 350p. [DC1496].

GREGORY -- Gregory, Lewis J. *Willis Gregory
Family History, 1785-1968.* Cincinnati, OH,
1969. 318p. [X388-FW].

GRETHER -- Grether. Frank. *Rev. John
Michael Grether and Wife.* Cleveland, OH,
Central Publishing House, 1928. 31p.
[D5300].

GRIESEMER -- Grismer, Beth. *Grismer -
Stomps Families.* __, U.S.A., B. Grismer,
1984. 33, 39, 28, iii leaves. 1. Stomps

family. 2. Griesemer family. 3. Dayton
(Ohio)-Genealogy. 4. Dayton (Ohio)-Biography.
[G274].

GRIESMER -- Griesmer, Howard Herbert. *The
Griesmers: A Century in Cleveland, Ohio,
1882-1982.* Cleveland, OH, Griesmer, 1984.
104 l. [C276].

GRIFFIS -- Aultz, Stanley Wright.
Chronicles of a Griffis Family. Miamisburg,
OH, S.W. Aultz, 1981. 147p. [C276].

GRIFFITH -- Griffith, D. Eugene. *The
Ancestors and Descendants of James William
Griffith and Mary Ellen O'Brien.* Salem, OH,
D.E. Griffith, D.C. Stratton, 1987. vi, 86p.
1. Griffith family. 2. O'Brien family. 3.
Grifith, James William, 1869-1950-Family. 4.
Griffith, Mary Ellen O'Brien, 1868-1970-
Family. [G274].

GRIMES -- Dillon, Anna Maria Totten. *The
Grimes Family of Early Bath and Pocahontas
Counties, Va. (W.Va.), and Their Descendants,
1770-1989.* Columbus, OH, A.M. Dillon, 1989.
119p. 1. Grimes family. 2. Virginia-
Genealogy. 3. West Virginia-Genealogy. 4.
Ohio-Genealogy. [G275].

GRISSOM -- NAS. *Grissom - Price Family of
Virginia and Ohio.* NP, n.d. 9p.
[X390-FW].

GRISWOLD -- Griswold, Edwin V. *The
Griswolds on the Olentangy.* Chicago, IL,
1939. 16p. [L7344].

GRISWOLD -- Griswold, Rev. Edwin V. *The
Griswolds of the Olentangy with a Supplement:
The Descendants of Worthington Franklin
Griswold.* Los Altos, CA, T. P. Ligda, 1953.
22p. [X391-SP].

GROSS -- Donner, Harold L. *The Antecedents
and Descendants of John Frederick Grose and
Augusta Whilhelmine Werth: Married November
28, 1878.* Cleveland Heights, OH, H. L.

Donner, 1984. 27 l., 1 leaf of plates. 1. Gross family. 2. Grose, John Frederick, 1853-1917-Family. [G277; C279].

GROSS -- Hall, William C. *The Andrew Jackson Gross Genealogy: Being a History of Andrew Jackson Gross, Born in Pa. and All His Descendants from Hardin Co., Ohio to Iowa and Thence to All Parts of the United States.* Nevada, IA, Hall, 1978. iv, 114p. 1. Gross family. [G277; C279; VP88].

GROSVENOR -- Grosvenor, Jeannette. *Descendants of Nathan E. Grosvenor and Laura Fuller, 1794-1973 (with his Ancestry) Removed from Mansfield, Conn. to Claridon, O. in 1854/ 55.* Chesterfield, OH, Baker Print. 1973. vi, 320p. [X392-FW].

GROVER -- Grover, Charles. *Grovers: The Only Direct Line for James Luther Brumfield enclosed... Gallia County, Ohio.* Maysfield, KY, Brumfield, 1990. 8 leaves. [DC1521]

GRUBB -- Hall, William C. *The John Grubb Genealogy: Being a History of John Grubb and His Wife Mary Ralston, Both Born in Ross Co., Ohio and Their Descendants.* Nevada, IA, Hall, 1982. iv 1, 237p. [C280].

GRUBER -- Gruber, Alice. *Gruber / Reissenweber: A Generation of Letters.* Cuyahoga Falls, OH, Gruber, 1978. 30p. [C280].

GRUBER -- Gruber, Alice. *Gruber / Reissenweber: A Generation of Letters Courtesy of the Ancestors / Related Material and Family History.* Cuyahoga Falls, OH, Akron, OH, 1978. x, 660p. [C280; NG48].

GRUBN -- McCafferty, Jane R. *Grübn - Grube Couzins: Germany 1803 to Gallia County, Ohio.* Fort Washington, MD. J. R. McCafferty, 1981. 111p. C lists as GRUBER. [C280; NG48].

GUCKES -- Harrell, Mary Edith. *Ancestry of Philip Ellsworth Guckes (1875-1928).*

Cincinnati, OH, Harrell, 1966. 21 leaves. X
gives 21 pages. [D5363; X393-FW].

GUISE -- Titus, Elroy Wilson. *A History of
the Guise, (Geiss, Gise) and Related
Families.* Columbus, OH, Titus, 1972, 173p.
[DS290: X394-FW/LA/OH/PH].

GULLETT -- Fisher, Joanne M. Gullett.
*Ezekiel Gullett and Descendants: North
Carolina to Indiana, 1780-1986.* Evansville,
IN, Whipporwill Publications, Union City, OH,
J. M. Fisher. 1986. xii, 265, 11p. 1.
Gullett family. 2. Gullett, Ezekiel, 1780-
1861-Family. [G280].

GUNN -- NAS. *The Jasper Gunn Line.*
Photocopy sent by Robert W. Gunn of Delta,
Ohio. NP, n.d. pni. [X394-IG].

GUNN -- Saxbe, William Bart. *Johann Genning,
1818-1898 and His Descendants: A Toledo
Family, with Notes on the Families of Rust,
Gunn, Kleinhans, Bruning, Holtgrieve, and
Nesper.* Baltimore, MD, Gateway Press, 1988.
xi, 292p. 1. Jennings family. 2. Genning,
Johann, 1818-1898-Family. 3. Rust family. 4.
Gunn family. 5. Ohio-Genealogy. [G280].

GURNEY -- Gurney, Elizabeth Niver. *One
Gurney Story.* Waverly, OH, E. N. Gurney,
1979. 341p. [C284].

GUSTINE -- Weaver, Gustine Courson. *The
Gustine Compendium.* Cincinnati, OH, Powell &
White, 1929. xv, 339p. [D5389].

GUTHRIE -- *A Sketch of Stephen Guthrie,
senior and His Children; A Pioneer Family of
the Ohio Land Company of 1787.* Zanesville,
OH, 1891. 35p. [L7441].

H

HAAG -- Haag, Wilbur Francis. *The Haags of
Jennings County, Indiana.* Dayton, OH, W Haag,
1979. ca. 200 leaves. [C285].

HADSELL -- Moore, Catharine B. *Hadsell Family.* Columbus, OH, 1969. 39 leaves. [X398-OH].

HAGANS -- Hagans, Uriah. *Autobiography of Uriah Hagans.* Toledo, OH, Pelton, 1906. 80p. [X399-FW].

HAID -- Haid, John. *The Official History of the August Haid Branch of the American Haid Family.* Hamilton, OH, J. Haid, 1984. 26 l. [DC1552].

HAINES -- Haines, Ruth C. *Ancestry and Descendants of Zimri and Elizabeth Compton Haines, and Other Genealogical Notes.* Waynesville, OH, 1954. 53 leaves. [X400-NY/OL].

HAISELUP -- NAS. *Descendants of Elijah Haiselup and Eleanor Eberhardt of state (sic) Virginia, Ohio and Bartholomew County, Indiana.* NP, 1978. 145 leaves. [D5429; VV82].

HAKEMOLLER -- Sanders, Rita Elisabeth Hakemoller Froschauer. *A Trunk Full of Memories: Christopher (Kleine) Hakemoller and Johann Lucas Lambers. The Story of Their Lines and Their Descendants.* Englewood, OH, R.E.H.F. Sanders, 1983. xv, 230p. [C287].

HALE -- White, Franklin H. [G289]. See above: CARTER. [G125].

HALE -- Williams, Kathryn E. *The Ancestry and Descendants of Jacob and Martha Harvey Hale.* Wilmington, OH, Author, 1969. 216p. [X400-FW/OH].

HALL -- NAS. *Biographical Notes of Our Beloved Parents, Mr. and Mrs. William Hall late of Cleveland, Ohio.* Cleveland, OH, 1876. 26p. [X401-LI/SL].

HALL -- Hall, Gilbert Edgerton. *Records of Captain John Hall, Born May 27, 1723, Died Aug. 6, 1777 in the Defense of His Country;*

with Some Account of His Ancestors and Descendants. Fremont, OH, John H. Stine's Print, 1904. 29p. [L7546; D5463].

HALL -- Hartley, Elizabeth J. H. *Descendants of Moses Hall, John Doudna, and Benjamin Hall (Quaker Fams. of Belmont County, Ohio, from Va., and N.C.).* Denver, CO,1958. xxii, 339p. [X401-DP/FW/NY; VV83].

HALL -- Spencer, Emily P. S. *Kate Wilt Hertzog Hall, 1844-1899, Wife of Alpheus Beede Stickney, 1840-1916, Their Descendants and Some of Her Ancestry, 1584-1972.* Cleveland, OH, 1972. 14, 2 leaves. [X402-MH].

HALL -- Weller, Eloise Barrick. *Johnathan Hall of Pennsylvania and Ohio His Ancestors and Descendants.* Evansville, IN, E. B. Weller, 1984. 182p. [DC1567; VP90].

HAMEL -- Hamel, Claude Charles. *Genealogy of the Hamel Family of Amherst, Lorain County, Ohio.* Amherst, OH, 1951. 1 v. various pagings. [L7613].

HAMILTON -- Cummings, Marian Sill. *Hamilton Family Records; Descendants of John and Jane Hamilton of Cayuga County, N. Y.* East Cleveland, OH, Waterbury Press, 1940. 4, 65p. D gives underscored part of title. [L7644; D5500].

HAMMON -- Hammond, Edith L. *Ancestors and Descendants of Jonathan Hammon (1776-1859) of Geneva, Ohio.* NP, 1975. 38p. [X406-FW/SL].

HAMPTON -- Doup, Mary Lou. [G293]. See above: BLEVINS. [G62].

HANG -- Schneider, Donald R. *Ancesteors (sic) and Descendants of Valentine Hang, 1815-1883.* Beloit, OH, D.R. Schneider, 1987. 107 leaves, 7 leaves of plates. 1. Hang family. 2. Hang, Valentine, 1815-1883-Family. 3. Ohio-Genealogy. 4. Gau-Algsheim (Germany)-Genealogy. 5. Germany-Genealogy. [G294].

HANCE -- Pierce, Doris Whittier. *The Thomas Hance Family of New Jersey and Bennington Township, Delaware County, O., later Morrow County, Ohio.* Galena, OH, Pierce, 1970. 149 leaves. [D5538].

HANCHETT -- Hanchett, Junius Tilden. *The Hanchett Family.* Middletown, OH, J. C. Hanchett, 1957. 113 leaves. [L7674].

HANITCH -- Dempsey, Helen H. *The Hanitch Family of Alsfeld, Germany and Dayton, Ohio with Related Families.* San Antonio, TX, 1950. 42p. [X408-LA].

HANK -- Rudolph, Myra H. *Genealogical Notes: Hank Family.* Warren, OH, 1930-56. 9 vols in 23(?). Contains also Berry and Bryan Families. [X408-SP].

HANK -- Rudolph, Myra H. *The Hank Family in America. Luke Hank of Eastwood, Notts, England and Chester County, Pa. and John Hank of Ilkeston, Derbyshire, England.* Warren, OH, 1932. 268 leaves. [X408-SP].

HANKS -- Baber, Adin (with a number of Hank descendants). *The Hanks Family of Virginia and Westward; A Genealogical Record from the Early 1600's, Including Charts of Families in Arkansas, the Carolinas, Georgia, Illinois, Indiana, Iowa, Kentucky, Missouri, Oklahoma, Ohio, Pennsylvania, and Texas.* Kansas, IL, 1965. Sold exclusively by A. H Clark Co., Glendale, CA. 1 v. (various pagings). [L7685; VV85; VP92].

HANNA -- Harvey, Kate Hanna. <u>The Book of Benjamin Hanna, His Children and Their Descendants</u>. Cleveland, OH, Press of Horace Carr, 1938. ix, 210p. D gives underscored title. [D5562; X408-FW/LA/OH].

HANNA -- Rice, Charles Elmer. *A History of the Hanna Family, Being a Genealogy of the Descendants of Thomas Hanna and Elizabeth (Henderson) Hanna, Who Emigrated to America* *in 1763. With an Appendix containing the Genealogy and History of the Wrights of Kelvedon Hall and Their Descendants in the United States.* Damascus, OH, Pim and Son, Printers, 1905. 238p. [L7692].

HANNA -- Rice, Charles Elmer. *A History of the Hanna Family.* Alliance, OH, Rice, 1905. 238p. [D5564].

HANNAFORD -- Eyster, Virginia Hannaford. *Journey of the Heart: A Loving Family Memoir.* New York, NY, Walker, 1986. 150p. 1. Hannaford family. 2. Eyster, Virginia Hannaford, 1924- -Family. 3. Ohio-Biography. 4. Missouri-Biography. [G294].

HANSON -- Hanson, Floyd H. *James Harvey Hanson and Sidna Gregg Hanson and Their Descendants, with Supplements.* Bedford, OH, 1973. 49 leaves. [X410-KH].

HARBAUGH -- Strock, Richard M. [G297]. See above: FUNK. [G246].

HARBINE -- Harbine, J. Thomas. *A Letter to T. Harbine Monroe, Tacoma, Washington from J. Thomas Harbine, Xenia, Ohio.* Xenia, OH, 1904. 51p. [X411-LI].

HARMON -- NAS. *Biographical Sketch of John B. Harmon and Family.* Cleveland, OH, Williams, 1882. 11p. [X414-FW/LI].

HARMON -- Harmon, Israel. *Souvenir of the Harmon Reunion at the Residence and Grounds of Charles Rollin Harmon, Aurora, Ohio, August 13, 1896.* Springfiled, MA, Harmon, 1896. 20p. [L7768].

HARMON -- Harmon, L. III. *Souvenir of the Harmon Reunion at the Residence and Grounds of Charles Rollin Harmon, Aurora, Ohio, 1896. Part Second, Special Family Record of Israel Harmon, (III) and Frances M. Cooley Harmon and Harmon Genealogy from John Harmon, First*

American Harmon of Record. Springfield, MA, L. Harmon, III. 119, 1 pages. [L7770].

HARRELL -- Harry, Robert Jesse. [G300]. See above. BRINTON. [G89].

HARNLEY -- Budd, A. D. *Harnly Family Surname Index for History of the Harnly Family, by E. H. Harnly, Pub. in 1903.* Ashland, OH, n.d. 12p. [X414-FW].

HARPER -- Ford, Jane C. *Records of the Harper Family.* Cleveland, OH, A. C. Rogers, 1905. 61p. [X415-FW].

HARPER -- Long, Byron R. *A Grave in the Wilderness; An Account of Capt. Alexander Harper, Who Settled Near Unionville, Ohio in 1798 and Died There the Same Year.* In Ohio Archaeological and Historical Quarterly, Columbus, OH, 1914. V. 23, p.81-104. [L7778].

HARRAUF -- Smith, Ned B. *Harrauf (Harroff) Families, 1753-1938.* Youngstown, OH, 1939. 7 leaves. [L7786].

HARRINGTON -- Harrington, Charles A. *The Descendants of Dr. John Harrington (1752-1802): A Physician of Brookfield, Vermont.* Shaker Heights, OH, Harrington, 1961. 87p. [DC1635; X415-FW/MH/NY].

HARRIS -- Harris, Charles. *Walter Harris and Some of His Descendants.* Cleveland, OH, Western Reserve Historical Society, 1922. 30p. L adds: "Appendices: Harrison family tree. - Patterson family tree. - Fragments of family trees. Graduates of Scio College; Non-Graduates of Scio College-1866-1910, inclusive. [L7819; D5666].

HARRIS -- Harris, Gale Ion. *Families of Elisha, Joseph and Woodruff Harris of Chenango County, New York and Geauga and Portage Counties, Ohio.* East Lansing, MI, G. I. Harris, 1981. 131p. [C300].

HARRIS -- McIntosh, Harris. *A Chronicle of the Harris and McIntosh Families.* Perrysburg, OH, H. McIntosh, 1980. 189p. [C300].

HARRISON -- Binkley, Jonathan A. *The Harrison - Willson Families; Binkley, Derrer, Delauney, Frederick, Guenzler, Keller, Lister, Van Delinder.* Toledo, OH, J. A. Binkley, 1981. 68p. [C301].

HARRISON -- Harrison, Joseph T. *The Story of the Dining Fork.* Cincinnati, OH, C. J. Krehbiel Co., 1927. 370p. [L7850; D5703].

HARSCH -- Harsch, James R. *Harsch, Harsh, and Orwig Genealogies; also Potter Genealogy.* Toledo, OH, Harsch, 1947. 58 leaves. [D5720].

HART -- Hart, William Lincoln. *Hart Family History; Silas Hart, His Ancestors and Descendants.* Alliance, OH, 1942. 198p. (NY Library gives 219p.) [L7883; X419-NY].

HARTER -- Harter, Mary. *Harter History.* Doylestown, OH, Harter, 1965. vxi, 155p. D gives date of 1964. [L7886; NG50; D5746].

HARTMAN -- Blaine, Harry S. and Vera E. Waldvogel. *Ancestry of Mary Whipking Hummel.* Toledo, OH, 1954. 32, 1 leaves. [L7893].

HARTPENCE -- Heer, Esther Leonard. *The Hartpence Family in America: Descendants of Johannes Eberhart Pence and Hannah Kitchen of Hunterdon County, New Jersey, 1735-1985.* Baltimore, MD, Gateway, Columbus, OH, Heer, 1989. ix, 269p. [G303].

HARTSON -- Hartson, Louis D. *A Hartshorn (Hartson) Genealogy.* Oberlin, OH, 1967. 19 leaves. [X419-NY].

HARTZELL -- Ware, Flossie E. B. *Some Descendants of Henry Hartzell and Martha (Moore) Hartzell of Adams County, Pa. and*

Darke County, Ohio. NP, 1970. 24, 15p.
[X420-FW].

HARVEY -- Harvey, Rev. Lanson B. and Edward
P. *Rev. Erastus Harvey and His Descendants.*
East Liberty, OH, Howard H. Harvey, 1912. 2,
36p. D gives no date. [L7910; D5761].

HARVEY -- Harvey, Rev. Lanson B. and Edward
P. *Erastus Harvey, Pioneer, Preacher &
Patriot: American Family History. Reprint
and Update Aug. 1985.* __, United Statees,
1985. Originally published: Rev. Erastus
Harvey and His Descendants, East Liberty, OH,
H. H. Harvey, 1912. With additional portraits
and family record updates. 54p. 1. Harvey
family. 2. Harvey, Erastus, 1789-1872-Family.
[G303].

HASKELL -- NAS. *Haskell Journal.*
Cincinnati, OH, Haskell Family 1985-. _v.
See Library Shelflist for Holdings.
[DC1675].

HASKINS -- Green, Charles R. *The Issac
Haskins Family and Genealogy; Including That
of His Son-in-Law, Henry T. Peck, Generally
Known as Harry T. Peck, All of Wakeman, Ohio.*
Olathe, KS, Printed by the Register Pub. Co.,
1911. 16p. D gives: 25 leaves. L adds:
Supplement added containing family history and
genealogy of Mrs. Mary Tuller Bacon also of
Wakeman, Ohio. [L7942: D5774].

HASKINS -- Green, Charles. *The Issac
Haskins Family and Genealogy; Including That
of His Son-in-Law, Henry T. Peck, Generally
Known as Harry T. Peck, All of Wakeman, Ohio.*
NP. 1911. 25 1. [D5774].

HASSELBACH -- Overmyer, John C. <u>History
and Genealogy of the Hasselbach Family in
America</u>; *Being a Record of John Peter, John
Phillip, Regina Elizabeth and Elizabeth
Margaret: Four Daughters of of John Jacob
Hasselbach, and of Their Descendants, 1781-*

136

1910. Fremont, OH, C. S. Bellman, 1910. 159p.
D gives underscored title. [L7956; D5778].

HASTINGS -- Hastings, Francis H. *Family
Records of Dr. Seth Hastings, Senior, of
Clinton, Oneida County, New York.* Cincinnati,
OH, Earhart & Richardson, Superior
Printers, 1899. 202p. [D5781].

HATFIELD -- Stephenson, S. K. *The
Descendants of Joseph and Anna Hatfield,
Married December 6, 1779...* Lebanon, OH,
Republican Press, 1897. 13 p. [L7973].

HATHAWAY -- Collacott, Margaret (Oliver) &
Grandin, Ruth T. *The Ancestors and
Descendants of Zephaniah and Silence Alden
Hathaway: With Notes on Allied FAmilies.*
Mentor, OH, Collacott, Grandin 1961. 277
leaves. NG gives underscored part of title.
[NG50; D5796].

HATHCOCK -- Haithcock, Richard. *Haithcock
Families of Ohio and the Allied Families from
North Carolina. Rev. 2nd ed.* Washington
Court House, OH, R. L. Haithcock, 1985. viii,
161p. 1, Hathcock family. 2. Ohio-Genealogy.
3. North Carolina Genealogy. [G304; C304].

HATHORN -- Gould, Rodney J. *Notes on the
Hathorn Family of Massachusetts and Maine.*
Canton, OH, 1931. Unpaged. [XA1072-WR].

HATTON -- Carvin, Joseph Franklin. *The
Family of Wiley G. and Nancy Hatton plus Other
Hattons.* Columbus, OH, J. F. Carvin, 1984.
ix [i,e.xix], 127 l., 18 leaves of plates.
[C304].

HAVEN -- Goodell, Amelia. *History of the
Haven Family, Also Reports of the Family
Reunions Commencing... 1895.* Garretsville,
OH, W. W. Sherwood, 1896. 15p.
[X424-MH/OH].

HAVERFIELD -- Taylor, Dr. Wallace. *A
Genealogy and Brief History of the Haverfield*

*Family of the United States, One of the
Pioneer Settlers of Jefferson County, Ohio,
later Harrison County.* Oberlin, OH, Press of
the News Printing Co., 1919. x, 316p. [L7998].

HAWK -- Aikin, Nancy & Schumaker, Beverly.
*The Hawk Family of New Jersey and Athens
County, Ohio in the Nineteenth Century.*
Guysville, OH, Aiken, Athens, OH, Schumaker,
1984. vi, 97 l. DC gives author as Arkin.
[C305; DC1686].

HAWKINS -- Cullison, Josephine Hawkins.
*"Roots and Wings": A History of the Family of
Elder and Elisabeth Hawkins, 1809-1987.*
Warsaw, Oh, J.H. Cullison, 1987. vi, 375p.
1. Hawkins family. 2. Hawkins, Elder, 1809-
1889-Family. 3. Ohio-Genealogy. [G305].

HAWORTH -- Hadley, Hattie E. H. *Lineage of
the Haworth Family.* Wilmington, OH, 1934.
23p. [X427-FW].

HAWORTH -- Hunt, C. M. *Hunt, A Partial List
of the Descendants of George Haworth, the
Immigrant.* Cincinnati, OH, Author, n.d. 78p.
[X427-FW].

HAWORTH -- Williams, Kathryn E. *Descendants
of Richard Milton Haworth and His First Wife,
Elizabeth West, and His Second Wife, Jane
Janney.* Wilmington, OH, Williams, 1967. 30
leaves. [D5839].

HAYES -- NAS. *Hayes Memorial: The Library
and Museum, Spiegel Grove, the Hayes Homestead
(of Pres. Rutherfod B. Hayes and His Wife
Lucy Webb Hayes).* Columbus, OH, 1950, 40p.
[X428-FW].

HAYES -- Hathaway, Bernice F. *Hayes -
Maddock - Stubbs and Allied Lines; Many of the
Ancestors and Descendants of Bailey Hayes and
Mary Stubbs, Married...1802. Early
Pennsylvania, Virginia, Maryland, North
Carolina, Georgia and Ohio Lines.* Denver, CO,
1969. [X428-DP/FW/MH/NY; VV90].

138

HAYNES -- Haines, Ruth C. *Ancestry and Descendants of Zimri and Elizabeth Compton Haines, and Other Genealogical Notes.* Waynesville, OH, Author, 1954. 53, 5 p. Includes Woolman, Compton, McPherson. [X429-FW].

HAYES -- Hayes, Royal S. *The Hayes Family.* Cincinnati, OH, Hayes, 1928. 532p. [D5850].

HAYES -- Hayes, Royal S. *The Hayes Family, Origin, History and Genealogy.* Norwood, OH, 1928. 453, 11p. [L8048].

HAYES -- Hayes, Stanley W. *A Mayflower Family of Central Ohio.* NP, 1963. 53p. [D5851].

HAYES -- Hayes, Stanley Wolcott. *A Mayflower Family of Central Ohio.* Richmond, IN, Stanley W. Hayes Research Foundation, 1963. Unpaged. [L8052].

HAYES -- Marchman, Watt P. *The Hayes Memorial.* Columbus, OH, Ohio State Archaelogical and Historical Society, 1950. 38p. [D5852].

HAYS -- Evans, John James. [G307]. See above: BELL. [G46].

HEADLEE -- Headlee, Ray L. *A History of the Headlee and Headley Families.* Akron, OH, William G. Headlee, 1959. 146p. [D5890].

HEARN -- NAS. *The Hearne Family in Ohio from N. Car. and Maryland.* Harrison, OH, E. M. Shaver, 1989. 1 v. (various foliations). 1. Hearn family. 2. Ohio-Genealogy. [G308].

HEATON -- NAS. *Heaton Family Records.* Akron, OH, Daughters of the American Colonists, Indian Trails Chap., Akron, OH, 1974. 14p. [X432-OH].

HECK -- Heck, Arch Oliver. *Descendants of Daniel David Heck, a Settler in the Lower Part of the Shenandoah River Valley near the Virginia Natural Bridge During the Latter Part of the 1700's.* Columbus, OH, 1970. [VV91].

HECK -- Heck, Earl Leon Werley. *The History of the Heck Family of America, with Special Attention to Those Families Who Originated in Indiana, Kentucky, Maryland, Ohio, Pennsylvania and Virginia.* Englewood, OH, Heck, 1959. 50p. D gives underscored title. [L8136; D5910].

HECKATHORN -- Sherwin, Ann C. *The Heckathorn Family: Charles Heckathorn and Nancy Whitla of Columbus and Carroll Counties, Ohio and Isabella County, Michigan.* Decorah, IA, Anundsen Publications Co., 1981. 77p. [C309; NG51].

HEIDENRICH -- Heidenrich, George Edward. *The Heidenrichs Then and Now.* Cincinnati, OH, Heidenrich, Washington, DC, Miller, 1972. 1 v. [D5918].

HEIER -- Raber, Nellie M. R. *Heier, Hire, Hyre, Hyer, Descendants of Lienert and Clara (L.) Heier.* Lakewood, OH, Author, n.d. (sic) 1971. Various pagings. [X433-FW].

HEISER -- Smith, Ned B. *Heiser Genealogy, 1783-1937.* Youngstown, OH, 1937. The Traveler Print Shop, 1938. 22p. [L8162].

HELBERG -- Helberg, Barbara K. *Helberg Family History.* Utica, KY, McDowell Publications, 1987. vii, 196p. 1. Helberg family. 2. Germany-Genealogy. 3. Ohio-Genealogy. [G310].

HELLER -- Irwin, Inez H. *The Heller - Stover Genealogy and Family History.* Olmstead Falls, OH, 1976. 217p. [X434-OH].

HELLER -- Heller, Dick D. *Heller Family of Monroe Township, Harrison County, O., 1819-1969.* Decatur, IN, 1969. 22p. [X434-FW].

HELLER -- Heller, Dick D. *Heller Family.* Decatur, IN, 1974. 46p. [X434-FW].

HELLER -- Heller, James L. *The History of Louis Heller of Dunn County Wisconsin, and His Descendants.* Tallmadge, OH, J. L. Heller, 1977. 27p. [C312; D5927].

HELWIG -- Richards, Sylvia. *Friedrich Helwig Memorial. Bicentennial ed.* Willard, OH, Richards, 1979. vi, 117p. 1. Helwig family. 2. Helwig, Friedrick-Family. [G311; NG51; D5933].

HEMMERT -- Hemmert, Dave. *The Story of Bavarian Immigrants: Hemmert.* Wapakoneta, OH, D. Hemmert, 1989. 176p. 1. Hemmert family. 2. Bavaria (Germany)-Genealogy. [G311].

HENDERSHOT -- Hendershot, Alfred E. *Genealogy of the Hendershot Family in America. (1710-1960)* Akron, OH, Hendershot, 1961. viii, 213p. D omits date in title. [D5945; X436-FW].

HENDERSON -- Lloyd, Emma Rouse. *The Henderson Family of Pennsylvania and Kentucky.* NP, n.d., Pages not shown. (Available for Consultation at Lloyd Library, 309 West Court Street, Cincinnati, OH.) [L8194].

HENDRICKS -- Hinds, Virginia Horner. *Hendrickson, Capt. James Ridgeway, First Burgess of McKeesport, Allegheny County, Pennsylvania 1812-1869, Some Ancestors and Descendants: Family History, 1470-1978, Migration from Holland to New Amsterdam, New Jersey, Pennsylvania, and Points West: Allied Lines, Bailey, Spielmyer, Imlay, Lawrence, Cox, Stout, Lanen Van Pelt (sic), Polhemius, Ten Eyck, Vanderveer, DeMandeville.* Waverly, OH, Hinds, xvii, 139p., 14 l. of plates. [C314; VP100].

HENKEL -- Van Henkle, et al. *The Ancestors and Descendants of Horace Russell Henkle and Effa Hope (Phelps) Henkle.* Lincoln, NB, Henkle Audio Visuals, 1983. Subtitle: Being the account of one family extending for a dozen generations from the five western European countries through early colonial America in Massachusetts, New York, Pennsylvania, Virginia, and North Carolina to the end of the ninteenth century in these states and West Virginia, Ohio, and Indiana, and then with the last year to the nineteenth century the start of five generations in Colorado. Privately printed. 1. Henkel family. 2. Henkle, Horace Russell, 1870-1949- Family. 3. Phelps family. [G312].

HENLEY -- Kilbarger, Harold. *Kilburger, Kiehlburger, Kilbarger, 1810-1987.* __, OH, H. Kilbarger, J. Kilbarger, 1987. a-f, 158p, [i,e. 208p.] (sic). 1. Kilbarger family. 2. Henley family. 3. Winters family. 4. Ohio-Genealogy. [G312].

HENRICK -- NAS. *History of Henrick and Associated Families 19th and 20th Centuries. Coschocton County, Ohio, Brown County, Illinois.* NP, n.d. Folder. [X438-OL].

HENRY -- Henry, Frederick A. *Captain Henry of Geauga, a Family Chronicle.* Cleveland, OH, The Gates Press, 1942. 735p. [X438-FW/IG].

HENRY -- Henry, Frederick Augustus. *A Record of the Descendants of Simon Henry, 1766-1854, and Rhoda Parsons, 1774-1847, his wife.* Cleveland, OH, Press of J. B. Savage, 1905. 5, 65p. [L8203; D5971].

HENRY -- Henry, Heber Homer. *Genealogy of the Descendants of John Henry of Bern Townwship, Athens County, Ohio.* Amesville, OH, Messenger Printery Co., 1922. 100, 12p. D gives 100p. [L8210; D5972].

HERRICK -- Herrick, Gen. Jediah. *Herrick Genealogy. A Genealogical Register of the Name and Family of Herrick from the Settlement of Henerie Hericke, in Salem, Massachusetts, 1629 to 1846 with Concise Notice of Their English Ancestry.* Revised Augmented and Brought Down to 1885 by Lucius C. Herrick, MD. Columbus, OH, Privately Printed, 1885. x, 516p. [L8257].

HERRMAN -- Heck, Earl L. W. *Augustine Herrman: Beginner of the Virginia Tobacco Trade, Merchant of New Amsterdam and First Lord of Bohemia Manor in Maryland.* Englewood, OH, Heck, 1941. ix, 123p. [D6016: X441-FW].

HERRON -- Faskett, Helen R. *History and Genealogy of Two Pioneers of Rich Hill Twp., Muskingum County, Ohio: William Herron, 1805, and Thomas Leedom... 1810.* New London, OH, 1971. 85 leaves. [X441-OH].

HERSHBERGER -- Miller, Jacob J. *History of Gabriel Hershberger and His Descendants: 1808-1968.* Blufton, OH, 1969. v, 286p. [X441-FW/NY].

HERSHBERGER -- Raber, Menno J. *Descendants of Eli W. Hershberger, 1861 to 1970.* Fredericksburg, OH, 1970. 32p. [X441-FW].

HERSHEY -- Freeburn, Dwight. *From Germany to America with Our Harshey and Allied Families.* Berea, OH, D. Freeburn, 1984. 257 leaves. 1. Hershey family. 2. Pennsylvania-Genealogy. 3. Ohio-Genealogy. [G315; C317].

HERTER -- Hott, Kathryn. [G315]. See above: FRITZINGER. [G242].

HESS -- NAS. *Genealogical Data: Hess - Brown, York and Bedford Counties, Pa., and Columbus, Ohio.* NP, 1916. Broadside. [X442-NY].

HESSER -- Hesser, Ernest George. *A History of the Hesser Family, 1708-1945.* Crestline, OH, 1947. xii, 249p. [L8287].

HESTER -- Hester, Martin M. *History and Genealogy of the Descendants of John Lawrence Hester and Godfrey Stough, 1752-1905.* Norwalk, OH, Hester, 1905. ix, 323, 43, 30p. D gives: 323, 30p. [L8288; D6033].

HICKEY -- Achor, Robert L. [G317]. See above: ACHOR. [G2]. (Two entries).

HICKMAN -- Burdette, Elizabeth Y. *Sotha Hickman and Some of His Descendants.* Akron, OH, 1975. iii, 23 6p. [X444-FW].

HIGBY -- Higbee, Lucy Ann. *The Diary of Lucy Ann Higbee.* Cleveland, OH, Privately Printed (H. and Nettie B. Carr), 1924. 57p. 1 leaf. An account of a journey partly by canal boat from Trenton, N.J. to Ohio, returning via Niagara Falls and Saratoga. Also the Higbee Family Genealogy. [L8331].

HIGGINS -- Hott, Richard. [G317]. See above: CHALFANT. [G131].

HIGGINS -- Wood, Anne Farrell Higgins. *The Paternal Lineage and the Descendants of Myrick Higgins of Vermont, Ohio and Iowa.* NP, Wood, 1956. 49 leaves. [X445-NY/SU].

HIGGINS -- Wood, Anne Farrell Higgins. *The Paternal Lineage and the Descendants of Myrick Higgins of Vermont, Ohio and Iowa.* NP, Wood, 1962. 2d ed. 114 leaves. D does not give ed. [D6079; X445-OH/SL/SU].

HIGGINS -- Wood, Anne Farrell Higgins. *The Story of Many Descendants of the Brothers Ichabod and Richard Higgins, 1603-1979.* Orinda, CA, Wood, 1979. 613p. A revision and enlargement of the 3rd ed. of the author's The Paternal Lineage and some of the descendants of Joseph Higgins of Massachusetts, Vermont, and Ohio, published in 1969. 1. Higgins family. [G318; C320].

HILDRETH -- Hildreth, Samuel Prescott. *Genealogical and Biographical Sketches of the Hildreth Family From the Year 1652 Down to the Year 1840.* Marietta, OH, Hildreth, 1840. L gives: Reprinted 1925. 4, 334p. X-LI gives 3, 336p. D gives 334p. [L8355; D6091; X446-LI].

HILDRETH -- Sheneman, Allen D. *Hildreth Genealogy: Ancestors and Descendants of William and Joannah Chalker Hildreth of Glastonbury, Connecticut: With Information on Tuthill, Wells, Chalker, Coleman, Hurlbut, Stokley, and Riley Families.* Defiance, OH, Hubbard, Co., 1982. viii, 135p. [C320].

HILL -- Arbogast, Kathryn Hill. *The House of Hill: The Story of Hill and Other Allied Families -- Covington, Hammond, Coleman, Florence, Galbreth, Gilliland, Kinnear, Sharp, Shawhan, Hamilton, Yoakum, McKinley, Litten, Whiteside, Gulick, Wilson, Schleich, Davis, Hott, Wttich (sp?) and Others.* Columbus, OH, Fish Graphics, 1982. xv, 272p. [C321; DS344].

HILL -- Furniss, John Neilson. *Hill and Allied Families of Central Ohio. Also, Wheeler, Keys, Gapen, Higbie, Varney, Ewalt, Douglas Families.* Baltimore, MD, 1974. 203p. [S1208; NG52].

HILL -- Hill, Leonard Uzal. *Descendants of Paul Hill and Rachel Stout through Charles Hill, and of Moses Edwards and Desire Meeker through Uzal Edwards.* Piqua, OH, 1953. 58, 31 leaves. [L8386].

HILL -- NAS. *Diary of a Journey From Ohio to New Jersey in 1838.* NP, New Jersey DAR.1950. 65 leaves. [D6113].

HILLES -- Hilles, Samuel E. *Memorials of the Hilles Family, More Particularly of Samuel and Margaret Hill Hilles of Wilmington,*

Delaware; with Some Account of Their Ancestory and Some Data Not Before Published; also Extended References to the Life of Richard Hilles or Hills, Principal Founder of the Merchant Taylors School in London, 1561... Cincinnati, OH, S. E. Hilles, 1928. 1 v. various pagings. D gives 239p. [L8393; D6118].

HILLYER -- Heck, Pearl Leona. *The Hillyer Family of Connecticut, Ohio and Florida, from 1640-1933.* NP, 1933. 65 l. [D6130].

HILLYER -- Pollock, Mabel C. H. *The Hillyer Family, Connecticut and Ohio.* Salem, MA, 1954. 12p. [X448-OH].

HILTY -- Shumacher, Verena. *Family Record of the Children of Peter Hilty, 1821-1892 and Elizabeth Neuenschwander Hilty, 1819-1894.* Pandora, OH, 1965. 32 leaves. [X448-FW].

HINA -- Hina, Charles E. *The Hina Family: Three Centuries.* Lisbon, OH, C. E. Hina, 1983. 351p. [C322].

HINDS -- Thomas, B. A. H. *Thomas, Hine, Root, Atwood, Hall, Manso Genealogical Records.* Akron, OH, Author, 1951. 133p. [X449-FW].

HINKLE -- Alban, William Rowland, Mrs. (Janet Nellie Hinkle). *The Genealogy of Christopher Hinkle, Jr., and His Wife Margaret (Allen) Hinkle, Jr.* Galina, OH, Mrs. W. R. Alban, 1982. xvi, 129p. [C323].

HINMAN -- Hinman, Adin Vincent. *A History of the Hinmans; Containing also an Abbrevaited Record of the Kindred Families Showing Their Relation to the Hinmans.* Youngstown, OH, Vindicator Press, 1907. 75p. [L8426; D6143].

HINSDALE -- Hinsdale, Albert. *Chronicles of the Hinsdale Family.* Cleveland, OH, J. B. Savage, 1883. 31p. [L8430].

HINTON -- Hinton, Herbert Lee. *Ancestors and Descendants of James Harley Hinton and Marth Alice Adams: Including Some Related Families.* Tiffin, OH, Hinton, 1979. 6, a-k, 146p. [C323].

HIRSCH -- Harsh, Robert C. *The Harsh Family Genealogy, 1740-1987: Being a Record of the Descendants of Juliana Veronica Hirsch, Widow of Hans Heinrich Hirsch; Derived from the Life-Long Collections of Harvey Edgar Harsh... et al.* Columbus, OH, R.C. Harsh, 1987. iv, 514, 121p., 1 leaf of plates. 1. Hirsch family. 2. Hirsch, Juliana Veronica-Family. [G320].

HITCHCOCK -- Hitchcock, Elizabeth G. *Some Descendants of Matthias Hitchcock, of East Haven, Connecticut, Concentrating on the Cleveland, Ohio Branch; also Extended Lineage of Helean Townsend Bradely, Mary Ann Canfield, Susanna Frisbie, Sarah Marshall, Eliza Jane Morley, Jemima Sill, Mary Sterling and Sarah Jane Wilcox.* Mentor, OH, Hitchcock, 1966. 23, xii l. [D6150].

HOAGLAND -- Hoagland, G. W. *Dirck Jansen Hoogland Family History, 1657-1976.* Cleveland, OH, Genie Repros, 1976. xiv, 374p. PH gives name as HOOGLAND. [X451-FW/PH].

HOAGLAND -- Warrick, John A. *Historical Sketch of the Clark - Hoagland Families of Coshocton County, Ohio and Iroquois County, Illinois...* Chicago, IL, Author, 1929, 11p.. [X451-FW].
    -- *Same Revised...* 1941. 22p. [X451-FW].

HOAR -- Horr, Norton T. *A Records of Descendants of Hezekiah Hoar of Taunton, Massachusetts; with an sic Historical Introduction.* Cleveland, OH, Horr, 1907. 56p. [D6165].

HOBSON -- Davis, Earl H. *Hobson Descendants of George and Ethel Hobson, Virginia, North*

Carolina, Ohio, Indiana. Long Beach, CA, Author, 1957. 323p. [X452-FW/MH].

HOCHSTETLER -- Hochstetler, Harvey. *Descendants of Jacob Hochstetler, The Immigrant of 1736.* Berlin, OH, Gospel Book Store, 1970. 1191p. Reprint of 1912 ed. plus appendix and indexes. [X452-DP].

HOCHSTETLER -- Hostetler, Damon S. *Descendants of Amos L. Hochstetler.* Clearwater, FL, Sunshine H.M., (sic), 1990. 1 v. (various pagings). 1. Hochstetler family. 2. Hochstetler, Amos L., 1868-1941-Family. 3. Ohio-Genealogy. 4. Hostetter family. [G321].

HOCHSTETLER -- Miller, J. Virgil. *Descendants of Noah H. Hochstetler and Barbara Schrock and Some European Background of the Hochstetler Family.* Wooster, OH, Atkinson's Print., 1972. 116p. [X452-FW].

HODGEN -- Burgner, Walter C. *Hodgen Family of Knox Co., Indiana.* Lima, OH, 197_. Unpaged. [X453-FW].

HODGES -- Hodges, Rufus. *A Record of the Families in New England of the Name of Hodges.* Cincinnati, OH, 1837. 22p. [L8474].

HOFFER -- Brown, Relva O. Spears and Richard E. Pride, II. *The Hoffer Families from Hoffer Hill, Rardon, Ohio, Scioto County.* Sardinia, OH, R. O. Brown, 1984. 205p. [C325].

HOFFMAN -- Huffman, Robert Louis. *The Huffman Family of Sonora, Ohio.* Wilington, DE, R.L. Huffman, 1988. 49p., 13p. of plates. 1, Hoffman family. 2. Ohio-Genealogy. [G322].

HOGG -- Stevenson, Robert A. *The Magee Family. Supplement.* Akron, OH, R.A. Stevenson, <1986- .> v. <7 >. Contents: -v. 7. The Hogue family in America, 1682-1982. 1. Magee family. 2. Hogg family. [G323].

HOGUE -- Hogue, Delos W. *History of the Hogue Family.* Springfield, OH, 1956. 120p. [X455-FW].

HOHL -- Moran, Soni Hohl. *The Hohl Family History, 1800-1983, John and Katherine Hohl.* Thornville, OH, S. H. Moran, [1983-] v. <1 > [C327].

HOHN -- Price, Vergie Farley. [G325]. See above: DROSTE. [G201].

HOING -- Hoying, David A. *In Praise of Our Ancestors: History of the Hoyng - Hoying Family.* Minster, OH, D.A. Hoying, 1990. 379p. 1. Hoing family. 2. Netherlands-Genealogy. 3. Ohio-Genealogy. [G325].

HOKE -- Berlekamp, Jean A. (Stiger) & McConnell, Hope L. *In the Name of God Almighty, Amen, I Hoke Bequeath.* Green Springs, OH, 1980. v, 572p. G lists under HOOK. 1. Hook family. [G328; NG53].

HOKE -- Hoke, George W. *A History of the Hoke Family.* Covington, OH, Printed by the Little Printing Co., 1953. 172p. See also just below. [X455-FW/SU].

HOKE -- Hoke, George Washington. *A History of the Hoke Family.* Covington, OH, Printed by the Little Printing Co., 1953. 172p. [D6208].

HOLDERBAUM -- Holderbaum, Bruce A. *The Holderbaum Family in America, 1751-1975.* Cleveland, OH, Halderbaum, 1975. iii, 106p. [X456-LA/OH/PH].

HOLE -- Rice, Charles Elmer. *A History of the Hole Family in England and America... With Appendices of the Hanna, Grubb, Douglas - Morton , Miller, and Morris Families.* Alliance OH, R. M. Scranton Pub. Co., 1904. 134p. D gives underscored title. [L8522; D6220].

HOLE -- VanFossan, W. H. *Histories of Certain Branches of the Hole, Preston and*

Morris Families of Columbiana County, Ohio.
NP, 1964. 68 leaves. [D6221].

HOLL -- Holl, Henry C. *History of the Hall - Schrantz Family; of the Descendants of Ephraim Hall.* Canton, OH, Repository Printing Co., 1891. 112p. [L8524].

HOLLEMAN -- May, Richard Holman. *A Supplement to The Abraham Holman Family of Ross County, Ohio (Including the Dreisbach and Eyestone Lines): A genealogy originally completed by Richard Holman May and published by the Godfrey Memorial Library, Middleton, Conn., in 1959.* Supplemented by Richard Holman May, Mill Valley, CA, May, 1979. 39p. [C328].

HOLLINGSWORTH -- Burtoft, Mrs. L. Ada Judkins. *Biographical Sketch of Hon. David A. Hollingsworth, Cadiz, Ohio with Selected Speeches, Incidents and (Genealogy).* NP, 1920. 8,339p. [X457-LI].

HOLLINGSWORTH -- Farmer, Walter I. [G327]. See above: FARMER. [G222].

HOLLIS -- Bell, Albert Dehner. *Hollis Notes, 1639, 1948.* Rockland, OH, Bell, 1948. 34 leaves. [L8543; D6237].

HOLLOWAY -- Holloway, M. C. *Holloway Bicentenniel: An Account of the Descendants of Elijah Holloway, 1754-1825, Worcester County, Maryland... to Ross County, O.* NP, n.d. 38p. [X458-FW].

HOLMAN -- May, Richard Holman. *The Abraham Hollman Family of Ross County, Ohio. A Genealogy of the Abraham and Leah Dresbach Holman, Their Ancestors and Descendants.* Middletown, CT, Godfrey Memorial Library, 1959. 49p. [L8553; NG53].

HOLMES -- Butler, Gold Jane. *The Descendants of George Holmes in America.* Zanesville, OH, Butler, 1928. 122p. [D6253].

HOLMES -- Francis, W. O. *A History of the Holmes Family.* Chillicothe, OH, Dave Webb Private Press, 1942. 11p. [L8560].

HOLMES -- Holmes, James T. *Genealogy and History of the Holmes Family and Some of Their Friends.* Columbus, OH, 1901. 1200p. Vol 2. Hectagraphed. [X459-OH].

HOLMES -- Holmes, Col. J. T. *The American Family of Rev. Obadiah Holmes.* Columbus, OH, Holmes, Stoneman Press, 1915. 247p. [L8557; D6255].

HOLT -- Tatum, V. Holt (from notes provided by Madue Holt Black & others). *The Holt Family in Europe and American, 1248-1971; A Brief Account of the Genealogy, History, and Armory in England and Germany in Europe: Also in the State of Massachusetts, Connecticut, Virginia, North Carolina, Tennessee, Mississippi and Utah in America.* Cincinnati, OH, 1971. [VV96].

HOLTON -- Holton, Edward P. *A Genealogy of the Descendants in America of William Holton (1610-1691) of Hartford, Conn., and Northampton, Mass.* Cleveland, OH, 1935. 73, xxvii p. [X460-MH].

HOLTON -- Holton, Edward P. *Genealogy of the Descendants in America of William Holton (1610-1691) of Hartford, Conn., and Northampton, Mass. Ed 2.* NP, 1965. 291p. [X461-MH].

HOLYCROSS -- Pompey, Sherman Lee. *Notes on the Surname of Holycross in Virginia and Union County, Ohio. Compiled from Census Records, Vital Records, and the Union County History published by Beer.* NP, 1981. 36 leaves. Library copy lacks leaf 33. 1. Holycross family. 2. Ohio-Genealogy. [G328].

HOMAN -- Schieltz, Ruth C. Wagner. *Der Stammbaum, May-Homan = The Family Tree, May-*

Homan. Versailles, OH, R. C. W. Schieltz, 1982. 252p. [C330].

HONEYWELL -- Honeywell, Samuel Willet. *The American Descendants of Samuel Honewell of Bideford, Devonshire, England, Lost at Sea in 1823.* Columbus, OH, Printed by Middleton Print Co., 1971. vi, 191, xi, p. [S1241].

HOOK -- Hooker, Malcolm D. *Descendants and Ancestors of Benjamin and Anne Frizelle Hooker, 1976, with 1977, 1978 & 1979 Supplements and Revisions Added. Revised ed.* West Liberty, OH, Hooker, 1979. 250 1. in various foliations. D lists under HOOKER; gives 1976 publ. date but adds: "Indexes bound with 1977 and 1978 Supplements and Revisions. [C331; D6291].

HOOK -- Hoover, Jesse W. *A History of the Hock (Anglicized) Hoke Family, 1405-1900. Limited. ed.* ___, OH, Hoke Historian (sic) Committee, 1990. vi, 426p. 1. Hook family. 2. Ohio-Genealogy. 3. Germany-Genealogy. [G329].

HOOVER -- Hoover, J. L. *History of the Hoover Families. August, 1907.* Circleville, OH, Lowe and Spencer Print., 1907. 15p. [X462-PH].

HOPKINSON -- Andrews, Thomas Sheldon. *Ira Andrews and Ann Hopkinson, Their Ancestors and Posterity. Including an Autobiography of the Author... Also a Treatise on Marriage, Divorce, and the Laws of Psychol and Constitutional Hereditary Transmissions.* Toledo, OH, Blade Printing Co., 1879. vi, 437p. [L8637].

HOPPES -- Hoppes, L. Edwin. *Hoppes and Related Families.* Springfield, OH, L. E. Hoppes, 1982. xii, 516p. [C332].

HOPPLE -- Parker, Kenneth L. *A Dozen Generations (1634-1971)... Starting in*

Maryland with the Greene and Wheeler Families and on through the Tudors to the Hopples in Cincinnati. Wilmot, OH, Author, 1971. 65p. [X464-OH].

HORN -- McCorkle, Elyzabeth S. *A Memorial Collection of the Revolutionary Ancestors of Floy Aileen Wiltrout Horn: Her Lineage from John Frederick Christian Alleman of Pa., William Priest of Va, Jacob Shidler of Pa, Frederick Schutt of Pa.* Ashland, OH, 1964. 22 leaves. [L8651; NG54].

HORNBROOK -- Bush, Thomas Lloyd. *The Times of the Hornbrooks: Tracing a Family Tradition.* Cincinnati, OH, T. L. Bush, 1977. xv, 386p., 12 leaves of plates. [C333].

HORNER -- Hinds, Virginia H. *Our Horner Ancestors, William of Fayette County, Pa., Sone of Thomas of Baltimore County, Md., Family Genealogy ca 1700-1973. Allied Lines: Preston, Gilbert, Mitchell, West, Snively, Bumgarner, Swearingen, Moore.* Waverly, OH, 1974. viii, 268p. [X465-DP/FW/LA/NY/PH].

HORNUNG -- Knack, Mary A. *Hornung Genealogy of New Bavaria, Ohio.* New Bavaria, OH, n.d. 10p. [X466-FW].

HORTON -- Horton, T. W. *A Tabulation of the Descendants of Joseph Horton, a Soldier of the American Revolution.* Milford Center, OH, Horton, 1924. 49 leaves. [D6348].

HORTON -- Parsons, Franc H. *The Horton Family.* Vermillion, OH, The News Press, 1936. 17p. [X466-SU].

HOSFORD -- Hosford, Henry Hallock. *Ye Horseforde Booke: <u>Horsford - Hosford Families in the United States</u> of America.* Cleveland, OH, Tower Press, Inc., 1936. 256p. X gives title: ... Horsfoed - Hosford... and 356p. D gives underscored title. [L8668; D6353; X466-PH].

HOSKINS -- NAS. *The Hoskins Genealogist.*
Chesterland, OH, (etc.) G. E. Russell, Jan
1956 - Mar 1960. 7 nos. in 1 vol. Semi-
annual (irregular). [X467-DP/MH].

HOSMER -- Hosmer, Mary R. *Hosmer Genealogy,
Ancestors and Descendants of Zechariah Hosmer
of Parkman, Ohio.* Freeport, IL, 194_. 46p.
[X468-SP].

HOSTETTER -- Hostetler, Damon. [G331].
See above: HOCHSTETLER. [G321].

HOUGH -- Hough, James Emerson. *Genealogical
Table of Moses (Huff) Hough and His
Descendants.* Cincinnati, OH, 1973. 1 Sheet.
[S1253].

HOUSE -- House, Harmon. *House Family from
Diersheim, Germany in 1817; with a Supplement
of Henry House, Morgan County, Indiana.*
Dayton, OH, House of Howard, 1971. 97p.
[X469-FW].

HOUSE -- Noe, Byron. *Genealogy of the House
Family.* Fairborn, OH, 1975. Various Pagings.
[X469-FW].

HOUSEMAN -- Frazier, Harry Houseman. *The
Houseman Family of Westmoreland County,
Pennsylvania.* Tiffin, OH, Frazier,
(Advertiser Press) 1937. 148p., 26 p. of
pictures. "Supplementary to the Houseman
Family", 3p. inserted at end. D gives 148p;
and no reference to supplement nor Advertiser
Press. [L8702; D6385; VP110].

HOUSTON -- Houston, Rev. Samuel Rutherford.
*Brief Biographical Accounts of Many Members of
the Houston Family.* Cincinnati, OH, Elm
Street Printing Co., 1882. v, 420p.
[L8706; DC1865].

HOUT -- Pittis, Margaret Birney. *The Hout
Family for Two Hundred Twenty-seven Years, Ten
Generations, 1725-1952. Johann George Haudt,*

*anglicized to John George Hout; His Sons
Jacob, Peter, George Michael, Rudolph and
Their Descendants in Berkely County, Virginia,
now in West Virginia. Allied Families with
Extra Records: Arnold, Birney, Horn, Knisley,
Livingston, McCulloch or McCullough, Müller,
or Miller, Munch, or Minich, Oberlin or
Overly, Pittis, Simpson, Streiter or Strider.*
Cleveland, OH, Pittis, 1952. 638p. D gives
underscored title. [L8719; D6394].

HOVER -- Breese, John Elmer. *Hover Family,
Descendants of Manuel Hover.* Lima, OH, 1938.
11 numb. leaves. [A329].

HOVEMEYER -- Hovemeyer, Eric E. and Family.
The Hovemeyer Family in Germany and America.
Cincinnati, OH, 1972. 32p. 50 copies
printed. [S1260].

HOWARD -- Weaver, Gustine Nancy (Courson).
*The Howard Lineage; The Ancestry of Ida Ann
Boydston Welch. Also Whitten, Rector,
Duckett, Lewis, Osborne, Claypoole Families.*
Cincinnati, OH, Powell and White, 1929. 230p.
D gives underscored part of title.
[L8742; NG54; D6414].

HOWE -- NAS. *Howe Genealogy; A Manuscript
Record of Families of Ancestors of James R.
Howe in Connecticut, New York, New Jersey, and
Ohio from 1702.* NP, n.d. 94p. [XA1072-WR].

HOWE -- White, Franklin H. [G334]. See
above: CARTER. [G125].

HOWELL -- Hammel, Ruth A. *Howell - Gardner
Family, from Ireland to Montgomery County,
Ohio to Tippicanoe County, Indiana.*
Lafayette, IN, Hammel, 1979. 219, 68p. [C336].

HUBBARD -- Hubbard, Frank Allison.
*Descendants of George Hubbard of Middletown,
Conn.* Sandusky, OH, 1918. 10, 2p. [L8819].

HUDSON -- Hudson, Roland V. *My Hudson
Ascendants.* Tiffin, OH, 1973. 95 l. [S1277].

HUDSON -- Hudson, Roy D. *Hudson Genealogy, 1634-1957, Including All Known Descendants of Ananias and Magdeline Willey Hudson and Those Who Have Married into the Family.* Bay Village, OH, 1957. 32 leaves. [X474-FW/LA/MH/NY/SU].

HUGHES -- Hughes, Nancy G. C. *Lineage, Genealogy, and History: Hughes Family Origin in Western Pa.; Aten or Eaton Family Origin in Brooklyn, N.Y., ... Western Pa.; Blackburn Family Origin in Western Pa., Schultz Family Origin in Ohio.* NP, n.d. 63p. [X476-FW; VP111].

HUGHES -- Hughes, Raymond Finley. *Hughes Family of Cape May County, New Jersey, 1650-1950.* Cincinnati, OH, Hughes, 1950. 265p. [D6497].

HULL -- Riley, Clifton Virginia Hull. *A Hull Pioneer to Ohio. Behind One Line of Descendants of Lot Hull and Inquiries into His Ancestry. A Family History and Genealogy.* NP, 1977, 127 leaves. [C340].

HUMPHREY -- Avery, Elroy McKendree. *John Humphrey, Massuchetts Magistrate; Did He Marry the Daughter of the Third Earl of Lincoln?* Cleveland, OH, 1912. 22p. L adds: An answer to the New York Times. D gives underscored title: [L8903; D6514].

HUNNEWELL -- Hunnewell, James M. *Descendants of Roger and Ambrose Hunnewell (Honneywell).* Columbus, OH, S. W. Honeywell, 1972. 275p. [X478-FW]

HUNT -- Hunt, Charles Cummins. *A Genealogical History of the Robert and Abigail Pancoast Hunt Family.* Columbus, OH, Champlin Press, 1906. 202p. [L8929; D6537].

HUNTER -- NAC. *Hunter Family History.* Urbana, OH, 1905. 46p. [L8943].

HUNTOON -- Waite, Frederick C. *Origin of the Name, Concord, Lake County, Ohio, and the*

Huntoon Family. NP, n.d. 2p. of mounted clippings. [X481-OH].

HUPP -- Fry, Eloise Latham. *Our Buckeye Tree: A Genealogy.* Cincinnati, OH, E. L. Fry, 1958. 1 v. various pagings. [C342].

HURD -- Hurd, Raymond W. *Genealogy of the Hurd Family, and Partial Genealogy of the Herd Family of Monroe County, Ohio.* Greensburg, PA, 1961. 20 leaves, 2 leaf supplement inserted. [X481-NY].

HURLBUT -- Deans, Arline Mary Hulbert and Nadine Hulbort Sullivan. *Hulbert Family, Descendants of Thomas Hurlbut of Saybrook, Connecticut, 1635 and the Allen Family of Ohio, Sabin Family of Ohio.* Alexandria, VA, Deans, 1976. 134 leaves, 2 leaves of plates. C gives underscored title; NG gives 134 leaves. [C343; NG55].

HUSS -- Scott, Fae Elaine. *The Family Tree of John Huss of Iowa.* Genoa, OH, Scott, 1978. xxviii, 222p. (Her descendants of Chester Co., Pa.). v. 2. [C343].

HUSTON -- Price, Hazel H. *(The) Hustons. Family of John C. and Ella Loder Huston.* Westerville, OH, 1972. 5 parts. Pt. 1, Hustons - Pt. 2, Morrisons and Montgomerys - Pt. 3, Loders - Pt. 4, Pecks and Lewises - Pt. 5, Brecounts and De Camps. [X482-CW/FW/OH].

HUTCHISON -- Barnes, M. E., MD & Rev. J. A. Barnes, DD. *James Hutchineson and His Descendants.* Greenville, OH, 1927. 1p., 6 numb. leaves. [L9031].

-- Copy 2 Bound with the Author's *James Sharp and His Descendants.* Greenville, OH, 1927. pni. [L9031].

HUTTON -- Hutton, C. Osborne. *Descendants of the Quaker Huttons of Pennsylvania.* Mentor, OH, 1965. [VP113].

HUXLEY -- Huxley, Jared. *Genealogical Descent of the Huxley Family in the United States...2nd ed. rev. and enlarged.* Youngstown, OH, The Vindicator Press, 1901. 77, 8p. [L9040].

HYDE -- Hyde, Edith Drake. *The Descendents (sic) of Andrew Hyde of Lenox Massachusetts, Sixth in Descent from William Hyde of Norwich Connecticut, Including the Descendents (sic) of Rebecca Hyde Aye of Morrow County, Ohio.* Ann Arbor, MI, Edwards Bros. Inc., 1937. v, 58p. [L9050].

HYDE -- Logan, Thos. A. *The John Hyde Association; Report of Thos. A. Logan.* Cincinnati, OH, 1880. 36p. [X484-LI].

I

IDEN -- Iden, V. Gilmore. *Sons and Daughters of Randall Iden.* Mt. Vernon, OH, Raymond J. Iden, 1941. 99p, 32 l. [D6636].

IMHOFF -- Imhoff, Rufus L. *Descendants of Peter Imhoff (1806-1893).* Wooster, OH, Author, 1959. 63p. [X487-FW].

IMLAY -- Imlay, Hugh and Nellie. *The Imlay Family.* Zanesville, OH, Imlay, 1958. 190p. D gives 190, 2p. [L9070; D6644].

INNIS -- Innis, James Robert. *Francis Innis, Pioneer of the Tuscarora Valley, Juniata County, Pennsylvania, and His Descendants: Being Principally, a Geneology (sic) of the Family Which Arose from James Innis, Son of Francis. From Research Papers of the Late Iona Geraldine Innis Austin, and of the Compiler and Others.* Cincinnati, OH, J. R. Innis, Jr. 1982. xiii, 401p. C & VP list under INNES. DS does not give pagination. [C348; DS383; VP114].

INGLES -- Hale, John P. *Trans-Allegheny Pioneers; Historical Sketches of the First*

158

*White Settlements West of the Alleghenies 1748
and After. Wonderful Experiences of the
Hardships and Heroism of Those Who First
Braved the Dangers of the Inhospitable
Wilderness and the Savage Tribes that then
Inhabited It.* Cincinnati, OH, The Graphic
Press, 1886. 2, 330p. [L9085].

INSKEEP -- Innskeep, Ruth Celia. *Meeth
Families of Inskeep and Garwood.*
Bellefontaine, OH, Inskeep, 175, 426p.
[S1316].

IRETON -- Ireton, Judith S. *The Ireton,
Irton Family.* Dayton, OH, 1972. 183p.
[S1317; NG56].

IRETON -- Ireton, Judith Smith. *The Ireton,
Irton Family.* Dayton, OH, Ireton, 1972.
168p. [D6665].

IRVIN -- Wolfe, Esther E. Hoff. *The Irvin
Family.* Cleveland, OH, Wolfe, 1964. 124p.
FW lists under IRVINE. [D6676; X489-FW].

IRWIN -- Irvin, L. J. *Family Records and
Memoirs.* Dayton, OH, Author, 1931. 105p.
[X489-FW].

J

JACKSON -- Doughman, M. P. *Some of the
Descendants of Edward William Jackson, Born
New Jersey, 1730, and Died Virginia, 1807.*
Lebanon, OH, 1966. 30, 5p. [X492-FW; VV103].

JACKSON -- Jackson, Harry L. *Some
Descendants of John and Elizabeth Cummins
Jackson in Kentucky: Kentucky Relatives of
Stonewall Jackson.* Cleveland, OH, Jackson,
Clarksville, TN, Jostens Publications. 1976.
154p. [C350; D6703; X492-FW/LA/OH].

JACKSON -- Jackson, Rev. Hugh Parks, Hugh
Hogue Thompson, DD and James R. Jackson, esq.
The Genealogy of the "Jackson Family".

Urbana, OH, Press of Citizen and Gazette Co.,
1890. 124, 18p. Also, Descendants of Mary
Jackson and Joseph Caldwell, p 63-72. Bound
with A List of Descendants of Samuel and Mary
Ann Jackson by William T. Jackson, 1934, 21p.
L gives 124p. [L9144; D6705].

JACKSON -- Robbins, Oscar Burton. *History
of the Jackson Family of Hempstead, Long
Island, N.Y., Ohio and Indiana.* Loveland, CO,
Robins, 1951. A-K, 356p. L omits author.
[L9168; D6718].

JACOBS -- Symmonds, Dorothy. *A History and
Genealogy of the Pritchett, Rimmer, Jacobs,
Hamilton, Eldridge, Etheridge, Smith, Brown,
and Davidson Families from North Carolina,
Tennessee, Illinois, Missouri, and Kansas in
the Early 1800s to 1900s.* Bellaire, TX, D.
Symmonds, 1985-<1989 >. v.<1-2 >. Vol.
2 has title: A History and Genealogy of the
families of Howland, Brown, Follett, Van Dyke,
Lamb, Spaulding, and Davidson with related
lines of Treat, Botsford, Parker, Burwell,
Clark,   Andrews,   Symmonds,   Burnaman,
Ashbaugh,and Smith from Holland, England,
Scotland, and   France to Massachusetts,
Connecticut, New York, New Jersey, Ohio, Iowa,
Indiana, Nebraska, Kansas, and Texas from "The
Mayflower" pilgrmins in 1620 to the 1980s .
Pritchard family.   2. Rimmer family.   3.
Jacobs family. [G345].

JACOBSON -- Jacobson, J. Larry. *Family
Histories: Jacobson of W. Prussia and Kansas,
Huffman of Virginia, Ohio, Kansas, Forgey &
Wakefield of Ohio.* NP, 1967. Various
Pagings. [X493-KH].

JAMES -- James, Charles G. *The James Family,
a Preliminary Report on the Descendants of
William James, Sr. and Jane Williams James,
Virginia and Warren County, Ohio.* NP, n.d.
Unpaged. [X494-OH].

JAMES -- Ohler, Clara Paine. *Ancestors and
Descendants of Captain John James and Esther*

Denison of Preston, Connecticut. Lima, OH, Ohler, 1912. 216p. [L9186; D6731].

JANSEN -- Miller, Betty A. *The Cornelius Jansen Family History, 1822-1973.* Berlin, OH, Miller, 1974. 73p. X gives: Includes also Janzen. G lists under JANZEN. 1. Janzen family. 2. United States-Genealogy. [G346; X494-FW/KH/NY/OH].

JANUSZEWSKI -- Lybarger, Donald F. *The Family of Joseph Januszewski; Notes Gathered from Many Sources.* Cleveland, OH, 1965. 15 leaves. [L9206].

JARVIS -- Yoho, Denver C. *Stevens - Jarvis Family History.* Gallipolis, OH, D. Yoho, 1984. 318p. 1. Stevens family. 2. Jarvis family. 3. West Virginia-Genealogy. 4. Ohio-Genealogy. C lists as STEVENS. [G346; C667].

JEFFERS -- Hagan, Erma Jeffers. The Descendants of John H. Jeffers and Gallia County, Ohio *and Related Families, 1844-1975.* Parsons, WV, McClain Print Co., 1976. xiv, 262p. D & X give underscored title. [C354; D6759; X496-FW; VV104].

JEFFRIES -- Jeffries, Mark Emerson. *Genealogical Sketch of the Robert Jeffries Family in America 1656-1928.* Columbus, OH, Empire Press, 1928. 22p. D gives 20p. [L9244; D6762].

JENNEY -- Carrol, Virginia E. *Descendants of John and Sarah (Carey) Jenney Through Ansel and Elizabeth (Brown) Jenney and Their Children.* Cleveland, OH, Carroll, 1973. 103p. 3 leaves. X gives 106p. and family names as JENNE. [D6779; X497-FW].

JENNINGS -- Jennings, William Henry. A Genealogical History of the Jennings Families in England and America... *Vol. 2. The American Families.* Columbus, OH, Press of Mann & Adair, 1899. 1 v. (600 Copies Printed). D gives: underscored part of title and Columbus, OH, Jennings, 1899. ix, 819p. [L9271].

JENNINGS -- Jennings, William Henry. *A Genealogical History of the Jennings Families in England and America.* Columbus, OH, 1899. 3 vols. Contents: Vol I. The English Families, Vol II. The American Families, Vol. III. Chart Pedigrees. HSP(sic) has only Vol. 2. [X498-PH].

JENNINGS -- Saxbe, William Bart. [G348]. See above: GUNN. [G280].

JESSUP -- Kahrl, Faith Jessup. *The Memoirs of Faith Jessup Kahrl.* Compiled by Rosemary O. Joyce. Columbus, OH, R.O. Joyce, 1989. xix, 315p. 1. Kahrl, Faith Jessup, 1902- - Homes and haunts. 2. Kahrl, Faith Jessup, 1902- -Family. 3. Lebanon-Social life and customs. 4. United States-Biography. 5. Jessup family. 6. Presbyterian Church-Missions-Lebanon. 7. Kahrl, George Morrow, 1904- . [G349].

JOHNSON -- Johnson, Evangeline H. *Record Books. Ed. by Wm. Cummings Johnson.* Hiram, OH, W. C. Johnson, 1961-1974. 5 Vols. Vol. 1. 1870-1896. - Vol 2. 1896-1909. - Vol. 3. 1909-1918. - Vol 4. 1918-1920. - Vol 5. 1920 - 1930. Memory Book on spine. Index with added family history by Hiram C. Johnson, 122, (61)p. [X502-NY].

JOHNSON -- Johnson, George H. *Johnson. Our Family Record.* Cleveland, OH, 1926. 21p. FW gives: Columbus, OH, 20p. and no date. [X500-LI & X501-FW].

JOHNSON -- Johnson, Lorand V. *The Descendants of William and John Johnson, Colonial Friend of Virginia.* Cleveland, OH, 1940. 196p. L adds: Data relative to earliers generations was taken largely from "The family of Johnston and of that ilk and of Caskbien" by Alexander Johnson, Jr., Edinburgh, 1832. [L9349; VV105].

JOHNSON -- Johnson, Lorand V. *The Descendants of William and John Johnson, Colonial Friend of Virginia.* Shaker Heights, OH, 1942. 32p. [X502-PH; VV105].

JOHNSON -- Johnson, Lorand V. *Selected References Relating to the Ancestry of William and John Johnson, Colonial Friends (Quakers) of Virginia; An Account of the Connections of the Family of Johnston of Caskieben, and of that Ilk, of the Garioch, Aberdeenshire, Scotland.* Shaker Heights, OH, 1972. 250p. NG gives underscored title. [NG58; VV105].

JOHNSON -- Johnson, Lorand V. *The Johnson - Moorman Family Connections; Unpublished Records of the Late Jesse Bryan.* Shaker Heights, OH, 1973, Author, 94 l. [S1366].

JOHNSON -- Smith, Robert Houston. *The Ancestry of Henry Van Dyke Johnson and Daniel Johnson: A Genealogical Chart. - 1st ed. -* Wooster, OH, R.H. Smith, 1989. 8p., 1 folded leaf of plates. 1. Johnson family, 2. Johnson, Henry Van Dyke, 1797-1830-Family. 3. Ohio-Genealogy. [G352].

JOHNSON -- Tilden, Emily Ester Irish. *Genealogy of the Johnson - Tozer Family and Historical Sketches.* Lorain, OH, 1917. xii, 262p. [D6862; X501-CH/FW].

JOHNSON -- Tilden, Emily Esther Irish. *Genealogy of the Johnson - Tozer Family. rep. 1917 ed.* Sandusky, OH, 1978. 262p. [NG57].

JOHNSON -- Johnson, William Cumming II, Ed. *John Cummings Johnson and Family of Ohio and Tennessee: Journals, Photos, Genealogy, Correspondence, etc.* Hiram, OH, Johnson, 1975. 179p. in various pagings. Covers years 1847-54. [X503-FW/NY/OH].

JOHNSON -- Johnson, William Cumming. *The Index to Memory Books, with Added Family*

History. Hiram, OH, W. C. Johnson, 1977. ii, 122, 61 leaves, 1 leaf of plates. "Edition of 80 copies planned." [C360].

JOHNSTON -- Johnson, Lorand Victor. *Selected References Relating to Johnston of Caskieben, Crimond, and Caiesmill, with Reference to Alderman Robert Johnson, Deputy Treasurer of the Virginia Company, The Ulster Plantation and the Somers Island.* Shaker Heights, OH, 1976. 351p. NG & X give date of 1975. [NG58; D6868; X504-DP/IG/LA/MH/OS/SP].

JONES -- Evans, Virgil H. *Family Tree of John Jones (Tirbach), Elder or Partirach of the Welsh Settlement of Jackson and Gallia...* Columbus, OH, 1929. 60p. [X506-FW].

JONES -- Hartzler, M. D. *Descendants of Joseph Jones and Elizabeth Miller; A Genealogy.* Franklin, OH, 1949. 24p. [X506-FW].

JONES -- Jones, Charles C. *Record of the Family of Daniel Jones including His Ancestors, Brothers and Sisters, and Descendants.* Wooster, OH, Jones, 1937. 21p. PH gives 23p. [D6909; X506-PH].

JONES -- Jones, David T. *The Two J. W. Joneses of Adams County, Ohio.* Kankakee, IL, Mimeo at Olivet Nazarene College, 1959. 12 leaves. [X507-FW/MH].

JONES -- Jones, David Tracy. *Some Pioneer Jones Families of Adams County, Ohio.* Kankakee, IL, Olivett Nazarene College (Mimeographed), 1960. 24 leaves. [L9435].

JONES -- Jones, John Morgan. *The Jones Family, 1764-1956. Andrew and Margaret (Wolfe) Jones and Their Descendants.* Rushsylvania, OH, Claren Corwin Jones, 1977. 8, 55 leaves, 1 leaf of plates. Written in 1956. [C363; D6917].

JONES -- Johnson, I. D. J. *Keeping Up With the Jonses; A Family History and Genealogy.* West Milton, OH, Author, 195_. 31, 11p. [X507-FW].

JONES -- Mote, Martha J. Taylor. *A Genealogy of the Jones Family in America.* Dayton, OH, 1908. 9 leaves. [X506-MH].

JONES -- Niday, Mary Elizabeth Walker. *Keeping Up With the Jonses.* Gallipolis, OH, M.E.W. Niday, 1985. 134p. 1. Jones family. 2. Ohio-Genealogy. [G354].

JONES -- Norris, Madalene Jones. [G354]. See above: BOONE. [G69].

JONES -- Wallace, Edna. *Jones, Ball, Wallace Genealogy.* Joseph Spencer Chapter (Ohio) DAR, G.R.C. NP, 1984. 60 leaves. [DC2033].

JORNS -- Carlisle, Robert Z. *The Gustav Jorns and Julia Ann Jones Family History.* Columbus, OH, R. Z. Carlisle II, 1980. 37 leaves. [C365].

JUDD -- Farmer, Walter I. [G356]. See above: FARMER. [G222].

JUDSON -- Weeks, Dr. F. E. *Biography of Deacon Benjamin Judson of Woodbury, Connecticut, with Names of His Descendants.* Norwalk, OH, Weeks, 1914. 20p. [L9470].

JUNGEN -- Eberle, Maxine Renner. *The Christian Jungen Family in Switzerland and America.* Millersburg, OH, Tope Village Printing, 1978. 124p. [D6967].

JUNK -- *Junk Journal.* Bowling Green, OH, P. W. Jones, 1986- . _v. See DAR Library Shelflist for Holdings. [DC2044].

JUVE -- Juve, Lucile Kaufman. *Juve Families in America.* Copley, OH, R. D. Juve, 1983. 66 leaves. 2 leaves of plates. [C366].

K

KAHN -- Rome, Melodia & Walter S. *The Story of Estate; Another Chapter of the Romance of Business in the Land of Opportunity.* Hamilton, OH, The Hill-Brown Publishing Co., 1937. 45p. History of the Estate Stone Company and the accomplishments of the Kahn family. [L9476].

KASLER -- King, Byron W. *Kasler Family of Athens County, Ohio.* Bay Village, OH, King, 1975. [D6980].

KASSERMAN -- Connor, Ralph. *Swiss Family Kasserman.* Chicago, IL, J.B. Barekman, 1985. iv, 44p. 1. Kasserman family. 2. Monroe County (Ohio)-Genealogy. [G359].

KAUFMAN -- Kaufman, Mannoah A. *Abraham Kaufman Family History: Descendants of Abraham Kaufman and Susanna Keck.* Fresno, OH, 195_. 100p. [X514-FW/NY].

KAUFMANN -- Novak, Lucile Kaufmann. *Kaufmann Families from Grindelwald, Switzerland: Christian and Uhlrich of Holmes County, Ohio, Rudolph of Teton County, Wyoming, Peter of Knox County, Ohio.* Nashua, NH, L. Novak, 1982. 282p. [C370].

KECK -- Grasselli, Johanna P. I. *Genealogical Record of the Keck Family.* Cleveland, OH, 1905. xi, 55p. [X515-FW].

KECK -- Keck, John Melvin. <u>The Keck Family</u> with Special References to the Decendants of Michael Keck Who Came to Ohio in 1806. Cleveland, OH, Keck, 1926. 71p. D gives underscored title. [L9510; D6993].

KEESE -- Keese, W. T. *Keese Family History and Genealogy From 1690-1911.* Cardington, OH, Independent Printing Co., 1911. 48p. [D7000].

KEIFLING -- Keifling, William. *The Keifling Ancestry.* Brookville, OH, W. H. Keifling, 1983. vii, 73p. [C372].

KEILEN -- Keilen, Daniel H. *Genealogical History (Descendents) of Jacob and Sophie Sager Keilen.* Mason, OH, D. H. Keilen, 1981. 85 leaves. Errata sheet inserted; leaf 73 omitted by error in numbering. [C372].

KEITH -- Sams, Catherine J. *Keith & Kin.* Caldwell, OH, Sams, 1989. ii, 116p. [DC2063].

KELBLEY -- Koop, Myra C. Studer. [G361]. See above: ELCHERT. [G210].

KELLER -- Keller, Rev. Eli. *History of the Keller Family.* Tiffin, OH, Press of W. H. Good, 1905. 192p. [L9536].

KELLER -- Shumaker, Rev. E. S., Amos Keller and Zarel (Lulie) Jones. *Descendants of Henry Keller of York County, Pennsylvania and Fairfield County, Ohio.* Indianapolis, IN, E. S. Shumaker, 1924. 594p. [L9538].

KELLEY -- Kelley, Hermon Alfred. *A Genealogical History of the Kelley Family Descended from Joseph Kelley of Norwich, Connecticut.* Cleveland, OH, Kelley, 1897. 122, xv p. D gives underscored title. [L9544; NG59; D7023].

KELLOGG -- Kellogg, Dale Cosnett. *Ancestry, Life and Descendants of Martin Kellogg, the 'Centanarian' of Bronson, Huron County, Ohio.* Elyria, OH, Kellogg, 1954. 86p. [L9560; D7026].

KEMP -- Abbott, Lyndon Ewing. [G362]. See above: DERR. [G186].

KEMPER -- Thrush, Lillian Kemper. *Kemper.* Worthington, OH, L. K. Thrush, 1986. 53p. [DC2073].

KENDALL -- Richards, Sylvia. *Johnathan Kendall Memorial. Bicentennial ed.* Willard, OH, S. Richards, 1978. xii, 74p. [C375; NG59; D7063].

KENDRICK -- Crawford, Andrew J. *Kindrick & Allied Families of Wayne Co., Kentucky.* Fairborn, OH, A.J. Crawford, 1989. 2 v. 1. Kendrick family. 2. Kentucky-Genealogy. [G363].

KENNER -- Cleveland, Paul Wood. *Kenner; A Compilation of Family Letters and Data Pertaining to the Kenner and Related Families, Their Early Life in Virginia and Subsequent Years After Migration to Ohio.* Erie, PA, 1966. 187 leaves. [L9615; VP122].

KEPLER -- Meredith, Jack R. *The Typhoid Tragedy: A History of Keplers in America.* Cincinnati, OH, Shasta Publications, 1981. x, 131p. [C377].

KEPLER -- Meredith, Jack R. *The Typhoid Tragedy: A History of Keplers in America - 2nd ed.* Cincinnati, OH, Shasta Publications, 1986. viii, 261p. 1. Kepler family. [G365].

KEPPEL -- Keppel, Robert G. *The Keppels in Seneca County, Ohio; with Notes on Rosenberg, Blue, and Shaull Connections.* Tiffin, OH, 1962. 2 vols. Also 2 boxes of ms. material. [XA1073-WR].

KERN -- Kern, Mason Henry. *Genealogical History of the Kern and Stetler Families.* Toledo, OH, Kern, 1946. 127 leaves. [D7095; X521-FW/PH].

KERR -- Kerr, J. M. *Notes on the Kerrs in America, Particularly... in Miami County, O.* Ontario, CA, Record Pr., 1904. 25p. [X521-OH].

KERR -- Tyson, Genevieve A. Kerr. *Kerr Genealogy: A Genealogical Records of Andrew*

168

Benson Kerr, Late of Gallia County, Ohio:
Together with Biographical Sketches and
Illustrated with Portraits and Documents.
Baltimore, MD, Gateway Press, 1984. xii,
170p. [C378].

KERR -- Warner, G. E. The Miami County
Kerrs... The Name Kerr and Origin of Family.
San Francisco, CA, Murdock, 1906. Pages not
given. [X521-OH].

KETCHAM -- Armbrust, Janet Lee Ketchum. A
Gathering of the Ketchum Kindred: The
Descendants of Benjamin and Rhoda (Benn)
Ketchum of Decatur County, Indiana: Including
Other Ketchum/Ketcham Families of Ohio,
Indiana, and Kentucky. Mount Vernon, WA,
J.L.K. Armbrust, 1990. viii, 167p. 1.
Ketcham family. 2. Ketchum, Benjamin, 1804-
1883-Family. 3. Ketchum, Rhoda, 1807-1888-
Family. 4. Middle West-Genealogy. [G367].

KEYES -- Keese, Willis T. Keese Family
History and Genealogy, from 1690-1911.
Dedicated to the Descendants of John and
Elizabeth Titus Keese. Cardington, OH,
Independence Printing Co., 1911. various
pagings. [L9670].

KEYSER -- Keyser, Philip Luther. Keyser
Family History. Dayton, OH, Keyser, 1974. 2
v. [NG59; X523-FW/PH].

KIDD -- Kidd, John D. Some Kidd, Herman,
Tuttle, Bennion Ancestors, 1596-1984.
Jackson, OH, J. D. Kidd, 1985. vii, 131p.
[C379].

KILBARGER -- Kilbarger, Harold. [G368].
See above: HENLEY. [G312].

KIMBROUGH -- Herman, Berthenia Davis.
[G369]. See above: BRIDGE. [G88].

KINCAID -- Kincaid, G. L. Kincaid
Genealogy. Sardinia, OH, Sardinia News Press,
1922. 44p. [D7173].

KINDER -- Kinder, George D. *Centennial Reunion of the Kinder Family, at the Old Homestead... near Franklin, Ohio... 1900.* Ottawa, OH, Sentinal Print., 1900. 41p. [X526-CH].

KING -- Chandler, Catherine Soleman. *A History of the King, Armstrong and Allied Families (Pennsylvania to Columbiana County, Ohio).* NP, 1964. 149 l. X gives 48 pages; omits "A" in title. [D7180; X527-FW; VP123].

KING -- King, George H. S. *(Genealogical Record of My Ohio Ancestors).* Fredericksburg, VA, 1941. 3 numb. leaves. [X527-OH].

KING -- Jonasson, Mildred King. [G370]. See above: BANNISTER. [G33; NGS8].

KING -- King, Isaac F. *Genealogical Leaflet of the Walter King Family.* Columbus, OH, 1892. 10p. [X526-OH].

KING -- King, Judith E. *The King Family; A History and Genealogy of Robert and Hannah Forker King.* Cincinnati, OH, 1970. v, 78 leaves. [A371].

KING -- Robert S. *The King Family of Suffield. Dayton Branch.* NP, 1969. 4 leaves. [X527-CH/FW/OH].

KINKADE -- Kinkade, John H. *A Sketch of the Kincade Family.* Marysville, OH, 1901. 20p. [X528-FW/SU].

KIRK -- Wilson, Clarence K. *The Kirk and Wilson Families Tree.* Cincinnati, OH, Hobson Press, 1943. ix, 128p. [L9800; D7223].

KIRKBRIDE -- Kirkbride, Sherman A. *A Brief History of the Kirkbride Family; with Special Reference to the Descendants of David Kirkbride, 1775-1830.* Alliance, OH, Alliance Leader Print, 1913. 64p. [L9803].

KIRKPATRICK -- Kirkpatrick, Albert R. *The Samuel Kirkpatrick Family, 1779-1938.* West Elkton, OH, Press of Albert R. Kirkpatrick, 1938. Unpaged. [X530-FW/IG].

KIRKPATRICK -- Kirkpatrick, D. M. *The Samuel Kirkpatrick Family, 1779-1938.* West Elkton, OH, Albert R. Kirkpatrick, 1938. 78p. [D7231].

KIRKPATRICK -- Korbitz, Ellen Kirkpatrick. *William Kirkpatrick, Died November 20, 1838: Immigrant Ancestor from Ireland to America, Clermont County, Ohio, and Edgar County, Illinois. A Directory of His Descendants.* Burlington, IA, 1958. 30p. [L9816].

KIRKPATRICK -- Phillips, John. *The Kirkpatrick Family.* Cabin John, MD, Capital Pub. Co., 1988. 17 leaves. 1. Kirkpatrick family. 2. Ohio-Genealogy. [G371].

KIRKWOOD -- Kirkwood, William W. *Descendants of William Kirkwood (1820-1898).* Findlay, OH, 1974. 59p. [X531-FW].

KISTLER -- Sprague, Floride Kistler. *Kistler Families Descended From George Kistler, Jr., of Berks County, Pennsylvania.* Chauncey, OH, Sprague, 1944. 46p. [L9820; D7237].

KLASSEN -- Klassen, Paul. *Descendants of Peter and Catharina Klassen.* Wadsworth, OH, Author, 1973. 44p. [X532-FW].

KLINE -- Kline, Helen. *The Kline Klan.* Wauseon, OH, Gilson Lithographing Co., 1960. 173p. [L9840; D7251].

KLINGSHIRN -- Koff, Lois Ann and Marion Quinn. *Faith, Joy & Tears: The Klingshirn Saga Continues.* Avon Lake, OH, Westfair Publishers, 1984. xii, 401p. [C385].

KLOCK -- Williams, Helen Laura (Clock). *Klick - Clock Family.* Euclid, OH, 1949. Variously numb. leaves. [L9843].

KLOCK -- Williams, Helen Laura (Clock). *Klick - Clock Genealogy.* Euclid, OH, 1952. 1 v. variously paged. [L9844].

KLOCK -- Williams, Helen Laura (Clock). *Klick - Clock Genealogy.* Revised, Euclid, OH, 1960. 1 v. Loose-Leaf. [L9845].

KNAGGS -- Ross, Robert B. *History of the Knaggs Family of Ohio and Michigan.* Detroit, MI, Clarence M. Burton, 1902. 56p. D gives 54p. [L9850; D7263].

KNAPP -- Neff, Tilla H. *The Knapp Family, Connection, New York, Ohio.* Lakewood, OH, 1952, 51, 5 leaves. [X534-FW/NY].

KNAPTON -- Barnes, Thomas Grady. *The Knaptons of Wescoe Hill, 1638-1962.* Marion, OH, Barnes, 1963. 186, 2p. Supplement inserted in FW's copy. [D7269; X534-FW/NY].

KNEISLEY -- Kneisley, J. S. *Kenisley Ancestral Notes.* Quincy, OH, 1927. 27p. [X535-FW].

KNIGHT -- Knight, Eugene Wallace. *Ancestry and Descent of Giles Knight, Jr., a Broadweaver of Rodborough, Gloucestershire Co., England.* Dayton, OH, E. W. Knight, 1984. 106, 44p. [C386].

KNIGHT -- Knight, Sarah Ann. *Knight Family Records. A History of the Long Ago, to the Present Time, 640-1951.* Bellafontaine, OH, 1951. 1 vol. Unpaged. X gives underscored title. [L9880; X535-FW/NY].

KNISELY -- Knisely, Isaac E. *Genealogy of the Family of David Knisely (1792-1877).* Toledo, OH, n.d. 105p. [X535-FW].

KOENIG -- Coffman, Dorothy Yoder. [G376]. See above: FOX. [G238].

KNOLLMAN -- Bodey, Leona E. *A Knollman Family History.* Cincinnati, OH, 1970. 54, x leaves. [A375].

KOHLER -- Caylor, Shelly L. *Johannes Kohler's Family.* Dayton, OH, Caylor, 1925. 28, 13 leaves. [D7306].

KOPPEMHAFER -- Hamel. Claude Charles. *Geneaology of a Branch of the Koppemhafer Family from Germany Which Settled in Vermillion Township, Erie, Co., Ohio.* Amherst, OH, 1948. 10 leaves. [L9913].

KOPPES -- Koppes, Charles W. *Chronological Outline and Genealogical Directory of the Koppes Family.* Cleveland, OH, Evangelical Pr., 1917. 85p. [X538-OH].

KORYTA -- Agricola, David V. *The Koryta Family of Karlov, Bohemia.* Cleveland, OH, D. V. Agricola, 1980, vi, 9p. [C389].

KRAUSE -- Carroll, Phyllis Bicknell. [G378]. See above: CROUSE. [G167].

KREHBIEL -- Krehbiel, Jacob. *Krehbiel History and Family Records... 2nd printing by Howard Raid.* Blufton, OH, 1974. 1 vol. (various pagings). Contains also Ruth and Galle Families. [X539-OH].

KREIDER -- Duty, Allene B. *Kreider Genealogy.* Cleveland, OH, 1953. 20 leaves. [X540-PH].

KREISCHER -- Schaadt, Mrs. Edwin. *Kreischer Family.* Van Wert, OH, 1955. 44p. [X540-FW].

KREKLER -- Schafer, Bessie K. Krekler and Related *Families.* Oxford, OH, 1963. 35p. [L9928].

KRIECHBAUM -- Krichbaum, Charles. *Krichbaum Family History, 1749-1918.* Quincy, IL, Kreigbaum Herigage, 1973. 30p. Reprint. Originally published Canton, OH, Commmittee on Publications appointed by the Ohil Krichbaum Reunion, 1918. [C390].

KROGNESS -- Krognes, C. George. *Ancestors and Descendants of Krogness and De Voe Families in the U.S.A. and of Four Interrelated Families, Bailey, Bonsness, Rud, (Ruud, Rude), Vigness.* Cleveland, OH, Krogness, 1980. 170p. [C390].

KRUEGER -- Fetzer, Richard Lee. *Krueger Genealogy.* Rocky River, OH, Fetzer, 1960. 67p. [D7332].

KUHN -- Kuhns, Ezra McFall. *Notes on the Kuhn Family.* Dayton, OH, Priv. Print., 1934. 35p. [L9942]

KUHN -- Venable, C. S. *History and Roster of the Peter Kuhn Family in the U.S.A.* Shelby, OH, 1932. 96p. [D7337; X541-FW].

KUHN -- Whelan, Kathryn S. *Christopher Kuhn, Born... 1808, Remish, Bavaria, Germany, and His Wife Ann Mary Barbara (Bores) Kuhn, Immigrated to Tiffin Twp., Ohio, in 1845.* Defiance, OH, 1964. 41, 13 l. [X541-OH].

KUHL -- Hamel, Claude Charles. *Genealogy of the Family of Charles Fred and Alice Caroline (Baatz) Kuhl of Erie County, Ohio.* Amherst, OH, 1951. 4 leaves. [L9944].

KUNKLER -- Geiger, Wilma M. *Daniel Kunckler / Kunkler, Pennsylvania Pioneer and His Descendants.* Strasburg, OH, Geiger and Kunkler, 1986. VII, 189p. [DC2145].

L

LADRACH -- Stein, Alberta. *The Family of Gottlieb (1833-1912) Magdelena (1838-1912) Ladrach.* Dover, OH, A. Stein, 1982. 168p. Eratta slip inserted. [C396].

LAKE -- Lake, Devereux. *A Personal Narrative of Some Branches of the Lake Family in*

America. Sandusky, OH, Lake, (Lorain, OH, Lorain Printing Co.), 1937. 8, 256p. [L9988; D7374].

LAMB -- Lamb, Scott G. *A History of the Lamb Family in Ohio.* Berwyn, PA, 1954. 75 leaves. Based on a manuscript by Sylvester Lamb. [X547-PH].

LAMB -- Lamb, Maud J. *Descendants of Anthony Lamb (in) Virginia, Ohio and Iowa.* NP, 1949. [VV112].

LAMB -- Lamb, Sylvester. *The Lamb Family of Ohio.* Bellair, FL, Marjorie Lamb McLean, 1985. 75 leaves. [DC2161].

LAMM -- Jennings, Elizabeth Robinson. [G384]. See above: CARRUTHERS. [G124].

LANDIS -- Landes, Alva D. *The William and Lucinda Landes Family of Montgomery County, Ohio.* Covington, OH, A.D. Landes, 1987. 83p. 1. Landis family. 2. Landes, William, 1850-1923-Family. 3. Ohio-Genealogy. [G385].

LANDIS -- Stewart, Catharine N. L. *History of David Landis, Sr. Who Migrated to Montgomery County, Ohio in 1837, and His Descendants.* Las Vegas, NV, 1963. 44p. [X548-FW].

LANDON -- Spellman, Robert A. W. *Ebenezer Landon and His Descendants: A Short Sketch, with Particular Reference to the Landon Family of Plain Township in Franklin County, Ohio.* New Haven, CT, 1962. 25 leaves. [X549-NY].

LANE -- Irby, Sharon Elaine Lapp. *The Lane Family of Muskingum County, Ohio.* Dresden, OH, S.E.L. Irby, 1985. 203p. 1. Lane family. 2. Muskingum County (Ohio)-Genealogy. [G385].

LANGDON -- Harcourt, Harry W. *John Langdon, Monroe and Morgan Counties, Ohio.* NP,

Harcourt, 1985. 66+p. Including an Appendix containing the Langdon Data from Herbert Furman. Seversmith's Colonial Families of Long Island. [DC2173].

LANGDON -- Williams, Harriett Langdon and Elam Chester Langdon. *From One Generation to Another...* Brooklyn, NY, H. N. Langdon and A. M. Smith, 1906. 2, 7-80p. Commeration of the 100th anniversary, December 20th, 1906, of the arrival overland from Vershire, Vermont of the Langdon family at Columbia, later, Cincinnati, Ohio. [L10061].

LANGENDORFER -- Agricola, David W. *The Langendorfer Family of Weingarten/Baden and Harmann, Missouri, 1695-1975.* Cleveland, OH, Agricola, 1975. iii, 16p. [S1517].

LANGENDÖRFER -- Agricola, David W. *The Langendorfer Family of Weingarten. 3rd rev. ed.* Cleveland, OH, D. V. Agricola, 1981, viii, 36p. Originally published in 1975 as The Langendörfer Family of Weingarten/Baden and Harmann, Missouri, 1695-1975. Cleveland, OH, Agricola, 1975. [C399].

LANGENECKER -- Langenecker, John. *Genealogical Diagram of the Descendants of Daniel Langenecker.* Wilmot, OH, 1903. 14p. [X550-SU].

LANGSTROTH -- Langstroth, T. A. *Langstroth and Mansfield Genealogies.* Cincinnati, OH, 1959. Pages not given. [X550-FW].

LAPE -- Lape, Charles Fred and Ella Foy O'Gorman (Mrs. Michael Martin O'Gorman). *Some Descendants of Gottlieb Lape and His Wife Catherine Jacobs of Zanesville, Ohio.* NP, 1935. 1p., 6 numb. leaves. [L10089].

LAPP -- Irby, Sharon Elaine Lapp. *The Lapp Families of Muskingum, Coshocton, Pike, and Jackson Counties, Ohio. Germany to Ohio.* Dresden, OH, S.E.L. Irby, 1987. 2 v. (435p). 1. Lapp family. 2. Ohio-Genealogy. [G388].

LARIMER -- Work, Jesse C. *Larimer Family, 1740-1959*. Lancaster, OH, Author, 1959. 66, 10p. [X552-FW].

LARKCOM -- Taylor, Calista S. *History of the Larkcom Family and Their Descendants*. Garrettsville, OH, Item Printing Co., 1886. 34p. [D7456].

LARRICK -- Larrick, W. Donald. *The Larrick Families of Guernsey County, Ohio*. Pickerington, OH, 1968. 41 1. [X553-SP].

LARSH -- NAS. *Larsh Reunion at "Crestwood" Sept. 11, 1938, Estate of Everett P. Larsh*. Dayton, OH, 1938. Unpaged. [X553-FW].

LATHAM -- Worden, Margaret Latham. *The Ancestry of Arthur Wood Latham and of His Wife Harriett May Phillips*. Largo, FL, Worden, 1980. xi, 253, 9 1. of plates. With notes of allied families including Bennett, Heath, Leeds, Smith, Stevens, Wheaton, Whittlesey, and Wood Families of Connecticut or Massachusetts; Barnett and Cook Families of New York; Buster, Famulener, Long and Shoop Families of Ohio; and an Evans Family of England. D shows only 253p. [C402; D7469].

LATIMER -- Durig, Grace. *The Latimer Chronicles: A Collection of Family Letters*. Xenia, OH, G. & R. Durig, 1987. vii leaves, 280p. 1. Latimer family-Correspondence. 2. Middle West-Biography. 3. Middle West-Genealogy. [G389].

LAUB -- Slabaugh, John M. *The Lauver Legacy of Life and Love: Jacob M. Lauver, 1871-1965 and Emma Graybill, 1870-1942: Their Ancestry and Their Descendants*. Uniontown, OH, J.M. Slabaugh, 1989. 180p. 1. Laub family. 2. Lauver, Jacob M., 1871-1965-Family. 3. Graybill, Emma, 1870-1942-Family. 4. Mennonites-Genealogy. [G389].

LAUGHLIN -- Abbott, Lyndon Ewing. [G390]. See above: EWING. [G219].

LAUGHLIN -- Laughlin, Emma E. *An Addition to the Laughlin History Prepared for the Third Quinquennial Reunion Held at Cambridge, Ohio, 1917.* Barnesville, OH, 1917. 8p. [X555-LI].

-- *Same for the Fourth Quinquennial Reunion.* 1922. 10p. [X555-LI].

-- *Same for the Fifth Quinquennial Reunion.* 1927. 11p. [X555-LI].

LAUGHLIN -- Laughlin, John W. *1807-1907, Laughlin History.* Barnesville, OH, Laughlin, 1907. 64p. [L10125; D7480].

LAUGHLIN -- Laughlin, John W. *1807-1907, Laughlin History for the Reunion Held at Bellecenter, Ohio, Thursday, August Twenty-second, Nineteen Hundred and Twelve. Rev ed.* Barnesville, OH, 1912. 104p. 10 l. [L10126].

LAWSON -- Clark, Lillian Bond. *The Lawson Family of Scioto County, Ohio and Greenup County, Kentucky.* Portsmouth, OH, Clark, 1976. 64p. X gives 63p. [D7500; X557-FW].

LAYCOCK -- Wolfe, Barbara E. S. *Joseph Laycock, 1740-1802 of Brown County, Ohio and Some of His Descendants.* Logansport, IN, Author, 1970. 106p. [X557-FW].

LEACH -- Leech, David Lloyd. *Genealogy and History of a Leech Family.* Glendale, AZ, v, 174p. 1. Leach family. 2. Ohio-Genealogy. [G392].

LEARY -- Greene, Rovert Ewell. *The Leary - Evans, Ohio's Free People of Color.* NP, Greene, 1979. 88p. [C405].

LECKLITER -- Netherton, Alene Lichlyter. *Leichleiter & Variants: Leckliter, Lichlyter, Lechliter, Licklider, Lecklider, Lickliter, and Lechleiter.* NP, 1978-86. (New Carlisle, Ohio: McGrego-Werner) 2 v. Vol. 2 has imprint: Whichita, Kan. 1. Leckliter family. [G393].

178

LeCLERCQ -- Curran, Joan F. *Descendants of Augustin LeClercq, Who with His Six Children came from France to Gallipolis, Ohio in 1790.* Baltimore, Gateway, 1988. ix, 166p. 1. LeClerq family. 2. LeClercq, Augustin, 1744-1801-Family. 3. France-Genealogy. [G393; DC2207].

LEE -- NAS. *Genealogy of Paul R. Lee on His Father's Side.* 7th ed. Mansfield, OH, Lee, 1975. 84p. [S1545].

LEE -- Lee, Harold R. *Lee Family Genealogy. (Revised 1973).* Columbus, OH, 1973. 14 leaves. [X560-OH].

LEEPER -- Leeper, Chauncey L. *Traces of the Family of Joseph and Caroline Leeper: Guernsey County, Ohio, Henry County, Iowa, Scotland County, Missouri, 1825-1973.* Kirksville, MO, C. L. Leeper, 1973, 54 leaves. [X561-SP].

LEEPER -- Leeper, Laura Alnetta. *Genealogy of Alexander Leeper.* Akron, OH, Leeper, 1926. 59p. [L10301; D7579].

-- *Supplement to the Alexander Leeper Family History.* Akron, OH, 1948. 44p. Bound with the Main Work. [L10301].

LEHMAN -- Yoder, Elva B. L. *Records of the Descendants of John Hardman Lehman and His Wife Mary (Lehman) Lehman, with Research Notes...* Columbiana, OH, Author, 1967. 19p. [X562-FW].

LEIDHISER -- Hamel, Claude Charles. *Genealogy of the Werner Leidhiser Descendants of Lorain County and Erie County Ohio.* Amherst, OH, 1951. 11 leaves. [L10340].

LEIS -- Lease, Florence Louise (Clark). *The Leis Family; M. Louis Leise, Charlotte Meir, Married in Germany, 1844, Settled North of Greenville, 1847.* Greenville, OH, C. Runke, 1948. 1 v. (unpaged). [L10351].

LEIST -- Webb, David K. *Leist Family. A True Copy of the Leist Family Record Taken From Original Documents Written About 1802 and Now in the Archives of the Ross County Historical Society Museum at Chillicothe, Ohio.* NP, 19__. 1 leaf. [L10353].

LEISTENSNIDER -- Leistensnider, Mary. *History of the Leistensnider Family.* Mansfield, OH, 1915. 8p. [X563-FW].

LEONARD -- Blaine, Harry S. *Some Ancestors and Descendants of Avery Leonard of Seneca County, Ohio.* Toledo, OH, Press of Gordon A. Blaine, 1933. 2p., 42 Numb. leaves. [L10403; D7617].

LEONARD -- Goodenough, Caroline Leonard. *Memoirs of the Leonard, Thompson, and Haskell Families with Their Collateral Families of Alden, Andrews, Bell,... and Many Others.* Yellow Springs, OH, The Antioch Press, 1928. 5, 3-344p. 1000 copies printed. [L10400].

LEONARD -- Russell, Mildred Huffman. *Some of the Descendants of Joseph Leonard of Washington County, Pennsylvania and Delaware County, Ohio.* NP, 1958. [VP135].

LESLIE -- Leslie, David E. *The Leslie Family: Scotland to Ireland to Pennsylvania to Loudoun County, Virginia, to Preble County, Ohio to Butler County, Ohio.* __, OH, D.E. Leslie, 1983. 1 v. (various pagings). [G398].

LEVERING -- NAS. *Proceedings of the Levering Family Reunion...Vol 1.* Columbus, OH, Published by Order of the Levering Family Association, 1892. 1 v. [L10444].

LEYDA -- Rudd, Dorothea. *The Ancestors and Descendants of Frederick Leyda (1796-1877) from Carroll Co., Ohio.* Ocoee, FL, Rudd, 1988. A3, 293p. [DC2250].

180

LIMING -- Liming, Melville D. *The Lineage of the Liming Family of Brown County, Ohio.* Newton Centre, MA, 1954. 9 numb. leaves. [X572-MH/SL].

LINDENMAN -- Schürch, Terry L. *Schurch-Lindenman Family Re-union Records.* Richwood, OH, T. L. Schurch, 1990. 1 v. (unpaged). Shirk family. 2. Lindenman family. [G402].

LINDSEY -- Cooke, Margaret A. W. *Lindsey Family; David (and) Hezekiah of Westmoreland County, Pa., Clermont, County, Ohio; Thomas Medaris Family... Daniel Camerer Family...* Springfield, IL, DAR, 1957. 45p. Also allied families: Spires, Hughes. McConnell, Bledsoe. [X574-FW].

LINDSEY -- Cooke, Margaret Watson. *The Hezekiah Lindsey Family (Lindsay, Lindsey) of Westmoreland Co., Pa., Clermont, Co., Ohio.* NP, 1963. 160 leaves. [D7723; VP136].

LINDSEY -- Lindsey, Helen B. *Thomas Noble Lindsey and Descendants.* Newport, KY, or Cincinnati, OH, 1928. 8p. [X574-FW/MH].

LINENBERGER -- Hall, Helen L. *Grandfather's Story.* Carthagena, OH, The Messenger Press, 1955, 45p. [X547-SU].
-- *Same. Centennial Edition.* Hutchinson, KS, 1973. 108p. [X547-SU].

LINENBERGER -- Toepfer, Amy & Dreiling, Agnes C. *The Linenberger Genealogy.* Carthagena, OH, Messenger Press, 1956. 432p. [L10564; NG63; D7729].

LINN -- Feller, Forest T. *Adam Linn of Guernsey Co., Ohio.* NP, 1973. 19 l. Bound with James Sargent, Sr., of Pike County, OH. (12 l.). NG gives 1964, pni. [NG65; D7733].

LINNELL -- Linnell, Mary Belle. *The Genealogy of Joseph Linnell. A Soldier of the American Revolution.* Sylvania, OH, Linnell,

1964. 108 leaves. D gives underscored
title. [L10571; D7737].

LINSCOTT -- NAS. *My Linscott Line; The
Descendants of George Linscott, Who Was the
Son of Israel, Who... Came to Athens County,
Ohio from Maine in 1797.* NP, 1969. 116
leaves. [X554-OH].

LINTHICUM -- Lincicome, Glen A. *My
Lincicome Heritage: Lincicome, Conner,
McKee, McPeek, and Related Families.* Urbana,
OH, G.A. Lincicome, 1987. iii, 144p. 1.
Linthicum family. 2, O'Connor family. 3.
McKee family. 4. Ohio-Genealogy. [G403].

LITZENBERG -- Litzenberg J. E. *The
Litzenbergs in America. A Biographical Record
of George Litzenberg and His Wife Grace
Coates, with a preview of Their Ancestors and
a Genealogical and Biographical Record of
Their Descendants.* Centerberg, OH,
Litzenberg, 1948. xvii, 629p. D gives title
as underscored. [L10601; D7766].

LLOYD -- Lloyd, John A. *Our Family. A Brief
History of the Lloyd, Thomas, Freund, Zell,
Miller, and Roberts Families...* Glendale,
OH, 1976. 84 leaves. [X578-OH].

LOGAN -- Green, Thomas Marshall. *The Logans.
(In Historic Families of Kentucky...1st
Series).* Cincinnati, OH, 1889. p.117-229.
[L10659].

LOGAN -- Logan, George William. *A Record of
the Logan Family of Charleston, South
Carolina.* VV indicates: New edition with
biographical additions. Cincinnati, OH,
Morrill, 1923. 70p. Originally published
Richmond, VA, 1874. New edition with preface
biographical additions and tables.
[L10661; D7811; VV119].

LOGSDON -- Logsdon, Harry C. *A Historical
Sketch and a Genealogical Record of the*

Endless Line of Logsdon and Kelly Families.
Millersburg, OH, 1965. 76p. [L10667].

LONG -- Ferguson, Sylvia Celicia Fuson. *Long Family History. William Henry Long, Sr., 1802-1863; Some Ancestors and His Descendants - 1st ed.* Oxford, OH, S. C. F. Ferguson, 1984. 187p. [C422].

LONG -- Ogier, Lois McNeil. *Longs and Leedys - Pioneers; A Chronological Record of the Long and Leedy Families of Maryland, Pennsylvania, Ohio and Points West.* Barberton, OH, Ogier, 1962. iii, 137, 13p. X gives iii, 137p. [D7828; X581-FW/NY; VP139].

LONGENECKER -- Longenecker, John. *Genealogical Diagram Dedicatory to the Lineal Descendants of Daniel Langenecker, through His Son David and Grandson Peter Langenecker to the Fifth Generation...* Wilmot, OH, 1903. Genealogical Table. [L10703].

LONGSWORTH -- Breese, Mary Esther (Longworth). *Longsworth Family History; Descendants of Solomon Longworth, Sr., of Maryland.* Lima, OH, Breese, 1951. 225p. NG and D give underscored title. [L10712; NG64; D7835].

LONGSWORTH -- Harrington, Dossie E. *Diary of Basil Nelson Longsworth... Covering the Period of His Migration from Ohio to Oregon.* Denver, CO, Author, 1927. 43p., 1 leaf. [X582-FW/PH].

LOOMIS -- Loomis, Elias. *Descendants of Joseph Loomis in America.* Berea, OH, 1909. 859p. [NG64].

LOOMIS -- Loomis, Elisha S. *Loomis... Pedigree... Collated, Verified and Formulated.* Cleveland, OH, (priv. print.) 1930. 1p. [X582-OH].

LOURENS -- Dallas, Zella Rogers. [G409]. See above: DALLAS. [G172].

LOTHROP -- Moorman, Irma Lothrop. *History of the Lathrop Family.* Swanton, OH, 1940. 32p. [L10749].

LOUTZENHEISER -- Loutzenheiser, P. V. *History of the Loutzenheiser Family, as Read at the Annual Reunion...1893.* Canton, OH, McGregor & Bolton, 1894. 39p. D gives underscored title. [D7862; X583-FW].

LOVE -- Davis, Neva Henderson. *The History and Genealogy of the Love Family: A Sketch, 1791-1956.* Davidsonville, OH, [X gives Clairsville, OH] Davis, 1956. 82p. D gives underscored title. [D7865: X583-FW].

LOVELAND -- Beard, P. C. *Supplement No. 2 to the Loveland Genealogy, Containing the Descendants of Eliza Loveland and Reuben Beard.* Toledo, OH, 1897. 39p. [X584-FW/LI].

LOVELAND -- Loveland, J. B. and George. *Genealogy of the Loveland Family in the United States of America, from 1635-1892, Containing the Descendants of Thomas Loveland of Weathersfield, now Glastonbury, Conn....* Freemont, OH, I. M. Keeler & Son, Printers, 1892-95. 3 v. [L10777].

LOWE -- Smith, Jessica Lowe. *Lowe Genealogy; Sept. 1933.* Newark, OH, B. B. Lowe, 10 l. [S1617].

LOWING -- Lowing, William. *History and Geneology sic of the Lowing Family.* Cleveland, OH, Prompt Printing and Pub. Co., 1922. 144p. [D7892].

LUCKENBACH -- King, Helen H., Erwin M. King, and D. Walter Hawk. *Descendants of John Gerradt Luckenbach and Conrad Hawk, 1740-1958.* Warren, OH, Riffle Photography, 1958. 100p. [L10812].

LUPFER -- Lupfer, Robert N. *A Family Record (Ancestors of Elizabeth Baker Lupfer, Baker, Miller, Dickinson, Melyn, Shellabarger,*

Morgan, Lupfer). Springfield, OH, 1963. Various pagings. [L10847].

LUTZ -- NAS. *The Ceremony and Address at the Celebration of the Golden Wedding of Jacob D. Lutz and Wife... 1863 with a Genealogical Table...* Circleville, OH, Print. Circleville Union, 1863. 16p. [X588-PH].

LUTZ -- NAS. *The Third Reunion of the Children of Jacob D. Lutz...* Circleville, OH, 1874. 4 p. [L10853].

LUTZ -- NAS. *Lutz and Wood Families.* NP, Ohio DAR, G.R.C., 1955. 17, 3 l. [D7942].

LYBARGER -- Lybarger, Donald F. & Jesse J. *A Brief History of the Lybarger Family.* Reading, PA, 1915. 8p. [L10857].

LYBARGER -- Lybarger, Donald Fisher. *History of the Lybarger Family.* Cleveland, OH, Lybarger, 1921. 101p. [L10858; D7945].

LYBARGER -- Lybarger, Donald Fisher. *History of the Lybarger Family.* Cleveland, OH, Lybarger, 1959. iii, 122 leaves. [L10859; NG65; D7946; XA1073-WR].

LYBARGER -- Lybarger, Donald Fisher. *The Story of the Dowler - Hartshorn, Fisher - Lybarger Families.* Cleveland, OH, 1938 (i.e. 1962). 63 leaves. [L10860].

LYMAN -- Lyman, Carolyn B. P. *Lyman; A Genealogical Record of the Lyman Family in Andover Township, Ashtabula County, Ohio.* Cleveland, OH, 1938. 24 l. [X589-NY].

LYNCH -- Heiser, Alta H. *Quaker Lady; The Story of Charity Lynch and Her People.* Oxford, OH, The Mississippi Valley Press, 1941. x p., 2 leaves, 15-273p. (Annals of America, V. 2). [X589-FW].

LYNN -- Fellers, F. S. *Linn - Sargent Families: Part 1: Adam Linn Revolutionary War*

Pension W.5023. Walhonding, OH, 1964. 36p. [X590-FW].

LYON -- Lamb, Burley Frank & Parker, Ivan W. and Elnor C. *Who's Who In The Lyon Family.* Columbus, OH, 1972. xx, 324p. [S1631; NG65].

LYTLE -- Lytle, Leonard. *The Descendants of William Lytle and His Wife Jane of Washington County, Penna. and Clermont County, Ohio.* Royal Oak, MI, Lytle, 1951. 21p. X gives 21 leaves. [D7966; X590-DP/FW/SW/SU; VP142].

LYTLE -- Winters, John. Lytel. *The Descendants of Edward Lytle of Pennsylvania, Butler Co., Ohio and Indiana.* West Newton, IN, 1959. 71 leaves. [D7967; X591-DP/FW/NY/PH/SP/SU; VP142].

M

MacDONALD -- Cox, Samuel. *A Record of John MacDonald and His Children.* Frazeysburg, OH, 1901. 10p. [X601-NY].

MacLEAN -- MacLean, J. P. *A History of the Clan MacLean from Its First Settlement at Duart Castle in the Isle of Mull to the Present Period Including a Genalogical Account of Some of the Principal Families Together with Their Heraldry, Legends, Superstitions, etc... Limited ed.* Cincinnati, OH, R. Clarke & Co., 1889. 490p. [L11197].

MacLEAN -- MacLean, J. P., PH. D. *Renaissance of the Clan MacLean, Comprising also a History of Dubhaird Caisteal and the Great Gathering of August 24, 1912. Together with an Appendix Containing Letters of Gen'l. Allan MacLean, Narrative of American Party, a MacLean Bibliography.* Columbus, OH, The F. J. Heer Printing Co., 1913. 208p. [L11202].

MacLEAN -- MacLean, J. P. *An Account of the Surname Maclean or MacGhillean, from the*

*Manuscript of 1751, and A Sketch of ...
Lachlen MacLean, with Other Information ...*
Xenia, OH, The Aldine Publishing House, 1914.
48p. [L11203].

MacLEAN -- MacLean, J. P. *A Mac Lean
Souvenir...* Franklin, OH, The News Book & Job
Print, 1918. 55p. [L11206].

MacLEAN -- MacLean, A. Kennedy. *A Brief
Historical Account of Angus and Rebecca
(MacMillan) MacLean, Pioneers and Their
Descendants and Married Relatives the Kennedys
of Glen Road and Ohio.* NP, 1963. 84p.
[L11210].

MacLEAN -- Sinclair, Brevard D. *An
Historical Account of the MacLeans of Duart
Castle, and the Genealogy of the Children and
Grand-children of Rev. John Campbell
Sinclair...* Columbus, OH, 1879. 37p.
Contains also sketches of the Davidson and
Brevard Families of Mecklenburg County, N.C.
[X610-PH].

MacPHERSON -- Pierce, Doris Whittier. *The
Family of James Ferson, Jr. and Mary (McNeill)
Ferson of Scotland, Ireland, New Hampshire,
and Orange Township, Delaware County, Ohio.*
Sunbury, OH, Pierce, 1975. Leaves b-d. 138
leaves, 2 leaves of plates. [S1682].

MacQUILLEN -- Honeywell, Mary Quillen. *The
Quillen Family, an Ohio Branch.* NP, 1966. 32
leaves. 100 copies printed. [L11275; S1683].

MACK -- Cotner, Katherine Borchers. *The
Descendants of John Christopher Miller and
Hanna Franciska Stratman...: A Genealogical
and Biographical History.* Wilmington, OH,
1985. 7 v. Contents: v. 1. And Their Seven
Children in the Miller, Mack, Martens, &
Roessler families -v. 2. Through Catharine
Margaret Miller and John George Mack -v. 3
Through Anna Catharine Miller and Frederick
August Martens -v. Through John Martin Miller
and Catharine Baker -v 5. Through Dorthea

Elizabeth Miller and Christian Roessler -v. 6. Through John Conrad Miller and Rebecca Rheidenhour -v. 7. Through Christopher Phillip Miller and Amanda Carpenter & Catharine Spears. 1. Miller family. 2. Miller, John Christopher, 1759-1822-Family. 3. Mack family. 4. Martin family. C lists under MILLER. [G415; C473].

MACY -- Shreve, Irene M. and Dix, Marilyn M., cp. *Shaking the Family Tree. Macy and Smith Families.* Columbus, OH, 1985. 104p. 11 p. of plates. 1. Macy family. [G416; NG68].

MAGEE -- Stevenson, Robert A. [G417]. See above: HOGG. [G323].

MAIBACH -- Schar, Jerry R. *Maibach Family: American Descendants of Benedicht Maibach (1775-1842) and Anna Barbara Matthys to the Fifth Generation.* Rittman, OH, J. R. Schar, 1981. 1 broadside. [C433].

MAINE -- Aspinwall, Algernon Aikin. *The Descendants of Ezekiel Maine of Stonington, Conn.* Delware, OH: Frances Main and Cleveland, OH: Florence Maine, 1954. 161, 18 leaves. [D8041].

MALLETT -- Mallett, Manley W. *The Toledo Malletts; A Genealogy, 1694-1974.* Columbus, OH, 1973. 16 leaves. [X619-FW/OH].

MALLORY -- Baldwin, C. C. *Mallery.* Cleveland Leader Printing Company, 1882. Pgs. 159-165. From the Authors Candee Genealogy, Cleveland, 1882. [L11340].

MALOTT -- Kroner, Ethel G. *History of the Malott Family of the State of Maryland and Clermont County, Ohio.* Cincinnati, OH, Author, n.d. 19p. [X619-FW].

MANN -- Mann, Pauline Bachman. *Shuah Strait Mann, 1829-1918, New Jersey, Ohio, Iowa: His Ancestors and Descendants.* Des Moines, IA, P.B. Mann, 1987. viii, 184p. 1. Mann

family.   2.   Mann, Shuah Strait, 1829-1918.
[G421].

MANNING -- Byrd, Helen Norris. [G421]. See
above: CAMP. [G117].

MANSPARGER -- Mansbarger, Charles.
*Photostat Copy of a Letter to the Library of
Congress Describing an Accompanying Coat of
Arms of the Mansparger Family.* Zanesville,
OH, 1939. [L11385].

MARCHAND -- Smith, Carol Marchand and Ralph
Marchand. *Marchand Family History and
Genealogy.*   Orrville, OH, Orrville Print.
Co., 1978. vii, 155p. [C437].

MARKEL -- NAS. *Lineage Record of the Family
of Jacob and Lydia Markel, Salt Creek
Township, Pickaway County Ohio.* NP, n.d. 7p.
[X622-OL].

MARKLEY -- NAS. *Historical Collections.*
Strongsville, OH, by members of "Descendants
of the Ohio Pioneer Markley Organization"
"before 1870" (sic), D. Carroll Print., 1988-
<1990 >. v. <1-3. > 1. Markley family. 2.
Ohio-Genealogy. [G423].

MARKLEY -- Carroll, Mary and Richard
Markley. *Markley Family Scrapbook.*
Strongville, OH, Dove Graphics, 1984. 230p.
[C438].

MARKLEY -- Markley, Joseph M. *History of
the Markley Relationship.* Canton, OH,
Markley, 1922. 18p. VP gives 1922-24.
[X623-LA/SP; VP144].

MARKLEY -- Markley, Joseph M. *The History
of the Markley Relationship.* Canton, OH,
Markley, 1922-24. 168p. [D8103].

MARKS -- Marx, Hazel R. Dick. *The
Descendants of John Fredrich Wilhelm Marx and
Heinrich Christian Freidrich Hornburg.*
Columbus, OH, Mr. & Mrs. George Marx, 1982.
a-b leaves, 127p. [C438].

MARKWITH -- Vance, Joseph Harvey. *Some Descendants of John C. Markwith (1774-1836) of Essex County, New Jersey, and Darke County, Ohio.* Lombard, IL, J. H. Vance, 1981. 11p. [C439].

MARSHALL -- Gladden, Sanford Charles. *Descendants of Moses & Mary (Adams) Marshall of Columbiana County, Ohio.* Also Adams, Aleshire, Clark, Darst, Edmundson, Families. Boulder, CO, 1965. 152p. NG gives 151p. D gives title as underscored. Only 100 copies printed. [L11459; NG68; D8125].

MARSHALL -- Hayes, Arthur M. *They Found a Country-The Marshall Family.* Frankfort, OH, 1966- -vols. V. 1. mostly the text of The Marshall Family, a history of the descendants of Wm. Marshall, Kittaning, Pa., 1884 by O. S. Marshall. [X624-OH].

MARSHALL -- Marshall, George Sidney. *The Daniel Marshall Family, with a Sketch of the Aaron Marshall Family.* Columbus, OH, 1949. 74p. [L11457].

MARSHALL -- Marshall, Ross Souley. *Working on the Railroad. Marshall Family.* Cleveland, OH, Gates, Legal Publishing Co., 1956. 179p. D & X give underscored title. [NG68; D8134; X624-FW].

MARSHALL -- Paxton, William. M. *The Marshall Family... Descendants of John Marshall and Elizabeth Markham, His Wife with Typewritten Notes of Some of the Marshall-Smiths.* Cincinnati, OH, Robert Clarke & Co., 1885. 415p. D gives underscored title. [L11447; D8136].

MARTIN -- Cotner, Katherine Borchers. [G425]. See above: MACK. [G415].

MARTIN -- Krulce, Ruth B. [G426]. See above: BROWN. [G99].

MARTIN -- Martin, Frank J. *The Martin Family of Cleveland.* Cleveland, OH, 1931.

2d. edition. 8p., 11-37 leaves.
[X625-GF].

MARTIN -- Mohler, Louise Morton. *The Martin Family of Ohio.* Washington, PA, L. M. Mohler, 1978-1982. 2 v. Contents: Book 1. Descendants of Peter Martin, son of Cavalier Martin. Book 2. Ancestors of Peter Martin plus additions and supplements to Book. [C442; VP145].

MARTIN -- Moorman, Christine H. *The Martin Family.* Cincinnati, OH, Printing Plus, 1980. 25p. [C442].

MARTIN -- Tinkey, James Calvin. *The Martin Family.* Mt. Vernon, OH, 1945. 23p. [L11495].

MARTINI -- Grof, H., Ed. *Martini Family News-Letter and Genealogical Information Bulletin. 1963.* Cincinnati, OH, Strasbourg, ? nos. Annual issued in English and French editions. [X628-NY].

MASON -- Mason, Dr. Philip. *A Legacy to My Children, Including History, Autobiography, and Original Essays.* Cincinnati, OH, Moore, Wilstach & Baldwin, Printer, 1868. 610p. [L11522].

MASSA -- Massa, David J. *The David Massa Family.* Mansfield, OH, 1958. 1 Vol. Part B. [X629-NY].

MAST -- Mast, Moses E. *Descendants of Joseph J. Mast and Mary Miller from the Year 1814-1958.* Strasburg, OH, Gordon-Spidell Prin., 1958. 76p. [X630-FW].

MAT(T)HIAS -- Seale, Dorothy Weiser. *Matthias (Mathias) Milestones; The Genealogy & Biographical History of Daniel Mathias, Senior (A Soldier of the Revolution) of Westmoreland Co., Pa, & Stark Co., Ohio, The Life of Michael Sanor (a Soldier of the Revolution), also Zehner Fam.* Boulder, CO, Westview Press,

1984. xxxiii, 431p. C lists as MATHIAS. DC gives: Mat(t)hias Milestones. Index with a related appendix. [C444; NG69: DC2393; VP147].

MATHIAS -- Shaver, Evelyne Mathias. [G429]. See above: DOLL. [G195].

MATTESON -- Matteson, Porter. *Mattesons in America*. Columbus, OH, 1948. 26p. [D8230].

MATTESON -- Matteson, H. Sheldon Porter. *Mattesons in America*. Columbus, OH, 1940-67. 2 Vols. Various pagings. Vol. 2 has imprint: Palm City, Fla. [X631-GF/IG/MH/NY/SW].

MATTHEWS -- Matthews, William J. *In Memorium*. Columbus, OH, F. J. Heer Printing Co., 1917. 105p. [D8234; X632-CH/OS].

MATTINGLY -- Mattingly, Herman E. *The Descendants of Henry Mattingly, c1750-1823; Progenitor of Western Maryland, Ohio, Indiana, Illinois and Many Other Mattingly Families*. NP,, 1969. vi, 236p. [L11594].

MAXWELL -- Maxwell, Fay. *Maxwell History and Genealogy and Maxwell Families of Ohio*. Columbus, OH, F. Maxwell, 1974. 157p. X-OH gives 156p. [DS462; X634-OH].

MAY -- May, Richard Holman. *The May Family of Kingston, Ohio; A Genealogy of Henry and Susannah McCutchen May and Their Descendants. Also Taylor Family*. Washington, DC (Ann Arbor, MI) 1969. 72p. [L11646; NG69].

MAY -- May, Richard Holman. *The May Family of Kingston, Ohio*. Washington, DC, May, 1969. 72p. [D8276].

MAY -- Schieltz, Ruth C. Wagner. *The Family Tree May - Homan = Der Stammbaum May - Homan*. Versailles, OH, R. C. W. Scheiltz, Fort Laramie, OH, R. W. Timmerman. 1982. 252p. [C447].

MAYHEW -- NAS. *Ancestors and Descendants of Joseph E. Mayhew.* Cleveland, OH, Priv. Print., 1957. 6-35p. [X635-PH].

MAYHEW -- Mayhew, F. F. *Family Tree of the Descendants of Thomas Mayhew Governor and Patentee of Martha's Vineyard, Nantuckett, and Elizabeth Isles.* Cincinnati, OH, 1901. pni. [X635-NY].

McCALL -- Nida, Jack E. *The McCall Family of Gallia County, Ohio.* Columbus, OH, Nida, 1942. 39 leaves. [D8324].

McCANDLISH -- Black, Elizabeth. *McCandlish - Black Family History.* Worthington, OH, Black, 1935. 160, 45p. "The Genealogical History of William McCandlish of County Ayr, Scotland and his descendants, and also of William Black of Ballymoney County, Antrim, Ireland, and his descendants. [L10933; D8331].

McCLAUGHERTY -- McClaugherty, James D. *The History of the Family McClaugherty.* Dayton, OH, C & M Printing, 1966. ca. 200p. [D8347].

McCLIMANS -- McCollister, Gertrude McClimans. *Some Notes on the McClimans and Johnston Families.* Columbus, OH, 1965. 37 leaves. [D8355].

McCLURE -- NAS. *The John McClure Family of Pennsylvania, Ohio, West Virginia, Indiana: 1696-1924.* Morgantown, WV, Clan MacLeod Society USA, 1986. 32p. 1. McClure family. 2. McClure, John, 1696-1757-Family. [G435].

McCLURE -- NAS. *The Richard McClure Family of Pennsylvania and Ohio: 1700-1924.* Morgantown, WV, Published by Scotpress for the Clan McLeod Society, USA, 1985. 28p. (Migration project publication series; no. 4.) 1. McClure family. 2. McClure, Richard, b.

ca. 1700-Family.   3. Pennsylvania-Genealogy.
4. Ohio-Genealogy.   [G435].

McCLURE -- McClure, Cicero Pangburn.
Pioneer McClure Families / of the Monongahela
Valley Their Origins and Their Descendants.
Akron, OH, McClure, Press of the Superior
Printing Co., 1924. 171p. D gives titles as
underscored. [L10965; D8360].

McCLURE -- McClure, Stanley W. *The McClure*
Family: A Record of McClure Families of
Harrison County, Kentucky, Franklin County,
Indiana, Hamilton County, Ohio, Junction City,
Kansas and Other Lines of Descent. NP, 1956.
26 leaves. 1. McClure family. [G435].

McCLURE -- McClure, Stanley W. *The McClure*
Family: A Record of McClure Families of
Harrison County, Kentucky, Franklin County,
Indiana, Hamilton County, Ohio, Junction City,
Kansas and Other Lines of Descent -- Rev. --.
Harrison, OH, S. W. McClure, 1983. 52 leaves.
[C451].

McCOLLOUGH -- Eaton, Mary Louise
McCollough. *The History of the John and*
Esther Gamble McCollough of Washington County,
Pennsylvania, Beaver County, Pennsylvania,
Harrison County, Ohio. Ellsworth, OH,
Ellsworth: Ellsworth, 1987. 180p.
[DC2447].

McCOLLOUGH -- McCollough, John Edmond. *A*
McCollough History, Mostly About the Family of
John McCollough, Jr. Shelby, OH, McCollough,
1991. 46, ix p. [DC2448].

McCONNELL -- Core, Zelma M. *The*
McConnells; Descendants of Alexander and
Elizabeth McConnell, 1693-1960. Rockford, OH,
Rockford Press, 1960. 28p. D gives
underscored title. [D8371; X598-NY].

McCONNELL -- McConnell, Joy Lee. *Ancestors*
and Descendants of Myron and Bessie McConnell

of Montroe Township, Kosciusko County, Indiana. Ancestors From Wayne, Stark and Other Counties of Ohio, New Jersey, New York, and Pennsylvania, Descendants Scattered From Coast to Coast. Salem, OR, J. L. McConnell, 1985. 166 leaves. [C452; VP149].

McCONNELL -- McConnell, Ralph I. *Genealogy of the McConnell Family (Descendants of Hugh McConnell and Jane Furguson).* Bridgeport, OH, 1955. 27p. D gives underscored title; also 27, 4p. [D8374; X598-NY].

McCORD -- Lofquist, Margaret U. *The Genealogical Record of Some McCord Families in America.* Glendale, OH, Carey P. McCord, 1965. 32 leaves. [D8377].

McCORMICK -- Garrard, Herbert L. [G435]. See above: GERARD. [G255].

McCORMICK -- McCormick, Edgar L. *Determined Lives: A Family's Odyssey, 1867-1954.* Grantham, NH, Tompson & Rutter, Kent OH, Distributed by the Brimsfield Memorial House Association, 1989. 164p. 1. McCormick family. 2. McCormick, Edgar L.-Family. 3. Ohio-Biography. 4. Ohio-Genealogy. [G436].

McCORMICK -- McCormick, Robert William. *The McCormicks of Fairfield, Ohio.* McCormick, 1979. 73p. [D8385].

McCOY -- McCoy, Lycurgus. *William McCoy and His Descendants; A Genealogical History of the Family of William McCoy, One of the Scotch Families Coming to America Before the Revolutionary War, Who Died in Kentucky about the Year 1818. Also a History of the Family of Alexander McCoy, A Scotsman Who Served through the Revolutionary War, and Died in Ohio in the Year 1820.* Battle Creek, MI, McCoy, 1904. 204p. [L10992].

McCRACKEN -- MacCracken, Constable. *A Records of the Descendants of John McCracken, Born Central Pennsylvania 1776, Died Xenia,*

Ohio, 2 Jan. 1828. Baltimore, MD, Gateway Press, 1979. xxi, 780p. [D8395; VP149].

McCREARY -- McCreary, Marjorie. *The John McCreary Clan, 1710-1777.* Cleveland, Oh, 1916. 20 leaves. [NG66].

McCREARY -- McCreary, Marjorie. *The John McCreary Clan, 1710-1777.* Cleveland, Oh, 1968-70. 7 parts in 4. Parts VIa and VIb subtitled Caughey Notes. PH has parts I, Index to Parts II, III, IV, VIa, and VIb, VII. [X600-FW/PH].

McCURDY -- McCurdy, D. E. & W. D. *Historical Geneology (sic) of the McCurddy Family; A Concise History of the McCurdys dating from 1489, Including a Record of Their Ancestry to Gilkrist Makurerdy, a Scottish Chief and to Robert II King of Scotland.* Denison, OH, 1915. 3, 9-76p. NG gives underscored title. [L11009; NG66].

McDONALD -- Burns, Norman. *The McDonald Family: Early Settlers in Wayne Township, Darke County, Ohio.* Arlington, VA, N. Burns, 1980. 47 p., 4 l. of plates. X gives 47p. and omits "The" in title. [C455; X602-FW].

McDONALD -- Millett, Stephen M. *The Heirs of Somerled: The Historical Origins of the MacDougalls and MacDonalds, 1100-1500: An Historical Account of the Career of Somerled, the Norse Slayer, Who Claimed the Title of King of Argyll and King of the Isles, and of the First Ten Generations of His Descendants, Including Their Involvement in the Creation of the Country of Scotland. - 2nd rev. and enl. ed.* Columbus, OH, Scottish Lore Press, 1990. v, 55p. 1. McDougall family. 2. McDonald family. 3. Somerled, ca. 1100-1164-Family. 4. Scotland-Genealogy. 5. Scotland-History-1057-1603. [G438].

McDONALD -- Welshimer, A. G. *The McDonald and Whitaker Families.* Bellefontaine, OH, Welshimer, 1967. 76p. [D8432].

McDOUGALL -- Millett, Stephen M. [G439]. See above: McDONALD. [G438].

McDOWELL -- Green, Thomas Marshall. *Historic Families of Kentucky with Special Reference to Stocked Immediately Derived from the Valley of Virginia; Tracing in Detail the Various Genealogies and Connexions and Illustrating from Historical Sources Their Influence upon Political and Social Developments of Kentucky and the States of the South and West .. 1st Series.* Cincinnati, OH, 1889 or 1890. iv, 304p. [L11039].

McFADDEN -- Amos, Sare McFadden. *Our Family.* Columbus, OH, Amos, 1976. 65, v p. [D8458].

McFADDEN -- McFadden, Albert. *McFadden Genealogical Records.* Wooster, OH, 1884. Unpaged. Manuscript. [XA1073-WR].

McFALL -- Kuhns, Ezra McFall. *Notes on the McFall and Allied Families.* Dayton, OH, Priv. Print., 1936. 39p. [L11065].

McFEELY -- Eaton, Mary S. *McFeely Family of Steubenville, Ohio.* Laguna Beach, CA, 1964. 83p. [X604-FW/OH].

McGRADY -- McGrady, L. J. *Daniel Hugh McGrady and His Descendants, b. 1852 - d. 1935.* Toledo, OH, 1964. 1 Sheet (Genealogical Table). [L11091].

McGRADY -- McGrady, L. J. *McGrady: Letters, Legend, Lore -- 1st ed. --.* Toledo, OH, L. J. McGrady, 1984. 54p. [C458].

McGRATH -- McGrath, William R. *A McGrath Family History with Registry of American McGraths.* Bath, OH, Halbert's, 1985. 61 leaves, 135p. [C458].

McGRIFF -- Dowling, Hannah F. B. *George McGriff Family and His Descendants, Who Lived* *in Ohio, Indiana, Iowa, and Missouri.* Dayton, OH, Dowling, 1970. 25p. [X605-FW].

McGRIFF -- Dowling, Hannah Foster. *George McGriff Family and His Descendants, Who Lived in Ohio, Indiana, Iowa, and Missouri.* Dayton, OH, Dowling, 1978 or 1979. 25 leaves. [C458].

McHOSE -- Knittle, Rhea Mansfield. *The Ancestors on the Maternal Side, the Descendants, and the Relationships on the Maternal Side of Alavesta Sevilla Hohenshil Myers.* Ashland, OH, Garber Publishing Co., 1923. 43p. [D8494].

McILRATH -- Cramer, Charles F. *1588-1927. Genealogies of the Following Ancestral Families of McIlrath, Cramer, Sands, Beers, Smith, Bradford, Dawes, Fisher, Clark, Jackson, and Their Descendants to Cousinry...* Lorain, OH, 1927. 34p. [XA1073-WR].

McINNIS -- Perkins, Shirley Campbell. *Our Search for Settlers, Savages, Scallawags, Saints.* Navarre, OH, Perkins, 1978- v. Errata slips inserted. [C459].

McINTIRE -- Puckett, Lillian Colletta and Leslie E. Tombstone Inscriptions of Cherry Fork Cemetary, Adams County, Ohio and Genealogical Gleanings. Denville, NJ, 1964. viii, 91p. [L11124].

McKEE -- Lincicome, Glen A. [G442]. See above: LINTHICUM. [G403].

McKEEVER -- Bushfield, Bernice Bartley. *The McKeevers and Allied Families of West Middletown, Washington County, Pennsylvania.* Toronto, OH, Bushfield, 1959. 159, 19p. [D8522; VP151].

McKINLEY -- NAS. *The Ancestors of William McKinley.* NP, Phil. Pr., 1897. 8p. [X608-FW].

McKINLEY -- Blue, Herbert T. O. *McKinley Family.* East Canton, OH, East Canton Print, 1927. 24p. Excerpts from Ohio History Sketches by the author; covers 5 generations of the... forebears of President W. McKinley. [X608-FW].

McKINNEY -- Powers, Robert P. *A Record of My Maternal Ancestors.* Delaware, OH, 1966. 366p. [L11175].

McKINSEY -- Barry, Ruby M. *The McKinsey's (sic) (McKensey, McKensie, McKinsey) Family; Descendants of George W. McKinsey and His Wife Sarah (Thomas) McKinsey of Newberry, S. C. and Warren County, Ohio and the Migration of Their Children into Indiana.* Indianapolis, IN, R. M. Barry, 1969. 216p. [X609-FW/NY].

McKISSICK -- Burgner, Walter C. *McKissick - Kissick Family of Fleming County, Kentucky, Knox County, Indiana, (and) Allen County, Ohio.* Lima, OH, n.d. Various pagings. [X609-FW].

McMILLAN -- NAS, . *The McMillans, 1750-1907.* Fairborn, OH, Historical Committee of the Clan McMillan, Miami Valley Publishing Co., 1957. 95p. Bound with Supplements 1957 (35p.), 1961 (30p.), 1970 (45p.). [D8552].

McMILLAN -- Cooper, James Henry and Martha Gertrude. *The McMillans, 1750-1907; a Record of the Descendants of Hugh McMillan and Jane Harvey from Scotland through Ireland to America.* Revised by the Historical Commission of the Clan McMillan 1937-1951. Fairborn, OH, Printed by the Miami Valley Pub. Co., 1951. 96p. [L11235].

McMILLAN -- Maffett, Mary Ellen. *A McMillan - Patton Family Connection.* [Decorah], IA, Anundsen; Eaton, OH, Distributed by Silver Press, 1990. 244p. 1. McMillan family. 2. Paton family. 3. Ohio-Genealogy. [G444; DC2504].

McNAGHTEN -- McNaghten , Tunis. *History of the McNaghten Family.* Columbus, OH, Press of the Hann & Adair Print. co., 1912. 66p. [X612-OH].

McNEILL -- Pierce, Doris W. *Family of James Ferson, Jr. and Mary (McNeill) Ferson of Scotland, Ire., New Hampshire, and Orange Twp., Delaware Co., Ohio.* Sunbury, OH, 1975. b-d, 138 leaves. [X613-FW].

McVICKER -- Smith, Shirley K. [G446]. See above: BENNETT. [G49].

MEACHAM -- Gerstman, Virginia Meachum. *A History of the Meachum Family of Van Buren County, Michigan: The Families of George, Sylvester, John, and Lafayette Meacham Who Were Born in New York, Moved to Medina, Ohio, in 1835, and Settled Van Buren County in 1852 with Lines Tracing Back to Jeremiah Meacham Who Settled Salem in 1630: Allied Families: Bigelow, Stockwell, Orton, Johnson, Brown, Walker, Foster, Manchester, Brooks, Andrews, Rowe, Miska, Krugler, and Spencer.* Decatur, MI, Heritage Valley Pub. Co., 1989. vi, 161p. 1. Meacham family. 2. Meacham, Jeremiah J., ca.1613-1695-Family. 3. Michigan-Genealogy. [G446].

MEADOR -- Moody, Edna Wallace. *Meador, Meadows, Lilly Genealogy.* For Joseph Spencer Chapter, (Ohio) DAR, G.R.C. NP, 1984. 57 l. [DC2523].

MECKSTROTH -- Meckstroth, Jacob A. *The Meckstroth Migration: An Account of the Migration from Germany and the Homesteading in America of the Family of Herman Heinrich Meckstroth. Collected from Oral Tradition.* Columbus, OH, J. A. Meckstroth, 1980. iv, 54p. [C465].

MEDARIS -- Cooley, Elizabeth Morrow. *The Medaris Family of Early Clermont Co., Ohio.* Fort Thomas, KY, Author, 1957. 11 l. X gives 9p. [NG70; X637-CH/FW].

MEEK -- Freeburn, Eleanor. *On the Trails with Our Meek Family in America: The Descendants of Guy Meeke and the Families Who Married Into This Meek Family in America.* Berea, OH, E. and D. Freeburn, <1987 >. v. <3 >. 'Up dating [sic] volumes I & II of 1987.' 1. Meek family. 2. Meeke, Guy, d. 1682-Family. [G449].

MEIER -- Fisher, Mildred M. *James 'Jim' Meier Family, 1801-1970; Grandmother's Family. Hugh McCollough, 1781-1864.* Wooster, OH, Atkinson's Print., 1971. 25 pages. [X638-FW].

MEFFERT -- Mefford, Betty Lou. *The German Mefferts: (Meffert, Mefferd, and Mefford).* Cleveland, OH, B.L. Mefford, 1985- v. <1 >. 1. Meffert family. 2. Germany-Genealogy. [G449].

MELL -- Smith, Ned Burton. *The Mell Family, 1679-1938.* Youngstown, OH, 1938. 3 l. [L11721].

MELLERIO -- Siegchrist, Mark. *Rough in Brutal Print: The Legal Source of Brownings Red Cotton Night-Cap Country.* Columbus, OH, Ohio State University Press, 1981. ix, 187p. [C466].

MELLETT -- Miller, Franklin. *The Mellett and Hickman Families of Henry County, Indiana.* Gambier, OH, Miller, 1974. 2 v. (628p.). Contents: -v. 1. Family origins. Early History - v. 2. Geneal. Table. [S1766; NG70; D8661].

MELLINGER -- Mellinger, Ruth M. *Melchoir Mellinger... His Early Ancestor's, Most of Whom Lived and Died in Germany and Switzerland.* Findlay, OH, Author, 1971. 430, 58p. [X639-FW].

MENDENHALL -- Anderson, Annie W. *Mendenhall Families (of America with Their Lateral Lines...)* Cincinnati, OH, 1964. Unpaged. [X640-FW].

MENDENHALL — Mendenhall, William and Edward. *The Mendenhalls of England and the United States...* Cincinnati, OH, Moore, Wilstach & Baldwin, Printers, 1865. 63p. [L11732].

MENDENHALL — Mendenhall, William, Edward, and Thomas A. *History, Correspondence, and Pedigrees of the Mendenhalls of England, the United States and Africa...* Greenville, Oh, T. Mendenhall, C. R. Kemble Press, 1912. 299p. D gives titles as underscored and note: "Original edition by William A. and Edward Mendenhall, 1865." See immediatelly above. [L11733; D8664].

MERION — Pedlar, Mary Martha Merion, et al. *Genealogy of the Merion, Kienzle and Allied Families.* Columbus, OH, 1956. 84p. [L11750].

MERRYMAN — Tracy, Elsie Howlett. *Merrimans (Merrymans) and Tracy (Traceys): Pioneer Community Builders from Maryland 1756 through Pennsylvania to Ohio from 1814-1820, to Family Migrations after 1828 to Michigan, Indiana, Illinois, and Points West.* LaJolla, CA, E. H. Tracy, 1976. 77 leaves. [C470; VP154].

MERSHON — Swiger, Loraine B. *History of Henri Marchand II Family in America with Descendants of Timothy Mershon, Sr., of Ohio.* Owensboro, KY, McDowell Publications, 1981. 210p. [C470].

MERSHON — Swiger, Lorraine B. *A Supplement to the Mershon Book.* NP, L. B. Swiger, 1983. 67p. [C470].

MERWIN — NAS. *Genealogical Outline of Charles L. Merwin Family of East Palestine, Ohio.* Washington, DC, 1959. Genealogical Table. [L11801].

— NAS. *Notes to Genealogical Outline of Charles L. Merwin Family.* Washington, DC, 1959. 10 leaves. [L11801].

MESSENGER -- Messenger, Amanda Long. *Ancestors and Descendants of Captain David Beckett Messenger and Hannah Higley Messenger.* Xenia, OH, Messenger, Greenfield, OH, Greenfield printing. 1952. 64p. [D8716; X644-FW/NY].

MESSENGER -- Reniger, Jerilyn Jacklin J. *The Messenger Family in Portage and Geauga Counties, Ohio, New Connecticut.* Lansing, MI, Reinger(sp?), 1966. viii, 338p. X gives underscored title. [D8719; X644-FW/NY/OH/PH].

METCALF -- Metcalf, Isaac Stevens. *Metcalf Genealogy; Prepared for the Children and Descendants of Isaac Metcalf... Born at Royalstown Mass. and Died in Boston, April 17, 1830.* Cleveland, OH, The Imperial Press, 1898. 62p. D gives underscored title. [L11820; D8724].

MEYER -- Meyer, Henry. *Genealogy of the Meyer Family.* Cleveland, OH, Lauer & Mattill, 1890. 131p. [D8733; X646-FW/LI/NY].

MEYLI -- Morris, David H. *The Faith of Our Fathers... A Brief Account of the Swiss Family Meyli...* Cleveland Heights, OH, 1936. 12p. [X646-FW/PH].

MICHAEL -- Shaver, Evelyne Mathias. [G453]. See above: DOLL. [G195].

MICKLEY -- Gruber, Alice M. *The Mickleys, the Dunns, and Related Families: Courtesy of Their Descendants.* Cuyahoga Falls, OH, 1980. ix, 454p. [C472].

MIDDLETON -- Coleman, Ruth M. *James Middleton of Centre County, Pennsylvania circa 1800-1820 and Some of His Descendants Who Migrated to Ross County, Ohio.* NP, R.M. Coleman, 1977. 100 leaves. [C472; VP154].

MILFORD -- Gruber, Alice Milford. *The Milford Connections in America, Australia,*

England and Wales. Cuyahoga Falls, OH, A. M. Gruber, 1982. viii, 382p. [C473; NG71].

MILFORD -- Gruber, Alice Milford. *Milfords Kinsmen and Countrymen, A Supplement of the Milford Family Connection.* Akron, OH, 1985. 144p. [NG71].

MILLARD -- Smith, Edward C. *Supplement to Outline for a Genealogy of the Family of Humphrey Millard of Reading, Mass.* Lakewood, OH, 1946. 35 leaves. [X648-NY].

MILLER -- NAS. *(Miller and Spangler) Bible Records... Copies of Pages from a Family Bible Owned by Otto Miller.* Cincinnati, OH, 1974. 6 leaves. [X650-NY].

MILLER -- Byler, Amanda J. *Miller Family Book, Record of the Descendants of Daniel D. and Mary P. Miller.* Middlefield, OH, 1955. 35p. 4 leaves. [X650-FW].

MILLER -- Cotner, Katherine Borchers. <u>The Genealogical and Social History of the Descendants of John Christoper Miller</u> and His Wife. Columbus, OH, Cotner, 1969. 643p. On Cover: Miller, Mack, Martens, Roessler. D gives underscored title. [D8765; X651-OH].

MILLER -- Cotner, Katherine Borchers. [G454; C473]. See above: MACK. [G415; C473].

MILLER -- Erb, Elizabeth J. M. *Family Record of Daniel C. Miller and Catherine E. Herschberger from 1851-1956.* Charm, OH, 1956. 28p. [X650-FW].

MILLER -- Glenn, Alva. *Family Record of Eli J. Miller and Veronica Weaver and Their Descendants.* Plain City, O H , 1 9 6 1 . unpaged. [L11908].

MILLER -- Gray, Alice L. *Family Tree of Anthony and Susanna Miller.* Montpelier, OH, 1975. 155p. [X653-FW].

204

MILLER -- Hovemeyer, Eric E. *Some Descendants of Griffin H. Miller.* Cincinnati, OH, 1972. iii, 44 leaves. [S1777].

MILLER -- Hovemeyer, Eric E. *The Descendants of Henry and Polly Miller of Bedford, New York, 1766-1977: Including Over Three Hundred Descendants of Griffin Henry Miller, with Additional Material Concerning the following Related Families, Brawner, Corson, Coulter, Crocker, Curtis, Dixon, Fancher, Fernyhough, Goldsberry, Harding, Hollister, Holmes, Horton, Hud, Jones, Kellogg, Lande, Lyon, Porter, Reynolds, Rundle, Silkman, Stevens, Tyler, Winthrop, and Many Others.* Cincinnati, OH, Hovemeyer, 1977. 362p. NG gives underscored title. [C474; NG71].

MILLER -- Johnson, Patricia Givens. *Elder Jacob Miller (1735-1815), A Founder of the Brethren Churches and Dunkard Settlements in Franklin County, Virginia (1775), Ohio (1780), and Indiana (1810), and Some of His Descendants.* NP, Johnson, 1977. 109P. [C474; VV131].

MILLER -- Mast, Eli D. *Descendants of J. Miller and Magdelena Weaver Family Records, 1776-1970.* Apple Creek, OH, Author, 1970. Unpaged. [X652-FW].

MILLER -- Miller, Chester I. *The John Miller Family.* London, OH, 1973. 9 leaves. [X652-OH].

MILLER -- Miller, Chester I. *The Samuel Sherman Miller Family of Symmes Township, Lawrence County, Ohio.* London, OH, 1973. 12 leaves. [X652-OH].

MILLER -- Miller, Elfer B. *The Miller Families of William, Ebenezer (Sr.), Ebenezer (Jr.), Noah, Samuel, Samuel Buell, Frank Buell, and Clifford Buell.* Peachtree City, GA, E.B. Miller, 1990. iv, 129 leaves, 8 leaves of plates. 1. Miller family. 2.

Miller, William, 1620-1690-Family. 3.
Connecticut-Genealogy.   4. Ohio-Genealogy.
[G455].

MILLER -- Miller, Emmanual J. *Family
History of the Descendants of Jeremiah Miller
and Lydia Troyer.* Wilmot, OH, n.d. 69p.
[X653-FW/NY].

MILLER -- Miller, Emmanual J. *Family
History of Joni Miller and His Descendants.*
Wilmot, OH, Miller, 1942. 123p. [D8784].

MILLER -- Miller, Flavil R. *Jacob Miller
and Jane Scarborough Kith' n' Kin'; Some
History and Genealogy of the Jacob Miller
Family from the Revolutionary Era and
Scarborough Data from the Sixteen Hundreds.*
Newcomerstown, OH, 1971. 222p. [S1776a].

MILLER -- Miller, Isaac. *Short History of
Samuel and Barbara Miller; Together with a
Complete Genealogical Family Register of Their
Descendants.* Lima, OH, C. N. Shook, 1966.
29p. [X648-FW].

MILLER -- Miller, J. Virgil. *History of the
Miller Family, with a Complete Record of the
Descendants of Daniel B. Miller.* Bluffington,
OH, 1970. 72p. [X652-FW].

MILLER -- Miller, John Peery. *The Genealogy
of the Descendants of Frederick and Mary
Elizabeth Peery Miller.* Xenia, OH, Smith
Advertising Co., 1913. 103p. [L11878].

MILLER -- Miller, Jonas D. *Family Record of
Jonas D. Miller and Elmina Miller and Their
Descendants.* Plain City, OH, 1964. 12p.
[X651-FW].

MILLER -- Miller, Jonas E. *Brief History of
Jonathan S. Miller and Mary J. Troyer.*
Millersburg, OH, 1958. 53p. [X650-FW].

MILLER -- Miller, Josiah C. *Genealogy and
History of the Descendants of Samuel Miller.*

206

Columbus, OH, F. J. Heer Print co., 1912.
278p. [X648-FW/OH].

MILLER -- Miller, Lovina. *Brief Historical Sketches of Five Generations.* Dundee, OH, Harvey Gardner, 1936. 46p. [D8794].

MILLER -- Miller, Maynard E. *Records of the Miller Family; Descendants of Jacob Miller of Lyme, Conn., 1700 -1953, with Historical and Biographical Notes.* New Lyme, OH, 1920. 57p. [X649-OH].

MILLER -- Miller, Morris. *A Short Historical Account of the Miller & Morris Families, Collated Partly from Tradition, but Mostly from Authoritative Records.* Knoxville, OH, Stokes Bros. Printers, 1876. 296, 5p. [L11868].

MILLER -- Miller, Oscar R. *Miller Family History. Descendants of Daniel D. Miller and Lydia B. Troyer, 1874-1974.* S gives underscored title. Berlin, OH, Miller, 1974. 90p. [S1779; X653-FW].

MILLER -- Miller, Oscar R. *Descendants of Jost B. Miller and Anna Yoder, 1873-1976.* Berlin, OH, Miller, 1976. 113p. [C475; X653-FW/OH].

MILLER -- Miller, Oscar R. *Miller Family History.* Berlin, OH, 1981. v. <2 >. Vol. I. - Descendants of Eli S. Miller and Maria Kaufman, Vol. II - Descendants of Isaac S. Miller and (1) Rachel Troyer (2) Fannie Erb, - - [2] Descendants of Solomon S. Miller and (1) Mary Herschberger (2) Barbara Christner. [C475].

MILLER -- Miller, Ruth Suitor. *Some Descendants of Daniel Miller (d. 1816) of Adams Co., Pennsylvania, and Mahoning Co., Ohio.* Asheville, NC, Ward Pub. Co., 1986. xii, 88p. 1. Miller family. 2. Miller, Daniel, d. 1816-Family. 3. Ohio-Genealogy. [G455; DC2569].

MILLER -- Miller, W. L. *Levi D. Miller Family History.* Millersburg, OH, 1958. 54p. [X651-FW].

MILLER -- Miller, Wm. H. *The Miller Family in the Ohio Valley; Sketches of John... Joseph... Robert... and Anderson Miller.* Columbus, OH, 1915, 52p. [X648-LI/OL].

MILLER -- Miller, Willis Harry. *The Descendants of Samuel S. Miller, 1812-1892, of Frederick County, Maryland, Seneca County, Ohio, and Steuben County, Indiana.* Hudson, WI, Star Observer Print. 1944. 28p. [L11901; NG71].

MILLER -- Norris, Emory. *The Isaac Miller Family.* Columbus, OH, 1938. 31p. [L11893].

MILLER -- Robertson, Helen Miller. *The Family of Daniel Miller and Allied Families.* Akron, OH, Robertson, 1986. 166p. [DC2572].

MILLER -- White, Marilyn Miller. *The James Millers of Adams County, Ohio.* Lexington, KY, Waterman Enterprises, 1984. 107 p., 7 leaves of plates. [C475].

MILLIKEN -- Smith, Mrs. C. E. *The Millken and Milligan Families of Pennsylvania and Ohio. A Collection of Data Relating to Milliken Ancestry of Sarah August (Prior) Smith...* Columbus, OH, 1920. 48 l. [L11917].

MILLIKEN -- Smith, Sarah Augusta. *Milliken and Milligan Families (of Pennsylvania and Ohio).* Columbus, OH, 1921. 1 v. (unpaged). [L11918; VP156].

MILLIKEN -- Evans, Roe (White) and Sarah A. (Prior) Smith. *Milligan (Millikan) Family. 1949 Addenda to 1920 Record.* NP, 1949. 12 leaves. [L11918].

MILLIKEN -- Smith, (Mrs. Charles E.) Sarah Augusta Prior. *Milliken War Data and Lineage* *of World War Soldiers.* Columbus, OH, 1934. 62p. War Records of Descendants of Abraham Stiles and John Milliken. [L11919].

MILLS -- Colton, G. H. *Historical Address Delivered at the Mills Family Reunion... 1879.* Garrettsville, OH, Warren, Peirce, Book printer, 1880. Pages not given. [X654-WR].

MILLS -- Mills, E. C. *Mills Genealogy. A Folded Genalogical Chart Designed to Accompany the Mills Genealogy manuscript notes by E. C. Mills.* Columbus, OH, 1946. 1 folded chart. [X654-OH].

MILLS -- Mills, Clarence A. *Mills - Wininger Genealogy; Eight Generations of Migration to and across America.* Cincinnati, OH, Author, 1968. v, 22 leaves, 24p. [X654-FW].

MILLS -- Mills, Orvis D. *Nathan Mills Descendants, 1750-1982.* Enon, OH, O. D. Mills, 1982. vi, 100p. [C476].

MINER -- NAS. *Centennial of Miner Family. (In Ohio Archaeogocial and Historical Quarterly.* Columbus, OH, 1906. v. 15, p.407-418. [L11948].

MINOR -- Green, C. R. *Volunteer Service in the Army of the Cumberland. Pt. first. History of the Volunteers from Clarksfield, Huron Co., Ohio,... Pt. second. List of Volunteers from Wakeman, O., the Whole War. And... since. Pt. third, Sergeant Benj. T. Strong's Biography and History of the Chickamauga Campaign... Pt. fourth. Descendants of Justus Minor, Who Moved from Conn. in 1821 to Wakeman, O.* Olathe, KS, 1914. 48p. [L11956].

MINOR -- Green, Charles. R. *Descendants of Justus Minor Who Was Born About 1775 in Connecticut, and Removed to the Firelands, Ohio, 1821.* Olathe, KS, 1914. 14p. [X655-OH].

MINOR -- Green, Charles. R. *A Historic Pamphlet. Wakeman, Ohio. Lines of the Volunteers in the Civil War. The Minor Family as Pioneers in Wakeman. Justus & Cyrus Minor, 1821, Charles Minor, 1866.* Olathe, KS, 1914. 22p. [L11957].

MIZE -- Miller, Franklin, Jr. *The Isaac Mize Family of Eastern Kentucky.* Gambier, OH, Miller, 1985. 396p. 1. Mize family. 2. Mize, Isaac, 1786-1809-Family. [G459; C478; NG71; DC2588].

MOFFETT -- Maffett, Everett L. *Henry Maffett of Loudon County, Virginia and Descendants.* Eaton, OH, Silver Press, 1987. 119, 9p. 1. Moffett family. 2. Maffett, Henry, d. 1799-Family. [G459].

MOGENSEN -- Morgensen, Otto Peter. *Morgensen / Mogensen: Three Brother from Barnholm, Denmark: Some Genealogical Memoranda.* Kettering, OH, Morenson, 1978. 19, 16 leaves. [C479].

MOHLER -- NAS. *The Mohler Family of Ohio. Descendants of Jacob Mohler, Grandson of Ludwig Mohler of Lancaster County, Pennsylvania.* Beaver Falls, PA, 1958. 92p. [L12008].

MOHN -- Troth, Matilda C. S. *Record of the Mohn Family From 1730.* Clyde, OH, 1906. 8 leaves. [X659-NY].

MOLES -- Moles, Millard H. *Moles Family.* Tallmadge, OH, 1973. x, 89p. [X659-FW].

MOLLAT -- Getz, Nadine M. *We Would Remember. A Near Complete Genealogical Compilation of the Mollat Immigrants of 1833 and 1851.* Baltic, OH, Getz, 1950. 264p. X gives 253p. D gives underscored title. [D8874; X659-IG].

MONTGOMERY -- Faris, David. *The Descendants of James Montgomery of Brush Creek, Adams County, Ohio.* Baltimore,

Gateway, 1987. 477p. 1. Montogmery family.
2. Montgomery, James, 1744-1820-Family.
[G462].

MONTGOMERY -- Montgomery, Frank. *History
of the Descendants and Connections of William
Montgomery and James Somerville.* Newark, OH,
Advocate Printing Co., 1897. 112p. [D8901].

MOORE -- Moore, Arthur Clayton. *Moore.*
Hudson, OH, A. C. Moore, 1982. 160 leaves.
[C483].

MOORE -- Moore, Elmer D. *Contriubtions
Biographical, Genealogical and Historical of
the Family of Mr. William Moore and Mrs. Mary
Parmer Moore, His Wife. From the Year 1756 to
... 1934.* Warren, OH, Mimeographed by the
Author, 1934. 419p. (Divided into 4 parts).
[X664-OH].

MOORE -- Moore, William A. *The James Moore
Family Genealogy: A Virginian and His
Derivatives.* Hamilton, OH, W.A. Moore, 1987.
7, 404, 32p., 1 leaf of plates. 1. Moore
family. 2. Moore, James, 1740-1790-Family.
3. Ohio-Genealogy. [G464].

MORAN -- Moran, Vinetta A. *The Descendants
Moran.* Worthington, OH, V. Moran, 1982. 88p.
[C484].

MORGAN -- Lincicome, Glen A. *My Mothers's
People.* Urbana, OH, G.A. Lincicome, 1986-
v. <1 >. 1. Pitts family. 2. Morgan
family. 3. Yoho family. [G466].

MORR -- Morr, Ralph B. *Supplement of the
Genealogies of the Morr and Myers Families.*
Akron, OH, Akron Craftsman Printing Co., 1971.
iv, 630p. [S1790b; D8984].

MORR -- Morr, Ralph B. *Morr Family History.*
Delta, OH, 1976. x, 58p. [X667-FW].

MORR -- Moyer, Calvin F. *Genealogy of the
Morr Family.* Ashland, OH, Sun Publishing Co.,
1896. 295p. [L12173; D8985].

MORRILL -- Morrill, Horace Edwin. *American Ancestry of Benjamin Morrill and His Wife Miriam Pecker Morrill, of Salisbury, Mass., and Their Descendants of 1901.* Dayton, OH, 1903. 21p. [L12175].

MORRIS -- Woodson, Edgar Thomas. *The Worthington-Morris Source Book.* Marysville, OH, E.T. Woodson, 1990. 24 leaves, 22 leaves of plates. 1. Worthington family. 2. Morris family. 3. Ohio-Genealogy. 4. Afro-American-Genealogy. [G468].

MORRISON -- Haag, Mary Helen Morrison. *Samuel Morrison of Bucks County, Pa., and Some of His Descendants. -- Rev. --.* Dayton, OH, M.H.M. Haag, 1981. 1 v. (various foliations). [C487; VP160].

MORRISON -- Morrison, Howard. *Some Descendants of William Morrison Revolutionary Soldier of Wells, Lebanon and Albion, Maine.* Albany, OH, Author, 1950. 16p. 2 leaves. [X669-FW].

MORRISON -- Puckett, Lillian & Leslie E. *Tombstone Inscriptions of Cherry Fork Cemetary, Adams County, Ohio and Genealogical Gleanings.* Denville, NJ, 1964. viii, 91p. [L12219].

MORROW -- Hall, William C. *The Thomas Morrow Genealogy: Being a History of Thomas Morrow, Born in Jackson County, Ohio and His Descendants.* Nevada, IA, Hall, 1978. iv, 229p. 3 leaves of plates. [C488].

MORROW -- Hickox, Lura Morrow. *Some of the Descendants of William Morrow, Irish Immigrant and Hannah His Wife and Allied Lines, Wells and Essex.* Columbus, OH, L. M. Hickox, 1982. 133 leaves. [C488].

MORSE -- Ballinger, Dwight Gail. *White-Morse Family History, 1790-1985.* Cincinnati, OH, Mr. & Mrs. D.G. Balliner, 1987. iv, 54 leaves. 1. White family. 2. Morse family. 3. North Carolina Genealogy. [G468].

MOSHER -- Stevens, Gerard Thomas. *The Moser Family.* Columbus, OH, Stevens, 1982. 194p. [C489].

MOUGEVILLE -- Sorell, Marsha. *Mougeville, Daudier, DeMange: French Lineage of Darke County, Ohio Settlers.* 2nd printing. Indianapolis, IN, Sorrell, 1989. x, 54p. [DC2663].

MOTE -- Mote, Luke S. *Sketch Book of Lineal Descent, or, Genealogical Register of the Mote and Mendenhall Families; Also, Some Account of the Jones, Hollingsworth, Wright, Gardner, Butler, and Other Families.* West Milton, OH, 1855. Various pagings. Photo offset copy of original mss., 1967. [X672-FW].

MOURNING -- Mourning, Kenneth William. *Roger Mourning and His Descendants.* Toledo, OH, 1948, 8, 8, 17 leaves. These papers delivered at annual meetings of the family. [L12301].

MOYER -- Jung, Paula M. *Moyer Family, Descendants of Jacob and Christena Moyer of Naked Creek, Rockingham Co., Va.* Akron, OH, 1974. 96p. [X673-FW].

MUCKLEY -- Muckley, Paul E. *Genealogy of Michael and Anna Barbara Muckley Family.* Waynesburg, OH, 1976. Pages not given. [NG73].

MULLETT -- Getz, Nadine Mullet. *We Would Remember; A Near Complete Genealogical Compilation of the Mollat Immigrants of 1833 and 1851.* Dayton, OH, Otterbein Press, 1950. 264p. [L12336].

MUNDELL -- Barry, Ruby M. *The Mundell (Mundle) Family; Descendants of James Mundell and His Wife, Margaret (Garrett) Mundell of New Castle County, Delaware, and Greene County, Pa. And the Migrations of the Children into Kentucky, Ohio, West Virginia* *and Other Western States.* Kansas City, MO, 1968. Pages not given. [X675-FW/NY; VP162].

MUNSON -- NAS. *The Obadiah Clan of Munsons; Supplement to the Munson Record, 1637-1887.* Columbus, OH, Munson Association, 1941. 117p. [X676-NY/OH].

MUNSON -- NAS. *Short Sketches of Some of the Descendants of Amer Munson and Hannah Galpin Munson, His Wife of Ashtabula, Ohio.* NP, 1946. 62 leaves. X has 17p. [X676-OH/WR].

MUNSON -- Monson, Marie. *A Genealogy of Richard Woodworth, 1758 Ireland-1843 Ohio, Revolutionary War, His Wife, Sarah Ann Robinson and Collateral Families.* North Bend, OR, Monson, 1975. iv, 78 leaves. S lists under WOODWORTH. 1. Woodworth family. 2. Munson family. [G472; S2767].

MURDOUGH -- Lightner, M. A. M. *History of the Murdough Family (1804-1933).* Granville, OH, 1933. 50p. [X677-FW].

MURPHY -- Towne, Ernest L. Mrs. *The Ten Children of Moses and Laura Murphy.* Painseville, OH, Mrs. E. L. Towne, 1982. ii, 124 leaves. [C495].

MURRAY -- Murrey, Arthur Junior. *Murreys and Related Families, 1787-1982 -- 1st ed.* -- Massillon, OH, A. J. Murrey, 1982. iii, 103p. [C496].

MUTCHNER -- Hawkins, Carl H. *Ancestors and Descendants of Jarrett Mutchner, Randolph and Wayne Counties, Indiana, Darke County, Ohio.* Richmond, IN, 1971. 17p. [X678-FW].

MYERS -- Binkley, Jonathan A. *The Meyers - Wilcox Families: Binkley, Brooks, Coffman, Christner, Foust, Hart, Kalp, Lohr, Shaffer.* Toledo, OH, J. Binkley, 1982. 24p. [C497].

MYERS -- Meyer, Henry. *Genealogy of the Meyer Family.* Cleveland, OH, Printed by Lauer & Mattill, 1890. 131p. [L12383].

MYERS -- Myers, James C. *Myers Family.* Gallipolis, OH, J. C. Myers, 1981 - . 1. v. loose-leaf. [C497].

MYERS -- Wilson, Lester T. *Myers and Eatherton Families of Hancock and Wyandotte Counties, Ohio, Allied Families with Those in Ohio; Koh, Kohe, Koher, Brown, Pratt, Treece, Clark, Kanouse, Rex, Keenan, Corbin, Lockwood.* St. Petersburg, FL, 1946. 12p. [L12387].

N

NAFZIGER -- Nafziger, Carroll. *Christian Nafziger, Emigrated to America in the 1840's, (sic) Settled in Hopedale, Illinois.* Grafton, OH, Nafziger Heritage News, 1984. 103p. 1. Nafziger family. 2. Nafziger, Christian, 1792-1873-Family. [G475].

NASH -- Nash, Emily. *Diary of Emily Nash, 1812-1888, Vital Records Only...* Akron, OH, 1934 (The Puritan Manuscripts). Pages not given. [X682-FW].

NASH -- Pabst, Anna Catherine Smith. *Nashes of Ireland; Richard and Alexander Nash of Eastern Shore, 1200-1956.* Delaware, OH, Pabst, 1963. 44 leaves, lxii, 44p. NG gives 44 leaves. D gives 44 leaves, 114p. and title as underscored. [L12411; NG73; D9166].

NASH -- Phillips, Vernon Sirvillian. *Francis Nash of Braintree, Mass., and 480 of His Descendants.* Columbus, OH, 1932. 45 numb. leaves. [L12409].

NASH -- Phillips, Vernon Sirvillian. *Francis Nash of Braintree, Mass., and 1550 of His Descendants.* Columbus, OH, 1933. 112p. (variously paginated). D gives 112 leaves. [L12410; D9167].

NAST -- Nast, William. *Correspondence, Genealogical Material and Miscellaneous Papers of the Rev. William Nast Family.* Cincinnati, OH, ca. 1763-1938. NP, n.d. 1 Box. [X682-OH].

NEABEL -- Erion, Daniel R. *Neabel Generation.* Milford, OH, Author, 1943. Unpaged. [X683-FW].

NEAD -- Wurstner, Betty L. M. *Genealogy of the Matthias Nead Family in America, 1753-1973.* Vandalia, OH, 1973. 27p. [X683-FW].

NEALE -- NAS. *Ancestry of Herbert R. Neal of Shaker Heights, Ohio.* NP, 1965. Unpaged. [X683-FW].

NEALE -- Neil, Julia Evans (Stone). *From Generation to Generation. The Genealogies of Henry Moore Neal, Abby Grosvenor Tillinghaste, Guy Mallon, Albert Neilson Slayton, Byron Lakin Bargar, Alfred Hastings Chapin.* Columbus, OH, The Champlin Press, 1915. 131p. [L12427].

NEAR -- Frashuer, Mary Near. *Our Canadian Nears and Early Kin: Descendants of Carl Naeher, Palatine Immigrant to Colonial America, 1710.* Akron, OH, MFC Print. & Pub. Co., 1973. 282p. 1. Near family. [G477; X683-FW/LA/NY].

NEFF -- Neff, Elizabeth Clifford. *A Chronicle, Together With a Little Romance Regarding Rudolf and Jacob Npaf (L gives: Näf) of Frankford, Pennsylvania, and Their Descendants, Including an Account of the Neffs in Switzerland and America.* Cincinnati, OH, Press of Robert Clarke & Co., 1886. 352p. [L12435; NG74; D9193; VP163].

NEFF -- Neff, Elizabeth Clifford. *Addenda, Naf - Neff History; With Revolutionary Records of Captain Rufolf Neff, Ensign Aaron Scout, Major Thomas Smyth, Jr.* Cleveland, OH, 1899. 35p. [NG74].

216

NEFF -- Neff, E. E. *Genealogy and Family History of the Neff, Bryson, and Glover Families.* Columbus, OH, 1906. 20p. [X684-OH].

NEELEY -- Neely, Bonnie. *Neeley/Neely Families Living in Ohio in 1850.* Woodbridge, VA, 1974. 10 l. [NG74].

NEIGHBOURS -- Mackoy, Harry Brent. *A Study in Heredity and Environment; Being a Historical and Genalogical Sketch of the Ancestors of Joseph Henry Assel, formerly James Joseph Neighbours of Cincinnati, Ohio.* Covington, KY, Mackoy, 1922. 94p. X gives no date; omits "A" in title. [D9200; X684-FW].

NEIGHBOURS -- Mackoy, Harry Brent. *A Study in Heridity and Environment; Being a Historical and Genealogical Sketch of the Ancestors of Joseph Henry Assel, Formerly James Joseph Neighbours of Cincinnatti, Ohio.* Cincinnati, OH, A. H. Pugh Print. Co., 1953. 94p. [X684-CH].

NEIKIRK -- Neikirk, Floyd Edwin. *Genealogy of Edna Marea Neikirk Greiner.* Clyde, OH, Neikirk, 1960. 106 leaves. [D9201].

NEIKIRK -- Neikirk, Floyd Edwin. *Ohio Descendants of Seventeenth Century Ancestors in Plymouth and Providence Plantations, Massachusetts Bay and Connecticut Colonies, New York, Pennsylvania, Virginia, Maryland, New Jersey, 1620-1960.* Clyde, OH, 1960. 112, 35 leaves. Contains sequel to genealogy of Clark Rathbun Cleveland and genealogy of Edna Marea Neikirk Greiner... story of Jonathan Rathbone Jr. [L12442; VV138].

NEIL -- Neil, Julia Evans Stone. *From Generation to Generation.* Columbus, OH, Champlin Press, 1915. 131p. [D9202].

NEISWANDER -- Neiswander, Harry A. *Neiswander Family History; Swiss Background of Immigration of Neuenschwander Family to*

America. Blufton, OH, Author, 1969. 58p. [X684-FW].

NELSON -- Nelson, Herbert L. *The Family Tree of Herbert L. Nelson, Jr.: Genealogy from 1806-1980.* Solon(?), OH, H. L. Nelson, Jr. 1985. 77 leaves. [C503].

NELSON -- Nelson, John F. *Geneology (sic) of the Daniel Nelson Family of Nelsonville, Ohio 1638- Thomas Nelson, Rowley, England, 1958.* Bowling Green, OH, 1958. 1 v. various pagings. [L12462].

NELSON -- Nelson, John F. *Journal of the Proceedings of the Daniel and Sarah Nelson Family Reunion... 1960.* Nelsonville, OH, Clarksburg, WV, 1960. 37p. [X685-OH].

NESBITT -- Brickhouse, Dorothy Louise Nesbit Laybourne. *The Ancestry of Dorothy Louise Nesbit and William Frank Nesbit, 1741-1987.* Bethesda, MD, Produced for private circulation by V. A. Hook, 1988. 61 leaves, 30 leaves of plates. 1. Nesbitt family. 2. Nesbit, William Frank, 1908-1961-Family. 3. Pennsylvania-Genealogy. 4. Ohio-Genealogy. [G479].

NESSLY -- Walkup, O. W., Reporter. *Complete Report of the Nessly Centennial Held at Brooklyn, W. Va., 1885.* Wellsville, OH, A. P. Howard, 1885. 36p. [X685-FW].

NETHERS -- Noyes, Mary Nethers and Dale Shaw Wright. *Line of Nathan Nethers and Jemima Berry.* __, OH, M. N. Noyes, 1979. 158 leaves. 3 folded plates laid in. [C504].

NEUKIRK -- Neikirk, Floyd Edwin. [L12481]. See above: NEIKIRK. [L12422; VV138].

NEUENSCHWANDER -- Lehmn, Adah L. *Christian Neuenschwander Family Record, 1812-1978.* Galion, OH, A. L. Lehman, 1979. ca.150p. [C504].

218

NEVILLE -- Jones, Ruth D. Neville. *The Descendants of Thomas M. Neville and Theresa Nevin.* Neville, OH, 1970. 14 l. [L12489].

NEWELL -- Baldwin, C. C. *Newell.* Cleveland, OH, Leader Printing, Co., 1882. 167-171p. (From the Author's Candee Genealogy, Cleveland, 1882. [L12510].

NEWHOUSE -- Bouic, M. E. M. *Newhouse History. Rev. ed.* Ostrander, OH, 1967. Unpaged. [X687-FW].

NEWTON -- NAS. *History of the Newton and Oviatt Families.* Columbus, OH, Chas M. Cott, Printer, 1875. 40p. [D9256; X688-FW/LI/NY].

NEWTON -- White, Franklin H. [G480]. See above: CARTER. [G125].

NICHOLS -- Bartlett, Robert F. *Historical and Genealogical Sketch of the Nichols - Thomas Family in Ohio, With Partial Ancestory and Collateral Relatives in Virginia.* Mt. Gilead, OH. 1909. 15p. NG gives NP. [NG74; X689-FW; VV138].

NICHOLS -- Nichols, William D. *Hoge, Nichols, and Related Families; Biographical - Historical; A Sequential Arrangement of Genealogical Data.* Fairview Park, OH, Author, 1969. xii, 300p. [X689-FW].

NICKOLS -- Bartlett, Robert F. *Historical and Genealogical Sketch of the Nickols - Thomas Family in Ohio, with Partial Ancestry and Collateral Relatives in Virginia.* Mt. Gilead, OH, 1909. 15p. [X690-LI].

NIXON -- Nixon, Robert Henry. *Nixon - Ellison Genealogy; The Nixon and Ellison Families Who Came to Adams County, Ohio in the 1790's and Early 1800's from County Tyrone, Ireland. Also Records of Hall, Lovejoys, and McCutchens.* Cincinnati, OH, 1970. viii, 203p. [S1812].

NOBLES -- Sherman, Roy V. *Sone of the Descendants of Luther Nobles, son of* _____ *& Harsha Nobles.* Akron, OH, 1969. 33p. [L12593].

NOLD -- NAS. *Nold History.* Leetonia, OH, 1956. 1 Vol., various pagings. [X692-NY].

NOLD -- NAS. *Nold History.* Leetonia, OH, Nold Family Re-union Association, 1959. A1-F, 11p. [X692-FW].

NORRIS -- Norris, Walter E. *Chronicles of William Norris, Sr. and Sarah Ann Graves Norris of Coshocton County, Ohio.* NP, 1972. 53 leaves. [D9318].

NORRIS -- Smith, Barbara Norris. *The Norris Family History.* New Concord, OH, B. N. Smith, 1980. 175p. [C511].

NORTHCOTT -- Northcott, H. C. *Biography of Rev. Benjamin Northcott.* Cincinnati, OH, Printed at the Western Methodist Book Concern, 1875. 111p. [D9322].

NORTHWOOD -- Dempsey, James G. *Norwood - Northwood Families of Kent, Warwickshire and Gloucestershire* - *2nd abridged ed.* Cincinnati, OH, J.G. Dempsey, 1987, 1983. 66p. 1. Norwood family. 2. Northwood family. 3. England-Genealogy. [G486].

NORTON -- Baldwin, C. C. *Norton.* Cleveland, OH, Leader Printing, Co., 1882. 173-181p. (From the Author's Candee Genealogy, Cleveland, 1882). [L12632].

NORTON -- Gibboney, Harold G. *The Nortons from the Norman Conquest through the Settlement of Guilford, Conn., in 1639 to the Present, 1066-1965. 2nd ed.* Athens, OH, 1966. 54 leaves. [X694-FW/NY/SU].

NORWOOD -- Dempsey, James G. [G486]. See above: NORTHWOOD. [G486].

NOYES -- Noyes, Horatio N. *Noyes Genealogy. A Record of the Descendants of Rev. James Noyes, Newbury, 1634-1656?* Cleveland, OH, Noyes, 1889. 32p. D gives underscored title. [L12648; D9350].

NÜBLING -- Edwards, Lucile. *The Descendants of Johannes Nübling.* Columbus, OH, G. Marx, 1984. 100p. 1. Nübling family. 2. Nübling, Johannes, 1812-1889-Family. 3. German Americans-Genealogy. [G487].

NYE -- Hasson, Ethel W. *Genealogy of the Nye Family.* Centerburg, OH, 1943. 8 leaves. Typewritten. [X695-OH].

NYE -- La Fontaine, Leo S. [G487]. See above: FONTAINE. [G234].

NYE -- Nye, George Hyatt. *A Genealogy of the Nye Family.* Cleveland, OH, Nye Family of America Association, 1907. 3, 704, 8p. D gives 704p. [L12662; D9361].

NYE -- Nye, George Hyatt. *A Genealogy of the Nye Family.* Cleveland, OH, 1907-67. v. 1-2. [NG75].

NYE -- Nye, George Hyatt. *A Genealogy of the Nye Family.* Cleveland, OH, 1907-67. 4 v. Vol 1 - Half Title: Banjamin Nye of Sandwich, Massachusetts, his ancestors and descendants. Vol 3 - has sub-title: Nyes of German origin. Vol 4 - has sub-title: Supplement to Vols, I, II, & III. [L12663].

NYE -- Nye, Willis. *Genealogy of George Nye (Nigh) Family, 1755-1965.* Galion, OH, Nye, Willis and Wanda, 1965. (1 v. loose-leaf). D gives 80p. [L12664; D9363].

O

OBEE -- Obee, Harold B. *The Family History of the Obee-Billing Association.* Bowling Green, OH, H. B. Obee, 1980. v. 203, 10p. [C514].

OBERG -- Howe, Helen Cooper. *The Family Tree of Friedrich Oberg.* Cincinnati, OH, Howe, 1979. 303p. [C514].

OBERHOLTZER -- Loomis, Elisha Scott. *Some Account of Jacob Oberholtzer, Who Settled, About 1719, in Franconia Township, Montgomery County, Pennsylvania and Some of His Descendants in America.* Cleveland, OH, Loomis, 1931. 412p. D gives title as underscored; omits pagination. Ltd. ed. 300 numb. copies. [L12675; NG75; D9369; VP167].

OBERTEUFFER -- Oberteuffer, Delbert. *Genealogy of the Oberteuffer Family.* Columbus, OH, 1935. Genealogical Table. A Chart prepared to accompany the author's manuscript of the Oberteuffer Family... at the Pennsylvania Historical Society and the New York Public Library. [L12676].

O'BRIEN -- Duryee, Harold Taylor. *An Ohio Family in Summit County.* Canfield, OH, Duryee, 1953. 37 leaves. [D9371].

O'BRIEN -- Griffith, D. Eugene. [G489]. See above: GRIFFITH. [G274].

O'CONNOR -- Lincicome, Glen A. [G489]. See above: McKEE. [G442].

O'CONNOR -- O'Connor, William G. [G489]. See above: BOLEN. [G65].

O'DANIEL -- O'Daniel, V. F. *Snatches of O'Daniel, Hamilton, and Allied Ancestry and History in Maryland and Kentucky.* Somerset, OH, Rosary Press, 1933. 101p. [L12700; D9377].

OEN -- Einhart, Mary M. *Family Tree of Henry Oen, 1825-1902. Corrected to July 1, 1966.* Toledo, OH, 1966. 22 leaves. [L12722].

OGDEN -- Kasler, John V. *A History of the Ogdin Family in America, Including the Descendants of Ignatius and Mary Ogdin, 1750-1987.* St. Petersburg, FL, Genealogy Pub.

Service, 1988. v, 227p. 1. Ogden family. 2.
Ogdin, Ignatius-Family. 3. Ohio-Genealogy.
[G490].

OHL -- Partridge, Ruth. *Ohl Genealogy and
History, 1710-1951.* Warren OH, Partridge,
1951. viii, 187p. D gives 187, 19p.
[L12747; D9404].

OLDFATHER -- Longman, Rufus A. *The
Genealogy of the Oldfather Family.*
Cincinnati, OH, Longman, 1911. 220p.
[L12762; D9411].

OLDFATHER -- Longman, Rufus A. *Post Office
Director of the Oldfather Family Relationship,*
Being a Supplement to the Family Genealogy
Published by R. A. Longman. Cincinnati, OH,
Longman, 1912. 39p. [L12763].

OLIN -- NAS. *Report of the Second Annual
Reunion of the Descendants of Ezra Olin and
Betsy Green, Held at Streetsboro, Ohio...
1897.* Ravenna, OH, Ravenna Repub. Print.,
1887. 14p. [X700-FW].

OLIN -- Taylor, Robert M. *Index to
Biographical Sketches and Records of the Ezra
Olin Family by George S. Nye, Chicago, 1892.*
Kent, OH, 197_. 21 leaves. [X700-FW/NY].

OLNEY -- Currie, Barbara Calder. [G492].
See above: CALDER. [G114].

OLWIN -- Mullen, Lena Belle Olwin. *Johann
Werner Ohlwein, 1775-1829, and His
Descendnants...* Versailles, OH, Versailles
Policy Pub. Co,, 1987. iv, 429p. 1. Olwin
Family. 2. Ohlwein, Johann Werner, 1756-1829-
Family. 3. Middle West-Genealogy. [DC2774].

OMWAKE -- Omwake, George L. *The Omwakes of
Indian Springs Farm.* Cincinnati, OH, 1926.
96p. [L12806; D9436].

O'NAN -- O'Nan, James Frederick. *Treasure Up
the Memory; Some Genealogical Notes Relating*

to the O'Nan and Allied Families. Cincinnati, OH, 1969. vii, 149p. [A507].

ONG -- Ong, Albert R. The Ong Family in America. Martins Ferry, OH, 1906. 171p. [L12812].

ORCUTT -- Richey, Virginia Emswiler. Descendants of Sylvester Orcutt. Delaware, OH, Richey, 1973. 85 leaves. [D9443].

ORTMAN -- Roll, Judith Janes. A Genealogy of the John Ortman Family, Ross County, Ohio. Kingston, OH, J. J. Roll, 1980. 30p., 3 pages of plates. [C519].

ORTON -- Jordan, Julia H. Orton. Supplement to An Account of the Descendants of Thomas Orton, be Edward Orton, Columbus, 1896: Supplement: Account of Azariah Orton of Farmington, Ill, and His Descendants. Burlington, IA, 1900. 23p. [X704-FW/LI].

ORTON -- Orton, Edward. An Account of the Descendants of Thomas Orton of Windsor, Conn. 1641 (principally in the male line). Columbus, OH, Press of Nitschke Brothers, 1896. 220p. D gives title as: An account of the descendants of Thomas Orr (sic). [L12844; D9457].

OTTARSON -- Moore, Catherine B. Ottarson Genealogy. Columbus, OH, n.d. Unpaged. [X706-OH].

OVERFIELD -- Boese, Virginia. Overfield Genealogy Research Notes. Troy, OH, 1968. 48 leaves. [X707-PH].
        -- Revised Edition. Troy, OH, 1970. iii, 105 leaves. [X707-PH].

OVERFIELD -- Boese, Virginia. Overfield Family. Troy, OH, Boese, 1968. 1 v. (various foliations). [D9482].

OVERFIELD -- France-Rice, Mary H. O. Overfield History. Troy, OH, Copied by Troy

Historical Soc., 1968. Various pagings.
[X707-NY/OH/SL].

OVERMYER -- Overmyer, Barnhart B. and John C. *Overmyer History and Genealogy From 1860 to 1905.* Fremont, OH, Chas. S. Beelman, Printer, 1905. 4, 297, 39p. [L12889; D9484].

OVERTON -- Anderson, William Pope. *The Early Descendants of Wm. Overton & Elizabeth Waters of Virginia, And Allied Families.* Also *Anderson, Barret, Boone, Brown families.* Cincinnati, OH, Anderson, 1938. 160p. D gives title as underscored. [L12890; NG76; D9485].

OWEN -- Owens, James Adolphus. *Kisses Sweeter Than Wine: Owens - Jeffcoat Family.* Akron, OH, 1974. 40 l. [S1879].

OWSLEY -- Owsley, Harry B. *Genealogical Facts of the Owsley Family, in England and America, from the Time of the Restoration to the Present.* Chicago, IL, 1890. Hubbard, OH, R. P. Owsley, 1971. 164p. Reprint of 1890 ed. [X708-FW/LA].

P

PAE -- Kyle, Phyllis Richards. *Pae Dirt. Digging into Some Old Records and Recent Recollections of Pae Families in England, Scotland, and the United States.* Rev and enl. Lakewood, OH, P.R. Kyle, 1986. iv, 115 leaves, 11 leaves of plates. 1. Pae family. 2. Great Britain-Genealogy. 3. Canada-Geneaalogy. [G499].

PAGE -- Page, Edith (Moyer). *George Page of Branford, Conn., And Some Of His Descendants, With Allied Lines.* Shaker Heights, OH, Page, 1977. 119p. D gives title as underscored. [C524; NG76; D9516].

PAINE -- Paine, Rev. Jason L. *Chart No. 3, Showing Ancestry and Descendants of Gen.*

Edward Paine, Founder of Painesville, Ohio.
Fayette, IA, 1902. Genealogical Table.
[L12945; NG76].

PAINE -- Ohler, Clara Price. *Ancestors and Descendants of David Paine and Abigail Shepard of Ludlow, Massachussetts, 1463-1913.* Lima, OH, 1913. 252p. Contents Paine - Ohler - Compton - Roby - Shepard - Spur - Leonard - Tileston - Bridgman - Adams - Webb - Pierce - Bass Families. [L12950].

PALMER -- Kellog, Dale C. *Palmer - Burlingham Genealogy; Descendants of Caleb Palmer (1775-1854) and Eliphalet Burlingham (c1785-c1840) Chiefly Descended from Their Grandchildren, H. Milton Palmer (1844-1918) and Isadore A. Burlingham (1849-1918) of Huron County, Ohio.* Elyria, OH, 1974. 177p. [S1888].

PALMER -- Kellog, Dale C. *Palmer - Burlingham Genealogy; Descendants of Caleb Palmer (1775-1854) and Eliphalet Burlingham (c1785-c1840). Also Carpenter Family.* Elyria, OH, 1974. 199p. [NG77].

PALMER -- Palmer, Larry Trenton. *Adam Palmer, 1770-1864 of Augusta County, Virginia: (Ancestors and Descendants).* Strasburg, OH, Gordon Print., 1981. 188p. [C524].

PANCOAST -- Koleda, Elizabeth P. *Some Ohio and Iowa Pioneers, Their Friends and Descendants.* Prineville, OR, Hutchinson Photo and print. co., 1973. 219p. [X715-OH].

PANZICA -- Panzica, Ignatius Anthony. *Our Family Vines = Nostra Famiglia Alberi.* Cleveland, OH, Panzica, 1978. iv, 46 leaves. [C525].

PARDEE -- Pardee, Aaron. *Genealogy of One Line of the Pardee Family.* Wadsworth, OH, Pardee, 1896. 69p. [L13007; D9558].

PARK -- Becker, Dorothy Robertson. *The Parke Family: Earliest Pioneers of New Jersey with*

Later Generations Who Pioneered in Old Frederick Co., Va., and On Into Ohio & Indiana. Ft. Worth, TX, Miran, 1979. xvi, 137p. [C526; VV142].

PARK -- Park, Charles C. *The Complete Record of the Descendants of Melvin Park, Son of Peter Park, a Native of Scotland.* Elyria, OH, Republican Steam Print. 1876. 14p. [X716-MH].

PARKER -- NAS. *A Brief Sketch of the Life of Perses Follett Parker,... of Family History (sic).* Columbus, OH, The Champlin printing co., 1893. 43p. [X717-LA/PH].

PARKER -- Ashley, Julia Linden Robertson. Richards, Sylvia. *Memorial To Thomas Richards, Fire Lands Pioneer -- Bicentennial ed.* -- Willard, OH, Richards, 1976. x, 114p., 1 leaf of plates. [C581; NG83; D10490].

PARKER -- Gray, Mary Parker. *My Revolutionary Ancestor: His Ancestors and Descendants.* Elyria, OH, M.P. Gray, 1984. 328p., 11p. of plates.. [C527].

PARKER -- Parker, Rufus H. and L. N. .... *History and Genealogy of the Family of Deacon Lovel Parker, Whom Emigrated from Barkhamsted, Conn., to Kinsman, Ohio in the Year 1816.* Syracuse, NY, The Mason Press, 1898. [L13052].

PARKER -- Stewart, Mildred Beth Wise. *Descendants of Hazekiah Parker, Sr. and Mary Ann Smith Parker.* Farborn, (sic) OH, Stewart, 1988. vi, 270p.. [DC2824].

PARKER -- Ward, Harvey Parker. *Glances at the Ancestors of John Parker (Born 1807, Died 1891).* Columbus, OH, 1895. 16p. The first Jewetts in America, p. 12-16. [L13051].

PARKHILL -- Parkhill, Forbes. *The Parkhill Family.* Darrowville, OH, School Pub. Co., 1933. 25p. [X718-DP/OH].

PARMENTER -- Parmenter, George Lisle. *Parmenter Family.* Lima, OH, n.d. 1 folded page. [X719-OH].

PARR -- Parr, Perry Louis. *The Descendants of Richard Parr, Pioneer of Licking County, Ohio. v. 1.* Palo Alto, CA, 1980 iii, 194p., 2 leaves of plates. NG omits pagination.. [C528; NG77].

PARR -- Parr, Miriam. *The Descendants of Richard Parr, Pioneers of Licking County, Ohio: Additions and Corrections.* Paolo Alto, CA, Heritage West, 1983. 124p. Supplement to the descendants of Richard Parry by Perry Louis Parr, 1980 (just above). 1. Parr family. 2. Licking County (Ohio)-Genealogy. [G504; C528; NG77].

PARSONS -- Parsons, Walter A. *The Parsons Family.* East Cleveland, OH, 1930. 2 vols. [X720-WR].

PATON -- Maffet, Mary Ellen. [G506]. See above: McMILLAN. [G444].

PATTEN -- NAS. *Fifty Years of Reunions of the Patten Counsins and Their Families; 1920-1970 by the Descendants of John and Hannah (Diehl) Patten of Ohio and Indiana.* NP, Patten Cousins Reunion Assoc., 1970. 283p. [X721-FW].

PATTERSON -- NAS. *Welcome to the Rubicon.* Dayton, OH, Patterson Memorial Commission, n.d. 9p. [X722-CH].

PATTERSON -- Bailey, Marshall Price. *Patterson Genealogy.* Salem, OH, 1965. 23p.. [X722-FW/MH].

PATTERSON -- Conover, Charlotte R. *Patterson Log Cabin.* Dayton, OH, National Cash Register Co., 1900. 44p. [X721-FW].

PATTERSON -- Conover, Charlotte Reeve. *Concerning the Forefathers.* Dayton, OH,

National Cash Register Co., 1902 432p. [D9651].

PATTERSON -- Ellis, Kathryn Young. [G506]. See above: FRAME. [G238].

PATTERSON -- Joy, Shirley Patterson. *William Patterson of Nova Scotia and His Descendants.* Madeira, OH, S.P. Joy, 1988. 95 leaves, 23 leaves of plates. 1. Patterson family. 2. Patterson, William, 1800-1878-Family. 3. Nova Scotia-Genealogy. 4. Canada-Genealogy. [G506].

PATTERSON -- Patterson Julia J. J. *Johnston and Patterson Families.* Dayton, OH, 1895. Various pagings. [X721-FW].

PATTERSON -- Patterson, Robert A. *The Patterson Family, a Geneological (sic) History.* Carrollton, OH, Press of the Chronicle, 1909. 18p. [L13140].

PATTON -- Puckett, Lillian & Leslie E. [L13153]. See above: MORRISON. [L12219].

PAYNE -- Payne, J. Barton. *Family Tree of George Payne (1777-1856) of Porter, Gallia County, Ohio.* Wheaton Coll., IL, 1960. Genealogical Tables. [L13179].

PEARMAN -- Carter, James Grafton. *Pierman and Clark Families of Putnam County, Ohio and Related Families of Henderson, Storch, and Grafton, 1790-1972.* Columbus, OH, 1972. 87 leaves. D lists as PIERMAN. [S1911; D9940].

PEASE -- Duty, Allene Beaumont. *The Ancestors and Descendants of the Honorable Calvin Pease and Laura Grant Risley Pease, His Wife of Suffield, CT., Rutland, VT, and Warren, OH.* Cleveland, OH, Duty, 1979. vi, 230p. C gives: 1st ed [C533; NG78; D9715].

PECKHAM -- Peckham, Charles Wesley. *The Charles Peckham Branch. Peckham Genealogy from England, Rhode Island, Pennsylvania,*

Ohio, Indiana, Wisconsin, Illinois, Texas and _Elsewhere._ Lebanon, OH, C. W. Peckham, 1978 171p. NG gives NP and underscored title. [C534; NG78].

PEDLAR -- Pedlar, Mary M. _The Pedlar - Solomon Family of Cornwall, England and Ontario, Canada._ Columbus, OH, 1955. 12p (folder). [X726-OL].

PEERS -- Richardson, Robert N. _Valentine Peers._ Middletown, OH, Richardson, 1976. 234p. [C534; D9740; X727-FW/LA/NY].

PELZEL -- Pelzel, Michael J. _The Descendants of Vincent Pelzel._ White Oak, OH, M.J. Pelzel, 1989. vii, 323 leaves. 1. Pelzel family. 2. Pelzel, Vincent, 1861-1938- Family. [G510].

PEMBERTON -- Rich, Miss Evelyn. _Notes on the Pemberton Family. Ancestors of Emilius Oviatt Randall._ Columbus, OH, 1898. p. 113-138. Detached from the "Old Northwest" Genealogical Quarterly, July, 1898. [L13264].

PENCE -- Carson, Beatrice. _Pence Family Genealogy; Descendants of Henry, Jacob, and Lewis Pence. Shenandoah Couty (sic) Va., and Champaign County, Ohio, 1749-1900._ Washington, DC, 1967. 109 l. [NG78].

PENCE -- Carson, Beatrice. _Pence Genealogy: A History of the Pences of Shenandoah County, Virginia Who Migrated to Champaign County, Ohio, 1749-1900._ Washington, DC, Beatrice Carson, 1967. 106 p., 3 l. May be same book as that just above. [X728-FW].

PENCE -- Heer, Esther Leonard. [G510]. See above: HARTPENCE. [G303].

PENCE -- Pence, Kingsley Adolphus. _The History of Judge John Pence and His Descendants, born in Shenandoah County, Virginia, January 15, 1775. Resided in_

Chapaign County, Ohio, Bartholomew County, Indiana and Henderson County, Illinois. Denver, CO, 1912 126p. [L13266].

PENCE -- Pence, Richard Allen. *A Guide to the Pence Families in America. Pt.I: Jacob and Valentine Pence, Augusta (Rockingham) Co., VA. incl. desc. in OH and West. Pt. II: Jacob, Lewis and Henry Pence of Shenandoah (Page) Co., VA, and Champaign Co., OH.* Fairfax, VA, 1982. 2 v. [NG78].

PENNELL -- Pennell, Andrew C. *The Lewis (1781-1850) and Sarah (1790-1863) Pennell Genealogy.* North Olmstead, OH, Pennell, 1987. a-d, 139 leaves. 1. Pennell family. 2. Pennell, Lewis, 1781-1850-Family. [G510; DC2862].

PENNELL -- Pennell, Andrew C. *The Pennells of Balderson, England and Their American Descendants.* No. Olmstead, OH, Pennell, 1990. a, 175 leaves. 1. Pennell family. 2. England-Genealogy. [G510].

PEOPLES -- Peoples, William L. *Genealogy of the Peoples Family.* Westlake, OH, W.L. Peoples, 1988. 117 l., 2 leaves of plates. 1. Peoples family. 2. Ohio-Genealogy. [G510].

PERDUE -- Perdue, Robert Hartley. *Descendants of William Perdue, Who Settled in Chester County, Pennsylvania in 1737-38 with His Wife Susanna (Pim) Perdue. Part II. Ancestors of Lucinda Maria (Smith) Perdue, giving Smith, Potter, and Hamilton Lines. John Purdue founder of Purdue University.* Cleveland, OH, 1934. v-xi, 168 numb leaves. [L13336; VP176].

PERKINS -- Crawford, Andrew J. [G512]. See above: BRENT. [G86].

PERKINS -- North, Joel R. *The Family of James K. and Alice J. Perkins of Lake Preston, South Dakota: With an Account of Their*

Descendants to the Present. Lima, OH, J.R. North, 1979. 39p., 3 leaves of plates. [C537].

PERKINS -- Perkins, Edward. *What I Know About My Ancestors and Their Families. Also Some Account of My Wife's Ancestors and Their Families.* Weymouth, OH, 1888. (Chicago, 1847). 3p., 33 numb. leaves. X adds: "The Perkins family" copied from the original manuscripts by Victor J. Andrew, 1947. [L13362; X731-DP/LA/MH/SU].

PERKINS -- Perkins, Paul M. *Genealogy and History of One Branch of the Perkins Family in America, Originating with Edward Perkins, Immigrant to America and to New Haven, Connecticut, before 1646.* Minerva, OH, P.M. Perkins, 1980. iii, 29, 103 leaves. [C537].

PERKINS -- Perkins, Ralph. *Volume II, Perkinsiana.* Cleveland, OH, Gates Press (1962-63), 214p. Companion volume to J. B.'s final bulletin by Jacob B. Perkins. [X731-FW].

PERRY -- Perry, Aaron Fyfe. *Memoranda Concerning Descendants of Joun Perry, John Strong, John Fyfe, Robert Gray.* Cincinnati, OH, G. E. Stevens & Co., 1878. 1, iii, 28p. [L13379].

PETERS -- Peters, James Marvin. *Peters Family of Scott County, Virginia: A Genealogy of Henry Peters (1763-1859), John Peters (1770-1846) and Jacob Peters, Jr. (1779-1862): Related Families, Baker, Bartram, Boggs...* New Carlisle, OH, J.M. Peters, 1986. xvi, 458p. 1. Peters family. 2. Peters, Henry, 1763-1859-Family. 3. Peters, John, 1770-1846-Family. 4. Peters, Jacob, 1779-1862-Family. [G513].

PETERSON -- Williams, Edgar M. *The Lineal Ancestors and Descendants of Caroline Van Evera and James Holman Peterson.* Akron, OH, 1962. 12 leaves. [X734-NY].

PETHTEL -- Pethtel, Rheba I. [G514]. See above: BRADFORD. [G81].

PETTIT -- Gregory, Jane E. *Notes on Pennsylvania and Ohio Pettits...* Lafayette, CA(?), Gregory, 1989. 99 leaves. [DC2884].

PETTY -- Petty, Gerald M. *Petty of England and Virginia.* Columbus, OH, Petty, 1973. 538p. [S1951; D9862].

PETTY -- Petty, Geral M. *Petty, of England & Virginia; Wright of Virginia, Kentucky & Missouri; Riley of Maryland, Kentucky & Missouri; and related Alexander, Copeland, Dale, Douglass, Givens, Hubbard, McClung, Owens, Patton, Paxton, Rowland, & Tedford Families.* Columbus, OH, 1973. [VV145].

PETTY -- Petty, Gerald McKinney. *Solomon Jackson Petty, 1850-1915: Amcestprs amd Descemdamts.* Columbus, OH, Petty's Press. 1981. 22p. [C540].

PFANDER -- Pfander, Homer Garrison. *Charles Pfander Famila, Iowa Pioneers from Ohio.* Clarinda, IA, 1949. 109p. [L13530].

PFAUTZ -- Miller, Marcella M. H. *Fouts, (Foutz, Pfoutz, Pfautz) Family.* Dayton, OH, Author, 1961. 3, 24p., 3 leaves. [X735-FW].

PFOST -- Morrison, Okey J. *The Slaughter of the Pfost - Greene Family of Jackson County, W. Va. A History of the Tragedy with Notice of the Early Settlers of Jackson County, a Sketch of the Family and John F. Morgan.* Cincinnati, OH, Gibson and Sorin Co., printers, 1868. 96p. [L13536; VV146].

PHELPS -- Van Henkle, Charles, et al. [G516]. See above: HENKEL. [G312].

PHELPS -- Hasson, Ethel W. *Phelp Family in America.* Centerburg, OH, 1943. 6 leaves. [X736-OH].

PHELPS -- Johnson, Bernice P. *A Genealogy of Allison Phelps.* Estherville, OH, Johnson, 1970. 191, xii p. [D9878].

PHELPS -- Phelps, Richard E. *Family of Jedediah Phelps.* Shadyside, OH, 1973. 17p. [X736-FW].

PHILLIPS -- Hackenbracht, Henry. *History of Richard and Francina (Hart) Phillips and Their Descendants; Including a Brief Account of Their Ancestry, Collateral Lines and Items of Interest.* West Lafayette, OH, Hackenbracht, 1951. 305p. [D9898].

PHILLIPS -- Phillips, A. P. *Record of the Phillips Family, 1739-1907.* Findlay, OH, Phillips, 1907. 31p. [D9901].

PHILLIPS -- Phillips, L. G. *Phillips Family, 1739-1969; Supplement to the Record of the Phillips Family, 1739-1907.* Ashland, OH, 1969. 56p., 4 leaves. [X737-FW].

PHILLIPS -- Phillips, Margaret Minch. *Ten Generations of the Phillips Family in America.* Amherst, OH, M.M. Phillips, 1983. 137p. [C543].

PHILLIPS -- Phillips, Vernon S. *John Phillips of Grafton, Rensselaer County, New York, and 120 of His Descendants.* The Puritan Manuscripts, Akron, OH, 1933. 1p., 19 numb. leaves. [L13560].

PHILLIPS -- Phillips, William L. *The Descendants of Samuel and Mary Phillips, 1886-1971.* Zanesville, OH, 1971. 30 leaves. [X737-OH].

PIATT -- Shaffer, James F. *Piatt's Landing Eastbend.* Cincinnati, OH, Cincinnati Gas & Electric Co., 1978. vii, 110p. [D9922].

PIERCE -- Abbott, Lyndon Ewing. [G518]. See above: ABBOTT. [G1].

234

PIERCE -- Pierce, David. *The Pierce Family et al.* Hamilton, OH, 1945. 42p. Relating to Thomas Pierce family; Henry Ross family; David Barnett family and Samuel Pottenger family.. [X739-CH].

PIERCE -- Smith, L. H. *Joseph Pierce and His Wife Sally Ann Hatch of Scituate, Mass., and Cincinnati, Ohio.* Clearwater, FL, 1971. Unpaged. LI has vols. 1-5 and 7. [X740-FW].

PIERROT -- Uhrbrock, Richard Stephen. *Pierrot - Liengme - Fleming - Gatewood Lineage.* Athens, OH, 1966. 32 l. [NG79].

PILCHARD -- Uhrbrock, Richard Stephen. *Pilchards of Delmarva.* Athens, OH, Uhrborck, 1967. 49 leaves. [L13623; D9956].

PILON -- McGovern, Alberta Pilon. *Genealogy and Family History of the Thomas Bernard Pilon Family.* Shaker Heights, OH, Corinthian Press, 1981. 277p. [C545].

PIM -- Pim, Rachel. *Ancestry and Descendants of Nathan Pim, 1641-1904.* Damascus, OH, 1904. 23p. [X741-LI].

PITTIS -- Pittis, Margaret Birney. *Pittis Genealogy; The Pittis Family in America, Four hundred and sixty-four Years ... 1580-1944. Allied Families... Arnold, Birney, Brooke, Dare, Godfrey, Hout, Isham, Legg, or Legge, McCullough, Stephens.* Cleveland, OH, Pittis, 1945. xv, 2, 315p. D gives underscored title and 315p. [L13656; D9977].

PITTS -- Lincicome, Glen A. [G521]. See above: MORGAN. [G466].

PLATTER -- Platter, D. E. *History of the Platter Family from 1656 to the Present Time.* Cleveland, OH, 1902. 76p. [X744-FW].

PLATTER -- Platter, David E. *The Platter Genealogy.* East Cleveland, OH, Author, 1919, 84p. [X744-CH].

POLING -- Trebbe, Lethe, L. M. *Our Poland Descendants of Highland Co., Ohio & Hendricks County, Ind., Kans, & Okla., 1792-1980's.* Wichita, KS, L.L.M. Trebbe, 1989. xx, 706p. 1. Poling family. [G523].

POLLOCK -- Pollock, Philip Hewison. *A Memoir of the Robert Middleton Pollock Family, Who Lived at 210 South Eighth Street, Fargo, North Dakota.* Columbus, OH, 1968. 49 leaves. [S1978].

POMEROY -- NAS. *Stephen Pomeroy of Northampton, Mass., and Huntsberg, Ohio. Showing Lineage from Eltweed Pomeroy to 1908.* Middlefield, OH, Press of the Middlefield Times, 1908. 30p. [X746-CH].

POMEROY -- NAS. *Pomeroy Pamphlet, 1-2, 1909-1916.* Toledo, OH, 1909-1916, Pomeroy Family Association. 2 vols. [X746-OH].

POMEROY -- Hoppin, Charles A. *Letter to Col. A. A. Pomeroy, Sandusky, Ohio Concerning the Pomeroy Family of Devonshir, England.* London, 1915. 24p. Typewritten. [X746-OH].

POMEROY -- Hoppin, Charles Arthur. *Pomeroy. Interesting English Records Supplemental to the History and Genealogy of the Pomeroy Family.* Toledo, OH, 1915. 29p. A letter from C.A. Hoppin of London to A. A. Pomeroy. [L13730].

POMEROY -- Pomeroy, Albert A. *Pomeroy. Information on the Descendants of Sir Ralph de Pomeroy of Normandy and England, Who Was Ancestor of Eltweed Pomeroy.* Sandusky, OH, 1909. 8p. [X746-LI].

POMEROY -- Pomeroy, Albert A. *Pomeroy Pamphlet No. 2: Name and Fame of the New England Historic - Genealogical Society, Prostituted to Screen Its Surreptitious Letter Writer.* Toledo, OH, Franklin Print. 1916. 16p. [X746-FW/MH].

POMEROY -- Pomeroy, Albert A. *Romance and History of Eltweed Pomeroy's Ancestors in Normandy and England.* Toledo, OH, Press of the Franklin Printing, Co., 1909. vii, 8p. [L13730].

POMEROY -- Pomeroy, Albert A. *Pomeroy.* Toledo, OH, Franklin Printing, and Engraving Co., 1909. 29p. [D10033].

POMEROY -- Pomeroy, Albert A. *History and Genealogy of the Pomeroy Family;* Comprising the Ancestors and Descendants of Eltweed Pomeroy... Toledo, OH, Franklin Printing, and Engraving Co., 1912-1922. 3 Parts in 2 v. Part 3 printed at Detroie by Geo. A. Drake & Co. D gives 3 v. and underscored title. [L13731; D10032].

POND -- Pond, Daniel Streator. *A Genealogical Rocord of Samuel Pond and His Descendants.* New London, OH, Record Office, G. W. Runyon, 1875. 1, 126p. D gives underscored title. [L13736; D10037].

POOLER -- Pooler, Marjorie Russell. *Zelotes Pooler and His Descendants.* South Charleston, OH, Pooler (C gives: B.P. Driever), 1983. iii, 28p. [C552; DS559].

POPE -- Ballinger, Dwight Gail. [G525]. See above: BELLINGER. [G47].

PORTER -- Porter, William L. *List of Porter Families in the United States at the Time of Taking of the 1790 Census.* Kansas City, MO, n.d. 19p. [X749-FW].

POSTLE -- Montgomery, Martha A. & Thomas, Joanne V. (Lewis). *Postle (Postles) in America; A Preliminary Survey of Possells / Postal / Postel / Postell / Postels / Postill / Postle(s) / Postly / Postol /; With Emphasis on Delaware and Ohio Families.* Kansas City, MO, 1984. v. <1 >. NG gives no volume or pagination indication. [C553; NG80].

POTTER -- Stuckey, Helen Potter. *Summer Memories of Ohio, 1895-1909.* South Strafford, VT, Kemp & Cary Press, 1985. 79p. 1. Stuckey, Helen Potter, 1895- . 2. Potter family. 3. Cleveland Region (Ohio)-Biography. 4. Rural Life-Ohio-Cleveland Region. 5. Cleveland Region (Ohio)-Social Life and Customs. [G527].

POWELL -- Christy, M. L. *Index: Authentic Genealogical Memorial History of Philip Powell of Mifflin County, Pa, His Descendants and Others... by Rev. John Powell.* Lima, OH, 1976. 23p. [X752-FW].

POWELL -- Moore, Jessie M. P. *Powell Genealogy.* Walhondig, OH, 1961. 29 leaves. [X752-LA].

POWELL -- Powell, Rev. John. *Authentic Genealogical Memorial History of Philip Powell and His Descendants and Others...* Dayton, OH, Powell, 1880. Vol. 1... D gives xxi, 447p. [L13821; D10104].

POWELL -- Powell, John. *Memorial History of the Powell Family and Others.* Findlay, OH, Hancock County Chapter, OGS, 1986. 447 columns(?) 1. Powell family. 2. Ohio-Genealogy. [G528].

POWELL -- Russell, George E. *The Powell Family on Timsbury... and the Descendants of William Powell of Maryland and Pennsylvania.* Chesterland, OH, 1955. 8 l. [X751-MH/SU].

POWERS -- Powers, Robert Benjamin. *A Record of My Paternal Ancestors.* Delaware, OH, Powers, 1967 (1969). 361p. [L13840; D10115].

PRATHER -- Collier, Wayne. *Genealogical Chart of the Prather Family.* Newark, OH, 1954. Genealogical Table. [L13849].

PRESTON -- Preston, Francis Andrew. *History and Genealogical Brochure of the Pioneer*

Samuel Preston and Descendants. Cleveland, OH, 1947. 64p.. [DC2946; X755-FW].

PRESTON -- Van Fossan, William H. *A Brief Sketch of the Preston Family in America (Quaker Branch)...* Lisbon, OH, 1941. 10 leaves. One section of the "History of the Van Fossan Family". [X755-NY].

PREYER -- Piercy, Caroline B. *The Preyer - Andreae Family History.* Cleveland, OH, 1937. 194p.. [X756-FW/OH].

PRICE -- Jones, Ralph E. K. *The German Family of Price, Whic Migrated to Ohio... (and) Indiana. The Virginia German Price Family, 1730's...* Warren, OH, 1935. 6p. [X756-OH/SL].

PRICE -- Moore, Lewis G. *Genealogy of the Price Family.* Salem, OR, Lyle Printing & Pub. Co., 1957. 48p. [D10162].

PRICE -- Price, John Marshall. *The Price Family Tree: A Keepsake for the Descendants of Thomas David Price, 1826-1900 and His Wife, Sarah Jane Jones, 1831-1917 of the Welsh Hills, near Newark and Granville, Ohio.* New York, NY, 1957. 32p. [L13915].

PRICE -- Slaughter, Raymond D. *Slaughter and Price Genealogy: Our Ancestors, Cousins, and Descendants.* Columbus, OH, R.D. Slaughter, 1990. iii, 399p. 1. Slaughter family. 2. Price family. DC lists under SLAUGHTER.. [G531; DC3361].

PRICE -- Smith, Ella, M.D. *An Adventure in Genealogy.* Columbus, OH, priv. print., n.d. 18p. [X757-OH].

PRICKETT -- Irwin, Ruth Beckey. [G531]. See above: GADDY. [G247].

PRIDE -- Pride, Richard D. II and Faye Pride Martin. *The Joseph Pride Family of Brown and Clermont Counties, Ohio.* Georgetown, OH,

Pride Print. Press, 1985. 206p. C gives 200p. 1. Pride family. 2. Pride, Joseph, 1795-1882-Family. 3. Ohio-Genealogy. [G531; C558].

PRIOR -- Smith, Sarah August (Prior) "Mrs. C. E. Smith". *Records of Timothy Prior and Nathan Prion, Feb. 10, 1922.* Columbus, OH, 1922. 56, 2p. [L13952].

PRITCHARD -- Symmonds, Dorothy. [G532]. See above: JACOBS. [G345].

PROWANT -- Tracy, Pauline Shafer. *My Religious and Paternal Heritage of the Church of the Brethern and Genealogies of the Prowants, Burkharts, Shafers, and Dickeys.* Fostoria, OH, Gray Printing Co., 1971. 416p. [D10199].

PRUGH -- Feicht, Robert N. *Prugh Genealogy, 1705-1973.* Dayton, OH, Feicht, 1974. 329p.. [S2013; D10202].

PRYE -- Potts, Genevieve M. *The Pry - Prye Family in Pike County, Ohio.* Columbus, OH, n.d. 2p., 2-4 leaves. [X759-OH].

PUDNEY -- Pudney, W. D. *Prospective History of the Pudney Family.* Cleveland, OH, 1900. 16p. [X759-FW/LI].

PULSE -- Scott, Eelizabeth J. P. *Memorial Sketches (of the Pulse, Scott, and Faris Family,* Hillsboro, OH, Author, 1884. 6, 294p. [X760-FW/LI].

PURCELL -- NAS. *The Purcell Family Genealogical Journal.* Dayton, OH, Quarterly Published by Purcell Family Genealogical Assoc. Vol. 1 - Apr 1972 - . [X760-FW/NY].

PURDY -- Purdy, James L. *The Journal of James L. Purdy: Hopewell Township, York County, Ohio and Points in between Plus Additional Brief Information about His Life, Correspondence, and papers with everyname* *(sic) and subject index.* York, PA, South Central Pennsylvania Genealogical Society, Inc., 1990. 55p. 1. York County (Pa.)-Genealogy. 2. Richland County (Ohio)-Genealogy. 3. Purdy family. 4. Purdy, James L., 1793-1866-Diaries. [G536].

PUTNAM -- Barnard, Judge Job. *Genealogical Sketch of the Andrew Putnam Family* for the *Chataugua County Historical Society, 1916.* Conneaut, OH, Conneaut Printing Co., 1919. 29, 2p. L indicates: (Partly revised 1918.) D gives underscored title and 29p.. [L14003; D100229].

PUTNAM -- Buell, Rowena. *The Memoirs of Rufus Putnam and Certain Official Papers and Correspondence.* Published by the National Soc. of the Colonial Dames of America in the State of Ohio. Bost and New York, Houghton, Mifflin, 1903. 460p.. [X761-GF].

PUTNAM -- Cone, Mary. *Life of Rufus Putnam, with Extracts from His Journal.* Cleveland, OH, 1886. 142p. [X761-LI].

PUTNAM -- Putnam, George H. *Beanamin Barnes Putnam Genealogy.* Marietta, OH, 1956. Unpaged. [X761-GF].

PYATTE -- Shaffer, James F. *Piatt's Landing Eastbend.* Cincinnati, OH, Cincinnati Gas & Electric Co., 1978. vii 1, 110p. [C563].

PYNCHON -- Baldwin, C. C. *Pynchon.* Cleveland, OH, Leader Printing Co., 1882. p.183-204 incl. (From the Author's Candee Genealogy, Cleveland, 1882). [L14014].

Q

QUIGG -- Ferguson, Sylvia Celicia Fuson. *John Quigg, Jr. (1779-1814). Immigrant 1802, His Ancestors and Descendants: with Allied Families of Quig, Swain, Frazier, Kramer, Wiechman, Klute, Miller, and Ferguson.* Oxford, OH, E. Freeburn, 1982. 80 1. [C565].

QUIGLEY -- Freeburn, Eleanor and Dwight. *The Union of Our Quigley and Munro Families.* Brea, OH, E. Freeburn, 1982. 80 l. [C565].

QUILLEN -- Honeywell, Mary Quillan. *The Quillen Family.* Columbus, OH, Honeywell, 1966. 32, 7 leaves. [D10253].

R

RABER -- NAS. *Raber Family History, 1837-1937. Reunion Held at Archbold, Ohio, 1937.* Archbold, OH, 1937. 20p. NP, n.d. [X765-FW].

RAMEY -- Clark, Louise Sheerman. [G521]. See above: BALES. [G32].

RAMSEYER -- Liechty, John A. *Brief Outline Containing List of Names of Families Connected with Ramseyer - Rich Reunion.* Louisville, OH, 1907. 87p. [X767-FW].

RAND -- Keen, Ray A. *Hayes Rand; Pioneer from Ohio to Kansas, 1854-1914.* Manhattan, KS, 1973. 58 leaves. [X767-FW/KH].

RANDALL -- Knack, Mary Ann. *Where Are Your Roots? Randall and Crockett Family History.* Baltimore, MD, Gateway Press, Toledo, OH, Knack, M.A., 1981. ix, 202p. [C569].

RANDALL -- Mallett, Manley William. *Our Randall, Largent, Cassady Ancestors.* Columbus, OH, Mallett, 1978. 48p., 4 leaves of plates. [C569].

RANDOLPH -- Randolph, Clarence Coulson. *Family History. A History of the Ancestors and Descendants of C. C. Randolph.* Alliance, OH, Review Pub. Co., 1908. 32p. D gives underscored title. [L14089; D10293].

RANKIN -- Koch, Felix, J. *Marking the Old 'Abolition Holes'. (In Ohio Archaelogical and Historical Quarterly).* Columbus, OH, 1913. v. 22., p. 308-318. An account of the family farm... at Ripley, Ohio where slaves were aided to escape after crossing the Ohio River. [L14103].

RARDIN -- Woodruff, Audrey L. W. *Guide to the Randolph Family File, The Records & Notes of Dr. Joseph Spangler Rardin of Portsmouth, Ohio (1862-1945) at the Fort Wayne Library, Fort Wayne, Indiana.* Kansas City, MO, 1970. 27 leaves. [X769-NY].

RANSOM -- Ransom, Mervin. *Four Ohio Ransom Lines from Robert Ransom (1636-1697).* Decorah, IA, Anundsen Pub. Co., 1990. 1. v. (various pagings). 1. Ransom family. 2. Ransom, Robert, ca.1636-1697-Family. 3. Ohio-Genealogy. [G542].

RATHBONE -- Neikirke, Floyd E. *The Story of Jonathan Rathbone, Jr.* Clyde, OH, Neikirke, 1960. 35 leaves. Reprint of weekly seriel published Oct 8, 1965 - Jun 23, 1960 by the Clyde (Ohio) Enterprise. [D10317].

RATHBONE -- Neikirke, Floyd E. *The Story of Jonathan Rathbone, Jr., a Kinsman of Sandusky County, Ohio by the Questing Yankee - Floyd E. Neikirk.* Bessemer, AL, 1960. 35 leaves. [X770-MH].

RAUCH -- Rauch, Charles A. *Peter and Anna (Bowen) Rauch Lineage.* Arcanus, OH, C. Rauch. 1961. 1 v. (unpaged). 1. Rauch family. 2, Rauch, Peter, 1807-1891-Family. 3. Ohio-Genealogy. [G543].

RAY -- Froehlich, Dean. *Ray Families in Noble County, Indiana, Guernsey County, Ohio, Ohio County, Virigina, and Washington County, Pennsylvania.* NP. 1982, xvii, 147p., 3p. of plates. [C572; DS580; VV154; VP184].

READ -- Rouse, Alice Read. <u>The Reads and Their Relatives</u> *Being an Account of Colonel Element and Madam Read of Bushy Forest, Lunenberg County, Virginia, Their Eight Children, Their Descendants and Allied Families.* Cincinnati, OH, Johnson & Hardin

Press, 1930. xi, 688p. D gives underscored title. [L14170; D10343].

READ -- Read, H. E. H. *Thirteen Generations of Reads in America*. Toldeo, OH, 1976. 41p. [X773-FW].

READE -- Meadows, Fanny L. S. *Descendants of Reads or Reed; William Reade and Mable (Kendall) His Wife, Supply Reed and Susannah (Byam) His Wife, John Reed and Rebecca (Bearce) His Wife*. Cleveland, OH, J. M. Ames, 1937. 225, 59p. [X773-FW/LI/MH/NY].

REAM -- Ream, Solomon. *A Genealogical History of the Ream Family in Fairfield County, Ohio*. Cleveland, OH, Central publ. house, 1908. 41p. [X773-FW/NY].

RECORDS -- Records, William H. *Ancestry and Family Record of Rev. Samuel Records*. Fairborn, OH, 1964. 37 leaves. Copy of book made in 1902, supplemented with additional material. [X774-KH/OH/SP].

RECTOR -- Eckert, Helen. *The Rector Family of Pickaway County, Ohio* "The Push to the West". Cleveland, OH, 1953. 18, 4, 4 leaves. D gives underscored title. X omits "Ohio" in title and gives 18p. [D10359; X774-OH/SL].

REDD -- Doolittle, Melissa R. *Nathaniel Redd and His Descendants*. Akron, OH, Doolittle, 1980. 56 leaves. [C573].

REDDEN -- Uhrbock, Richard Stephen. *The Stephen J. Redden Family of Worcester County, Maryland*. Athens, OH, Uhrbock, 1960. 20 leaves. [L14195; NG82; D10361].

REDDEN -- Uhrbock, Richard Stephen. *John and Nehemiah Redden of Worcester County, Maryland*. Athens, OH, Uhrbock, 1966. 10 leaves. [L14196; NG82].

REDDING -- Ingersoll, Louise Van Harlingen. *One Branch of the Redding Family; Deniston Family of Preble County, Ohio; Van Harlingen* *and Related Families; Bible Records.* NP, 1946-47. 108 leaves. [DS585].

REDFOX -- Titus, Elroy Wilson. *A History of the Redfox and Related Families; with Detailed Information on the Families of Kesselring, Sparling, and Hewson... and... Alger.* Columbus, OH, Titus, 1975. 447p. [DS589; X774-FW/LA/OH/PH].

REED -- Bartlett, Vera M. *Descendants of John Leonard Reed, Leonard Reed, John Reed, and David Reed.* Magnolia, OH, 1944, 18 l. Supplement to the History and Genealogy of the Reed Family by W. H. Reed, 1929. [X775-FW/NY].

REED -- Lipsett, Linda Otto. *Pieced From Ellen's Quilt; Ellen Spaulding Reed's Letters and Story - 1st ed.* Dayton, OH, Halstead & Meadow's Pub., 1991. 223p. 1. Reed, Ellen Spaulding-Family. 2. Reed, Ellen Spaulding-Correspondence. 3. Reed family. 4. Spalding family. 5. Women-United States-Biography. 6. Pioneers-Wisconsin-History-19th century. 7. Ludlow (Vt.)-Biography. 8. Ludlow (Vt.)-Genealogy. 9. Friendship quilts-United States-History-19th century. [G546].

REED -- Charles I. *The Reeds of Belmont, Guernsey, and Noble Counties in Ohio.* Columbus, OH, 1968. 15, 19 l. [X775-OH].

REEMSNYDER -- NAS. *Family History of Herman Frederick Reemsnyder and His Descendants.* Columbus, OH, 1908. 238p.. [X776-FW].

REESE -- Reese, Helen J. *Descendants of Johannes Ries / Reese.* Boardman, OH, H.J. Reese, 1990. ix, 164p. 1. Reese family. 2. Ries, Johannes, 1753 or 4-ca. 1840-Family. 3. Ohio-Genealogy. [G547].

REEVES -- Bacus, Elizabeth R. *Reeves Family of Missouri, (by way of England, Virginia, Kentucky, Ohio, and Indiana.)* NP, n.d. 7, 4p., 5 leaves. [X776-FW; VV155].

REEVES -- Haney, Alice Blue. *Thomas and Mary Reeves, Charles County, Maryland.* Columbus, OH, Haney, 1967. 36 leaves. [D10401].

REICHELDERFER -- Reichelderfer, Laura A. B. *Genealogy of Some Pioneer Families Originating in Pickaway County, Ohio and Vicinity.* Delaware, OH, 1965. 63p. [X777-FW].

REIFF -- Rife, John Merle. *John George Reiff and His Descendants.* New Concord, OH, Reiff Press, 1960. 73p. [L14230].

REINHART -- Ardner, Rose A. *Reinhart (Family).* Tiffin, OH, 1971. 172p. [X778-FW].

REINOEHLS -- Reiser, Mary K. *The Reinoehls, Beginning 1758.* Portsmouth, OH, Jacksonville, FL, 1941. 33 (i.e. 35p.) [X778-OH/OL].

REISING -- Hamel, Claude Charles. *Genealogy of the Family of Antony and Ella M. (Baatz) (Derby) Reising of Florence, Florence Twp., Erie County, Ohio.* Amherst, OH, 1951. 3 leaves. [L14232].

REISINGER -- Ayres, Thomas D. *Reisinger Genealogy: Some of the Descendants of Jacob Reisinger of Columbia Twp., Ohio. - 2nd ed.* Saginaw, MI, Ayres, 1977. 44 leaves. C gives: "Based upon 'The Reisinger Family Tree' of 1946 by Hazel M. Reisinger." 1. Reisinger family. 2. Resginger, Jacob, 1808-1885- Family. 3. Ohio-Genealogy. [G548; C576].

REISINGER -- Ayres, Thomas D. *Reisinger Genealogy: Descendants of Jacob Reisinger of Columbia Twp., Ohio. - 3rd ed.* Simsbury, CT, T.D. Ayres, 1986. 100 leaves. 1. Reisinger family. 2. Resginger, Jacob, 1808-1885- Family. 3. Ohio-Genealogy. [G548].

REPPERT -- Foot, Eunice M. *Reppert and Related Lines.* Akron, OH, Crawford, Co., 1975. 104p. [S2070; D10431].

REX -- Snith, Sarah Augusta (Prior) "Mrs. C.E. Smith". *James Rex and Wife Rhonda (Milliken) Rex Family and Family Military Data.* Columbus, OH, 1922. 1, 2p. [L14265].

REYNOLDS -- Brown, Jean Casteel Reynolds. *The Reynolds Family of Dayton.* Dayton, OH, Reynolds & Reynolds, Co., 1949. 87p. [D10437].

REYNOLDS -- Ellis, Carolyn B. *Reynolds Family History and Genealogy, 1603-1933.* Findlay, OH, 1934. 2, 2-49 numb. leaves. [L14284].

REYNOLDS -- Imhof, Olive Reynolds. *Reynolds of Anne-Arundel and Washington Counties Maryland and of Lawrence County, Pennsylvania.* Wooster, OH, Bell & Howell Micropublishers, 1973. ca. 200p. [D10438; VP186].

REYNOLDS -- Strock, Richard M. [G551]. See above: FUNK. [G246].

RHODES -- Anderson, Alvin L. *Rhoades and Allied Families: Descendants of David and Celia (Copple) Rhoades.* Canton, OH, A. L. Anderson, 1989. iv, 204p. 1. Rhodes family. 2. Rhoades, David, 1810-1876-Family. 3. Middle West-Genealogy. [G552].

RHODES -- Rhodes, Troas Etta. *Some of the Early Settler of Pennsylvania, Virginia, Missouri, North Carolina, Indiana, Ohio, Illinois.* Palm Desert, CA, Artisan Printing Co., 1977. iii, 236, iv p.. [D10465; VV156].

RICE -- Rice, Charles Elmer. *By the Name of Rice; An Historical Sketch of Deacon Edmund Rice, the Pilgrim (1594-1663) Founder of the English Family of Rice in the United States and of His Descendants to the Fourth Generation...* Alliance, OH, Press of the Williams Printing Co., 1911, 96, 2p. [L14313].

RICH -- Booher, Emma Rich. *Rich Hill, Westmoreland County, Virginia, 1740 to Rich*

Hill, Noble County, Ohio, 1880. Senecaville, OH, Booher, 1976. 167p. [C580; X784-FW; VV156].

RICH -- Howells, Joseph. *Pioneer Life in Ashtabula County. (In Ohio Archaeological and Historical Quarterly).* Columbus, OH, 1927. Vol. XXXVI, p. 551-562. [L14328].

RICH -- Rich, George. *Genealogy. Descendants of Jonathan Rich...* Columbus, OH, Press of the Nitschke Bros. 1892. 1, 5-39p. [L14325].

RICH -- Rich, George. *Early Rich History.* Cleveland, OH, Rich, 1922. 46p. Bound with: Genealogy: Descendants of Jonathan Rich, 1892. 39p. [D10484].

RICHARDS -- Smith, Ophia D. *The Life and Times of Giles Richards (1820-1860).* Columbus, OH, The Ohio State Archaeological and Historical Society, 1936. xii, 130p. [L14334].

RICHARDSON -- Currie, Barbera Calder. *Richardson Pioneers in Southeastern Minnesota: Descendants of Thomas Stoddard Richardson.* Fairborn, OH, B.C. Currie and J.F. Vogt, 1987. 1 v. unpaged. 1. Richardson family. 2. Richardson, Thomas Stoddard, 1780-1853-Family. 3. Minnesota-Genealogy. [G553].

RICHARDSON -- Currie, Barbera Calder, ed. *Richardson Chronicles 1590-ca 1700, Westmill, England thru Woburn, Mass. Bay Colony.* Collected by Richardson Descendants. Fairborn, OH, B.C. Currie, 1988. 2 v. 1. Richardson family. 2. England-Genealogy. 3. Massachusetts-Genealogy. [G553].

RICHARDSON -- Richardson, John E. *The Richardson Family in America.* Cincinnati, OH, Author, 1939. 11p. [X785-CH].

RICHARDSON -- Richardson, Robert N. *John Cunningham Richardson (1788-1820) and His*

Descendants. Middletown, OH, Richardson, 1979. 85p. [C581; D10504].

RICHEY -- Whedon, Nellie Woods. *Richey - Woods - Baum of Ohio.* Ann Arbor, MI, Edwards Brothers, 1940. vi, 97p. [D10514; X786-FW/LA].

RICHMOND -- Hamel, Claude Charles. *Genealogy of a Branch of the Richmond Family Which Came from Rhode Island to Ohio and Settled in Amherst Township, Lorain County, Ohio.* Amherst, OH, 1949. 9 l. [L14368].

RICHMOND -- Hamel, Claude Charles. *Genealogy of the Richmond Family Which Came from Rhode Island to Ohio and Settled in Amherst Township, Lorain County, Ohio. Rev. 1955.* Amherst, OH, 1955?. 10 l. [A561].

RICKETTS -- Davis, W. E. *The Records Lineage: John, John, Jr., Josiah, Spencer Alexander, John, etc.* Glendale, OH, W.E. Davis, 1985. 1 v. (various foliations) 1. Ricketts family. 2. Kentucky-Genealogy. [G554].

RIDDLE -- Hoeman, Andree Sieverin, et al. *A Partial History of the Riddle - Beavers Families of Botetourt County, Virginia, Highland County, Ohio, Decatur and Page Counties, Iowa: Including Cook, Rader, Bender, Painter, Harschbarger, Ammen, Ranck, and Other Allied Families.* Des Moines, IA, R. E. Hays & Associates, Dallas Ctr., IA, for the Bernard Riddle Reunion, 1981. 409p. D gives no pagination. D & VV give underscored title. [C583; D10523; VV156].

RIDENOUR -- Ridenour, John. *The Ridenour Family: History and Genealogy.* Stone Creek, OH, Ridenour, 1973. 90, 2p. FW gives (10), 90p. [DC3081; D10524; X787-FW].

RIFE -- Rife, Geo. W. *John and Mary J, Rife of Green County, Ohio. Their Ancestors and Descendants.* Richmond, IN, J. Merle Rife,

1935. 42p. L indicates: 3rd ed. rev. by J. Merle Rife. [L14401; D10534].

RIFE -- Rife, John Merle and William Randolph Rife. *John and Mary J. Rife of Greene County, Ohio. Their Ancestors and Descendants.* Amelia, OH, Reiff Press, 1980. x, 73p. Previous ed. published in 1960 under title: John George Reiff and Descendants. [C584].

RIGHTER -- Righter, C. B. *Righter Genealogy, The Ohio Branch.* Iowa City, IA, 1974. 104, 8 leaves. [X789-FW].

RILEY -- Orlaska, Irene Mary. *The Roots and Branches of Nicholas and Hannah Riley, Knox County, Ohio, 1800-1985.* U.S., I.M. Orlaska, 1987. 190, 5p. 1. Riley family. 2. Riley, Nicholas, ca. 1778-1866-Family. 3. Ohio-Genealogy. [G556].

RILEY -- Riley, Jesse Keyser. *The Eight Volumes of the Riley Manuscripts.* Galena, OH, Mrs. W.R. Alban, 1989. ii, 248p. Revision of: Second printing of the Riley Family history. 1. Riley family. [G557].

RIMMER -- Symmonds, Dorothy. [G557]. See above: JACOBS. [G345].

RINEHART -- Hasson, Ethel W. *Rinehart.* Centerburg, OH, 1943. 9 leaves. [X789-OH].

RINEHART -- Henning, Emma. *The Ulrich Reinhart Family and Descendants, 1704-1985.* Dayton, TN, E.A. Henning, 1986. x, 432p. 1. Rinehart family. 2. Rinehart, Ulrich, 1704-1787-Family. 3. Ohio-Genealogy. [G557].

RINGS -- Hirschler, Paul. *Johannes Rings, Sr. Family History, Dec 4, 1779 to 1966.* Bluffton, OH, 1966. 175p. [X790-FW].

RISELING -- Orland, Frank Addison. *A Survey of the Riseling Family, Anderson Jackson*

Riseling Branch. Centerburg, OH, 1961. iii, 35, 8, 6 leaves. [L14421].

RISSER -- Bassett, Josephine R. *The Risser Family. A History of the Family and Genealogy of Those Descendants of John Risser "of Osthofen in the Palatinate" Who Emigrated to the United State and Settled in Ohio and Iowa.* Minneapolis, MN, 1947. 3, 3, 4-62 leaves. [X791-FW/MH].

RITTER -- Smith, Ned Burton. *The Ritter Families, 1705-1938.* Youngstown, OH, 1938. 1 leaf. [L14432].

RIVES -- King, Margaret Rives. *A Memento of Ancestors and Ancestral Homes, Written for Nieces and Nephews.* Cincinnati, OH, R. Clarke & Co., 1890. 139p. [L14434].

ROBENS -- Miller, Janic (sic) H. *The Robens Family, Connecticut, New York, Ohio and Unpublished Records of Carpenters and Bentley, New York.* Washington, DC, 1961. 81 leaves. [X793-FW/NY].

ROBINSON -- Barnes, Milford E., Mary E. (Robinson) Barnes, Ross A. Robinson. *Five Pioneer Robinson Families in Guernsey County, Ohio; A Genealogical Study on the Families of Samuel Robinson, Henry Robinson, William Robinson, James Robinson, and Mary (Robinson) Thomas.* Iowa City, IA, 1965. 50 leaves. [A566].

ROGERS -- Dallas, Zella Rogers. [G563]. See above: DALLAS. [G172].

ROGERS -- Jones, Orville W. *Descendants of John Rogers and Katherine P. (Johnson) Rogers.* Felicity, OH, Jones, 1971. 3 v. DAR has volume 1 only. [A567; D10690].

ROHR -- Smith, Gladys Marie Rohr. *Family Tree of Michael Rohr <u>b. 9/29/1811, d. 3/12/1909 and</u> Mary Eva Lenhart (Leonard)<u>, b.</u>*

2/22/1822, d. 1/21/1904 - 2nd ed. Navarre, OH, G.M.R. Smith, 1984. 2 v. (v, 111 leaves). 1. Rohr family. 2. Ohio-Genealogy. C omits underscored part of title and gives: <[1984- > v. <2 >. [G564; C592].

ROHRBOUGH -- Rohrbough, Merrill H. *A Family Genealogy.* Dayton, OH, M. H. Rohrbough, 1969- . 1 Vol. (Loose Leaf). FW gives 69 p. (paging irregular). [X801-FW/NY].

ROHRER -- Weiss, Lister O. *The Saga of a People.* A History of Johannes Rohrer with a Genealogy of His Descendants. Akron, OH, Weis, Lancaster Penn, Getz, (L gives Mt. Joy, Pa. Bulletin), 1939. 41p. D gives underscored title. [L14622; D10713].

ROHRER -- Weiss, Lister O. and Edna M. *Supplement to the Johannes Rohrer Family History, 1939-1967.* Orville, OH, 1967. 51 leaves. [L14622].

ROMIG -- Romig, W. H. *Renunio of John Romig's Descendants and the Centennial Celebration of the Settlement of the Homestead. Historical Papers on the Ohio Branch of the Romig Family.* Washington, IA, Gazette Print., 1903. 15p. [X802-FW].

ROSBRUGH -- Rosebraugh, Wilson F. *The Roseborough Family.* Newark, OH, 1955. 11 leaves. [L14672].

ROSE -- Linnell, Mary Belle. *A Partial Genealogy of the Rose Families of Granville, Ohio.* Toledo, OH, (L gives: NP), Linnell, 1968. 58 leaves. [L14681; D10743].

ROSE -- Rose, Charles Ensign. *A History of the Roses.* Warren, OH, Rose, 1939. 37 l. [D10746].

ROSE -- Rose, Charles E. *History of the Roses and Genealogy of One Branch and Their*

Allied Families in America. Warren Ohio, Warren Business College, 1939. 33p. [X803-FW].

ROSE -- Smith, Sarah Augusta Prior (Mrs. Charles Ellsworth Smith). *Rose, Miller, Pryor, (Prior) Ekelberry. Charts and Records.* Columbus, OH, 1922. 2, 86p. [L14676].

ROSLEY -- Rowley, Charles Scott. *The Village of North Fairfield, Ohio, and a Rolling Stone: An Autobiography of Charles Scott Rowley, 1878-1960... Materials toward a Genealogy of the Rowley Family...* Baltimore, MD, A. G. Rose, 1975. xii, 109 l. [S2131].

ROUSE -- Lloyd, Emma Rouse. *Clasping Hands With Generations Past.* Lloyd, (Cincinati, OH, Wiesen-Hart Press), 1932. 6, 3-228, 7p. D gives 228p. Contents: Rouse family, - Zimmerman family, - Tanner family, - Henderson family, - McClure family, - Porter family, - Allied families, - Our colored folk. [L14741; D10779].

ROUSH -- NAS. *In Memoriam. Godfrey Roush and Wives... 50th Annual Reunion of Stark Co. (Ohio) Roush and Allied Families...* North Canton, Ohio. Columbus, OH, 1939. 5p. [X807-OH].

ROUSH -- Rouse, Nancy E. *John Rouse of Virginia and His Descendants, 1717-1980.* Cincinnati, OH, Estate of Nancy E. Rouse, 1982. viii, 250p., 4 leaves of plates. [C599; VV161].

ROUSH -- Roush, Rev. L. L. *The Roush Family in America (Their Contributions to the "New Country").* In Ohio Archaeological and Historical Quarterly, Columbus, OH, 1927. Vol XXXVI, p. 116-144. [L14743].

ROUSH -- Roush, Lester L. *Military Service of Nine Brothers in the Cause of American*

Independence (Revolutionary War). Gallipolis, OH, 1971. 11p. [S2129].

ROUSH -- Roush, Lester Le Roy. *The Roush Family in America. History of the Roush Family in America, from Its Founding by John Adam Rausch in 1736 to the Present Time.* Strasburg, VA, Shenandoah Pub House, 1928 - (63). 3 v. v 3. Athens, Ohio, printed by Lawless Press. X gives underscored title and Vol. 3 of 3 vol. set and showing printed by Shenandoah Pub. House, 1963. [L14744; X807-LA].

ROWLAND -- NAS. *Rowland Genealogy, Joseph Rowland of Lancaster Co., Pa. and Ashland and Wyandotte Cos., Ohio, 1760-1927.* Lansing, MI, Mich. State Lib., 1952. 11p. [X808-FW; VP192].

ROWLAND -- Clay, Roy U. [G572]. See above: FULTON. [G245].

ROWLEY -- Rowley, Charles Scott. *The Village of North Fairfield, Ohio, and a Rolling Stone: An Autobiography of Charles Scott Rowley, 1878-1960.* Baltimore, MD, A. G. Rose, 1975. xii, 109 leaves, (The family document series, No. 11.) [X809-FW/NY/OH].

ROY -- Roy, Elmon Harold. *Our Roy Ancestors. - Rev.* Springfield, OH, E.H. Roy, 1985. 42 leaves. 1. Roy family. [G572].

ROY -- Roy, Elmon Harold. *Roy Family Historical Documents.* Springfield, OH, E.H. Roy, 1985. 112 leaves. 1. Roy family. [G572].

ROYER -- Francis, Jay G. *Royer (Family).* Dayton, OH, G. B. Eley, 1967. Various pagings. Reprinted from his Royer Family in America, pub. 1926. [X809-FW].

RUBINS -- Wood, Anne Farrell (Higgins). *The Story of Most of the Descendants of Edward*

Rubins, Jr. and Ann Blow of Lincolnshire, England and Ohio. NP, 1973. 253 leaves. [S2133].

RUCHTI -- Brady, Mary Ann Ward. Ruchti, Deppen, Yeakley, Stonebraker, Fruits, Newkirk, Ward Genealogy... Maumee, OH, Brady, 1982. iii, 190p. [DC3175].

RUFFNER -- Ruffner, Doris E. L. Peter Ruffner and His Descendants. Pickerington, OH, 1966, 377p. [X811-FW].
-- Supplement. 1969. 378-543p. [X811-OH].

RUNYON -- Runyon, Forrest M. History of the Runyon Family. Columbus, OH, 1949. 2 vols. [X812-FW].

RUPLE -- Osborn, C. M. Ruple Family; History of the Descendants of Baltus Ruple (B. 1740). Chiefly in Cuyahoga County, Ohio. Cleveland, OH, 1923. 1 vol. [X812-WR].

RUPP -- Rupp, Allen E. Descendants of Johannes Rupp. Marietta, OH, 1976. 199p. [X812-FW/OH].

RUSSELL -- Ewing, Ettie Misner. History of the Robert Russell Family. Canfield, OH, Mahoning Dispatch Press, 1936. 67p. [D10858].

RUSSELL -- Knouf, Osee O. J. Russell Family History; Record of the Known Descendants of John -- Russell, Sr. Who Was in Adams County, Ohio by March 1798, His First Wife, Frances... La Grange County, IL, D.A.R., 1968. 183p. [X814-FW].

RUSSELL -- Pooler, Marjorie Russell. A Russell History, Valentine Russell and His Descendants. Urbana, OH, Pooler, 1983. iii, 21p. C gives underscored title. [C604; DS630].

RUSSELL -- Russell George Ely. Russell Families of Seventeenth Century England.

Chesterfield, OH, 1955. 25p.
[L14586; NG86].

RUST -- Griffin, William L. *Rust: A History
of the Clark County, Ohio, Pioneer Family.*
1st ed. Chicago, IL, Adams Press, 1973.
177p. FW gives 180p. and does not indicate
edition. [S2143; X815-FW].

RUST -- Saxbe, William Bart. [G577]. See
above: GUNN. [G280].

RYBOLT -- Norris, Rita. *The Family of
Michael Rybolt & Rachel H. Scudder.* Harrison,
OH, E. Shaver, 1987. 1 v. (various pagings).
1. Rybolt family. 2. Rybolt, Michael, 1782-
1870-Family. 3. Scudder, Rachel H., 1777-
1846-Family. 4. Scudder family.
[G577].

S

SAFFORD -- Culbertson, Sidney Methiot. *The
Ohio Valley Saffords.* Denver, CO, The Kistler
Press, 1932. 2, vi, 240p.
[L14907; NG86; D10895].

SAGER -- Sager, Ward. *Sager Genealogy.*
Ravenna, OH, n.d. 25 leaves. [X818-FW].

SAMPSON -- Ellis, Carolyn B. *Sampson Family
History and Genealogy, 1753-1939, Maryland,
Ohio.* Findlay, OH, 1938. 3, 108p.
[X820-MH/OH].

SAMPSON -- Marg-An. *Genealogical Faces: Of
Seen and Unknown Persons: Chapbook.*
Cincinnati, OH, Marg-An, 1983. 24, ix-xii p.
[C609].

SAMPSON -- Todd, Edwin S. *New Light on the
History of the Sampson Family; with Special
Reference to the Line of Descent from Jane
Sampson to Her Granddaughter Marietta Wood
Todd.* Springfield, OH, 1939. 10 numb. l.
[L14947].

SAMPSON -- Turner, Van Edwin. *Descendants of John and Elizabeth Sansom*. N. Ridgeville, OH, V. E. Turner, 1982. viii, 72p. [C609].

SANDERS -- Harris, Mrs. Merie Hicks. *The Sanders Family of Virginia, Kentucky, Ohio & Iowa*. Cedar Rapids, IA, 1977. 28 leaves. [NG87].

SANDERS -- Rich, George. *Genealogy, Ancestors and Descendants of John Sanders, Fort Covington, N.Y.* Cleveland, OH, 1922. 1, 5-42, 6p. [L14962].

SARCHETT -- Sarchett, Cyrus Parkinson Beatty. *The Genealogy of the Sarchett Family, from the Island of Guernsey to Cambridge, Ohio in 1806*. Cambridge, OH, Herald Print, 1902. 11p. [L14996].

SATER -- McClure, Stanley William. *Sater, Hadges, Johnson, Wakefield, McClure, and Hathaway Families, Hamilton County, Ohio*. Harrison, OH, 194_. 14 leaves. Library copy imperfect: McClure and Hathaway families? wanting. [L15016].

SATER -- McClure, Stanley William. *The Descendants of William Sater (1793-1849), Crosby Township, Hamilton County, Ohio*. Harrison, OH, S.W. McClure, 1986. 89, xii, 6 leaves, 21 leaves of plates. 1. Sater family. 2. Sater, William, 1793-1849-Family. 3. Ohio-Genealogy. [G583].

SAUNDERS -- Rich, George. *Genealogy, Ancestors and Descendants of John Sanders, Fort Covington, N.Y.* Cleveland, OH, 1922. 42, 6p. [L15024].

SAYRE -- Sayre. Harrison Monell. *Descendants of Deacon Ephraim Sayre*. Columbus, OH, 1942. viii, 75p. [D11004].

SAYRE -- Sayre, Mortimer Freeman. *Brown and Sayre Ancestry; Three Centuries in Northern,*

New Jersey. *Limited ed.* Columbus, OH, 1971. 132p. [S2177].

SCAGGS -- Sparks-Edwards, Lucille. *A Perspective on The Family Skaggs called Big Sandy Skaggs.* Lima, OH, Edwards Enterprises, 1978. v. <1 >. [C613].

SCARBOROUGH -- Boone, Roger S. *Some Quaker Families: Scarborough, Haworth.* Springfield, OH, R. S. Boone, 1983-. _ v. See DAR Shelflist for Library Holdings. [DC3216].

SCARRITT -- Pearson, Ralph E. *The History of the Scarritt Clan in America.* Middletown, OH, Pearson, 1938. 68p. [D11011].

SCHALES -- Schales, Otto. *The Shales Book.* Columbus, OH, 1983. 396p. 1. Schales family. 2. Germany-Genealogy. [G586; C614; NG87].

SCHEID -- Scheid, George. *Scheid Book; A Genealogy, History, and Biographical Story of the Scheid Family in Germany and America, 1635-1952.* Monroeville, OH, Author, 1952. 2 vols. [X828-FW].

SCHELLHOUSE -- Hamel, Claude Charles. *Genealogy of the Shellhouse Family of Vermillion Township, Erie, Co., Ohio, Which Married into the Koppenhaffer and Leidheiser Families.* Amherst, OH, 1948. 6 l. [L15080].

SCHERGER -- Gardiner, Duncan B. [G587]. See above: ANTL. [G16].

SCHERGER -- Scherger, Roger F. *The Schergers Who Voyaged to America.* Piqua, OH, R. F. Scherger, 1983. 151p. [C615].

SCHERRETTS -- Richards, Sylvia. *Arnold Scherretts Memorial.* *Bicentennial Ed.* Willard, OH, Richards, 1979. 64p. [NG87; D11032].

SCHLABACH -- Miller, Emanuel J. *Daniel Schlabach Family History; Descendants of*

Daniel Schlabacg and Sally Kaufman. Sugar
Creek, OH, Royal Printing Co., 1942. 32p.
[L15097].

SCHLABACH -- Slabaugh, John M. *Knit
Together in Love: Moses Schlabach, 1859-1932,
and Lydia Yoder, 1868-1959: Their Ancestry
and Their Descendants.* Uniontown, OH, J. M.
Slabaugh, 1987. 170p. 1. Schlabach family.
2. Yoder family. 3. Schlabach, Moses, 1859-
1932-Family. 4. Yoder, Lydia, 1868-1959-
Family. 5. Pennsylvania-Genealogy. 6. Ohio-
Genealogy. [G588].

SCHLEGEL -- Schlegel, Kenneth P. *Johann
Frederick Schlegel: 1775-1856; History of
Johann Frederick Schlegel and Descendants,
1777-1970.* Coschocton, OH, 1970. 2A, 282p.
[S2189].

SCHLEGELMILCH -- Baldwin, John D.
*Descendants of the Widow Elizabeth
Schlegelmilch of Cleveland, Ohio.* Cleveland,
OH, 1943. 34p. Mansucript. [X830-WR].

SCHLIESSER -- Eberly, Catharine L. S.
*Schliesser's (sic) of Okolona and Related
Families.* Toledo, OH, 1976. 26p.
[X830-FW].

SCHLOSSER -- Sabins, Emma Jo Schlosser.
*Family History and Descendants of Jacob
Schlosser (1829-1906) and His Wife, Eva
Margaret Karrer (1829-1892).* Rocky River, OH,
1971. i, 149p. [S2190].

SCHLOTE -- Arndt, Barbara. *Dorothea Schlote
and Her Family: A Remembrance.* Cleveland,
OH, B. Arndt, 1989. xix, 99p. 1. Schlote
family. 2. Schlote, Dorothes, 1888-   -
Family. 3. Ontario-Genealogy. 4. Canada-
Genealogy. 5. Mennonites-Ontario-Genealogy.
[G588].

SCHMIDT -- Singer, Dorothy. [G589]. See
above: FLATH. [G231].

SCHNELL -- Schnell, Harry A. *Schnell - Bader Family.* Orrville, OH, 1946. 25p. [X832-FW].

SCHOENBERG -- Ginnery, Penny & Katy. *The Schoenenberger - Shonebarger Family, 1832-1984.* Lancaster, OH, P & K Ginnery, 1984. ix, 185p. [C617].

SCHOONOVER -- Lunsford, Ollie Collett. *The Families of Van Schoonhover, Schoonhoven, Schoonover: Mostly Descendants of Benjamin Schoonover of Randolph County, Wast Virginia.* Cortland, OH, O.M.C. Lunsford, [between 1983 and 1986]. viii, 162p. 1. Schoonover family. 2. Schoonover, Benjamin, 1745-1838-Family. 3. West Virginia-Genealogy. [G590].

SCHOTT -- Schott, Gleneta. *The Schott Family, Descendants of Johann Andreas Schott, of Ehrbach, Germany, and from Hessendarmstadt, Bavaria, Germany, and Jacob Schmidt Family, Descendants, Ancestor to Mary Schmidt, Wife of Adam Schott.* Dublin, OH, 1975. 12, 3p. [X833-OH].

SCHOTTENSTEIN -- Schottenstein, Morris. *The Schottensteins: A Family Biographical Essay: "the Heshel Schottenstein Family in Columbus, Ohio".* Columbus, OH, Orion Publications, 1987- v. <1 >. Contents: v. 1. 1908-1930. 1. Schottenstein family. 2. Schottenstein, Heshel, 1861-1941-Family. 3. Columbus (Ohio)-Genealogy. 4. Jews-Genealogy. 5. Lithuania-Genealogy. [G590].

SCHRACK -- Schneider, Norris F. *Nell Schrack.* Zanesville, OH, 1949. 10p. Reprinted from the Sunday Times Signal, March 27 and April 13, 1949. Zanesville, Ohio. [X833-OH].

SCHUBERT -- Davis, W. E. *The Schubert Family: Friedolin, Emma, Matilda, Rosa, George, Josphine, Frank, William.* Glendale, OH, W.E. Davis. 1985. 1 v. (various

foliations). 1. Schubert family. 2.
Schubert, Friedolin, 1832-1892-Family.
[G591].

SCHWALM -- NAS. *Johannes Schwalm, The
Hessian.* Lyndhurst, OH, Johannes Schwalm
Historical Association, 1976. viii, 296p.
[C620; X836-FW/NY/PH].

SCOFIELD -- NAS. *Scofield - Schofield
Family of Connecticut, Maryland, Ohio.* NP,
1973, 16 leaves. [X836-OH].

SCOGIN -- Lindsey, Helen B. *Elisha Scogin
and Family of Ohio and Indiana.* NP, Author,
1931. 35 1. [X837-FW].

SCOTT -- Benes, Frances Scott. *Our Scott
Heritage. An Account of the Ancestors and
Descendants of John Hillis Lettson Scott
(1822-1904) and His Wife Eliza Jane Prouty
(1830-1907) of Ohio, Iowa, and Missouri.* Palm
Desert, CA, Benes, 1989. 90, 9 1. [DC3236].

SCOTT -- Dayton, Lewis Scott. *Descendants of
Thomas Scott of Muskingum and Coshocton
Counties, Ohio.* La Moille, IL, 1956. 29, 2
leaves. A re-issue of the 1956 ed. with a few
corrections and a "Supplement: Corrections and
additional data received after publication
(leaves 22-31). [A594]

SCOTT -- Harrell, Mary E. *The Scott Family;
An Account of Lieutenant Colonel William Scott
of Peterborough, N.A.(?) and Greenfield,
Saratoga, Co., N.Y. and His Descendants.*
Cincinnati, OH, 1967. ii, 57 leaves.
[X837-NY].

SCOTT -- Russell, Patrick. *The Moore Scott
Family.* Columbus, OH, P. Russell, 1977. iii,
128p. [C621; NG88; D11093].

SCOTT -- Vercoe, Josephine McCord. *A
Genealogical History of the Scott Family;
Descendants of Alexander Scott Who Came to*

Augusta County, Virginia, ca. 1750; with A History of the Families with which They Intermarried. Columbus, OH, 1940. 8p. 182 numb. l. [L15179; VV164].

SCUDDER -- Kloos, Roberta Scudder. *Scudder Family in Ohio.* Lattabra, CA, Kloos, 1987. 3, 135 l. [DC3240].

SCUDDER -- Norris, Rita. [G594]. See above: RYBOLT. [G577].

SCRIVEN -- Dawson, Lucy Scrivens. *The Descendants of William A. Scrivens, February 1816 - July, 1975.* Middleburg Heights, OH, Dawson, 1976. 25p. [C622].

SEAGER -- Seager, Cordelia Theis and Charles William Seager. *The Seager Families of Colonial New England: Including Descendant Lines Principally from Massachusetts, Connecticut, Rhode Island, and Certain Families of New York and Ohio.* Illahee Hills, Brevard, NC, Seager, 1978. viii, 132p. [C622].

SEARS -- Sayre, Harrison Monell. *Descendants of Deacon Ephraim Sayre.* Columbus, OH, (Ann Arbor, MI, Edwards Bros. Inc., Lithoprinters), 1942. viii, 2, 75p. [L15234].

SEARS -- Sears, Edmund H. *Pictures of the Olden Time as Shown in the Fortunes of a Family of Pilgrims.* Boston, MA, Crosby, Nichols; Cincinnati, OH, G. S. Blanchard (etc.), 1857. viii, 342, 10p. [X839-FW/PH].

SEBALD -- Wilmer, Richard A. *Sebald.* Middletown, OH, R.A. Wilmer, 1988. 108p. 1. Sebald family. 2. Sebgald, Johann Michael Carl, 1771-1838-Family. [G595].

SECHRIST -- Nye, Sarah C. *A History of the Sechrist Family.* West Salem, OH, J. Sechrist, 1919. 18p. Copied by Minn. Hist. Soc., 1979. [X840-MH].

SEEKINS -- Seekins, Paul Orville. *The Seekins Genealogy; Aaron Seekins, 1690-1750, of Middleborough Massachusetts, with Most of His Descendants.* Columbus, OH, 1970. xiv , 201p. [A597].

SEIDENSTICKER -- Shuck, Larry G. [G596]. See above: FLESHMAN. [G232].

SELBY -- Fowler, Fred Edwin. *A Short Sketch of Some of the Descendants of William Selby, Who Was Born, June 15, 1717, and His Second Wife Dorothy Booge...* Brookfield, OH, 1939. 1 v. Loose-leaf. [L15256].

SELBY -- Fowler, Fred E. *A Short Sketch of Some of the Descendants of William Selby and His Second Wife Dorotha (sic) Booge...* Brookfield, OH, 1940. 119 l. [X841-WR].

SELBY -- Fowler, Fred Edwin. *A Short Sketch of Some of the Descendants of William Selby, Who Was Born, June 15, 1717, and Dorothy Booge His Second Wife. (Revised ed., 1937-1942).* NP, 1942. 220 leaves. [X841-WR].

SELBY -- Fowler, Fred Edwin. *A Short Sketch of Some of the Descendants of William Selby, Who Was Born, June 15, 1717, and His Second Wife Dorothy Booge... 2nd ed. enl.* Brookfield, OH, 1950. 1 v. various pagings. [L15257].

SELDERS -- Warner, E. F. *Whither Comest Thou? A Brief History of the Selders Family Descendants of George Selders and Ann Leaper Selders.* Bellvue, OH, (Priv. Print.) 1911. 16p. Title changed to "Whence Comest Thou?". [X841-OH].

SELLMAN -- Sellman, W. Marshall. *John Sellman of Maryland and His Descendants.* Cincinnati, OH, Sellman, 1975. vi, 234p. [D11175; X842-CH/FW/OH].

SELLS -- Jaeger, Eva S. *Lineage of Eva Sells Jaeger.* Columbus, OH, 1929. 9 leaves. Contains clippings from New York Evening

Journal of Sat. Oct. 26, 1929.
[X842-NY].

SELLS -- Stivison, David. *The Sells - Gessells and McQuaide Families.* Union Furnace, OH, Stivison, 1979, 1979. 58, 23 leaves, 2 leaves of plates. [C625].

SEMANS -- Seamans, W. O. *Family Record of the Descendants of William Semans, Who Lived on the Eastern Shore of Maryland During the Latter Part of the 18th Century.* Delaware, OH, 1891. 69p. [X842-LI].

SENFT -- Getz, Dennis E. *Family Tree (Christmas Greetings, 1952 in Memory of My Grandparents, George Adam Senft and Wife.)* Baltic, OH, Author, 1952. Unpaged. [X842-FW/IG].

SENIOR -- Hirschler, Paul. *Johannes Rings Senior Family History, Dec. 4, 1779 to 1966. 2nd printing.* Bluffton, OH, Howard Raid, 1974. 175p. [X842-OH].

SEBREE -- Guss, Willa I. *Sebree Studies: Lineage of Charles Jenkins Sebree (1854-1913) and Collateral Lines Traced to colonial Virginia: Conjugate Lines including Barnett, Butler, Butts, Carter, Gibbs, Hord, Jarrell, Johnson, Sage, Shreves, Thomason, Watts, Wilson.* Goleden, CO, 1984. [VV165].

SEYRE -- Sayre, Harrison M. *Descendants of Deacon Ephraim Sayre.* Columbus, OH, Author, 1942. viii, 75p. [X844-OH].

SHADE -- Hoffman, Walter R. *Pioneers of Pennsylvania, Ohio and Alabama; Empire Builders Extraordinary.* Piedmont, CA, 1966. 23 leaves. [X844-OH; VP201].

SHAFER -- Abbott, Lyndon Ewing. [G599].
See above: DERR. [G186].

SHAFER -- Tracy, Pauline S. *My Religious and Paternal Heritage of the Church of the Brethren; and Genealogies of the Prowants,*

Burkharts, Shafers, and Dickeys. 1708-1968.
Fostoria, OH, Gray Print., 1971. 403p.
[X845-FW].

SHAFFNER -- Pinkerton, Mina G. *History and Descendants of Martin Shaffner.* Tiffin, OH, 1959. 256p. [X845-OH].

SHANE -- Snyder, Vivian L. *The Family of James and Elizabeth Shane.* Stubenville, OH, Jefferson County, Genealogical Society Library, 1984. 186, 111p. [C628].

SHANK -- Longenecker, John. *Gemealogical Diagram; Dedicatory to the Lineage of Adam Shank, Through His Son Henry to the Fourth Generation.* Wilmot, OH, 1908. Genealogical Table. [L15361].

SHANK -- Richards, Sylvia. *James Shanks Memorial. Bicentennial ed.* Willard, OH, Richards, 1976. xiii, 222p. [C628].

SHANKS -- Blaine, Harry S. *Ancestry of James Shanks of Huron County, Ohio.* Toledo, OH, Blaine, 1951. 60, xi p. D gives 69, xi pages. [L15263; D11217].

SHANKS -- Richards, Sylvia. *James Shanks Memorial.* Willard, OH, 1976. 222p. NG gives no pagination. [C628; NG88; D11219].

SHARP -- Barnes, M. E., M.D. and The Rev. J. A. Barnes, D. D. *James Sharp and His Descendants.* Greenville, OH, 1927. 13 numb. leaves. Bound with Authors' James Hutchison and His Descendants. REPLACED BY MICROFILM 8746 CS. [L15375].

SHARP -- Eastwood, Elizabeth Cobb Stewart. *Henry Sharp (c1737-1800) of Sussex County, New Jersey and Fayette County, Pennsylvania, and His Wife Lydia Morgan. Chalfant, Depuy, Silverthorn, and Wheatley Families.* Cleveland, OH, 1975. xii, 263p. [NG88; D11226; VP202].

SHARP -- Eastwood, Elizabeth Cobb Stewart. *The First Supplement of Additions and Corrections to the Henry Sharp (of Sussex Co., N.J. and Fayette Co., Pa.) Genealogy.* Cleveland, OH, Eastwood, 1978. iv, 58p. [C628; X846-FW/NY/SP; VP202].

SHATTUCK -- Hamel, Claude Charles. *Genealogy of A Branch of the Shattuck Family, Early Settlers in Brownhelm, Lorain County, Ohio, about 1850.* Amherst, OH, 1948. 12 l. [L15387].

SHAUM -- Mumaw, Catharine. *Shaum Family History.* Wooster, OH, C.Mumaw. n.d. 60p. [X847-FW].

SHAUM -- Rutt, Harvey S. *History of Chester Township, Wayne County, Ohio and the Shaum and Holdeman Families.* Smithville, OH, H.S. Rutt, 1930. x, 155p. [NG89; D11240; X847-OH].

SHAW -- Dumford, Anna. *Shaw Genealogy.* Cincinnati, OH, Published by the Cincinnati Branch Genalogical Library, 1969. 128p. [X947-OL].

SHAW -- Shaw, Ivyl W. *Descent and Descendants of John L. Shaw (1809-1890) of Morrow County, Ohio.* NP, nd, In Vertical File at the Library of Congress. [L15402].

SHAW -- Shaw, Ivyl W. *The Descent and Descendants of John L. Shaw (1809-1890) of Morrow County, Ohio.* Chanute, KS, L. W. Breyfogle, 1964. 14p. [X847-NY/PH/SU].

SHEARER -- Starkey, William Lowell. *A Genealogy of the Jacob Shearer Family: Descendants of Jacob Shearer, 1744-1823 and Elizabeth Deal, 1750-1825, Who Came From Cordorus Township, York County, Pennsylvania to Washington County, Pennsylvania and then to Mapleton, Stark County, Ohio in 1813.*

Fremont, CA, W. L. Starkey, 1978. i v.
(various pagings). Limited edition of 8
copies. [C629; VP203].

SHEEHAN -- Sheehan, Thomas W. *The
Sheehan(d) Family.* Cleveland, OH, 1969. iv,
93 leaves. [S2253].

SHEEHAN -- Sheehan, Thomas W. *The Ancestry
of The Sheehan Brothers and Sisters.*
Cleveland, OH, 1972. viii, 230 l. [S2254].

SHEEHAN -- Watt, Artiss N. *Descendants of
Watt, Sheehan & Allied Families.* Napolean,
OH, Gibbs Pub. Co., 1988. 1 v. (various
pagings). 1. Watt family. 2. Sheehan family.
[G603].

SHEETS -- NAS. *History and Genealogy of
the John Sheets Family.* Convoy, OH, 1940.
36p. 4p. insert at end. [L15412].

SHELBURNE -- Stevenson, Kenyon. *Shelburnes
of Old Virginia: From the Arrival of Thomas,
The Emigrant, in 1607 to the Time When the
Children of Augustine Came From Kentucky to
Indiana.* Akron, OH, n.d. [VV167].

SHELDON -- Sheldon, Keith M. *Sheldons at
Bicentennial.* Bay Village, OH, Sheldon, 1979.
906p. [DS647].

SHELDON -- Sheldon, Rev. Henry Olcott. *The
Sheldon Magazine; or, A Genealogical List of
the Sheldons in America, with Biographical
Data and Historical Notes, and Notices of
Others Families with which They
Intermarried...* Loudonsville, OH, 1855-57.
variously paged. Issued in 4 no.: no. 1,
1855, no 2-4, Jan., Apr., Oct., 1957.
[L15440].

SHELDON -- Sheldon, Rev. Henry Olcott. *The
Sheldon Magazine; or, A Genealogical List of
the Sheldons in America, with Biographical
Data and Historical Notes, and Notices of
Others Families with which They*

Intermarried... Sidney, OH, S. H. Matthers 1857. 1 v. various pagings Reprinted with Corrections and Additions. Edited and Transcribed by Leland Locke Sheldon. New York Genealogical Committee, Sheldon Family Association, 1961. [L15444].

SHELLHOUSE -- Hamel, Claude Charles. [L15449]. See above: SCHELLHOUSE. [L15080].

SHELTON -- Sheldon, Keith, M. *Sheldons at Bicentennial.* Bay Village, OH, K. M. Sheldon, 1979. ii, 906p. [C631].

SHELTON -- Sheldon, Keith, M. *John Shelton of Providence and Records of His Descendants.* Bay Village, OH, K. M. Sheldon, 1984. 932p. [C631].

SHEPHERD -- Hodgman, Roderick H. *History and Genealogy of the John Shepherd Family.* Cleveland, OH, 1913, 243p. [X850-FW].

SHEPHERD -- Shepherd, John F. *History and Genealogy of James and Sarah Shepherd and Their American Descendants.* Toledo, OH, H. D. Paasch, printer, 1912. 67p. [X850-FW/OH].

SHEPPARD -- Sheppard, Carl Dunkle. *The Benjamin Kirk Sheppard Family, with Brief Data About Allied Families of John Kennedy, James Dunkle, James Pilcher, Robert Sage, Robert Aiken, Barnett Vandervort, and John Henry.* Akron, OH, 1964. 64 leaves. [L15476].

SHERMAN -- Clark, Louise Sheerman. *The Sheerman Family in America, Australia and England, and Allied Families of Bales, Ramey, West, and Yocom.* Springfield, OH, L. S. Clark, 1984. xiii, 62p. 1. Sherman family. 2. Bales family. 3. Ramey family. 4. Ohio-Genealogy. [G605; C632].

SHERMAN -- Sherman, Roy V. *Some of the Descendants of Philip Sherman, the First Secretary of Rhode Island.* Akron, OH, Sherman, 1968. 662p. [L15501; D11296].

SHERMAN -- Sherman, W. J. *Ancestry of Margaret and Elizabeth Sherman.* Toledo, OH, 1910. Negative photostat of chart. [X851-NY].

SHETLER -- Shetler, Andy J. *Christian Shetler Family History, 1804-1965, Including Some More Distant Shetler Relatives and Fannie Nisley Relatives.* Fredericksburg, OH, A. J. Shetler, 1965. Unpaged. [X851-FW/NY].

SHIELDS -- Raber, Nellie M. R. *William Shields of Augusta County, Virginia and Trumbull County, Ohio.* Lakewood, OH, Author, nd. Unpaged. [X853-FW; VV167].

SHINKLE -- Abbott, Louisa J. S. *The Shinkle Genealogy, Comprising the Descendants of Phillip Carl Schenckel, 1717-1987.* Cincinnati, OH, Press of Curts and Jennings, 1897. 348p. [X853-CH/FW/LI/MH/NY].

SHIPLEY -- Hall, Frank Nelson. *A Story of the Shiplett (Shipley) Family of Muskingum County, Ohio (near Zanesville) and Related Families: David Roland Shiplett from Culpeper, Virginia, Charles Franklin from Maryland, Catharine Councilman (Franklin) from Baltimore, Maryland, William Perley (Caleb) Hughes from New Jersey, Amy Allen (Hughes) from New Jersey, Fred Hall of Belvidere, Ill. The Descendants of Nelson and Ephraim Shiplett.* Denton, TX, 1962. [VV167].

SHIRK -- NAS. *The Genealogy of the Family of Uhlrich Shirk of Conton Berne, Switzerland, 1555.* NP, Ohio DAR, G.R.C., 1953. 76 l. [D11335].

SHIRK -- Schürch, Terry L. *Schürch Family of Switzerland.* Huber Heights, OH, T.L. Schürch, 1985-<1990 > v. <1-2 >. Vol. 2 has Title: Schürch family history. Cover title: Schurch, Schuerch family history. 1. Shirk family. 2. Switzerland-Genealogy. [G606].

SHIRK -- Schürch, Terry L. [606]. See above: LINDENMAN. [G402].

SHIRK -- Schürch, Terry L. *Schürch von Seeberg: A History of Jacob Schürch, Sr.* Huber Heights, OH, T.L. Schürch, 1986- v. <1 >. 1. Shirk family. 2. Schürch, Jacob, 1837-1911-Family. 3. Switzerland-Genealogy. [G606].

SHOEMAKER -- Shoemaker, Charles W. *Jacob Shoemaker and His Descendants in America.* Waterville, Oh, 1927. 12p. [X854-PH].

SHORB -- Shorb, Mary P. *John Shorb Family, 1761 to 1955.* Massillon, OH, 1959. 21p. [X855-FW].

SHORT -- Short, Georgia Spencer. *A Short Short Story.* Fairborn, OH, Short, 1988. 57, 2 leaves. [DC3316].

SHOVLIN -- Shouvlin, Daniel R. *The Shouvlin Family, 1863-1984. Prepared for the First Shouvlin Reunion, June 22-24, 1984.* Springfield, OH, D. R. Shouvlin, 1984. 55, 25p. [C635].

SHROCK -- Miller, Oscar R. *Descendants of Henry Schrock and Barbara Mitler, from the Year 1807-1971.* Berlin, OH, 1971. 121p. [S2281].

SHROYER -- Herring, Elder R. *Some Genealogical Facts about the Shroyer Family.* __, OH, 1933. 14 leaves. [X856-PH].

SHUCK -- Shuck, Larry G. [G608]. See above: FLESHMAN. [G232].

SHUEY -- Shuey, D. B. *History of the Shuey Family in America.* Galion, OH, Shuey, 1919. 381p. [L15602; D11375].

SHUPE -- Hamel, Claude Charles. *Genealogy of the Shupe Family, Early Settlers in Amherst,*

Lorain County, Ohio. Amherst, OH, 1948. 7 1. [L15612].

SHUSTER -- NAS. *Daniel Shuster (1752-1818) Geneological (!) and Historical Records of His Descendants to 1943.* Columbus, OH, Hollenbeck Press, 1944. 112p. [L15616].

SHUSTER -- NAS. *Supplement to: Daniel Shuster (1752-1818) Genealogical and Historical Records of His Descendants to 1972.* Lakewood, OH, 1972. 134p., I-XII p. [X857-GF].

SIDWELL -- NAS. *A Geneology of the Pennsylvnai, Maryland and Ohio Branches of the Sidwell Family.* Washington, DC, By a member of the family. 1930. 1, 58 numb. leaves. [L15633; VP207].

SIEBENALER -- Manley, Sondra Miller. *Mathias Siebenaler and American Descendants, 1823-1973.* Montpelier, OH, 1974. 386p. [S2285].

SILL -- Rudder, Edith Attkinson. *My Mother's Family, Shannon - Sill, Pennsylvania, Ohio, Hamilton-Robinson, Virginia, and Indiana.* Salem, IN, 1942. 38p. [L15643; VP208].

SIMMONS -- Duty, Allene Beaumont. *The Ancestors and Descendants of Ephraim Simmons, 1769-1837, of Little Compton, Rhode Island, Cleveland, and Peru, Ohio.* Cleveland, OH, 1977. i, 112 p. D gives underscored title. [C637; NG90; D11419].

SIMMONS -- Simmons, Franklin Bruce. *Simmons.* Akron, OH, Simmons, 1981. 165p. [DS659].

SIMON -- Hoyt, Helen E. *Simon and Otterbein Families.* Toledo, OH, 1952. 34p. [X860-FW].

SIMON -- Hudson, Roland V. *My Simon Ascendants.* Tiffin, OH, Hudson, 1975. 61 leaves. [S2296].

SIMONS -- Simons, Ira W. *Adam Simons Family.* Cleveland, OH, 1973. Unp. [X860-OH].

SIMONSON -- McClure, Stanely W. *The Simonson Family: A Record of the Simonson Families of Crosby, Harrison, and Whitewater Townships, Hamilton County, Ohio and Harrison Township, Dearborn County, Indiana and Other Lines of Descent.* Harrison, OH, S. W. McClure, 1981. 69 leaves, 4 leaves of plates. [C638].

SIMRALL -- Riker, Frances Simrall. *The Book of Simrall.* Cincinnati, OH, The Ebbert & Richardson Co., 1927. 198p. [D11442].

SINCLAIR -- Baker, Wilma S. L. *Father and His Town. A Story of Life at the Turn of the Century in a Small Ohio River Town.* Pittsburgh, Pa., Three Rivers Press, 1961. 143p. [X861-SU].

SINCLAIR -- McGrady, L. J. *Sinclair: A Family History Beginning with William Sinclair - 1st ed.* Toledo, OH, L.J. McGrady, 1986. iii, 61 leaves. 1. Sinclair family. 2. Sinclair, William, b. 1804-Family. [G612].

SINCLAIR -- Sinclair, Brevard D. *An Historical Account of Duart Castle with the Genealogies of the Children and Grandchildren of Rev. John Campbell Sinclair, Together with an Obit of the Latter.* Columbus, OH, Columbus Steam Printing Works, 1879. 33p. A short sketch of the Davidson and Brevard families of Mecklenburg, North Carolina. P. 35." [L15685].

SINGER -- Singer, John. *Singer Family Tree.* Springfield, OH, J. Singer, 1980. 184 leaves. [C639; NG90].

SINNETT -- Sinnett, Rev. Chas. N. *James Sinnett, Pioneer of Granville, Ohio, Colony: Ancestry and Descendants.* Brainerd, MN, 1920. 1, 19 numb. leaves. [L15701].

SKIDMORE -- Skidmore, Warren. *Thomas Skidmore (Scudamore), 1605-1684 of Westerleigh, Gloucestershire, and Fairfield, Connecticut: His Ancestors and Descendants to the Ninth Generation.* Akron, OH, W. Skidmore, 1980. v, 350p. "250 copies." 1. Skidmore family. 2. Skidmore, Thomas, 1605-1684- Family. [G613; C641; NG90; D11471].

SKIDMORE -- Skidmore, Warren. *The Scudamores of Upton, Scudamore: A Knightly Family in Medieval Wiltshire, 1086-1382.* Akron, OH, W.F. Skidmore, 1983. vi, 623p. [C641].

SKIDMORE -- Skidmore, Warren. *Thomas Skidmore (Scudamore), 1605-1684 of Westerleigh, Gloucestershire, and Fairfield, Connecticut: His Ancestors and Descendants to the Ninth Generation -- 2nd ed.* -- Akron, OH, W. Skidmore, 1985. vi, 505p. [C641].

SKIDMORE -- Skidmore, Warren and William F. Skidmore; *Rickmansworth, England-Delaware-North Carolina and West, 1555 to 1983.* Akron, OH, W. F. Skidmore, 1983. vi, 623p. [C641; NG90].

SKINNER -- Rearick, W. S. *The Family Tree of Samuel and Elizabeth Skinner.* Fremont, OH, Rearick, 1914. 31p. [D11479].

SLAUGHTER -- Slaughter, Raymond Dare. [G614]. See above: PRICE. [G531; DC3361].

SLOCUM -- Slocum, Charles Elihu. *History of the Slocums, Slocumbs, and Slocombs of America, Genealogical and Biographical, Embracing Twelve Generations of the First Named Family from A.D. 1637 to 1908, with Their Marriages and Descendants in the Female Line as far as Ascertained...* Defiance, OH, Slocum, 1908. xv, 543p. Supplement to and issued as vol. 2 of the 1882 ed. [L15762].

SMAILES -- Smailes, Thomas. *A Memorandum Book kept by Thomas Smailes, Senior of New York State and Virginia Township, Coshocton*

County, Ohio, Beginning in 1826 and Periodically...until 1864. Hilliard, OH, R. K. Bradley, 1971. 4, 40 leaves. [S2315].

SMALLEY -- Smalley, Matthew F. *John Smalley and His Descendants in America, June 5, 1632-Jan 1, 1960.* Canton, OH, M. F. Smalley, 1960. 122p. [X866-FW/LA/NY/OH/PH/SU].

SMELSER -- Pollock, Alvie Lee. *Asters At Dusk.* Dayton, OH, Pollock, 1961. v, 278p. [D11519].

SMILEY -- NAS. *A Composite Smiley Family History.* NP, Ohio DAR, G.R.C., 1969. 42 leaves. [D11520].

SMITH -- Harris, Marvin Eugene. *The Book of John Smith and His Descendants. (1st ed).* Columbus, OH, 1955. 141pages. [L15895].

SMITH -- Hartman, Blanche T. *The Smiths of Virginia; A History and Genealogy of the Smiths of "Big Springs Plantation", Frederick County, Virginia, Together with a Chronicle of the Drugan and the Carnahan Families of Pennsylvania and Ohio.* Pittsubrgh, Pa. 1929. 99p. [L15860; VV171; VP211].

SMITH -- Hays, Hugh Howard. *The Chronicles of the Descendants of Ephraim Smith.* Cleveland, OH, 1942. unpaged. -- *Extension.* (Patton, CA, 1961). 85p. [L15880].

SMITH -- Jones, Dorothy Almond. *From Whence We Came.* Rocky River, OH, Jones, 1979. v. [C646].

SMITH -- Koop, Rita Bone. *Bazel & Mary Howell Smith and Their Descendants of 'Smith Holler,' Wayne Township, Monroe County, Ohio.* NP, 1983. 184p. [NG91].

SMITH -- Miller, John Peery. *The Genealogy of the Descendants of Samuel Smith, sr., and Elizabeth (McCleave) Smith.* Xenia, OH, The Aldine Publishing House, 1922. 118p. [L15846].

SMITH -- Pabst, Anna C. Smith. *The John Richey Smith and Sarah B. Martin Smith Family History.* Delaware, OH, Pabst, 1967. 203 l. [D11567].

SMITH -- Pabst, Anna C. Smith. *The John Richey Smith and Sarah B. Martin Smith Family History.* Delaware, OH, Pabst, 1967. 177, xviii leaves. [L15914].

SMITH -- Rasor, Jean Smith. *The Ancestry and Descendants of Clarence Mitchell Smith.* Columbus, OH, J.S. Rasor, 1990. 121p. 1. Smith family. 2. Smith, Clarence Mitchell, 1853-1939-Family. 3. Ohio-Genealogy. [G617].

SMITH -- Smith, Chloris O. *John H. Smith Family History Updated.* North Canton, OH, C. O. and G. F. Smith, 1981. i, 84p. [C647].

SMITH -- Smith, Clarence M. *Genealogy of Smith and Patterson Family.* Columbus, OH, The F. J. Heer Printing Co., 1929. 91p. CH & OH omit both date and pages; give "Families" in title. MH gives date of 1931. [D11583; X868-MH also X873-CH/OH].

SMITH -- Smith, Mrs. Charles E. *Records and Charts of the James, Didenhover, Dowling, Brown, Christian Smith , Reed, Huston, Prutzman, and Elder Families.* Columbus, OH, 1928. 21 leaves. [L15858].

SMITH -- Smith, Edward C. *The Ancestors and Descendants of Samuel Smith, senior, of Middlefield, Mass.* Lakewood, OH, 1947. ix, 18-60 l. Also: *Supplement* by Edward C. Smith, Lakewood, OH, 1955. 77-86 leaves. [X869-FW/NY].

SMITH -- Smith, Jesse Lowe. *Smith Genealogy (Absalom Smith) Sept., 1933.* Newark, OH, 1964. 12 leaves. [L15907].

SMITH -- Smith, Lucius. *Original Records, Gathered by Lucius Smith for the Descendants of John Smith of Hadley, Mass.* Strongville, OH, 189_. 3 vols. [X867-WR].

SMITH -- Smith, Sarah Louise Gillespie. *Descendants of John Smith, Revolutionary War Soldier, Lived in Butler County, Ohio.* Oxford, OH, S.L.G. Smith & R. W. Smith, 1989. 179 leaves. [DC3390].

SMITH -- Stoner, Vera Barnhart. *The Family of John Smith of Trotwood, Montgomery County, Ohio; A Genealogy, 1750-1964.* Ladoga, IN, 1964. 49p. [S2319].

SMITH -- Waters, Margaret R. and Donald D. Murphy. *Smith Family, Descendants of George and Barbara (Bash) Smith of Westmoreland County, Pennsylvania, and Coshcoton County, Ohio, Whose Children Migrated Westward... with Allied Families of Bash, Waters, Ruby, Hogle, and Murphy.* Indianapolis, IN, 1946. 3, 280p. [L15885; VP212].

SMITH -- Watson, Estelle Clark. *Some Smiths, Osborns, and Allied Families of New England and Ohio.* Skokie, IL, Guild Press, Inc., 1964. 69, 27p. D gives 69, 25p. [L15908; D11623].

SMITH -- Weary, Frank Orlando. *Smith - Weary Chronology.* Akron, OH, Weary, 1921. 45p. [D11624].

SMITHSON -- Achor, Robert L. [G619]. See above: ACHOR. [G2]. - 2 Entries.

SMOCK -- Tuttle, Alva M. *Smocks in the Censuses, 1790-1840, with Plans for the Cooperative Compilation of Complete Histories of the Smock, Stayner, and Ryker Families.* Columbus, OH, 1954. 1a-16a, 1c-14c, 5-6p. [X873-FW/NY/OS/SU].

SNAVELY -- Snavely, Olan D. *Snavely Genealogy.* Toledo, OH, 1969. 14p. [X874-FW].

SNOOK -- Snook, Maurice Edward. *History and Genealogy of the Snook Families of Frederick County, Md. (Including a Delineation of the Snoke Family of Fairfield Co., Ohio).* Athens,

GA, Snook, 1980. 257p., 6 leaves. of plates.
[C650].

SNOW -- NAS. *Memory Book, Russ Snow
Centenniel, 1835-1935.* Cleveland, OH, Gates
Press, 1935. 136p. Program of Centennial at
Brecksville, Ohio. [X875-OH].

SNOW -- Wilcox, Owen N. *History of the
Family of Benjamin Snow, Who is a Descendant
of Richard Snow of Woburn, Massachusetts.*
Cleveland, OH, The Gates Legal Publishing
Company, 1907. 5, 386, 7p. D gives
underscored title and 385p.
[L15940; D11652].

SNYDER -- Price, Maude S. *Our Ancestors:
Snider, Skillen, Brannon, Sleeth, and
Carpenter Families.* Cincinnati, OH, 1953.
12p. [X875-FW].

SNYDER -- Schneider, Donald R. *Descendants
of Jakob Schneider of Seftigen, Switzerland.*
Beloit, OH, D.R. Schneider, 1981. vi, 220p.
1. Snyder family. 2. Schneider, Jakob, 1806-
1879-Family. 3. Switzerland-Genealogy. 4.
Ohio-Genealogy. [G620].

SNYDER -- Snyder, Orville A. *Peter B. & Ida
(Grabill) Snyder.* Wooster, OH, 1956. 14p.
[X875-FW].

SOUTHWORTH -- Southworth, George C. S.
Descendants of Constant Southworth, 1614-1685.
Salem, OH, 1892. 11p.
[X877-FW/LI/MH].

SPACKEY -- Bowers, , Charles M. *Genealogy
of the Spackey Families in America.* Fostoria,
OH, 1976. 49p. 7 leaves. [X878-FW].

SPAID -- Secrest, Abraham Thompson. *Spaid
Genealogy. Also Secrest, Hellyer, Anderson,
Frye Families.* Columbus, OH, (Pleasant City,
OH, Secrest), 1922. viii, 395p. D gives
underscored title. 500 copies printed.
[L15993; NG92; D11691].

SPANGLER -- Farley, Belmont. *Eight Centuries of Spanglers; twenty-two generations from 1150 A.D. to 1939 A.D.; Descendants of George Spangler (1150-1190)... with Special Reference to those Sons of Rudolph Spangler of Adams County, Pennsylvania, Who Emigrated to Ohio Between 1800 and 1825.* Washington, DC, 1939. 60p. [L15996].

SPARROW -- Held, Ruth Varney. *James Sparrow and Eliza Payne Morse of Boardman and Lower Salem, Ohio: Their Ancestors and Descendants.* San Diego, CA, Held, 1979. 113p., 5 leaves of plates. [C656].

SPARROW -- Held, Ruth Varney. *The Sparrows in Boardman, Ohio: 1982 Supplement to the Sparrow-Morse Book.* NP, R. V. Held, 1982. 8p. [C656].

SPEAKER -- Singer, Dorothy Louise Balzer. *Andrew Lewis Speakman, 1850-1912, Ancestors, Decendants Sibblings (sic): Proved Relationship to King Edward III, 1312-1377, England and U. S. President Richard M. Nixon.* Springfield, OH, D. L. B. Singer, 1985. 270p. [C656].

SPECHT -- Eberle, Maxine Renner. *History and Genealogy of the Specht - Hisrich Families, 1838-1976.* Berlin, OH, Berlin Printing, 1976. 130, 12p. Enlargement of the original book by O. H. Younger (1933). [X879-OH; D11709].

SPECK -- Speck, Isaac G. *Genealogy of the Speck and Benjamin Reed Families from 1754-1900; Also, Historical Reading of Great Interest.* Dupont, OH, 1900. 149p. 3 leaves. [X879-FW].

SPEICHER -- Speicher, David. *Descendants of Barbara Weaver and Abraham Speicher.* Bluffton, OH, 1958. 5p. [X879-FW].

SPENCER -- Hasson, Ethel W. *Spencer Family.* Centerburg, OH, 1943. 9 leaves. [X880-OH].

SPENCER -- Spencer, Emily Stickney. *Some Ancestry and Kindred of Meade Ashley Spencer.* Cleveland, OH, Spencer, 1976. 49 leaves, 4 leaves of plates. [C657].

SPIRA -- Speyer, Donald L. *The Family and Descendants of George and Appolonia Speyer.* Dayton, OH, D.L. Speyer, 1990. 58 leaves. 1. Spira family. 2. Speyer, George, 1832-1902- Family. 3. Ohio-Genealogy. [G626].

SPITLER -- Honeyman, Gale Edwin Spitler. *The House of Spittler - Spitler, 1736-1976: Descendants of Johannes and Catharina (Schaffner) Spittler, Emigrants from Bennwil, Canton Basel, Switzerland to Bethel Township, Lancaster County, Pennsylvania.* Laura, OH, Honeyman, 1977. 370p. [C658; VP216].

SPITLER -- Spitler, Arlie H. *Spitler Family.* Millersport, OH, Spitler, 1949. 474, 60p. [D11735].

SPITLER -- Spitler, Arlie H. *Spitler Family; (Descendants of Abraham and Jacob, Sons of John Spitler).* Millersport, OH, Author, 1949. 2 vols. By Hickory Grove Chapter D.A.R., Illinois. [X881-FW/OL].

SPOONER -- Spooner, Thomas. *Memorial of William Spooner, 1637, and of His Descendants to the Third Generation; of his great-grandson, Elnathan Spooner, and of his Descendants to 1871.* Cincinnati, OH, Robert Clarke & Co., 1871. vii, 242p. Priv. ed. 500 copies. D gives underscored title. [L16054; D11741].

SPOONER -- Spooner, Thomas. *Records of William Spooner of Plymouth, Mass., and His Descendants. v. 1.* Cincinnati, OH, Press of F. W. Freeman, 1883. 694p. This work intended to supplement and complete author's "Memorial of William Spooner, 1637" (immedieately above). COPY REPLACED BY MICROFILM (No. not indicated). [L16055].

SPRAGUE -- Weston, William Bradford. *Supplement to Sprague Families in America.* Chaucey, OH, Sprague, 1940. 212 leaves. [L16060; D11754].

SPRINGER -- Irwin, Ruth Beckey. [G627]. See above: GADDY. [G247].

SPRINGER -- Rizer, Kathleen. *The Springer Family Place and Part in History.* Tipp City, OH, Rizer Research, 1986. 15, 7 leaves. 1. Fayette County (Pa.)-History, Local. 2. Springer family. 3. Dwellings-Pennsylvania-Fayette County. 4. Historic buildings-Pennsylvania-Fayette County. 5. Fayette County (Pa.)-Biography. [G627].

SPROUL -- Wright, Hazel Sproul. *Robert Sprouel of Miami County, Ohio, Formerly of County Tyrone, Ireland.* Lincoln, RI, Wright, 1966. 36, 6 leaves. [D11770].

SPROULE -- Wright, Hazel Sproul. *Robert Sprouel of Miami County, Ohio, Formerly on County Tyrone, Ireland, and Some of His Descendants with Lineage of Families by Marriage 1775-1966.* Lincoln, RI, 1966-68, 2 v. [L16098].

SPRUILL -- Imlay, Nella C. *The Spruill Family, 1668-1973.* Zanesville, OH, 1973. 40p. [X882-OH].

SQUIER -- Hamel, Claude Charles. *Geneaology of a Branch of the Squier Family That Settled in Erie, Co., Ohio and Married into the Baatz Family of That County.* Amherst, OH, 1948. 8 leaves. [L16095].

SQUIER -- Hamel, Claude Charles. *Geneaology of a Branch of the Squier Family That Settled in Erie, Co., Ohio and Married into the Baatz Family of That County. Rev.* Elyria, OH, 1960. 7 leaves. [L16096].

STAFFORD -- Stafford, Horace W. *Genealogy and Biographical Sketch of the Stafford*

Families of Ohio and Indiana. Springfield, OH, 1927. 143p. [X884-FW].

STAHL -- Hull, Lillian Eleanor (Elder). *Genealogy of the Family of William Stahl and His Wife Elizabeth Boger Stahl.* Mansfield, OH, Richland Printing Company, 1945. 184p. D gives underscored title. [L16110; D11792].

STAHL -- Stahl, Jacob Peter. *The Stahl Family History.* Dayton, OH, Stahl, 1924. 2, 9-140p. [L16109; D11793].

STAHL -- Stahl, Noah. *Stahl Family,* Fostoria, OH, 1909. 20 leaves. [X884-FW].

STAINBROOK -- Stainbrook, Margaret Collins. *The Stainbrook - Steinbrook Family.* Zanesville, OH, M. C. Stainbrook, 1983. 928, 212p. [C660].

STAMM -- Davis, W. E. *The Stamm Family: Philipp Peter, Philipp Peter, Jr., Mary Elizabeth, Philipp Peter III, Frederick, Caroline C., Martin, Margaret, Elizabetha, Jacob, Phoebe, Karolina, Phillip, Julenrietta, Carl, etc.* Glendale, OH, W.E. Davis, 1985. 36 [i.e. 72], 29 leaves. 1. Stamm family. [G628].

STAMPER -- Stamper, Oliver. *Descendants of James Stamper, 1750-1826.* Cleveland Heights, OH, Stamper, 1945. 35p. [D11801].

STANDISH -- Blue, Herbert T. O. *A Genealogical History through Eleveln Generations of the Descendants from Captain Miles Standish Thru Rose Ellen Standish Treiber.* Canton, OH, 1950. 89 leaves. X-libraries show 93p. NG gives underscored title. [NG92; X885-FW/IG/LA/OH].

STANDISH -- Blue, Herbert T. O. *A Genealogical History Through Eleven Generations of the Descendants from Captain Miles Standish, Leader of the Pilgrin Fathers.* Canton, OH, Blue, 1950. 91 p. [D11806].

STANTON -- Doughman, Matella Pricket. *Genealogy of Some of the Ancestors and Descendants of Jesse F. Stanton (1808-1873) in Indiana.* Wilmington, OH, Doughman, 1950. 24 leaves. [D11820; X887-FW].

STARBUCK -- McConnell, George Edward. *Our Family's Starbuck Ancestry, 1604-1963.* Mount Vernon, OH, G. E. McConnell, Boston, MA, D. R. McConnell, 1963. 106p. D gives underscored title. [L16170; D11830].

STARK -- Linnell, Mary Beth. *The Genealogy of Joshua Stark, an Early Settler of Granville County, Ohio.* NP, 1966. 38 l. [L16183].

STARLING -- Sullivant, Joseph. *A Genealogy and Family Memorial.* Columbus, OH, Ohio State Journal Book and Job Rooms, 1874. 372p. [D11841].

STAUFFER -- Herman, June W. *Stauffer Ancestors from Northampton County, Pennsylvania to Ohio.* Rockville, MD, Herman, 1982. 30 l. [NG92: DS687].

STAUFFER -- Rupp, Allen E. *John Stauffer - Ann Steiner: Their Ancestral Charts for Four Generations in Europe and Their Descendants in America.* Marietta, OH, 1973. 121p. [X889-FW/OH].

STAUFFER -- Stauffer, Rev. Henry. *Historical Address Delivered by Rev. Henry Stauffer at the First Stauffer Family Reunion...* Akron, OH, Press of the Capron and Curtice Co., 1893. 40p. [X888-PH].

STAVELY -- NAS. *The Stavely Family of Frederick W. Stavely; the Early Staveleys, the Staveleys of Ireland (and) the Stavelys of America.* Akron, OH, 1969. 175p. [L16207].

STECHER -- Stecher, Robert Morgan. *A Stecher - Stecker Saga: The Story of Several German Families and Their Descendants in America.* Cleveland, OH, Western Reserve

Historical Society, 1977. xvii, 209p. C and NG omit "in America" from title. [C663; NG92; D11866].

STECHER -- Stecher, Robert M., Willie Stecker and Karl Vorework. *Cord Stecker and His Descendants in Europe and America.* Cleveland, OH, 1961. 1 v. [L16222].

STEDDOM -- Fisher, Herschel I. *The Steddom Reunion of 1915...* Lebanon, OH, Author, 1915. Unpaged. [X890-CH/OH].

STEDDOM -- Steddom, Arthur R. *Tracing the Steddom Name.* Cincinnati, OH, 197_, 18p. [X890-FW].

STEEN -- Moses, D. A. *The Steen Family in Europe and America... Extending from the Seveenteenth to the Twentiety Century.* Cincinnati, OH, Montfort & Company, 1900. 562p. D title underscored. [L16236; D11882].

STEEN -- Moses, D. A. *The Steen Family in Europe and America... Extending from the Seveenteenth to the Twentiety Century.* Cincinnati, OH, Montfort & Company, 1917. 740p. L gives: 2d ed. rev. and enl. D gives underscored title. [L16237; D11881].

STEFFEN -- Cook, Rohease B. *Record of the Descendants of John Adam Steffen of Northumberland Co., Pa. and His Son Frederick Steffy of Jefferson Co., O.; and of Henry Heisler of Harrison Co., O.* Erie, PA, 1974. 119p. Also includes Couts, Wagner, and Dinger Families. [X891-FW].

STEFFY -- Cook, Rohease B. *Genealogical Information Regarding the Families of Steffen of Northumberland Co., Penna,; Steffy of Jefferson Co., O.; Heisler of Harrison Co., O.* NP, 1954. 80 leaves. [D11889].

STEIN -- Koplowitz, Hannah. *The Stein Family of Reichensachsen and Their Descendants.* Cincinnati, OH, 1975. 8p. [X891-FW].

STEINBACH -- DeVerter, Paul Logan. *The Steinbach or Steinbaugh Family Province of Lower Rhine, Alsace-Lorraine and Ohio and Indiana, U.S.A.* Baytown, TX, 1958. 13 l. [L16246].

STEINER -- NAS. *Steiner Memoir, Sketch of the Steiner Family, 1311-1878.* Cincinnati, OH, R. Clarke & Co. Press, 1880. 21p. [X892-CH/FW/MH/PH].

STEINER -- Steiner, Clayton. *From Switzerland to Sonnenberg. The Story of Steiner, Amstutz, and Zuercher Families from Wayne County, Ohio.* Goshen, IN, 1976. 181p. [X892-FW].

STEINER -- Steiner, Florence S. *Brief History of the Steiner Family, 1783-1927.* Wooster, OH, 1927. Unpaged. [X892-FW].

STEPHENS -- Scalf, Henry P. *Stephens Family.* Dayton, OH, C. E. Shepard, 1970. 68p. Reprint of Data Gathered by Henry Stephens and published in the Floyd Co. (Ky.) Times. Contains Chart of C. E. Shepard. [X893-FW].

STEPHENS -- Stephens, Bascom Asbury Cecil. *The Stephens Family.* Lima, OH, Bower, 1910. 47 l. [D11905].

STERNER -- Sterner, Pauline L. [G634]. See above: BATCHELDER. [G39; C666; D86].

STEVENS -- Yoho, Denver C. [G635]. See above: JARVIS. [G346; C667].

STEVENSON -- Stevenson, George H. *History of the Stevenson Family of Frederick County, Maryland, and Sandusky County, Ohio.* Clyde, OH, 1938. 8p. Mounted newspaper clippings. [X895-FW].

STEVENSON -- Williamson, Ralph and Eva Anderson Williamson. *Stevenson and Anderson Families of New Jersey, Ohio, Indiana, and*

Kansas. Trenton, NJ, Parker Print Co., 1976. ix, 170p. [X896-CH/NY/OH/PH].

STEWART -- Kirk, Anna F. *History of the Stewart Family.* Fostoria, OH, The Gray Printing Co., 1928. 58p. [D11955].

STEWART -- White, Francenia Stewart. *Genealogy of Hugh Stewart and Descendants.* Columbus, OH, F. J. Heer, Printing Co., 1914. 181, 12p. [D11967].

STICKNEY -- NAS. *Alpheus Beede Stickney, His Descendants and Some of Their Ancestors, 1558-1965. Beede, Berkey, Burley, Boulter, Prescott, Shaw, Swaine, Wiggin, Sleeper, Stickney.* Cleveland, OH, 1965, 38 leaves. [L16322].

STICKNEY -- Moore, Howard P. *Biographical Sketch of Major Benjamim Franklin Stickney (1775-1852), Son-in-Law of General Stark, One of the Founders of Toledo, Ohio.* NP, 1953. 6 leaves. [X897-FW].

STIEG -- Stieg, Frank Henry. *Stieg History and Genealogy.* Fairfield, OH, 1970. 21 leaves. [NG93; X897-CH/FW/NY].

STILES -- Smith, Mrs. Sarah Augusta Prior. *Abram Stiles (Styls and Styles); John Milliken (Milligan and Milligin).* Columbus, OH, 1920. 35 leaves. [L16330].

STILES -- Stiles, Jessie Vernan. *The Family of Jonathan Stiles of Guernsey County, Ohio.* Indianapolis, IN, Stiles, 1957. 398p. [NG93; D11976].

STINSON -- Lillie, Leroy D. *The Stinson Family: David, 1784-1863, and Elizabeth McCauley Stinson, 1792-1870, and Descendants , Wayne County, Ohio.* Ames, IA, Lillie & Way, 1971. viii, 400p. Also contains addendum to March, 1973. 27p., and Addendum No. 2 to June, 1975. 21p. [X899-FW/NY].

STOKES -- Stokes, William J. Worth. *The Ohio Branch of the Stokes Family.* Dayton, OH, 1899. 1, 5-17, 1p. [L16376].

STOKES -- Stokes, William J. Worth. *The Stokes' (sic) from the Rancocas.* Dayton, OH, 1899. 19p. [X900-LI/PH].

STOKES -- Stokes, William J. Worth. *A Chronolical Genealogy of the Stokes Family in Ohio, from Thomas Stokes, the First Settler in This Country to the Present Time.* Dayton, OH, n.d. 19p. [X900-FW/LI].

STOMBERGER -- Stomberger, Paul George. *Family and Forefathers.* Clayton, OH, Stomberger, 1974. vii, 179p. [D12013].

STOMPS -- Grismer, Beth. [G636]. See above: GRIESEMER. [G274].

STOMPS -- Horvath, Leonard Stomps. *Brief History and Genealogy of the Stomps Family.* Engelwood, OH, 1971. 68 1. [S2410].

STONE -- Neil, Julia Evans (Stone). *From Generation to Generation. The Genealogies of Dwight Stone and Olive Evans.* Columbus, OH, The Champlin Press, 1907. 169p. [L16393].

STONESTREET -- Skidmore, Warren. *Thomas Stonestreet of Birchden, Withyham, East Sussex, and of "Birchden" in Charles County, Maryland, With His Posterity Down to the Sixth Generation.* -- 2nd rev. ed. -- Akron, OH, 1983, iv, 119p. C gives: "1985". 92p. 1. Stonestreet family. [G637; C670].

STONESTREET -- Skidmore, Warren. *Thomas Stonestreet of Birchden, Withyham, East Sussex, and of "Birchden" in Charles County, Maryland, With His Posterity Down to the Sixth Generation.* 3rd ed. Akron, OH, 1985. 92p. [NG93].

STOUT -- Conrad, Edna Keim. *Stout History.* West Salem, OH, Conrad, 1968. 26 1. [D12046].

STOUT -- Stout, Herald F. *Staudt - Stoudt - Stout Family of Ohio and Their Ancestors at Home and Abroad. Preliminary ed.* Dover, OH, 1935. 276, 49p. [X902-FW].

STOUT -- Stout, Herald F. *The Staudt - Stoudt - Stout Family of Ohio.* NP, 1935. 2 v. [D12050].

STOUT -- Stout, Herald F. *Stout and Allied Families.* Dover, OH, 194_. 1 v. various pagings. [L16439].

STOUT -- Stout, Herald F. *Richard Stout of New Jersey; A History of Patronymic Descendants.* Dover, OH, 1941. 2p., iii, 256 numb. leaves, 40 leaves. [L16440].

STOUT -- Stout, Herald Franklin. *Stout and Allied Families.* Dover, OH, 1943. 75, 343 l. [L16441].

STOUT -- Stout, Herald F. *Stout and Allied Families, 1733- 1968.* Dover, OH, The Eagle Press, 1951. xxii, 813, 70p. NY gives 1 vol. and omits date in title. [D12051; X902-NY].

STRADER -- Strader, Hartzel G. *The Strader Family History, 1737-1976.* Miamisburg, OH, 1976. 171 leaves. [X904-FW/OH].

STRALEY -- Shoemaker, Leah Custer. *The Descendants of Christian and Christina Straley Leah Custer Shoemaker.* Columbus, OH, Shoemaker, 1985. 94p. [DC3513].

STRATTON -- Stratton, David C. *"I'm Claiming the Promise": A History and Genealogy of William Henry and Edith (Townsend) Stratton.* Salem, OH, Stratton, 1977. 122p. 1. Stratton family. 2. Stratton, David Casner, 1942- . [G639; C672].

STRAUCH -- Kahler, Stephen. *The Ancestry and Descendants of Daniel and Susannah Strauch of Hancock County, Ohio.* Lexington, MA, S. Kohler, (D gives: NP, Strauch), 1988. 111p.

C gives: 111, 14p. 1. Strauch family. 2. Strauch, Daniel, 1796-1880-Family. 3. Hancock County (Ohio)-Genealogy. [G639; DC3517].

STROCK -- NAS. *Genealogical Sketch of the Joseph Strock Family.* Warren, OH, 1932. 91p. [X907-FW].

STROCK -- Strock, Richard M. [G640]. See above: FUNK. [G246].

STROUD -- Barr, Wallace. [G641]. See above: BARR. [G36].

STROUP -- Stroup, Hazel B. *Stroup Genealogy.* Hamilton, OH, n.d. Various pagings. [X908-FW].

STRONG -- Strong, Earl Poe. *The Strongs of Loudonville, Ohio, Descendants of Elder John Strong.* Mansfield, OH, Strong, 1936. 73 numb. leaves. [L16497].

STUART -- NAS. *The Stewarts of Coitsville, A History of Robert and Sarah Stewart of Adams County, Pa., and Their Descendants with a Part of Their Ancestors.* Youngstown, OH, T. Kerr & Sons, printers, 1899. 190p. [L16541].

STUART -- Smith, Berniece C. [G643]. See above: DAVIDSON. [G176].

STUART -- White, Francenia Stewart, Esther Stewart Hunt and Emma Stewart Lymann. *Genealogy of Hugh Stewart and Descendants.* Columbus, OH, F. J. Herr Print Co., 1914. xv pages, 2 leaves, 181, 12p. [L16555].

STUART -- Hamel. Claude Charles. *Geneaology of John Stewart, Brother of Walter Stewart of Londonderry, N.H., Boxford, Hopkinton and Blandford, Mass., and Suffield Conn.* Amherst, OH, 1951. 5 leaves. [L16568].

STUART -- Hamel. Claude Charles. *Geneaology of the Family of Walter Stewart of Londonderry, N.H., Boxford, Hopkinton and*

Blandford, Mass., and Suffield Conn. Amherst, OH, 1951. 50 leaves. [L16569].

STUDEBAKER -- NAS. *The Studebaker Story vol 1* -Indianapolis, IN, 1965. Quarterly published by the Studebaker Family National Association. [X911-FW/LA/NY/OH/PH].

STUDEBAKER -- NAS. *The Studebaker Story vol 1 - Summer, 1966 -* Tipp City, OH, Studebaker Family National Assoc. Three issues a year. Slightly irregular. Vol. 1 no. 1 preceeded by an introductory issue dated 1966. FW has volumes 1-8. [X911-FW/LA/NY/OH/SU].

STUDEBAKER -- NAS. *The Studebaker Family.* Tipp City, OH, The Studebaker Family Association, 1966-1974. 3 v. Quarterly. Library Holdings vs 1 (1966-1969), 4. no. 11-12 (1982), 14-16 (1983), 5 (1984-1987]. [DC?*****].

STUDEBAKER -- NAS. *The Studebaker Family.* Tipp City, OH, The Studebaker Family National Association, 1966-74. 2 v. [D12120].

STUDEBAKER -- NAS. *The Studebaker Story.* Indianapolis, IN, The Studebaker Family National Association, 1966-68. 4 v. in 1. [D12121].

STUDEBAKER -- Carlock, Walter. *The Studebaker Family; A Preliminary Genealogical Report.* Minneapolis, MN, 1964. 20 leaves. [X911-MH].

STUDEBAKER -- Carlock, Walter. *The Studebaker Family in America, 1736-1976.* Tipp City, OH, The Studebaker Family Assoc., 1976. xx, 910p. D omits date from title. [C675; NG94; D12122; X911-FW/NY/PH].

STUDEBAKER -- Carlock, Walter, et al. *The Studebaker Family in America.* Tipp City, OH, The Studebaker Family Assoc., 1976-1986. 2 v. [1] 1736-1976 [2] 1736-1986. 1. Studebaker family. 2. United States-Genealogy. [G644].

STUDEBAKER -- Hoy, Virginia Senseman. *What Beautiful People: The Story of Samuel and Nancy Studebaker.* Hamilton, OH, V. S. Hoy, 1984. 167p. [C675].

STUDEBAKER -- Miller, E. Irene. *A Pioneer Family (1736-1966).* Tipp City, OH, 1966. 7p. [L16581].

STUDEBAKER -- Studebaker, Ruth Epler & Emmert. *The Studebaker Family in America.* Tipp City, OH, The Studebaker Family Association, 1986. xvi, 877p. [DC3535].

STURGEON -- McCoy, Claudius T. *A Genealogical History of the Sturgeons of North America.* Cincinnati, OH, Sturgeon, 1926. 239, 12p., D gives: 239p., 3 leaves, 39p. [L16589; D12131].

SULLIVAN -- NAS. *Jeremiah Sullivan of Summit County, Ohio, His Descendants and Collateral Lines.* St. Paul, MN, 1942. 6 numb leaves. [L16616].

SULLIVANT -- Sullivant, Joseph. *A Genealogy and Family Memorial...* Columbus, OH, Ohio State Journal Book and Job Rooms, 1874. 1, 372, 3p. [L16618].

SUMMERBELL -- Summerbell, Rev. Carlyle. *Public Activities of Rev. J. J. Summerbell, D.D.* Dayton, OH, The Christian Pub. Assoc., 1916. 169p. [L16619].

SUTER -- Suter, Elam. *Family Record of the Abraham and Elizabeth Suter Family.* Pandora, OH, 1968. 18p. [X914-FW].

SUTTON -- Shafer, Twila Birnie. *Descendants of the Sutton - Beasley Family of Brown County, Ohio.* NP, 97p. [D12176].

SWAIN -- Butler, Jean Fuller. [G647]. See above: FULLER. [G245].

SWANDER -- Swander, John I. *History of the Swander Family.* Ann Arbor, MI, University

290

Microfilms International, 1979. 143p., 14
leaves of plates. Reprint of the 1899 ed.
published by T. S. Falkner and H. D.
Pittenger, Tiffin, OH. [C678].

SWANDER -- Swander, John I. *History of the
Swander Family.* Tiffin, OH, E. R. Good &
bro., 1899. 143p. OH adds: "11 leaves of
index." [X917-FW/LI/NY/OH].

SWANGO -- Swango, B. F., et al. *A History
of the Swango Family.* Eaton, OH, Distributed
by J. Cornwell, 1959. 132p. [S2435].

SWANK -- Murphy, Helen A. *Genealogical and
Historical Record of Christian Swank Family of
Pa., Ohio and Points West.* Toledo, OH, 1967
Various pagings. [X917-FW].

SWARTZ -- Eberhart, Elsie Swartz. *George
Henry Swartz and His Descendants of Fairfield
County, Ohio.* Rockford, IL, Ancestry Trails
and Tales, 1988. 111 leaves. [DC3564].

SWARTZ -- Swartz, Philip Allen. *The Swartz
Family of Shenandoah Valley, Va.* Poughkeepsie,
NY, Swartz, 1955. 293p. Bound with George B.
Gooding, (1795-1856): Inkeeper, Farmer of
Dighton, Massachusetts and Delaware County,
Ohio / comp. by Anna C. Smith Pabst, 34 1.
[D12187].

SWARTZBAUGH -- Hord, Virginia E.
Swartzbaugh: A Swartzbaugh Family Tree --
Printed ed. -- Dayton, OH, V. E. Hord, 1976.
126, 2, 32 leaves. Includes supplemental
leaves to 1980 and index (printed 1980).
[C678].

SWARTZENTRUBER -- Yoder, Joe D.
*Swartzentruber Family History: Lineal
Descendants of Daniel D. Swartzentruber, Jr.:
1842-1988.* Baltic, OH, J.D. Yoder
(Gordonville, Pa, Gordonville, Penna. Print
Shop). 1. Swartzentruber family. 2.
Swartzentruber, Daniel D., 1892-1977-Family.
3. Ohio-Genealogy. 4. Amish-Ohio-Genealogy.
[G647].

SWASEY — Swasey, Benjamin Franklin. *Genealogy of the Swasey Family Which Includes the Descndants of the Swezey Family of Southall, Long Island, New York, and the Descendants of the Swazey Families of Roxbury, now Chester, New Jersey.* Cleveland, OH, Priv. Print. 1910. 3, 5-525p. [L16664].

SWEET — Gross, Genevieve Ellis. *A Sweet Family History: Amos and Mercy (Carpenter) Sweet, His Ancestors, Their Descendants, and Related Families.* North Olmstead, OH, G.E. Gross: J.L. Sweet, 1990. xvi, 311p. 1. Sweet family. 2. Sweet, Amos, 1766-1838-Family. [G647].

SWINGLE — Swingle, Solomon L. and Grace E., et al. *John George Swingle, His Ancestors and Descendants, 1537-1980.* Zanesville, OH, J. G. Swingle Family Association, 1980. x, 448p. [C679].

SWITZER — Switzer, Robert M. *Genealogy of the Switzers; Descendants of Valentine Switzer Immigrant to America, Oct. 13, 1749.* Gallipolis, OH, 1938. 18p. [X919-FW].

T

TAFT — NAS. *Robert Taft (Family Tree).* Cincinnati, OH, nd, Ehrgatt, Farbiger, Lithio. [L16719].

TAFT — Washburn, Mabel Thacher Rosemary. *Ancestry of William Howard Taft. Also Torrey, Rawlson, Wilson, Hooker, Emerson Families.* New York, NY, Frank Allaben Genealogical Co., 1908. 52p. D gives title as underscored. [NG95; D12229].

TAFT — Ross, Isabel. *An American Family, The Tafts, 1668-1964.* Cleveland, OH, World Publishing, 1964. 468p. X gives: Ross, Ishbel with notation: "Author is possibly Rose" and dates as "1673-1964". [DC3572; X921-CH/FW/LA/PP].

TANEY -- Malloy, Dorothy Palmer. *Saga of the Taney Rainbow Trails*. Cincinnati, OH, Malloy, 1976. 6 parts in 3 v. [D12248].

TANNER -- Richards, Sylvia. *Memorial to Benjamin Barber Tanner, Fire Lands Pioneer*. Bicentennial ed. Willard, OH, Richards, 1978. 127p. D gives underscored title. [C682; NG95; D12254].

TAPPAN -- Myers, Merrible E. *The Tappan Family of Ravenna, Ohio*. NP, 1952. 31 leaves. [D12261].

TAPPAN -- Tappan, W. R. *Cooking with the Tappans - 1st ed.* New York, NY, Vantage Press, 1986. 91p. 1. Tappan family. 2. Tappan, W. R.-Family. 3. Businessmen-United States-Biography. 4. Mansfield (Ohio)-Biography. 5. Stove industry and trade-Ohio-Massillon-History. [G650].

TAYLOR -- NAS. *The Taylor - Livingston Centenary in Franklin County*. (In Ohio Archaelogical and Historical Society Quarterly) Columbus, OH, 1904. v. 13, p. 486-503. [L16811].

TAYLOR -- Duty, Allene Beaumont. *The Taylor Family*. Cleveland, OH, Duty, 1972. 88 leaves. [D12285].

TAYLOR -- Genther, Clara Sesler. *Ancestors and Descendants of Taylor and Hager Families of Madison and Union Counties, Ohio*. Cincinnati, OH, Genther, 1984. vii, 282p. DC gives 282, 21p. [C684; NG95; DC3595].

TAYLOR -- Helgeson, Betty Taylor and Geneva Taylor Koons. *Some Descendants of Isaac Anderson Taylor and Eleanor McFarland*. Garland, TX, B. T. Helgeson, Enon, OH, G. T. Koons, 1983. 50 leaves of plates. [C684].

TAYLOR -- Mills, Edward C. *The Taylor Family of Dentists*. (In Ohio Archaelogical

and Historical Society Quarterly) Columbus,
OH, 1947. v. 56, p 392-398. [L16832].

TAYLOR -- Taylor, Edward Livingston. *The
Old House and the Taylor - Livingston
Centenary.* Columbus, OH, F. J. Heer Printing
Co., 1907. 69p. D gives 67p.
[D12301; X925-FW/NY/OH].

TAYLOR -- Taylor, Margaret W. *Crystal Lake
Reflections.* Cleveland, OH, Tecohio Pub. Co.,
1985. 105 leaves, 1 leaf of plates. 1.
Taylor, Margaret W. (Margaret Wischmeyer),
1920- 2. Taylor family. 3. Crystal Lake
Region (Mich.:Lake)-History. 4. Crystal Lake
Region(Mich.:Lake)-Social life and customs.
[G653].

TAYLOR -- Taylor, Wallace. *Genealogy and
Brief History of the Thomas Taylor Family; One
of the Pioneer Settlers of Jefferson County,
Ohio, later Harrison County.* Oberlin, OH,
News Print, 1920. 172p. [X926-FW].

TAYLOR -- Taylor, William O. *The Family
Genealogy... Tricentenary ed.* Archbold, OH,
1930. 30p. [X926-NY].

TEAGARDEN -- Vogt, Helen Elizabeth.
*Genealogy and Biographical Sketches of
Descendants of Abraham Tegarden, from Arrival
in America, Including European Background.*
Berkeley, CA, Printed by Consolidated Pinters,
1967. 696p. 1. Teagarden family. [G653].

TEAGARDEN -- Vogt, Helen Elizabeth.
*Genealogy and Biographical Sketches of
Descendants of Abraham Tegarden, from Arrival
in America, Including European Background -
Rev. ed.* Willowick, OH, G. and S. Teegarden
(sp?), 1988. vi, 890p. 1. Teagarden family.
2. Tegarden, Abraham, 1688 or 9-1753-Family.
[G653].

TEAPE -- Day, Jesse H. *The Descendants of
John Teape and Elizabeth Bunce.* Athens, OH,
J. H. Day, 1984. xii, 304p. [C685].

TEMPLE -- Temple, Albert R. and Danny D. Smith. *The Rise of the Temple, A Millenium of Power & Progress, 716 A.D. to the Present & Genealogy.* 1st ed. Cincinnati, OH, Temple Family Association, 1973. vii, 108p. 100 copies printed. [S2468].

TEMPLE -- Temple, Albert R. *The Rise of the Temple, A Millenium of Power and Progress, 716 (A.D.) to the Present.* Rev. 3d. ed. Cincinnati, OH, Temple Family Assoc., 1973. xvi, 125p. [X929-MH/NY].

TEMPLE -- Temple, Albert R. and Danny D. Smith. *The Rise of the Temple, A Millenium of Power and Progress, 716 A.D. to the Present, and Genealogy.* -- 4th ed. -- Cincinnati, OH, Temple Family Association, 1979. V. [C686].

TENNEY -- Tenney, Horace A. *Genealogy of the Tenney Family, More Particularly of Daniel Tenney, and Sylvia Kent, His Wife, Late of Laporte, Lorain County, Ohio from 1634 and 1638 to 1875.* Madison, WI, M. J. Cantwell, printer, 1875. 76 (i.e. 80)p. [L16884].

THATCHER -- Briggs, Samuel. *Memoir of Hon. Peter Thatcher of Cleveland, OH.* Cleveland, OH, 1883. 8p. Reprinted from the N. E. Historical and genealogical register for January, 1883. [L16919].

THOBURN -- Thoburn, C. Stanley. *The Ancestry of Irish-American Thoburns.* Cleveland, OH, 1955. vi, 163 leaves. [X932-FW/NY/OH/SU].

THOMAS -- Miller, Stella. *A Genealogy of the Thomas Family, 1625-1911.* Mt. Sterling, OH, 1911. 39p. [X932-LI].

THOMAS -- Thomas, Alfred A. *To My Boy Thomas Head Thomas. A Genealogical Sketch of the Thomas Family.* Dayton, OH, 1885. 39p. [X932-CH/FW/LI/MH/NY/OH].

THOMAS -- Thomas, C. Robert. *Thomas and Related Families.* Strasburg, OH, C.R. Thomas [1986]- <v. 1-3 in 1> Vol. 3 has title: Thomas Doll-Dreher and related families. 1. Thomas family. [G658].

THOMAS -- Wingert, Grace Harper. *Our Kinsmen, A Record of the Ancestry and Descendants of Griffith Thomas, a Pioneer Resident of Orange County, North Carolina.* Springfield, OH, 1938. 135p. [L16963].

THOMPSON -- NAS. *Revolutionary War Soldier James Thompson Buried in Cashocton County, Ohio.* NP, 1988. 10, 32 leaves. DC3639].

THOMPSON -- Agricola, David V. *Descendants of John Thompson, 1783-1854, of Lawrence County, Kentucky.* Lakewood, OH, Agricola, 1976. iii, 19p. [C690; X937-FW].

THOMPSON -- Grover, Amy U. T. *Thompson - Beeson Family Record, 1682-1927.* Cheshire, OH, 1927. 35p. [X935-FW].

THOMPSON -- Holter, Patricia. *From Candelight to Sattelite: Thompson - Beeson Family History: Including Ancestors and Descendants of Pierce Clancy Thompson and Elisabeth Beeson United in Holy Matrimony, September 3, 1823. -- 1st ed. --* Cheshire, OH, History Book Committee, 1985. x 324p. [C690].

THOMPSON -- Moore, Sophia J. *History of The Thompson.* Damascus, OH, 1911. 79 l. [NG96].

THOMPSON -- Moore, Sophia J. T. *History of The Thompson(s).* Rev. by Rev. J. G. Black. Damascus, OH, A. Pim, 1911. 79 p. [X934-FW].

THOMPSON -- Thompson, Margilou J. *Thompson Genealogy: Being the Descendants of Christian Thompson, Down Seven Generations from 1791-1953.* Geneva, OH, 1953. 16p. [X935-FW].

THOMPSON -- Thompson, R. C. *Thompson Family History and Genealogy.* Toledo, OH, 2 vols. in 1. Monthly. [X934-NY].

THOMPSON -- NAS. *Thompson and Given Families, with Their Ancestral Lines and Present Branches: Rev. Samuel F. Thompson and Ellen Kerr Givens.* Hamilton, OH, Brown & Whitaker, 1898. 238p. [L16989].

THOMPSON -- Thompson, T. W. *The Thompson Geneology (sic). 3rd ed.* Dover, OH, Express Press, 1979. 196, 24, 15p. [C691].

THOMPSON -- Williamson, "May" Thompson. *Our William Thompsons of Ireland and Pennsylvania and Some Descendants.* Youngstown, OH, Williamson, 1941. xi, 3, 161p. [L17006].

THORNBURGH -- Thornburgh, William W. *History of the Thornburgh Family.* Urbana, OH, 1929. 152p, 38 leaves. [X937-FW].

THOROMAN -- Crawford, H. M. *Thoromans of Adams County, Ohio.* Poughkeepsie, NY, 1975. iii, 138p. 17 leaves. [X938-FW].

THREADGILL -- Miller, Janis Heidenreich. *Threadgills, Book II.* Baltimore, MD, Gateway Press, Hudson, OH, J. H. Miller, 1983. ii, 325p. Companion to Threadgills in America. [C693].

THROCKMORTON -- Swiger, Lorain B. *Family Sketches of the Throckmortons of Southern Ohio.* Waverly, OH, Swiger, 1975. 289p. [S2494].

THRUSH -- Thrush, Lilliam Kemper. *A Thrush Family History.* Worthington, OH, L. K. Thrush, 1984. 20, 26 leaves. 5 leaves of plates. [C693].

THRUSTON -- NAS. *A Tribute to General Gates Phillips Thruston.* Dayton, OH, United Bretheren Publishing House, 1914. 1, 129p. [L17058].

TICKNOR -- Teachenor, Richard Bennington... *A Partial History of the Tichenor Family in America, Desecendants of Martin Tichenor of Connecticut and New Jersey, and a Complete Genealogy of the Family Descending from Isaac Tichenor, of Ohio, Spelling the Name Teachenor with Some Reference to the Probable Collateral Lineage Descended from Ticknor of Massachusetts.* Kansas City, MO, 1918-20. 39p. [L17082].

TIDD -- Tidd, Howard H. *A History of the Tidds of Ohio.* NP, 1958. D gives: 1962. 175p. [L17084; D12483].

TIFFIN -- Gilmore, William E. *Life of Edward Tiffin, the First Governor of Ohio.* Chillicothe, OH, Harney, 1897. 149, 2p. [X941-FW].

TILTON -- Lochner, Edwin F. *The Ancestry of Earle Barrett Tilton, 1899- . Also Lochner and Payner Families.* Colombus, OH, E. B. Tilton, Philadelphia, PA, E. F. Lochner, 1983. 40 l., 168[i.e. 335]p. NG gives 168p. C notes: "authorized by Earle Barrett Tilton". [C695; NG96].

TILTON -- Richardson, Robert H. *Tilton Territory: A Historical Narrative , Warren Township, Jefferson County, Ohio, 1775-1838.* Philadelphia, PA, Dorrance, 1977, viii, 300p. [C695].

TIMMONS -- Beaver, Norman and Frances T. *The Timmons Story.* Otterbein, OH, Beaver, 1959. 39p. [X942-MH].

TINKER -- Tinker, A. B. *The Ancestors of Silas Tinker in America. From 1637. A Partial Record Read at the Annual Reunion of the Descendants of Silas Tinker at Ashtabula, Ohio. August 15, 1889.* Akron, OH, The Werner Printing and Litho. Co., 1889 11p. [L17120].

TINKEY -- Tinkey, James C. *1946 Supplement to the Tinkey and Martin Books.* Mt. Vernon,

298

OH, 1946. Ed. 2. Pagination not given.
[X942-FW/MH].

TINNEY -- NAS. *The Adamic Lineages, the Royal Lineages, the Ancestrial (sic) Lineages of Thomas Milton Tinney of Ohio, Utah, and California.* NP, 1971. 8 leaves. [S2510].

TIPTON -- Heinemann, Charles Brunk. *Tipton Family of Maryland, Virginia, Tennessee, Kentucky, Ohio, Indiana, Illinois, Missouri.* Washington, DC, 1934. [VV185].

TISDALE -- Hamel, Claude Charles. *Genealogy of a Branch of the Tisdale Family, Vermillion Township, Erie County, Ohio.* Amherst, OH, 1951. 5 leaves. [L17133].

TITUS -- Titus, Elroy Wilson. *A History of the Titus - Capron and Related Families: Originally of New England and the State of New York.* Columbus, OH, E. W. Titus, 1984. 3 v. (iii, 1486p.) DC gives underscored (cover) title. C omits "Capron" in title. [C696; DC3663].

TODD -- Becker Frederick. *A Todd Family History and Genealogy, 1749-1987: Todds of Somerset County, New Jersey and Hamilton County, Ohio - Principally the Ancestors and Descendants of John and Ann Phoenix Todd.* Decorah, IA, Anundsen Pub., 1987. 152p. 1. Todd family. 2. Todd, Adam, d. ca. 1765-Family. 3. New Jersey (State)-Genealogy. 4. Ohio-Genealogy. [G664].

TODD -- Tod, John. *Some Account of the History of the Tod Family and Connections.* Youngstown, OH, 1917. 5, 180p. Only 50 copies printed. [X944-CH/FW/LI].

TOMLINSON -- Casari, Robert B. *A Brief History of the Tomlinson Family of Ross County, Ohio.* Chillicothe, OH, R. B. Casari, 1982. 37 leaves. in various foliations, 2 leaves of plates. [C697].

TONG -- Stout, Harold F. *Tong, Tongue and Allied Families.* Dover, OH, 1947. xv, 101p. [X945-FW/NY].

TONG -- Stout, Harold F. *Tong, Tongue and Allied Families. Ed. 2.* San Diego, CA, Finley-Stout-Tong Family Association, 1974. 201p. [X945-FW].

TOPE -- Tope, M. *A History of the Tope Family; Setting Forth a full Account of the Trials, Successes, Peculiar Characteristics, Occupations &c.. of This Race of People in This Country Down to Date.* Bowerston, OH, The Patriot Office, 1896. 78p. [L17176].

TORRENCE -- Dieckmann, Paul. *Ancestry of the Torrence and Findlay Families of Cincinnati, Ohio.* New Kensington, PA, 1965. 32 leaves. [X946-CH; VP228].

TORRENCE -- Torrance, John Findlay and William Torrence Handy. *Chart of the Torrence, Findlay, Brownson, Paull, Irwin, McDowell, and Smith Families of Pennsylvania.* Cincinnati, OH, The Henderson-Achert-Krebs Litho Co., 1894. Genealogical Table. [L17182; VP228].

TOTMAN -- Hawks, Alice T. *The Totman Family of Western New York, Ohio and Wisconsin and Their Descendants.* Bellows Falls, VT, 1939. 14 leaves. [X946-NY].

TOWNSEND -- Cummings, Marian Sill. <u>William Townsend of Tyringham Massachusetts.</u> His Ancestors and Descendants in Allied Lines: *Tolman, Sill, Skinner, Hitchock, Bennett, and Hiller.* East Cleveland, OH, Waterbury P ess, 1932. 4, 3-42, 8p., D gives 42p. and underscored title. [L17230; D12591].

TOWNSEND -- Geissinger, Lulu Townsend Armstrong. *My Lovely World.* Columbus, OH, Geissinger, 1969. 174p. [L17234; D12592].

TOWNSEND -- Townsend, Hollis L. and LLoyd R. *The Genealogy and History of the Solomon Townsend Family, 1754-1962.* Cuyahoga Falls, OH, R. F. Plummer Co., 1962. 202p. [L17233; D12595].

TRACHT -- Miller, Minnie C. *The Tracht Family Tree.* Galion, OH, Wilson Printing Co., 1935. 33p. Errata sheet inserted at p. 19 [L17237;D12606].

TRAVIS -- Travis, Boyd W. *Descendants of Robert and Phoebe (L'Estrange) Travis.* Decorah, IA, Anundsen Pub., Co., Bluffton, OH, B. W. Travis, 1981. vii, 210, 4 pages of plates. [C701].

TREADWAY -- Lewis, Ailene Fitch. *The Tredway, Gooch, Embry, Cyphers, and Allied Lines, from England to Maryland, Virginia, Ohio, Kentucky, Illinois: West to North Missouri, Kansas, 1597-1983.* Holden, MO, A. F. Lewis, 1948. 33 leaves, 2 leaves of plates. [C701; VV186].

TRENT -- Trent, Ivan. *May We Remember--: A History of the Trent and Painter Families of Virginia.* Columbus, OH, J. Leezer, 1981. 222p. [C702].

TRIMBLE -- Tuttle, Mary McA. T. and Henry B. Thompson. *Autobiography and Correspondence of Allen Trimble, Governor of Ohio, with Genealogy of the Family...* Columbus, OH, 1909. v, 240p. p. 1 Reprint from the "Old Northwest" genealogical society "Genealogy of Trimble", p. 237-240. [L17303].

TRIPLETT -- Lytle, Leonard. *The Descendants of Joseph Triplett of Hardy County, West Virginia, and Summit and Licking Counties, Ohio.* Ballycastle, NJ, J. C. Scarlett & Son, printer. 1955. 12p. [L17309; VV187].

TROTT -- Trott, Jacob. *Record of Trott Family; from Great-Grandfather Meier, Born Early Sixteenth Century.* Clyde, OH, 1907. 7p. [X952-CM/MH/OH].

TROYER -- Troyer, Milo R. *Descendants of John F. Troyer and Pauline J. Mullett, Adella Mueller Ryser.* Wooster, OH, Author, 1974. 80p. [X953-FW].

TROYER -- Yoder, Kate (Hershberger). *Descendants of Jeptha A. Troyer, Born in Holmes County, Ohio, A.D. 1825.* Napponee, IN, Evangel Press, 1957. 175p. [L17338].

TRUAX -- Hires, Thura Colby Truax. *Thura Truax Hires Manuscripts: A Genealogical Study of the Names du Trieux, Truax, Trueax, Truex (sic) in the States of Pennsylvania and Ohio.* Ann Arbor, MI, Association of Philippe Du Trieux Descendants, 1983. V. <1 >. V. 1. Pennsylvania, Ohio. [C703; VP230].

TRUAX -- Hires, Thura Colby Truax. *Thura Truax Hires Manuscripts: A Genealogical Study of the Names de Trieux, Truax, Trueax, Truex (sic) in the States of Pennsylvania and Ohio.* Ann Arbor, MI, Association of Philippe De Trieux Descendants, 1983-<1985 >. v. <1,2 >. v. 1. Pennsylvania, Ohio. -v. 2. New York and Canada. 1. Truax family. [G671].

TRUESDELL -- Truesdell, Wesley E. *Twelve Generations from the Colonial Immigrant to the Present Time; Three Hundred Years in America.* NP, 1938. 11p. Massachusetts, Connecticut, New York, Vermont, Ohio Truesdell Family Record. [L17345].

TUELL -- Heuss, Lois Ione Hotchkiss. *The Ancestors and Descendants of David Prince Tuell and Charlotte Elizabeth Miller, Including Their Kinship with Allied Families of Prince, Short - Stover, Miller, Applegate, Daily, Wise.* Akron, OH, Heuss, 1977. 90 leaves. X gives 90 pages typewritten; omits date. [C705; X954-FW].

TUFTS -- Tufts, Jay Franklin. *Tufts Family History.* Cleveland Heights, OH, Tufts, 1963. 280, xxxxx (sic) p. [D12696].

TULLIS -- Little, Lawrence. *A Record of Descendants of Moses Tullis, Sr. of Berkeley Co., Va. and Thomas Little of Hunterdon Co., N.J.* Urbana, OH, Little, 1972. 76 leaves. [D12702].

TUPPER -- Hasson, Ethel W. *Tupper Family in America.* Centerburg, OH 1943. 2 leaves. [X955-OH].

TURNER -- Turner, V. E. *The Ancestors and Relations of Clarence Lester Turner: A Genealogy and Autobiography.* Delaware, OH, 1970. 134 leaves. [X956-OH].

TURPIN -- Holt,Florrie Bell. *Antique Turpin Dolls.* Cincinnati, OH, Talaria, 1961. 94p. [L17414].

TURRITTIN -- Doughten, Thomas Edson. *The Story of Samuel Turrittin and His Children.* Toledo, OH, Author, 1965. 56 l. X gives 56p. [NG98: X957-FW/LA].

TUTTLE -- Tuttle, Alva M. *Tuttle - Tuthill Lines in America.* Columbus, OH, Estel Print., 1968. 2 vols. (726p.) [X957-FW].

TWITTY -- Gregory, Lewis J. *Twitty Family in America, 1671-1976.* Columbus, OH, 1976. xvi, 431p. [X957-FW].

U

UHRBROCK -- Uhrbrock, Richard Stephen. *The Uhrbrock Family of Schleswig-Holstein, Hannover New York and Maryland.* Athens, OH, 1966. 30 leaves. [L17474].

ULERY -- NAS. *John and Elizabeth Ulery; A Brief Historical Sketch of Ancestry, Relationship and a Partial List of Descendants.* Springfield, OH, Ulery Reunion Assoc., 1930. 17p. [X959-FW].

ULERY -- NAS. *Ulery Family in Ohio and Pennsylvania.* NP, n.d. 25p. VP lists as ULREY. [X959-OL; VP232].

UNCAPHER -- Leeka, Caryl Ellis. *George A. Uncapher of Marion County, Ohio, 1815-1895.* NP, 1954. 66 leaves. [D12762].

UNDERWOOD -- Kellogg, Dale C. *Antecedents and Descendants of Levi Underwood, 1831-1885, and Related Families.* Elyria, Ohio, Kellogg, 1965. 105p. D gives underscored title. [L17491; D12766].

V

VAIL -- Engellant, Beulah Alm. *Descendants of Thomas Vail in Belmont County, Ohio in 1802.* Gt. Falls, MT, Engellant, 1981. 78 1. [D12797].

VAN BUSKIRK -- Kuesthardt, Anita M. *Who Was in the Van Buskirk Family; Early Generations, 1660-1800.* Port Clinton, OH, 1944. 17 leaves. [X965-NY].

VAN BUSKIRK -- (Van B.) Kuesthardt, Anita M. *The Genealogy of the Van Buskirk Family...* Port Clinton, OH, 1947. 1 vol. [X965-NY].

VAN CLEVE -- Van Cleve, Benjamin. *Memoirs of Benjamin Van Cleve.* Dayton, OH, Dayton Pub. Lib., n.d. 170p. 6 leaves. [X966-FW].

VAN DEEST -- Van Deest, Velma. *The Van Deest Family: A Genealogy, 1745-1988.* Johnstown, OH, USA, V. Van Deest, 1989. 166p. 1. Van Deest family. [G682].

VANDAVEER -- Vandaveer, Frederick Ewart and Kenneth Eugene Vandaveer. *The Vandaveer Family of Green County, Illinois.* Fairview Park, OH, Printed by West Side Blue, 1970. xi, 197p. [A678].

VANDERCOOK -- Neikirk, Floyd Edwin. *Some Descendants of Isaac Vandercook, b. 1662, d. 1750, Through Michael Vandercook, Member of the Committee of Safety, Soldier of the Revolution, Albany Militia.* Clyde, OH, 1953. 54 leaves. [S2594].

VANDEUSEN -- Pratt, Cherry Laura Van Deusen. *The Genealogy of Rev. W. H. Van Deusen (Son of Jacob Dean Van Deusen and Julia Maria Custer McIntosh Van Deusen) and Custer, Hendrickson, Belton, Chelf, Evans, and Stayton Families.* Rockford, OH, Rockford Press, 1969. 83p. A lists as: Van Deusen D gives underscored title. [A679; NG98; D12858].

VAN ETTEN -- Scott, Eva Alice. *Jacobus, Jansen Van Etten. Some Ten Generations in America of Jacobus Jansen Van Etten, Immigrant from... Holland to Kingston, New York about 1663.* Youngstown, OH, Scott, 1950. xx, 164p. D gives xx, 164, 17p. Ltd. ed. 100 numb. copies. [L17602; D12872].

VANFOSSEN -- VanFossen, Katherine Hobson. *The VanFossen (Van Fossen) Family in America.* Columbus, OH, VanFossen, 1949, 1952. 192p. D gives: xv, 192p. [L17605; D12875].

VAN HYNING -- Ely, June Herman. *VanHyning Family History: Descendants of Henry VanHyning (1737-1839) from New York State to Ohio.* Baltimore, MD, Gateway Press, x, 381, 22p. 1. Van Hyning family. 2. VanHyning, Henry ca. 1737-1839-Family. 3. New York (State)-Genealogy. 4. Ohio-Genealogy. [G682].

VAN HYNING -- Nance, Margery Ellen Van Hyning. *Genealogy of Henry Van Hyning, Revolutionary War Patriot and Ohio Pioneer: with Special Emphasis on the Family of Sylvester and Melissa (Hollister) Van Hyning.* Sun City, AZ, M. E. V H Nance, 1981 or 1982. 22 leaves. [C715].

VAN METER -- Van Meter, James T. *Van Meter Pioneers in America. Prepared for Van Meter*

Family Reunion, Putnam City, Ohio, June 25, 1978. Minnetonka, MN, Van Meter, 1978. 28 leaves. [C715].

VAN PELT -- Tilden, Ella E. Van Pelt. *History of the Van Pelt Family.* Cleveland, OH, 1930. 1, 32 numb. leaves. [L17634].

VAN SICKLE -- Van Sickle, John W. *A History of the Van Sickle Family in America.* Springfield, OH, Van Sickle, 1880. viii, 9-236p. D gives 236p. [L17648; D12913].

VAN SICKLE -- Van Sickle, John W. *Genalogical Notes and Abstracts of Church Records Relative to the Van Sickle Family.* Springfield, OH, 188_. 241 leaves. [X971-NY].

VANTREES -- Van Trees, Robert V. *A Decade of Digging: Vantrees, Van Trees, Vantreese, Van Treese, Vantrease, Vertrees, Von Trees, etc. Genealogy.* Huber Heights, OH, R. V. Van Trees, 1983. 42 leaves. [C717].

VANEMAN -- Vaneman, George. *George Vaneman, Hancock County Presbyterian Minister: His Daybook and Genealogy.* Findlay, OH, Hancock County Chapter OGS, 1988. 35, 5p. 1. Hancock County (Ohio)-Genealogy. 2. Vaneman, George, 1786-1877-Archives. 3. Vaneman family. 4. Marriage records-Ohio-Hancock County. [G685].

VARIAN -- Briggs, Sam... *The Book of the Varian Family, with Some Speculation as to Their Origins, etc.* Cleveland, OH, T. C. Schenk & Co., 1881. 4, 102p. [L17667].

VASS -- Anderson, Alvin L. *Vass and Allied Families: The Descendants of John and Mary (Cosner) Vass.* Canton, OH, Anderson, 1975. iv, 169 leaves. [X972-FW/NY].

VAUGHAN -- Adams, Martha V. *Forebears and Kindred.* Hanover, OH, Author, 1951. 47p. [X973-FW].

VEALE -- Shoemaker, Frank R. *History of the Veale Family*. Clayton, OH, 1964. 80p. [X973-FW].

VEITCH -- Emerson, Ann-Jannette. [G688]. See above: ELLIS. [G212].

VENABLE -- Brown, Henrietta Brady. *The Ancestors and Descendants of William Henry Venable*. Cincinnati, OH, Brown, 1954. 198p. D gives 198, 8p. [L17701; D12957].

VENABLE -- Brown, Henrietta Brady. *Some Vanables of England and America*. Cincinnati, OH, Kinderton Press, 1961. x, 463p. [L17702; D12958].

VERMILLION -- Burgner, W. C. *Vermillion and Stevenson - Stephenson Families of Allen County, Ohio*. Lima, OH, n.d. 68p. [X974-FW].

VINCENT -- Vincent, Boyd. *Our Family of Vincents: A History, Genealogy, and Biographical Notices*. Cincinnati, OH, Priv. Print., Stewart Kidd Co., 1924. 158p. [L17747].

VINCENT -- Vincent, Eli B. *Vincents Who Came from Providence, Rhode Island and Settled in Ohio about the Year 1800*. Marietta, OH, Priv. Print., 1932. 37p. [X976-OH].

VOGEL -- Clark, Faith. [G691]. See above: CLARK. [G141].

VOGT -- NAS. *The Vogt (Foucht) Family History, 1720-1947*. NP, Vogt (Foucht) Family Reunion Association of Ohio, 1937. 77p. PH gives no date. [D12987; X977-PH].

VON der Au -- Cochran, Richard M. *The Von der Au Genealogy: German Ancestors and American Descendants of Johannes and Elisabeth von der Au of Ernsthoffen, Hesse-Darmstadt, Cumberland County, Pennsylvania and Union County, Ohio: Including the Allied Families of Ruhl, Weidman, and Kinnel*. New

Concord, OH, R. M. Cochran, 1984. vii, 367p., 27 leaves of plates. [C724].

VONDERBURG -- Whedon, Nellie Woods. *The Vonderburg-Funderburg Family of Maryland and Ohio.* NP, 1954. 67 leaves. [D12990].

VON SCHRILTZ -- Kahn, Edythe T. *Our von Schriltzs in America, 1790-1988.* LaSalle, MI, E.T. Kahn, 1988. xvii, 783p. 1. Von Schriltz family. 2. Ohio-Genealogy. [G692].

VON VILLE -- McGrath, Mary Martha Von Ville. *Von Ville, Vonville, Vonwille, Vonwill, Vonvill, Families of Ohio, Maryland, U.S.A., Alsace, France.* Alpha, NJ, M. M. V. McGrath, 1984. 74p. [C724].

VORCE -- Vorce, Charles Marvin. *A Genealogical and Historical Record of the Vorce Family in America.* Cleveland, OH, Vorce, 1901. 111p. L lists under VORSE. [L17770; D12993].

W

WADDELL -- Smith, Guy H. *The Waddell Family.* Columbus, OH, n.d. 9 leaves. [X981-OH].

WADSWORTH -- Baldwin, C. C. *Wadsworth.* Cleveland, OH, Leader Printing, Co., 1882. pages 205-215 incl. (From the Author's Candee Genealogy, Cleveland, 1882). [L17799].

WADSWORTH -- Wadsworth, Mary Jane Fry. *The Wadsworth Family in America, 1632-1977.* Wilmington, OH, Wadsworth, 1978. 600p. [C725; D13011].

WAGNER -- Kintner, Nancy (Wagner). *History of the Wagner Family.* Carrollton, OH, Carroll Chronicle Press, 1917. 12p. [L17812].

WAGNER -- Moffat, Charles D. *Charles C. Waggoner, Auglaize County, Ohio, 1805-1879 and Allied Families of Layton, Bitler, Heidrick,*

Brackney, Hague, Bayliff. Decorah, IA, Anundsen Pub. Co., 1989. viii, 86p. 1. Wagner family. 2. Waggoner, Charles C., 1805-1879-Family. 3. Ohio-Genealogy. [G693].

WAGNER -- Wagner, Clark R. *History and Genealogy of the Wagner, Waggoner, Wagoner Family, 1941.* Arlington, OH, Advertiser Press, 1941. 304p. [L17815; D13019].

WAGNER -- Wagner, Clark R. *History and Genealogy of the Wagner, Waggoner, Wagoner Family.* Rochester, IN, Fulton County Historical Society, 1978. 304p. A reprint of the 1941 ed. published by the Advertiser Press, Tiffin, Ohio. [C727].

WAGNER -- Woodruff, Audrey L. (Mrs. Howard W.) [G694]. See above: ABELL. [G2; C727; DC3787].

WAITE -- Waite, Stuart G. *The Waite Family of Mass. and Ohio.* Springfield, MA, 1963. 70 leaves. [X983-LA].

WAKEFIELD -- McClure, Stanley W. *The Wakefield Family of Crosby Township, Hamilton County, Ohio.* NP, McClure, 1984. 39 leaves, 15 leaves of plates. [C727].

WALBORN -- Walborn, Herman W. *Walborn (Walburn) Genealogical History of America, Descendants from the Settlements of 1710, Including Data on Allied Families...* Piqua, OH, Hammer Graphics, 1975. 413p. NG gives: St. Paris, OH, omits printer. [NG99: X984-FW].

WALDSCHMIDT -- Matthews, Ruth K. V. *Christian Waldschmidt Family Record and History.* Findlay, OH, 1958. 34p. [X984-FW].

WALKER -- Mitchell, Morton, L. *A History of the Walkers and Millers of Stark County, Ohio.* NP, 1973. 25 leaves. [D13051].

WALLACE -- Hooper, Osman C. *The Story of Moses and William Wallace and Their Descendants: Barton, Hunter, Wolfe.* Columbus, OH, 1918. 47p. [X987-CH/FW/LI/NY].

WALLACE -- Warren, Ray B. *A Perspective of the Wallace - Warren - Stover Families.* Sidney, OH, 1970. 64 leaves. [X988-OH].

WALLS -- Brumfield, Marcia Conrad. *John P. Walls, 1834/N.C.--1898/Ohio.* Maysville, KY, Brumfield, 1990. 28p. [DC3805].

WALLS -- Knicely, Marilyn R. M. *Descendants of James Walls.* Coshocton, OH, 1971. 70p. 17 leaves. [X988-FW].

WALTER -- Hurd, Raymond W. *Genealogy of the Families of Jacob and Anna Ritz Walter and Jacob and Katherine Duerr Walter of Monroe County, Ohio. Revised.* Greensburg, PA, 1963. 23 leaves. [X989-NY].

WALTERS -- Walters, Raymond W. *One Branch of the Walters Family from pre-Revolutionary Days to the Present.* Cincinnati, OH, 1956. 17p. [X989-CH/FW/NY].

WALTZ -- NAS. *Waltz Family History and Genealogical Record, in Family Classification. Comprising Upward of 300 Names of Lineal Decendants (!) of Frederick Reinhart Waltz.* Dayton, OH, Reformed Publishing Company, Printers, 1884. xvi, 17-128p. [L17930].

WAMBOLDT -- Wombold, Elmer. *Wamboldt Family.* Dayton, OH, 1917. 67-122 leaves(?). Typewritten. [X991-MH].

WARD -- Ward, Harriett W. *Brief Account of Some of the Descendants of William Ward of Sudbury, Mass.* Euclid, OH, 1930. 47p. [X992-FW].

WARD -- Ward, Harry Parker. *Notes on the Family of Ward of Columbus, OH, Formerly of*

Great Yarmouth, England. Columbus, OH, 1898. 113p.? [L17954].

WARD -- Ward, Harry Parker. *A Memorial of Hudson Champlin Ward (1830-1897)... and a Chapter Memorial of His Deceased Son, William Vines Ward.* Columbus, OH, 1898. 163p. ltd. ed. 50 copies. [L17955].

WARD -- Ward, Harry Parker. *The Life of Dr. Isaac Blowers Ward (1800-1843) and His Wife Ann Vines (1803-1852) together with Some Account of Their Near Relatives, Particular Mention being made of the Late Caleb Vines, Esq. of London; Some Brief Genealogical Notes on the Wards of Norfolk and Suffolk and Vines Family of Berkshire; Also, the Complete Genealogy of Dr. Ward's Descendants to A. D. 1900.* Columbus, OH, 1900. 6, 13-251p. Ltd. ed. 35 copies. [L17957].

WARMAN -- NAS> *A History of the Warman and Related Families, Chiefly of Monongalia County, West Va.* Columbus, OH, 1972. On cover: A history of the Warman - Wells and related families. 155p. [X993-FW/LA/OH.PH; VV193].

WARMAN -- Titus, Elroy Wilson. *History of the Warman Family and Related Families.* Columbus, OH, Titus, 1972. 155p. [DS737].

WARNER -- Osler, Harold W. *Warner History.* Salesville, OH, 1935. 89p. Special attention to the Ancestors and Descendants of John Lewis Warner. Coat of Arms of Bye, Ellicott, and Ely Families. [L18006].

WARNER -- Strong, Doris Wolcott. *Ancestry and Descendants of Justus Warner, 1756-1856, One of the First Group of Settlers in 1811 in Liverpool (now Valley City) Medina County, Ohio in the Connecticut Western Reserve.* Washington, DC, 1941. 1, 18 leaves. [L18008].

WARNER -- Warner, Esther Mae Winget. *Descendants of William and Ann (Dyde)*

Warner, 1627-1954. Xenia, OH, Warner, 1954. 119p. D gives 128p. [L18010; D13155].

WARNIMONT -- La Fontaine, Leo S. [G700]. See above: FONTAINE. [G234].

WARNS -- Miller, N. Emerson. *The Cherokee Blood Trickles On: Stories and History of Martin and Martha Smith Warns and Their Descendants.* Nappanee, IN, Evangel Press, 1990. vi, 92p. 1. Warns family. 2. Warns, Martin, ca. 1797-1834-Family. 3. Warns, Martha Smith, ca.1790-ca.1846-Family. 4. Ohio-Genealogy. 5. Cherokee-Genealogy. [G700].

WARREN -- Duty, Allene Beaumont. *The Warren Family; Ancestors and Descendants of Moses Warren of Warrensille, Ohio From John Warren of Watertown, Massachusetts with Allied Families - 1st ed.* Cleveland, OH, Xerox Reproduction Center, 1985. iv, 207p. [C733; NG100; DC3825].

WARREN -- Swickheimer, Mary E. Rodman. *The Family of Thomas Warren,II and Margaret Milner Warren.* Delaware, OH, Swickheimer, 1972. 114p. [D13169; X995-FW].

WARREN -- Warren, Ray B. *Perspective of the Stover - Warren - Wallace Families.* Sidney, OH, 1970. 64 leaves. [X995-FW].

WARTENBE -- Ford, Mary Esther. *Wartenbe Genealogy: Ancestors and Descendatns of William and Catherine White Wartenbe of New Jersey, Virginia, and Ohio.* Baltimore, MD, Gateway Press, 1987. vi, 210p. 1. Wartenbe family. 2. Wartenbe, William, ca. 1760-1821-Family. [G701; NGS11; DC3828].

WASHBURN -- Parkinson, Mildred J. Smith. *A Genealogical History of the Washburns of Huron County, Ohio.* Milwaukee, WI, Parkinson, 1954. 92, xiv p. [L18052; D13182].

WASHINGTON -- Hoppin, Charles Arthur. *The Washington Ancestry and Records of the*

McClain, Johnson, and Forty Other Colonial American Families. Greenfield, OH, Edward Lee McClain, 1932. 3 v. [L18106; D13192].

WATERS -- Waters, Wilson. *Ancestry of the Waters Family of Marietta, Ohio.* Marietta, OH, Priv. Print. 1882. 2, 3-31p. [L18139].

WATERS -- Sisson, Eliza Paddock (Waters). *Reminiscences of the Bradford and Waters Families.* Marietta, OH, Printed by J. Mueller & Son, 1885. 16p. [L18140].

WATSON -- Stephen, David. *A Genealogy of the Watson Family: Descendants of Jonathan Watson of Washington County, Tennessee.* Mansfield, OH, S.D. Watson, 1986. iv, 73p. 1. Watson family. 2. Watson, Jonathan-Family. 3. Tennessee-Genealogy. [G703].

WATSON -- Watson, Clarence C. *Watson - Johnston (Johnson) Family History, 1815-1982.* Akron, OH, C. C. Watson, 1982. 33 leaves, 1 leaf of plates. [C736].

WATT -- Watt, Artiss N. [G703]. See above: SHEEHAN. [G603].

WAUGH -- French, Minerva W. *Historical Sketch of the Waugh Family... Read at the Reunion of the Waugh Family at Wakeman, Ohio, August 11, 1897.* NP, 1897. 10p. [X1001-FW].

WAUGH -- French, Minerva W. *"Thicker Than Water"; Genealogy of Dan Waugh Family.* Berlin Heights, OH, 1939. 80p. Begun in 1897 by M. W. French; continued by Elsie French. [X1001-FW].

WAUGH -- Lyman, H. H. *Dan Waugh Family. Information Tabulated from the Pamphlet by Minerva Waugh French of Wakeman, Ohio.* Oswego, NY, n.d. 11p. [X1001-FW].

WAUGH -- Waugh, Patricia Lee Russ. [G704]. See above: BOWERS. [G77].

WEAKLEY -- Weakley, Francis J. *The Weakley Family in America, 1703-1904.* Dayton, OH, 1904. 114p. [X1002-FW/LI].

WEAKLEY -- Weakley, Francis J. *The Weakley Family in America.* [United States, 1982] 114p. Reprint: Originally published as: The Weakley Family in America, 1703-1904. NP, 1904. (Dayton, OH, Press of the U. B. Pub. House.) [C737].

WEARY -- Weary, Frank Orlando. *Chronological Story of an Old Line Patriotic Pioneer All American Family with a Historic Published Record Extending Back Two Full Centuries.* Akron, OH, 1921. 45p. Cover Title Smith-Weary Chronology. [L18187].

WEAVER -- Bouic, Margaret E. M. *Jacob J. Weaver Family.* Ostrander, OH, 1974. 40p. [X1003-FW].

WEAVER -- Campbell, Mary Mae Cupp. *A Sense of Place: Virginia to Ohio and States West. Descendants of Peter Weaver and J. Jacob Kopp.* Lima, OH, Campbell, 1986. vi, 368p. [DC3857].

WEAVER -- Imhoff, Olive R. *Weaver Family of Maryland, Pennsylvania, Ohio, Illinois.* Pittsburgh, PA, 1962. [VP238].

WEAVER -- Weaver, Monroe A. *Benjamin Weaver (1839-1919) A Family History.* Shreve, OH, 1961. Unpaged. Paging irregular. [X1003-FW].

WEAVER -- Weaver, Monroe A. *Weaver Family.* Shreve, OH, 1961-66. Unpaged. [X1003-DP].

WEAVER -- Weidel, Helen T. *All the Descendants of Sarah Flora Weaver until 1963.* Kettering, OH, 1963. Unpaged. [X1003-CH].

WEBB -- Davis, W. E. *The Webb Lineage: James F., etc: George W., etc.* Glendale, OH, W.E. Davis, 1985. 1 v. (various foliations).

1. Webb family. 2. Webb, James F., 1820-1863-
Family. 3. Webb, George Washington, , d.
1915-Family. [G705].

WEBB -- Hamel, Claude Charles. *Genealogy of
a Branch of the Webb Family Which Came to
Amherst Township, Lorain County, Ohio in 1814
or 1815.* Amherst, OH, 1948. 4 l. [L18203].

WEBB -- Turner, Ronald R. *Webb Families of
the Virginias.* Fairview Park, OH, 1983. v,
162p. [C738; VV197].

WEBB -- Webb, Earl F. *"Oh," How I Have
Searched History and Genealogy: The Webb
Genealogy.* Dayton, OH, E. F. Webb, 1982. iv,
75 leaves. DS gives title: The Webb Family
History and Genealogy. Cover Title adds
dates: "1769-1982". [C738; DS744].

WEBB -- Webb, Samuel D. *The Genealogy of the
Webb Family.* Columbus, OH, 1932. 41 leaves.
[X1004-OH].

WEBBER -- Washburn, Lucy Adelia. *The
Richard Webber Family, a Genealogy from the
First Settlement in America.* Medina, OH, The
A. I. Root Co., 1909. 2, 21p. [L18208].

WEBER -- Hamel, Claude Charles. *Genealogy of
the Weber Family of Elyria, Lorain County,
Ohio Which Married Into the Hamel Family of
Amherst, Ohio.* Amherst, OH, 1948. 4 leaves.
[L18213].

WEBER -- Hamel, Claude Charles. *Genealogy of
the Weber Family of Elyria, Lorain County,
Ohio Which Married Into the Hamel Family of
Amherst, Ohio.* Elyria, OH, 1960. 6 leaves.
[L18214].

WEBER -- Weber, Minnie E. *David and Peter
Weber and Their Descendants.* Woodsfield, OH,
Author, 1961. 158p. Collected by Minnie
Weber about 1953 and closed by Clara Weber,
1961. [X1004-FW].

WEBSTER -- Webster, Frederick. *Legends of the Indian Hollow Road.* Elyria, OH, Lorain County Chapter, Ohio Genealogical Society, 1987. 36p. "Compilation of columns contributed... to the Elyria chronicle in 1912 and 1913". "Prepared from his interviews of the older area residents between 1906 and 1913". 1. Lorain County (Ohio)-History, Local-Sources. 2. Webster family. 3. Lorain County (Ohio)-Biography. [G705].

WEEKS -- Weeks, Dr. Frank Edgar. *Genealogy of Francis Weekes... and Collateral Lines; Bowne, Burrowes, Carpenter, Cooke, Cornell, Davenport, DeForest, Emery, Feake, Fones, Freeman, Goodwin, Fowler, Hoag, Ireland, Jansen, Kierstede, Kip, Montagne, Mosher, Paddy, Reddocke, Sands, Stevenson, Sutton, Taber, Thorn, Warren, Winthrop.* Kipton, OH, 1938. 746 numb. leaves. [L18243].

WEIS -- Weis, Lister O. (Bowers) and Edna M. (Fetzer) Weis. *A History and Genealogy of Nicholas Weiss and His Descendants.* Orrville, OH, 1862. 112p. [L18262].

WEISER -- Weiser, Frederick S. *Letters from the Mahatonga Valley; Correspondence from Jacob Weiser in the Mahatonga Valley, Northumberland County, Pennsylvania to Frederick Weiser, His Brother in Delaware County, Ohio.* Manheim, PA, John Conrad Weiser Family Association. 1967. 12p. [S2680; VP240].

WEITKAMP -- Weitkamp, Arthur Robert. *The Genealogy of the Weitkamps.* Cincinnati, OH, 1941. 3, 51 numb. leaves. [L18268].

WELCH -- Weaver, Gustine Courson. *Welch and Allied Families.* Cincinnati, OH, Powell & White, 1932. 312p. [L18275; D13308].

WELLER -- Weller, Cassius M. and Herbert C. *The Weller Family, Genealogy and Sketch Book, Especially the Ancestors and Descendants of*

Joseph Weller (1793-1814) Toledo, OH, H. C. Weller, 1946. 132 leaves. [L18292].

WELLS -- Cunningham, Ruth Coward. [G709]. See above: CUNNINGHAM. [G169].

WELLS -- Montgomery, Florence C. *Wells and Related Families That Moved from Maryland to the Ohio River Valley.* Hilton Village, VA, 1951. 221, 21p. (2 parts). [X1009-FW].

WELLS -- Roe, Mary Josephine. *Genealogy of Gen. James Wells and Descendants... Compiled 1883-1892.* Cincinnati, OH, The Webb Stationery & Printing Co., 1892. 142p. [L18304].

WELLS -- Wells, R. S. *Wells Family History.* Tippecanoe, OH, 1912. 29p. [X1009-FW].

WELSH -- Chamberlain, Georgianna Welsh (Mrs. Verne). *The Welsh Family from the Revolution to the Bicentennial, 1776-1976.* Wooster, OH, Chamberlain, 1976. 111p. X gives dates: "1776-1796"? and "Includes Cole descendants." [D13345; X1010-CH/FW/OH/SP].

WELSH -- Welsh, Doris V. *The Welsh Family of Maryland, Virginia, and Ohio, Descended from Major John Welsh.* 1980. 51 leaves. [NG101].

WENRICK -- Wenrick, Thomas K. *Wenricks of Bradford, Ohio and Their 1500 Descendants: A Bicentennial Survey.* Greenville, OH, 1976. 57p. [X1011-FW].

WERTZ -- Ungerer, Robert N. Mrs. (nee Thelma Shafer). *The Wertz Family, 1595-1978: Old Ties and New Links to Our Wertz Chain.* Wooster, OH, Mrs. R. N. Ungerer, 1978. 94p. [C744].

WESLEY -- Wakeley, Rev. J. B. *Anecdotes of the Wesleys; Illustrative of Their Character and Personal History, with an Introduction by Rev. J. M'Clintock.* New York, NY, Carlton & Lanahan, Cincinnati, OH, Hitchock & Walden, 1969. 391p. [L18360].

WESTERBECK -- Schmidt, Marjory. *Westerbeck Family History.* St. Marys, OH, M. Schmidt, 1989. 149p. 1. Westerbeck family. 2. Ohio-Genealogy. [G711].

WESTBROOK -- Coulter, W. J. *Vital Records of the Westbrook Family & Allied Families as Found in Orange Co., N.Y., Sessex Co., N.J., Pennsylvania, Ohio, Michigan, Illinois of the 1850-1960 Period as Noted.* Zephyrhills, FL, Coulter, 1953. 130 leaves. [D13387; VP242].

WESTFALL -- Baer, Mabel Van Dyke. *Westfall - Jakes, (Jacques) Families of Indiana, Ohio and Maryland.* NP, 1972. 223 l. [D13395].

WESTFALL -- Durett, Ralph. *Westfall Family of New York, Virginia, West Virginia and Ohio.* NP, 1974. 55 leaves. [D13396; VV198].

WESTHEIMER -- Westheimer, Irvin F. *Family of Ferdinand Westheimer.* Cincinnati, OH, Author, 1970. Unpaged. [X1014-CH].

WETHERILL -- Franklin, Leallah. *William Peter Wetherill: Ancestors and Descendants: Pioneers of Ohio.* Baltimore, MD, Gateway Press, 1988. viii, 365p. 1. Wetherill family. 2. Wetherill, William Peter, 1789-1830-Family. 3. Ohio-Genealogy. [G711].

WEYGANDT -- Powell, Esther Weygandt. *The Weygandt- Frase - Bechtel Family Record, 1523-1965.* Akron, OH, Powell, 1965. 104p. D gives 104, 12p. [L18408; D13404].

WHALLON -- Whallon, Rev. Edward Payson. *Some Family Records... Partial Histories of the Whallon, Hagaman, Bickle, Bridgeland, Kitchell, Pierson, Ball, Bruen, Crist, Hughes, Vincent, Bloodgood, Jans, Farrand, and Tuttle Families.* Cincinnati, OH, F. L. Rowe, 1934. 147p. "Kitchell family genealogy,.. by Mary Ellen Kitchell, supplementary to this book and to 'Robert Kitchell' and 'The Willis Family' p. (129) - 147. [L18416].

318

WHELAN -- Anderson, Alvin L. *Wheeland /
Wieland / Wheland / Weyland and Allied
Families.* Canton, OH, A. L. Anderson, 1984 -
<1986 >, V. <1-2 >. Contents V. 1. The
Wheeland, Wielad (sic), Weyland Family
History. V. 2. Descendants of Michael and
Elizabeth (Hildabittel) Wheeland. 1. Whelan
family. 2. Wieland family. [G712; C747].

WHETHERILL -- Franklin, Leallah. *Willim
Peter Whetherill: Ancestors and Descendants,
Pioneer of Ohio.* Baltimore, Gateway, 1988.
vii, 365p. [DC3897].

WHIPPLE -- Kappahan, Ruth Whipple and James
Grafton Carter. *Genealogy of the Whipple,
Paddock, Bull, Families in America, 1620-1970.*
Columbus, OH, 1969. 69 1. [A704].

WHITAKER -- Whitaker, Andrew M. *Whitaker
Family.* Cleveland, OH, 1846. 10p.
[X1017-FW].

WHITE -- Allen, L. P. *The Genealogy and
History of the Descendants of Mercy Shreve and
James White.* Greenville, IL, 1897. 8, 135p.
[X1018-LI].

WHITE -- Allen, L. P. *Sketches of Thomas
White of Ohio (Son of Mercy Shreve and James
White), His Children and Grandchildren.*
Greenville, IL, 1897. 110p. Bound with
above. [X1018-LI].

WHITE -- Davis, W. E. *The White Lineage:
William White, Hezekiah K. White, Mary K.
White, J. Emmett White, J. Lawrence White, W.
Cleve White, etc.* Glendale, OH, W.E. Davis.
1985. 32 leaves. 1. White family. 2, White,
William, 1799-1865-Family. [G713].

WHITE -- Fletcher, James A. *Family History
of the Home of George Jamison White of
Hampton, Adams Co., Pa. and Hester Jeneva
Murphy White of Millersport, Fairfield County,
Ohio.* Chillicothe, OH, 1963. 20p. 2 leaves.
[X1020-FW].

WHITE -- Ford, Mrs. Horatio. *Ancestors and Descendants of Thomas Howard White.* South Euclid, OH, 1928. Genealogical Table. [L18514].

WHITE -- Ford, Ella White. *Descendants of Thomas White, Sudbury, Mass., 1638.* Cleveland, OH, 1952. 93p. [L18528; D13461].

WHITE -- Reber, Marian J. *The White and Huffman Families of Franklin Township, Franklin County, Ohio.* NP, 1979. 166p. [D13473].

WHITE -- White, Fanny Marie. *Fanny Marie White Her Journal 1849-1876 Masschusetts and Ohio.* General James Breckenridge Chapter (Va.) DAR, G.R.C. NP, 1984. 199 l. [DC3918].

WHITE -- White, Franc and Andrew J. *Family History of James White and Fannie Pittinger and Their Descendants.* Painesville, OH, Acorn Printing, 1932, 142p. [X1019-FW].

WHITMARSH -- Bates, Newton Whitmarsh. *Genealogy of the Descendants of John Whitmarsh of Weymouth Mass.* Ashtabula, OH, P.H. Fassett, Printer, 1916. 85, 12p. [L18569; D13517].

WHITTECAR -- Abbott, Lyndon Eugene. [G716]. See above: ABBOTT. [G1].

WHITTIER -- Pierce, Doris Whittier. *Whittier Family of Philander Ellis Whittier and His Wife Mary Parker Tufts: Their Descendants and Some of Their Ancestry.* Sunbury, OH, D. W. Pierce, 1983. c-j, 228p. [C752].

WHITTLESEY -- NAS. *Military Record of the Descendants of John Whittlesey and Ruth Dudley, Who Were Married at Saybrook, Conn., June 20, 1664.* Cleveland, OH, Fairbanks, Benedict & Co., Printers, 1874. 14p. [L18610].

320

WIEGAND -- Wiegand, Madelon. *Roots, Branches and Twigs of Our Family Tree.* Conneaut, OH, M. Wiegand, 1979. 39p. Library of Congress copy gives: "ms note at head of title: Weigand, Burger, Bell, Hemingway, Richardson." [C753].

WIELAND -- Anderson, Alvin L. [G717]. See above: WHELAN. [G712].

WIGTON -- Carter, James Grafton. *Wigton - Carter Family, 1066-1975, and Related Families Crooks, Fawcett, Gates, Horner, Lisle, Porter, Tharp, Wallace.* Columbus, OH, Carter, 1975. 308 leaves. X gives date as 1974. [D13562; X1025-NY].

WILCOX -- Wilcox, Owen N. *Wilcox Family History.* Cleveland, OH, Wilcox, 1911. 63p. [L18560; D13571].

WILDER -- Langstroth, Theodore A. *Wilder Family.* Cincinnati, OH, 1959. 13 leaves, 21p. [X1027-FW].

WILDER -- McGregor, Margaret, Hattie McGregor, Mary McGregor Miller. *Descendants of James Wilder and Susan Wilmarth.* Springfield, OH, 1959. 16 l. [L18673].

WILDER -- Turner, Mary Rose (Wilder). *Extracts from the Book of the Wilders by which the Lineage of the Rhode Island Wilders Is Traced to Nicholas Wilder of England, 1485. Also, a Sketch of the Wilkinson Family.* Springfield, OH, 1927. 1, 19 numb. l, 2 leaves of plates. [L18669].

WILDMAN -- Wildman, George E. *Descendants of Eden Wildman, First Settler of East Farmington, and Early Wildman History.* Mesopotamia, OH, 1974. 23, 24p. [X1027-FW/NY].

WILEY -- Wylie, Jennie Dwight. *The Wylie Family from Pennsylvania and Ohio.* New York,

NY, 1959. 32p. NY lists under WYLIE.
[A711; XA1076-NY; VP242].

WILKINSON -- Wilkin, J. B. *The Genealogical Record of the Wilkin Family.* Leavitt, Carroll County, OH, J.B. Wilkin, 1876 [i.e.1986?]. 19 leaves. 1. Wilkinson family. 2, Ohio-Genealogy. [G719].

WILLARD -- Willard, D. H. *Willard Memoir. Sketch of the Life of Major Simon Willard, with Notice of Some of His Descendants to the Ninth Generation.* Cincinnati, OH, 1879. 10p. [X1028-FW/LI].

WILLARD -- Willard, Stephen F. *The Family of John Willard Ford, Youngstown, Ohio: Eight Generations Removed from Simon Willard...* Wollaston, MA, Author, 1964. 8 leaves. [X1028-MH].

WILLARD -- Willard, Stephen F. *The History of the Willard Family Association of America.* Wolloston, MA, Author, 1964. 38p. [X1028-NY].

WILLIAMS -- Lones, Lela Lillian. [G720]. See above: CRAWFORD. [G164].

WILLIAMS -- Fox, Margaret Elizabeth. *The Williams Family: Our Quaker Ancestors of Colonial New Jersey and Ohio.* [U.S.] M. E. Fox, 1983. 55 leaves, 9 l. of plates. [C755].

WILLIAMS -- Lewis, Percy Williams. *The Ancestors and Descendants of Ebenezer and Martha Porter Williams of Painesville, Ohio.* La Grange, IL, Lewis, 1974. 213, xxvi pages. [D13654; X1033-FW].

WILLIAMS -- Rendt, Gloria Woods. [G720]. See above: BOWSER. [G79].

WILLIAMS -- Smith, Loire Perkins. *Descendants of the Williams Family of the Second Century (by Loire Perkins Smith) and*

The Willimas Family's Hundred Years (by Edward Hall), 1901. Akron, OH, Smith, 1975. 77 leaves. 1. Williams family. [G721].

WILLIAMS -- Williams, Herman Joseph. *The George Philip Williams of Craig Co., Virginia, and Aylett Weaver of Monroe Co., West Virginia.* Portsmouth, OH, H.J. Williams, 1981. 264p. [C755; NG103].

WILLIAMS -- Williams, Jessie E. Palmer. *The John Waters Williams Family of Maryland and Ohio.* Washington, DC, 1949. 35, 5 leaves. FW & NY give 40 l. [NG103; X1031-FW/NY].

WILLIAMS -- Williams, Jessie Palmer. *The John Waters Williams Family of Maryland and Ohio.* New York, NY, 1949. 35 leaves. [D13678].

WILMS -- Wilms, Joyce Fox. *The Wilms Family from Northern Holland to the USA, 1866-1965.* Canfield, OH, J. F. Wilms, 1985. vii, 27 leaves. [C757].

WILLSEY -- Bell, Carol Willsey. *The Honorable Jacob Wilsey's Journal, 1831-1860.* Youngstown, OH, Bell, 1970. 67p. [D13718].

WILLSON -- Willson, Elizabeth L. *Journey in 1836 from New Jersey to Ohio.* Morrison, IL, Shawver Pub. Co., 1929. 47p. [X1035-DP].

WILSON -- Brien, Lindsay D. M. *Wilson Families of Southern Ohio; Family, Court and Cemetary Records from Counties of Butler, Greene, Miami, and Montgomery.* Fort Wayne, IN, Pub. Lib., 1966. 33p. [X1037-FW].

WILSON -- Richards, Lynda Wilson. *Wilson - Shepherd Family History, 1592-1983.* Massillon, OH, W. Richards, 1983. xiii, 252p., 4 pages of plates. [C758].

WILSON -- Travis, Boyd W. *Descendants of Mathew and Elizabeth (Culbertson) Wilson.* Decorah, IA, Anundsen Publishing Co.,

Bluffton, OH, B. W. Travis, n.d., vi, 121p., 2 pages of plates. [C758].

WILSON -- Westwater, Martha. *The Wilson Sisters, a Biographical Study of Upper Middle-Class Victorian Life.* Athens, OH, Ohio University Press, 1984. x, 250p. [C759].

WILSON -- Wilson, Merritt. *The Wilson Family of Western Maryland and West Virginia, and Associated Families: Ashby, Cresap, Harvey, Moon.* Athens, OH, Lawhead Press, 1971. [VV203].

WILSON -- Wilson, Richard Eugene. *The Willson Family, 1672-1959.* Kent, OH, 1959. 324 leaves. *Supplement No. 1* 1960- Kent, OH, 1960. [L18854].

WILSON -- Wilson, Roy E. *The William Wilson, Sr., 1722-1851, Family.* Zanesville, OH, Wilson, 1977. 113p. [D13761].

WILTROUT -- McCorkle, Elizabeth S. *A Memorial Collection of Notes on the Revolutionary Ancestors of Floy Aileen Wiltrout Horn.* Ashland, OH, 1963. 22 leaves. [X1038-FW/OH].

WILTROUT -- Wiltrout, Dale E. *Wiltrout Genealogy; Being an Attempt to Trace All of the Wiltrouts Who Ever Lived.* Ashland, OH, 1976. 333p. [X1038-FW].

WINANS -- Baldwin, John Dwight. *Winans; Descendants of Jacob Winans (1726-1910).* Cleveland, OH, 1943. 27 leaves. [X1038-WR].

WINEBRENNER -- Gibbony, A. G. *Winebrenner Genealogy.* Newark, OH, 1961. 110p. Reprint of 1949 edition. [X1039-FW].

WINEMILLER -- Wood, Helen Winemiller. *Our Family History.* Lima, OH, H. W. Wood, 1977. xviii, 228p. DS adds: "3 folded leaves". [C760; DS768].

WINGATE -- Warner, Esther Mae Winget. *The Wingate-Winget Families in America.* Osborn, OH, Herald Print Shop, 1931. 188p. [D13781].

WINTERRINGER -- Smith, G. K. *Names from John Winterringer's Ledger*, Martinsburg, Knox County, OH, 1830. pni. Typewritten. [X1041-OH].

WINTERS -- Bengtson, Corrine Wineteer. *The Wineteers, Part of Their Story: in New York, Virginia, Kentucky, Indiana, Illinois, South Dakota, Nebraska, Kansas, Missouri, Oklahoma, Wyoming, Montana, Idaho, Ohio, Oregon, California, Texas, Colorado, Washington, Iowa.* Ojai, CA, C.W. Bengtson, 1985. iv, 210p. 1 Winters family. [G729].

WINTERS -- Kilbarger, Harold. [G729]. See above: HENLEY. [G312].

WINTERS -- Winters, Jonathan. *A Sketch of the Winters Family.* Dayton, OH, United Brethern Publishing House, 1889. variously paged. [L18917].

WISE -- Champlin, Grace M. B. *Family Wise: The Story of the Kausler - Wise Family of Maryland, Pennsylvania, Ohio, Indiana, 1753-1975.* Minneapolis, MN, Champlin, 1975. 114p. Includes Shuggert family. [X1041-MH; VP248].

WISE -- Huffman, Hazel Wise. [G729]. See above: BRIGHT. [G88; C761].

WISE -- Stewart, Mildred Beth Wise. *The Dared To Be Wise: The Ancestors and Descendants of James Thomas Wise.* Fairborn, OH,, Stewart, 1990. ix, 254p. [DC3998].

WISE -- Wise, Ronnie W. *The Wise Family Chronicles.* Cleveland, OH, Wise, 1985. 186p. [DC4001].

WISE -- Timman, H. R. *In Schwarz und Weiss: The Family of Frank and Catharine Hagler Wise.* Norwalk, OH, 1975. 82p. [X1041-FW].

WISE -- Wise, Jack W. *Wise Family History from Pennsylvania to Ohio to Texas.* New Braunfels, TX, J.W. Wise, 1990. iii, 132, 16 leaves. 1. Wise family. 2. Pennsylvania-Genealogy. 3. Ohio-Genealogy. 4. Texas-Genealogy. [G729].

WISEMAN -- Wiseman, Charles M. *The Wiseman Family and the Old Church at Salem.* Gallipolis, OH, 1887. 13 leaves. [X1042-SU].

WITMER -- Witmer, Nettie. *Witmer Record.* Columbiana, OH, 1961. 28p. [X1043-FW].

WITZEMAN -- Witzeman, Bertha Evangeline Rowe. *Consider the Years. Witzeman with Ancestral Histories by James C. Rice - 1st ed.* Akron, OH, B. E. R. Witzeman, 1981. 419p. [C762].

WOLFE -- Atkinson, Nora E. W. *The Wolfe Family History.* Athens, OH, Lawhead Press, 1964. 332p. [X1044-FW/MH/NY/SP].

WOLFE -- Wolff, Frederick Lawrence,... *A Genealogy of the Descendants of John N. Wolff, (1729-1771) Veteran (1746) of the Third Inter-Colonial War, a Resident of Lancaster County, Pennsylvania, and Particularly of the Descendants of His Son John Wolff (1764-1831) Veteran of the War of the Revolution, a Resident of Lancaster County, Pennsylvania and Byron, Ohio. A Bicentennial Memorial of John Nicholas Wolff (Born 1729) and Anna Marie Bower Wolff, His Wife.* Omaha, NB, 1929. 3p., 65 numb. leaves. [L18988].

WOLFF -- Koogle, Bernice B. Wolfe. *History of the Ancestors of William Ernest Koogle of De Graff, Ohio.* St. George, UT, Wood, 1976. 210p. [D13863].

WOLPERS -- Abbott, Lyndon Eugene. [G733]. See above: SHAFFER. [G599].

WOOD -- NAS. *History and Genealogy of the Descendants of Abinah Wood and Susannah Humphreys.* Andover, OH, Press of the

Citizen, 1903. 80p. D gives 77p.
[L19015; D13858].

WOOD -- Terrill, Merwin Sherman. *The James Wood Family Record, 1771-1899.* Cincinnati, OH, 1899. 21p. [L19012].

WOOD -- Wood, Arthur. *The Descendants of William Wood and Currilar Murfield.* Columbus, OH, 1975. 35p. [X1046-OH].

WOOD -- Wood, Seely. *The Golden Wedding of Seely and Nancy B. Wood; Also a memorial of Mrs. Nancy Burnet Wood.* Urbana, OH, 1893. 37p. [X1045-LI].

WOODARD -- Matteson, Harry S. P. *Calvin Woodard Family.* Columbus, OH, 1946. 8p. [X1047-FW].

WOODIN -- Woodin, Ralph J. *The Geauga Woodins, 1834-1984.* Columbus, OH, R. J. Woodin, 1984. vii, 257p. [C766].

WOODMANSEE -- Perkins, H. E. *James W. Woodmansee, Clermont County, Ohio.* Indianola, IA, 1949. 22p. [X1048-FW].

WOODROW -- Woodrow, John F. *Our Kith and Kin.* Granville, OH, Denison Univ. Pr., 1948. 293p. Story of the life of John F. Woodrow... and genealogy. SP lists date of 1952 and has 2 vols. [X1048-FW/SP].

WOODS -- Whedon, Nellie E. Woods. *The James Woods Family of Pennsylvania and Ohio; An Account of of the Descendants of Allen Sr., Samuel Sr., and Nathaniel, Sr. the Three Sons of James Woods, 1736-1942.* Ann Arbor, MI, Edwards Brothers, 1942. 154p. D shows date of 1943.
[D13909; X1049-FW/LA; VP250].

WOODS -- Teetor, Henry D. *Historical Sketches of the Woods Family of Great Britain; of Which Willaim Woods of Cincinnati, OH, is a Descendant.* Cincinnati, OH, 1888. 34 leaves. [X1048-library not given].

WOODWARD -- Gibson, Nancy Brigham. *The History of the Woodward Family of Fulton and Henry Counties, Ohio. Immigrant Ancestor: Richard Woodward of Watertown, Ma., 1643.* El Redondo Chapter, California DAR, G.R.C. 1987. 137 leaves. [DC4023].

WOODWORTH -- Monson, Marie. [G735]. See above: MUNSON. [G472; S2767].

WOOLERY -- Woolery, L. C. *Life and Addresses of W. H. Woolery, Third President of Bethany College (with Ancestry).* Cincinnati, OH, 1893. 12, 426p. [X1050-LI].

WOOLWORTH -- NAS. *Ancestral Chart of Elisa Gertrude Woolworth, Who Married, 1913, Otto Miller of Cleveland, Ohio.* Cleveland, OH, 1930. 2 charts. [X1051-NY].

WORK -- Work, John C. and Rhoda Work Fisher. *Work Family History. 1792-1941.* Cleveland, OH, 1941. 75p. [X1051-FW/OH/OL/SU].

WORTHINGTON -- Woodson, Edgar Thomas. [G736]. See above: MORRIS. [G468].

WORTHINGTON -- Sims, Henry U. *The Genealogy of the Worthington Family of Alabama, South Carolina, Virginia, and Ohio, Being Descendants of Robert Worthington, Who Emigrated from Ireland to New Jersey in 1713, with an Appendix of the Symcock Family of Pennsylvania Down to 1716.* Birmingham, AL, 1937. 38(i.e.40), 10(i.e.12), 9 leaves. [X1052-NY].

WORTHINGTON -- Worthington, George. *A Genealogy of the Worthington Family.* Cleveland, OH, 1894. 2, 9-489p. [L19133].

WRIGHT -- NAS. *The Wright Family of Cincinnati, Ohio.* Cincinnati, OH, 19__. 62p. [X1052-NY].

WRIGHT -- Lawrence, Marianna Taussig. *The Wright Family of Cincinnati.* NP, nd. 62 l. "Written about 1932". [DC4041].

WRIGHT -- Roehl, Katherine M. *Enoch Wright and Wife, Susan Abshire, Their Lineage, Their Lives, Their Family; Resided Va., Ohio, Ind., Calif.* Lexington, MI, 1971. 28p. [X1053-FW; VV206].

WRIGHT -- Taussig, John W. *The Wright Family of Cincinnati, Ohio.* New York, NY, 1934. "Pages not known." [X1053-CH].

WRIGHT -- Wright, Edmon Wait. *Wright Family History.* Elyria, OH, variously paged. [L19160].

WRIGHT -- Wright, Gladys A. *The John Wright History: Beginning Bedford Co., Penn., 1790, Perry Co., Ohio, and Darke Co., Ohio, with Descendants Across the Country.* Winter Haven, FL, G.A. Wright, 1988. 52 leaves, 14 leaves of plates. 1. Wright family. 2. Wright, John, 1790-ca. 1860-Family. 3. Pennsylvania-Genealogy. 4. Ohio-Genealogy. [G737].

WRIGHT -- Wright, Jay B. *Joseph and Elizabeth Wright of Bedford County, Va. and Columbiana County, Ohio.* DeWitt, NY. 1974. 20 leaves. [NG105; X1054-FW/NY; VV206].

WURSTER -- Aid, Marie Dorothy, Anna Mabel Wurster and Dorothy Wurster Rout. *The Wurster Family, Chillicothe, Ohio.* Chillicothe, OH, D. W. Rout, 1971. 64p. [S2778].

WURSTER -- Wurster, Keith E. *The Wurster's (sic) of Mercer County, Ohio: as of December, 1985.* Oberlin, OH, K.E. Wurster, 1985. 32 leaves. 1. Wurster family. 2. Mercer County (Ohio)-Genealogy. [G737].

WYLIE -- NAS. *Notes on the Wylie, Jeffrey, Sills, Saure, Sharrock Families, Guernsey County, Ohio...* NP, n.d. Daughters of the American Colonists. 17p. [X1055-CH].

XY

YANEY -- Bigham, Thelma E. Y. *Jenne, 1818 to Yaney, 1975, Descendants of Johann Jacob Jenne...* Eaton, OH, Workshop at Eaton City Sch., 1975-6, ix, 451p. [X1057-FW].

YEARICK -- Yearick, Harry W. *Memoirs of Harry Warren Yearick and His Ancestors to Five Generations.* Toldeo, OH, Author, 1899. 17p. [X1058-FW].

YERGIN -- Yergin, Helen G. *The Yergin Family; A Record of the Descendants of Henry Yergin of Huntingdon County, Pa., later of Ohio.* New York, NY, 1949. 131p. [X1058-NY].

YETTER -- Stark, W. C. *Genealogy of the Yetter Family of Medina and Henry Counties, Ohio.* Cleveland, OH, 1974. iii, 10, 5 leaves. [X1058-FW].

YODER -- Coffman, Dorothy Yoder. *Census Records for Yoder Families, 1840, Pennsylvania & Ohio: From Microfilm at the National Archives.* Malvern, PA, D.Y. Coffman, 1986. 1, 2, 4p. 1. Yoder family. 2. Ohio-Genealogy. 3. Pennsylvania-Genealogy. 4. Pennsylvania-Census, 1840. 5. Ohio-Census, 1840. 6. United State-Census-, 6th, 1840. [G739].

YODER -- Slaubaugh, John M. [G740]. See above: SCHLABACH. [G588].

YODER -- Stutzman, Perry A. *Descendants of Elias J. Yoder from Years 1842-1959.* Millersburg, OH, Barton Print., 1959. 51p. [X1059-FW].

YODER -- Yoder, Christian C. *Family Record of Michel Yoder from Germany and those Related to Him by Inter-Marriage from the Year 1822-1932.* Sugarcreek, OH, 1932. 30p. [X1058-FW].

YOHO -- Lincicome, Glen A. [G740]. See above: MORGAN. [G466].

YOHO -- Yoho, Denver C. *Charlie Yoho -- His Family: 200 Years Along the Ohio River.* Gallipolis, OH, D. C. Yoho, 1982. 311p. [C774].

YOUNG -- Young, Henry S. *History and Family Records of the Young Family; Descendants of Frederick Young.* Tiffin, OH, The Adv., 1910. 107p. [X1060-FW].

YOUNG -- Young, Lewis E. C. *Biography of the Young Family... 1759-1904.* Fremont, OH, Fremont Print., n.d. 95p., 9 l. [X1061-FW].

YOUNKER -- Stiffler, R. Ewing. *Descendants of Joel B. Younker (1809-1879) and Sarah (Stiffler) Younker (1813-1893). A Genealogy Listing 325 Descendants of a Pioneer Family of Pennsylvania "Dutch" Ancestry, Married in New Philadelphia, Ohio, Migrated to Iowa, and Back Trecked to Geneseo, Illinois.* Denver, CO, 1947. a-j, 30p. First ed. limited to 50 copies. [L19278].

Z

ZANE -- Martzolff, Clement L... *Zane's Trace.* Columbus, OH, Press of F. J. Heer, 1904. 297-331p. "Reprinted from Ohio Archaelogical and Historical Society publications." [L19291].

ZEHE -- Sheehan, Thomas W. *The Zehe Family History.* Cleveland, OH, 1972. iv, 62 l. [S2793].

ZEHNER -- Carpenter, Mrs. Ellen Priscilla (Zehner). *The First Zehner - Hoppes Family History; Adam Zehner, John Michael (Habbas) Hoppes of Schuykill County, Pennsylvania, and Descendants, Pioneer Farmers and Millers, by the Zehner Indiana Branch of the Pennsylvania,*

Ohio, Indiana, Illinois, Wisconsin Relative Societies. South Bend, IN, Mirror Press, Inc., 1939. (variously paged.) [L19297].

ZIMMER -- Hamel, Claude Charles. *Genealogy of a Branch of the Zimmer Family from Robens Housa, Hesse-Cassel (now the Prussian Province of Hessen-Nassau) Germany.* Amherst, OH, 1948. 7 leaves. [L19301].

ZIMMERMAN -- Garman, Leo H. *The Family of Henry Zimmerman of Pennsylvania and Ohio: A Genealogical History.* Elmhurst, OH, 1985. xii, 533p. [C778].

ZIMMERMAN -- Zimmerman, Eric C. *Hans and Christian Zimmerman and Their Descendants. Ed. 3, rev.* Akron, OH, Author, 1968. 219p. First ed. pub. in 1949. [X1064-FW].

ZINN -- Jones, Ralph E. *The John Jacob Zinn Family of Lancaster, Penna.* Warren, OH, 1935. 2p. [L19307].

ZINN -- McFatridge-McCloskey, Mabel. *History and Genealogy of the Zinn Family.* N.P. 1937. 58p. [L19308].

ZOLLNER -- Ratcliffe, Susan Keller. *The Descendants of Henry Zoellner, 1801-1872: Hamilton, Ohio, Marysville, Ohio, Sandusky Ohio, Stuttgart, Arkansas.* Delaware, OH, Ratcliffe, 1976. iii, 167 leaves. D gives iv, 167 leaves. X lists as ZOELINER. [C779; D14106: X1065-FW/NY/OH].

ZOOK -- Mumaw, Clara B. Z. *Jacob and Barbara Zook Family History; A Short Sketch of the Ancestry of Jacob Zook and The Record of His Lineage.* Wooster, OH, Author, 1962. 38p. [X1065-FW].

ZORBAUGH -- Zorbaugh, Charles Louis. *Ancestral Trails; History of the Zorbaugh Family, the Evans Family, the McClure Family, the Harvey Family, the Clapp Family.* Wooster,

OH, The Collier Printing Company, 1941. 267p.
Ltd. ed. 100 copies. Errata sheet mounted on
p. 4. [L19313].

ZUMWALT -- Reed, Paul L. *The Andrew Zumwalt
Family.* Cleveland, OH, Zumwalt Historical
Committee (Baltimore, MD), Deford & Co., 1964.
ix, 180p. [D14113].

LIBRARY OF CONGRESS GENEALOGIES CONVERTED TO MICROFORM

A list of older genealogies in the United States Library of Congress, which have been converted to microfilm follows this brief introduction on availability of microfilms and other materials from the Library of Congress.

Where conversion to microfilm has taken place, there is usually no original volume in the Library's collection. Microfilm reels in the Library are 35mm. All listings are on 1 reel unless otherwise indicated.

The list of microfilmed genealogies in this volume can be used as a borrowing tool for librarians and those doing research on a particular family name can purchase the microfilm reels directly or paper copies made from them.

Library policy does not allow circulation of genealogy on interlibrary loan, but microfilm copies may be circulated. The Library may be able to assist in purchasing photocopies of out-of-print items. The interested researcher may obtain free upon request a circular entitled Out-of-Print Materials and Reprinted Publications. Requests should be addressed to: Library of Congress, Humanities and Social Science Division, Washington, DC 20540.

Copies of microfilm listed below may be ordered from the Photoduplicating Service at the address given above at a cost of $30.00 per reel, which includes postage and handling. Requets for "Copyflow" prints on paper may also be ordered. The researcher needs to inquire regarding specific prices.

Provided there are no copyright restrictions, photcopies of any item in the Library's genealogical collections may be obtained under the conditions specified in the

order form, which may be obtained from the
Library of Congress Photoduplication Service,
Washington, DC 20540. As an example of the cost
involved The Library indicates that the charge
for prparing an unbound photocopy of a 200-page
book (page sixe 9" x 6") would be about $50.
Note that in requesting photocopy services, the
specific pages and material to be copied must be
cited in the request.

The following short bibliographies on
genealogical subjects are available without
charge from the Library of Congress, Humanities
and Social Science Services Division:

Guide to Genealogical Research, a
Selected List of Publications, which tells how
to trace an ancestor.

Surnames, a Selected List of
References to books on family names and national
origins.

Immigrant Arrivals, A Short Guide to
Published Sources, of possible help in
identifying ships and passenger lists.

Heraldry, a Selected List of
References to books on the origins, use, design,
and identification of coats of arms.

Note that there is some duplication between
the works shown as being in the Library
collection as those listed below as being on
Microfilm. It is probable, that were
duplication exists, the original work is no
longer available other than in Microfilm.

The cross-index at the end of this volume
includes both microfilm and paper holdings
listed in the Libraries collections.

OHIO GENEALOGIES ON MICROFILM

A

ABBOTT -- Abbott, Amos Shinkle. *Chart of seven generations of descendants of James Abbott of Somersetshire, England who settled in Fosters Meadow, Long Island 1701 [microform]* - Bethel, OH, 1892. 1 chart, genealogical table. MICROFILM 84/7858 (C). <MicRR>. [G1123].

ACHOR -- Achor, Robert L. *Notes and materials on the Achor family of southwestern Ohio [microform]: including Richoux and Borne families of Louisiana, Worz, Smithson, and Hickey families of Ohio.* Miami, FL, 1970. iv, 51p. MICROFILM 85/8119 (C) <MicRR>. [G1124].

ALLEN -- Walden, Blanche L. *Pioneer families of the Midwest [microform].* Ann Arbor, MI, Edwards Bros., Inc. 1939-<1941-   > v. <1-3>. Paged continuously. Vols. 2-3 have imprint: Athens, O. Contents: v. 1. Harper, Rainey, Boal, Hope, Dewees and Francis families - v. 2. Smith, Dorr, Coe, Fuller, and Deweese families - v. 3. Allen, Pratt, Davis, True, Argo, and Plumly families. MICROFILM 87/7238 (C). [G1123].

ANDREWS -- Andrews, Adele. *The ancestors and descendents of Laban Andrews, revolutionary patriot and his wife, Prudense Stanley Andrews [microform].* Norwalk, OH, 1943. 136 [i.e.139] leaves. MICROFILM 87/5475 (C) <MicRR>. [G1128].

ANDREWS -- Andrews, Thomas Sheldon. *Ira Andrews & Ann Hopkinson, their ancestors and posterity [microform]: including the autobiography of the author...: also a treatise on marriage, devorce, and the laws of psychol and constitutional hereditary transmissions...* NP, Toledo: Blade Print and

Paper Co., 1879. vi, 437p., 1 leaf of plates.
MICROFILM 84/7846 (C) <MicRR>. [G1128].

AVERY -- Avery, Catharine Hitchcock.
*Revolutionary ancestry of Catharine Hitchcock
(Tilden) Avery [microform].* Cleveland, OH,
Daughters of the American Revolution, Western
Reserve Chapter, 1899. 11p.
MICROFILM 84/8246 (C) <MicRR>. [G1130].

AVERY -- Avery, Elroy McKendree. *The Groton
Averys, Christopher and James [microform]: the
founders of the family.* Cleveland, OH, 1893.
20p. MICROFILM 48010 (C). [G1129].

B

BALDWIN -- Baldwin, C. C. *The Baldwin
Genealogy, from 1500-1881 [microform].*
Cleveland, OH, Leader Print. Co., 1881. 974p.
MICROFILM 33347 (C). [G1131].

BALL -- Gans, Emmett William. *A Pennsylvania
pioneer [microform]: biographical sketch, with
report of the executive committee of the Ball
Estate Association.* Mansfield, OH, R. J.
Kuhl, 1900. 704p. MICROFILM 19347 (C).
[G1131].

BARKER -- Newhall, Barker. *The Barker
family of Plymouth Colony and Country.*
Cleveland, OH, F. W. Roberts Co., 1900. 102p.
1 leaf of plates.
MICROFILM 84/7837 (C) <MicRR>. [G1132].

BATTLE -- Battelle, Lillian S. *Batelle
genealogical record [microform].* Cincinnati,
OH, Press of R. Clarke, 1889. 20p.
MICROFILM 82/6140 (C). [G1133].

BENTLEY -- Brinkerhoff, Roeliff. *The
Bentley family [microform]: with genealogical
records of Ohio Bentleys and known as the
tribe of Benjamin.* Mansfield, OH, 1897. 20p.
MICROFILM 84/7881 (C) <MicRR>. [G1135].

BEST -- Best, Nolan Rice. *History of Peter and Mary Best and their family [microform]: read before a reunion of their descendants, held near the old homestead, in Hilliar township, Knox County, Ohio, on the centenary of the birth of Peter Best, May 13th, 1897.* NP, 1897. 15p. MICROFILM 84/7114 (C) <MicRR>. [G1136].

BOYDSTUN -- Weaver, Gustine Nancy Courson. *The Boydstun family [microform].* Cincinnati, OH, Powell & White, 1927. 5-149p., 3 leaves of plates. MICROFILM 87/6336 (C) <MicRR>. [G1140].

BRIGGS -- Briggs, Samuel. *A partial record of the descendants of Walter Briggs of Westchester, N. Y. [microform]: to which is added some account of his ancestry, collateral brances, origin of the family name, ancient pedigrees, wills* ... Cleveland, OH, Fairbanks, Briggs & Co., (printed for private circulation only), 1878. 50p. Limited ed. of 200 copies MICROFILM 78536 (C). [G1142].

BRIGGS -- Briggs, Samuel. *The archives of the Briggs family [microform]* Cleveland, OH, T. C. Schenk, 1880. xiv, 264p MICROFILM 76418 (C). [G1142].

BROUGHTON -- Phillips, Vernon S. *Amos Broughton, 1743-1837, of Hoosie, Renssalaer County, New York and some of his descendants [microform].* Columbus, OH, 1932. 9 leaves MICROFILM 86/6301 (C) <MicRR>. [G1144].

BRYAN -- Baldwin, C. C. *Alexander Bryan, of Milford, Connecticut [microform]: his ancestors and his descendants* Cleveland, OH, 1889. Leader Print., Co., 27p. MICROFILM 85/5801 (C) <MicRR>. [G1145].

BUCKINGHAM -- Buckingham, James. *The ancestors of Ebenezer Buckingham, who was born in 1748, and of his descendants [microform].* Chicago, IL, R. R. Donnelley & Sons Co., 1892.

256p., 3 leaves of plates.
MICROFILM 84/7850 (C) <MicRR>. [G1145].

BURGNER -- Burgner, Jacob. *History and genealogy of the Burgner family, in the United States of America, as descended from Peter Brugner, a Swiss emigrant of 1734 [microform] - 1st ed.* Oberlin, OH, Oberlin News Press, 1890. vi, 172 [i.e. 184]p., 18 leaves of plates. MICROFILM 84/8339 (C) <MicRR>. [G1146].

BURROUGHS -- Burrought, L. A. *Genealogy of the Burroughs family [microform].* Garretsville, OH, Peirce Print. Co., 1894. 24p. MICROFILM 57714 (C). [G1147].

C

CARPENTER -- Clark, William Caleb. *A Circular Relating to the genealogy of the Carpenter families in America, and a request for aid in obtaining information concerning the same [microform].* Cincinnati, OH, W. C. Clark, 1879. 7p.
MICROFILM 84/8087 (C) <MicRR>. [G1150].

CATLIN -- Baldwin, C. C. *Catlin [microform].* Cleveland, OH, Leader Print. Co., 1882, p. 14-147. From the author's Candee genealogy, Cleveland, 1882.
MICROFILM 78653 (C). [G1152].

CAVEN -- Hill, Leonard Uzal. *The genealogical records of George and Elizabeth Caven, immigrants from Ireland, and pioneer settlers in Springcreek Township, Miami County [microform].* Piqua, OH, 1949. 45 leaves.
MICROFILM 86/5688 (C)<MicRR>. [G1152].

CHAMBERLAIN -- NAS. *A loving record of how we kept the golden wedding at home [microform]: together with some family history, 1827-1877.* NP, 1877. 74p. "The golden wedding of Leander and Susanna

Chamberlain... in Solon Cuyahoga Country (sic), Ohio, September 6, 1877". MICROFILM 84/8092 (C) <MicRR>. [G1152].

CHASE -- Case, C. V. *Genealogical records of the Chace and Hathaway families from 1630-1900 [microform].* Ashtabula, OH, Wilson-Clark Co., 1900. 42p MICROFILM 85/5582 (C) <MicRR>. [G1154].

CLEVELAND -- Cleveland, H. G. *An account of the lineage of General Moses Cleaveland of Canterbury (Windham County) Conn. [microform]: the founder of the city of Cleveland, Ohio; also sketch of his life from the January (1885) number of the Magazine of western history by Harvey Rice.* Cleveland, OH, W. W. Williams, 1885. 14p. MICROFILM 84/8111 (C) <MicRR>. [G1158].

CLEVELAND -- Cleveland, Edmund Janes. *The genealogy of the Cleveland and Cleaveland families [microform]: an attempt to trace in both the male and female lines, the posterity of Moses Cleveland...* Hartford, CT, Case, Lookwood & Brainard, 1899 3 v. MICROFILM 8532 (C) <MicRR>. [G1158].

COE -- Coe, David Benton. *Record of the Coe family and descendants [microform] / from 1596-1856 (compiled by Daniel B. Coe); from 1856-1885 (compiled by Eunice A. Lloyd).* Cincinnati, OH, Standard Pub. Co., 1885. 16p. "Record of the Coe family and descendants from 1596 to 1856" first published in 1856 by David Benton Coe. Errata slip inserted. MICROFILM 84/8115 (C) <MicRR>. [G1159].

COLE -- Cole, Frank T. *The early genealogies of the Cole families in America [microform]: (including Coles and Cowles): with some account of the descendants of James Cole of Hartford, Connecticut, 1635-1652 and of Thomas Cole of Salem, Mass., 1649-1672.* Columbus, OH, Printed by Hann & Adair for the author, 1887. 307p. MICROFILM 24764 (C). [G1160].

COURTRIGHT -- Courtright, Dudley Vattier. *History of the Van Kortryks, or, Courtrights [microform]: allied families Staudt, Vattier, Moore.* Columbus, OH, F. J. Heer Print. Co., 1924. 105p. MICROFILM 86/6249 (C) <MicRR>. [G1163].

CRAIG -- Craig, Winchell McKendree. *The Craig family [microform]: genealogical and historical notes about the Craigs of America, Fayette County, Ohio, United States, Canada.* Rochester, MN. 1956. 149p. MICROFILM 86/6583 (C) <MicRR>. [G1164].

CRATER -- Craytor, Doyle M. *Descendants of Moritz Crater, 1703-1772 [microform].* Lakewood, OH, 1939. 51 leavess. MICROFILM 86/7000 (C). [G1164].

CRISPIN -- Crispin, William Frost. *A biographical and historical sketch of Captain William Crispin of the British Navy [microform]: together with protraits and sketches of many of his descendants and representatives of some families of English Crispins: also an historical research concerning the remote ancestry of English and American Cripins: and a tracing of the name from 361 B.C. to the present, including genealogies of the Crispin families and some account of related families - the Penns, the Holmes, the Masons: to which is added a section of genealogy and ancestry.* Akron, OH, Commercial Print. Co., 1901. 144p., 5 leaves of plates. MICROFILM 86/8890 (C) <MicRR>. [G1164].

CROWELL -- Crowel, Henry. *Crowel history, or, "Foot-prints in the sands of time" [microform].* Dayton, OH, 1899. 55, 64p. With: "Supplement to Crowell History, or "Foot-prints in the sands of time" by H. Crowel, Dayton, OH, 1904. MICROFILM 84/7785 (C) <MicRR>. [G1165].

D

DAVIDSON -- Harbaugh, Elizabeth Davidson. *The Davidson genealogy [microform]*. Ironton, OH, Edwards bros., 1949, c1948. x, 482p. MICROFILM 85/4736 (C). [G1168].

De CAMP -- De Camp, James M. *Record of the descendants of Ezekiel and Mary Baker De Camp of Butler County, Ohio [microform]*. Cincinnati, OH, Western Methodist Book Concern, 1896. 177p., 8 leaves of plates. MICROFILM 84/8021 (C) <MicRR>. [G1169].

DODD -- Dodd, Bethuel Lewis. *Ancestors and descendants of Lewis Dodd and Elizabeth [Baldwin] Dodd [microform]*. Cleveland, OH, C. C. Baldwin, 1889. viii, 11p. Partially reprinted from Baldwin genealogy. MICROFILM 72351 (C) <MicRR>. [G1171].

DOTY -- VanSant, Effie E. *Doty family history and genealogy, 1620-1935 [microform]*. NP, 1935 (Findlay, OH, Kistler's Print Shop) 104p. MICROFILM 84/3202 (C). [G1172].

DOZER -- Dozer, Eadid E. *Chronological record of the Dozer family, from August 31, 1805 to July 1924 [microform]*. Zanesville, OH, 1924. (Zanesville: Danker Print Co.) 54p. MICROFILM 86/8762 (C) <MicRR> [G1173].

DUNHAM -- Dunham, Chester Forrester. *The Dunham genealogy [microform]: related families: Billings, Powell, Hice, Gray, Root, Andrus*. Toledo, OH, 1956. 160 leaves, 2 leaves of plates. MICROFILM 86/6837 (C) <MicRR>. [G1174].

E

EASTMAN -- Higgins, Marie Washburn. *The Eastman - Washburn book [microform]: the* *ancestry and posterity of Hannah Eastman Washburn.* Akron, OH, M.W. Higgins, 1928. 43p., 2 leaves of plates: geneal. table. MICROFILM 86/6594 (C) <MicRR>. [G1175].

ELLIS -- Ellis, Frank R. *Descendants of Rowland Ellis and Sallie Abrams Ellis of Massachusetts [microform].* Cincinnati, OH, F.R. Ellis, 1893. 6 leaves, 2 leaves of plates. MICROFILM 85/5551 (C) <MicRR>. [G1177].

ELLIS -- Foos, Katharine J. Strickle. *The Ellis Family [microform].* Dayton, OH, U.B. Pub. House, 1900. 128p. MICROFILM 84/7797 (C) <MicRR>. [G1177].

F

FAIRBANKS -- Fairbanks, Charles H. *Fairbanks family record [microform].* Cleveland, OH, A.W. Fairbanks, 1886. 30p. MICROFILM 67838 (C). [G1178].

FAY -- Fay, Orlin P. *Fay genealogy [microform]: John Fay of Marlborough and his descendants.* Cleveland, OH, Press of J.B. Savage, 1898. 420p. MICROFILM 35168 (C). [G1179].

FELCH -- Felch, W. Farrand. *The memorial history of the Felch family in America and Wales. [microform]: the earliest and latest records, 1641-1881.* Columbus, OH, J.F. Earhart & Co., 1881. 49p., 1 leaf of plates. MICROFILM 84/8147 (C) <MicRR>. [G1179].

FOLLET -- Ward, Harry Parker. *A brief sketch of the life of Persis Follett Parker [microform]: together with a few not of family history.* Columbus, OH, Chamnplin Print. Co., 1893. 43p., 2 leaves of plates. "The Follett Ancestors"; p. 27-35. "The Fassett Ancestors"; p. 36-41. MICROFILM 85/4114 (C) <MicRR>. [G1181].

FOLLET -- Ward, Harry Parker. *The Follett - Dewey, Fassett - Safford ancestry of Captain Martin Dewey Follett (1765-1831) and his wife Persis Fassett (1767-1849) [microform]: being a compilation of family records and extracts from various histories, official records, and genealogical publications.* Columbus, OH, Champlin Print. Co., 1896. 277p. MICROFILM 84/8077(C) <MicRR>. [G1181].

FOREMAN -- Forman, Wm. P. *Records of the descendants of John Foreman, who settled Monmouth County, New Jersey, about the year A.D. 1685 [microform].* Cleveland, OH, Short & Forman, 1885. 29p., 1 leaf of plates. MICROFILM 85/5553 (C). [G1182].

FRINK -- Hamel, Claude Charles. *Genealogy of a branch of the Frink family from New York State, who were among the early settlers of Lorain County, Ohio [microform].* NP, 1948 4 leaves. MICROFILM 84/3279 (C). [G1183].

GEORGIA -- Brooks, Elmore L. *A genealogical record and history of the Georgia family in America [microform]: being the children and descendants of William and Sarah (Cable) Georgia and the children and descendants of Elijah Burr (1st) and Keziah (Stewart) Georgia: these were the first tow men of this name to come to America: both male and female lines are carried out complete.* Cleveland, OH, 1924. 314p. MICROFILM 85/7432 (C). [G1185].

GIBSON -- Gibson, W. T. *Capt. James Gibson and Anna Belle, his wife and their descendants [microform]: pioneers of Youngstown, Ohio.* NP, 189_. 52p. MICROFILM 84/8278 (C). [G1186].

GOTT -- Gott, Phillip P. *An Ohio Gott family, ancestors and descendants [microform]: the first Gotts in America.* Pittsburgh, PA, Reproduced on multility offset press by M.J. Moshier, 1940. 4p. MICROFILM86/8590 (C) <MicRR>. [G1188].

GOTT -- Gott, Phillip P. *Season's greetings, December 1940 [microform]: to kin, far and near, present and future: to genealogical* students and librarians. Washiungton, DC, P.P. Gott 1940. 1 sheet. A circular letter accompanying the author's work, "An Ohio Gott family". MICROFILM 86/8591 (C) <MicRR>. [G1188].

GUTHRIE -- Guthrie, Stephen Hand. *A sketch of Stephen Guthrie, senior, and his children [microform]: a pioneer family of the Ohio Land Company of 1787.* Zanesville, OH, 1891. 35p. MICROFILM 84/7893 (C) <MicRR>. [G1190].

H

HARMON -- Harmon, Israel. *Souvenir of the Harmon reunion, at the residence and grounds of Charles Rollin Harmon, Aurora, Ohio, Aug. 13, 1896 [microform]: published in compliance with the request of the secretary of the association for a copy of the address of the occasion by the speaker, Israel Harmon.* Springfield, MA, 1896. 20p. MICROFILM 85/6031 (C) <MicRR>. [G1193].

HARMON -- Harmon, Israel. *Harmon [microform]: history, genealogy.* Springfield, MA, 1898. 1 sheet. MICROFILM 84/8266 (C) <MicRR>. [G1193].

HASTINGS -- Hastings, Francis H. *Family record of Dr. Seth Hastings senior of Clinton, Oneida County, New York [microform].* Cincinnati, OH, Earhart & Richardson, 1899. 202p. MICROFILM 82/5147 (C). [G1195].

HATFIELD -- Stephenson, S. K. *The descendants of Joseph and Anna Hatfield, married December 6, 1779 [microform].* Lebanon, OH, Republican Print., 1897. 13p. MICROFILM 84/8368 (C). [G1195].

HINSDALE -- Hinsdale, Albert. *Chronicles of the Hinsdale family [microform] compiled by Albert Hinsdale in the seventy-third year of his age.* Cleveland, OH, J.B. Savage, 1883. 31p. MICROFILM 84/8379 (C) <MicRR>. [G1198].

HODGES -- Hodges, Rufus. *Record of the families in New England of the name of Hodges [microform].* Cincinnati, OH, R. Hodges, 1837. 22p. MICROFILM 84/714 (C). [G1199].

HOLL -- Holl, Henry C. *History of the Holl-Schrantz family, or, The descendants of Ephraim Holl [microform].* Canton, OH, Repository Print. Co., 1891. 122p. MICROFILM 84/8539 (C) <MicRR>. [G1200].

HOLMAN -- May, Richard Holman. *The Abraham Holman family of Ross County, Ohio [microform]: a genealogy of Abraham and Leah Dresbach Holman, their ancestors and descendants.* Middletown, CT, Godfrey Memorial Library, 1959. xi, 49p., 2 leaves of plates MICROFILM 85/7454 (C) <MicRR>. [G1200].

HOSFORD -- Hosford, Henry Hallock. *Ye Horseforde booke [microform]: Horsford - Hosford families in the United States of America.* Cleveland, OH, Tower Press, Inc., 1936. 259p., 11 leaves, 1 leaf of plats. Revised 1939 by Henry Hallock Hosford. MICROFILM 86/6839(C) <MicRR>. [G1201].

HOUSTON -- Houston, Sam'l. Rutherford. *Brief biographical accounts of many members of the Houston family [microform]: accompanied by a genealogical table.* Cincinnati, OH, Elm Street Print Co., 1882. 420p. MICROFILM 37455 (C). [G1201].

J

JACKSON -- Jackson, Hugh Parks. *The genealogy of the "Jackson family" [microform].* Urbana, OH, Press of Citizen and Gazette Co., 1890. 124p. MICROFILM 85/9509 (C) <MicRR>. [G1205].

JACKSON -- Jackson, Job Hayes. *Sketch of Nicholas Jackson of England [microform]: with a genealogical account of his descendants in America.* Clyde, OH, B.F. Jackson, 1891. 34p. Library/Congress copy imperfect: title page and all prior to p.5 wanting. MICROFILM 85/9509 (C) <MicRR>. [G1205].

JENNINGS -- Jennings, William Henry. *A genealogical history of the Jennings families in England and America [microform].* Columbus, OH, Mann & Adair <1899 > v. <2 >. Limited ed. of 200 copies - v. 2. The American families. MICROFILM 34457 (C). [G1206].

K

KELLEY -- Kelley, Hermon Alfred. *A genealogical history of the Kelley family [microform]: descended from Joseph Kelley of Norwich, Connecticut...* Cleveland, OH, 1897. 122, xv p., 32 leaves of plates. MICROFILM 84/7023 (C) <MicRR>. [G1209].

KELLY -- Kelly, Richard Thomas. *History of James and Catherine Kelly and their descendants [microform].* Springfield, OH, The Springfield Pub. Co., 1900. 114p., 3 leaves of plates. MICROFILM 84/7022 (C) <MicRR>. [G1209].

KNIGHT -- Knight, Sarah A. *Knight family records [microform]: a history of the long ago, to the present time, 640-1951. 109 leaves.* MICROFILM 87/6696 (C) <MicRR>. [G1212].

L

LAPE -- Lape, Charles Frederick. *Some descendatns of Gottlieb Lape and his wife Carolina Jacobs of Zanesville, Ohio [microform].* NP, 1935. 6 leaves. MICROFILM 86/7900 (C) <MicRR>. [G1214].

LAUGHLIN -- Laughlin, John W. *Laughlin history prepared for the re-union held at Bellecenter, Ohio, Thursday, August twenty-second, nineteen hundred and twelve [microform].* Barnesville, OH, 1912. 104, 19p., 4 leaves of plates. MICROFILM 86/6989 (C) <MicRR>. [G1214].

LOWE -- Smith, Jesse Lowe. *Lowe genealogy, Spet. 1933 [microform].* Newark, OH, B.B. Lowe, 1964. 10 leaves. Typescript (mimeographed). MICROFILM 86/5230 (C) <MicRR>. [G1219].

M

McCLURE -- McClure, Cicero Pangburn. *Pioneer McClure families of the Monongahela Valley [microform]: their origins and their descendants.* Akron, OH, Superior Print. Co., 1924. 171p., 2 leaves of plates. MICROFILM 86/7904 (C) <MicRR>. [G1220].

McCLURE -- McClure, Stanley W. *The McClure family [microform]: a record of the McClure families of Harrison County, Kentucky, Franklin County, Indiana, Hamilton County, Ohio, Junction City, Kansas, and other lines of descent.* Washington, DC?, 1956. 26 leaves. Typescript. MICROFILM 87/6323 (C) <MicRR>. [G1221].

McNEIL -- Pierce, Doris Whittier. *The family of James Ferson, Jr. and Mary (McNeill) Ferson of Scotland, Ireland, New Hampshire, and Orange Township, Delaware County, Ohio. [microform].* Sunbury, OH, 1975. b-d, 140 leaves. MICROFILM 86/5096 (C) <MicRR>. [G1223].

MALLORY -- Baldwin, C. C. *Mallery [microform].* NP, 1882. p. 159-165. From the author's Candee genealogy, Cleveland, 1882. MICROFILM 85/5328 (C) <MicRR>. [G1224].

MASON -- Mason, William L. *A record of the descendants of Robert Mason, of Roxbury, Mass. [microform]: including representatives at Dedham, Medfield, Northfield, Barre, Worcester, Sturbridge, Medway, Shrewsbury, Hubbardstown, Boston, Mass., New York City, Orange N.J., Brunswick, Maine, Cincinnati, Ohio, and Washington, D.C.* Milwaukee, WI, 1891 (Milwaukee: Burdick, Armitage & Allen), 8p., 9-35 leaves, 36-39p. MICROFILM 84/8288 (C) <MicRR>. [G1226].

METCALF -- Metcalf, Isaac Stevens. *Metcalf genealogy [microform].* Cleveland, OH, Imperial Press, 1898. 62p. MICROFILM 85/5304 (C) <MicRR>. [G1228].

MILLER -- Miller, Morris. *A short historical account of the Miller & Morris families [microform]: colatd partly from tradition, but mostly from authentic records.* Knoxville, OH, Stokes Bro"s., 1876. 296p. MICROFILM 85/5631 (C) <MicRR>. [G1228].

MORR -- Moyer, Calvin Fisher. *Genealogy of the Morr family [microform].* NP, C.F. Moyer, 1896 (Ashtabula, OH, Sun Publ. Co.,) 295p. MICROFILM 84/7957 (C) <MicRR>. [G1230].

MORR -- Morr, Ralph B. *Supplement of the Genealogies of the Morr and Myers families [microform].* Akron, OH, Akron Craftsman, 1971. iv, 630p. "Commerative medal" inserted in pocket. MICROFILM 86/5087 (C) <MicRR>. [G1230].

MOURNING -- Waddell, Kenneth Mourning. *Roger Mourning and his descendants [microform].* Toledo, OH, 1948. 1 v. (various foliations). Contents: The old Kentucky home - the story of a pioneer Illinois family - Some original sources of Mourning family history. MICROFILM 84/723 (C). [G1231].

MEYER -- Meyer, Henry. *Genealogy of the Henry Meyer family [microform].* Cleveland,

OH, Lauer & Mattill, 1890. 131p.
MICROFILM 71472 (C). [G1232].

N

NASH -- Phillips, Vernon S. *Francis Nash of Braintree, Mass. and 1550 of his descendants [microform].* Akron, OH, 1933. xii, 112p. "The Puritan Manuscripts, Vernon S. Phillips". MICROFILM 85/8509 (C) <MicRR>. [G1232].

NEFF -- Neff, Elizabeth Clifford. *A chronicle together with a littl romance regarding Rufolph and Jacob Näf of Frankford, Pennsylvania and their descendants [microform]: including an accounts of the Neffs in Switzerland and America.* Cincinnati, OH, R. Clarke & Co., 1886. 352p. MICROFILM 85/7392 (C) <MicRR>. [G1233].

NEFF -- Neff, Elizabeth Clifford. *Addenda [microform]: Näf - Neff history, regarding the origin and meaning of the name of Neff: together with revolutionary records of Captain Rudolf Neff, Ensign Aaron Scout, Major Thomas Smythe.* Cleveland, OH, E.C. Neff, 1899 (Cleveland, Plain Dealer Pub. Co.) 35p. MICROFILM 85/5808 (C). [G1233].

NOYES -- Noyes, Horatio N. *Noyes' genealogy [microform]: record of a branch of the descendants of Rev. James Noyes Newbury, 1634-1656.* Cleveland, OH, 1889. 32p. MICROFILM 85/5118(C) <MicRR>. [G1234].

O

ORTON -- Orton, Edward. *An account of the descendants of Thomas Orton, of Windsor, Connecticut, 1641 (principally in the male line) [microform].* Columbus, OH, Nitschke Bros., 1896. 220p., viii leaves of plates (some folded). MICROFILM 76420 (C). [G1235].

P

PAINE -- Ohler, Clara May Paine. *Ancestors and descendants of David Paine and Abigail Shepard of Ludlow, Massachusetts, 1463-1913 [microform].* Lima, OH, C.P. Ohler, 1913. 246p., 18 leaves of plates. MICROFILM 86/8228 (C) <MicRR>. [G1236].

PARDEE -- Pardee, Aaron. *Genealogy of one line of the Pardee family and some memoirs [microform].* Wadsworth, OH, 1896. 69p. MICROFILM 18502 (C). [G1236].

PARKER -- Parker, Rufus Henry. *History and genealogy of the family of Deacon Lovel Parker [microform]: who emigrated from *Barkhamsted, Conn., to Kinsman, Ohio, in the year 1816.* Syracuse, NY, Mason Press, 1898. 80p., 10 leaves of plates. MICROFILM 85/5678 (C) <MicRR>. [G1237].

PATTERSON -- Patterson, Robert A. *The Patterson family [microform]: a geneological (sic) history.* Carrollton, OH, Press of the Chronicle, 1909. 18p. MICROFILM 84/3170 (C). [G1238].

PERRY -- Perry, Aaron Fyfe. *Memoranda concerning descendants of John Perry, John Strong, John Fyfe, Robert Gray [microform].* Cleveland, OH, G. Stevens & Co., 1878. iii, 28p. MICROFILM 85/7466 (C) <MicRR>. [G1239].

POWELL -- Powell, John. *Authentic genealogical memorial history of Philip Powell of Mifflin county, Pa., and his descendants and others [microform]: with miscellaneous items and incidents of interest.* Dayton, OH, 1880. 447p. MICROFILM 8671 (C). [G1243].

PROUT -- Prout, Charles H. *Prout family history [microform]. Cornwall, England,*

Cleveland, U.S.A. - 2nd ed. Milwaukee, WI, 1973. 65 leaves, 6 leaves of plates. MICROFILM 85/8422 (C) <MicRR> . [G1245].

PYNCHON -- Baldwin, C. C. *Pynchon [microform].* Cleveland, OH, Leader Print Co., 1882. p.183-204. Detached from Candee genealogy. Cleveland, 1882. MICROFILM 85/5126 (C) <MicRR>. [G1245].

QR

RICH -- Rich, George. *Genealogy [microform]: descendants of Jonathan Rich.* Columbus, OH, Nitschke Bros., 1892. 39p. MICROFILM 85/7473 (C) <MicRR>. [G1247].

RICHMOND -- Hamel, Claude Charles. *Genealogy of a branch of the Richmond family which came from Rhode Island to Ohio and settled in Amherst Township, Lorain Co., Ohio [microform].* (Amherst, OH,) 1949. 9 leaves. MICROFILM 84/3190 (C). [G1248].

RUGGLES -- Ruggles, Henry Stoddard. *Ancestors of Benjamin Ruggles, Senator from Ohio, 1815-1833; John Ruggles, Senator from Maine, 1834-1840; Nathaniel Ruggles, M.1 from Massachusetts, 1813-1819, Charles Herman Ruggles, M.1. from New York, 1821-1823.* U.S.A. 19__. 61 leaves. MICROFILM 86/6679 (C) <MicRR>. [G1253].

S

SAMPSON -- Todd, Edwin S. *New light on the history of the Sampson family [microform]: with reference to the line of descent through Jane Sampson to her granddaughter Marietta Wood Todd.* Springfield, OH, 1939. 10 leaves. MICROFILM 84/703 (C). [G1253].

SCHELLHOUSE -- Hamel, Claude Charles. *Genealogy of the Schellhouse family of Vermilion Township, Erie County, Ohio* [microform]: which married into the Koppenhafer and Leidheiser family. Amherst, OH, 1948. 6 leaves. Typewritten. MICROFILM 85/8424 (C) <MicRR>. [G1255].

SCHLEGEL -- Schlegal, Kenneth P. *Johann Frederick Schlegel: 1777-1856 [microform]: history of Johann Frederick Schlegel and descendants, 1777 to 1970.* Coshocton, OH, 1970. 2A, 282p. MICROFILM 85/8469 (C) <MicRR>. [G1255].

SCHREINER -- Sheenah, Thomas W. *The Schreiner family history [microform].* Cleveland, OH, 1969. iv, 84 leaves. MICROFILM 85/8428 (C) <MicRR>. [G1257].

SCOTT -- Scott, E. Harrison. *Arthur Martin Scott, 1777-1858 [microform]: his ancestors and descendants.* Dayton, OH, Otterbein Press, 1951. 131p., 12 leaves of plates. MICROFILM 86/5979 (C). [G1257].

SELBY -- Fowler, Fred Erwin. *A short sketch of some of the descendants of William Selby, who was born June 15, 1717, and his second wife Dorothy Bogge [microform].* Brookfield, OH, F.E. Fowler, 1939. 119 leaves, 1 leaf of plates. MICROFILM 86/5741 (C). [G1257].

SHATTUCK -- Hamel, Claude Charles. *Genealogy of a branch of the Shattuck family, early settlers in Brownhelm, Lorain County, Ohio, about 1850 [microform].* Amherst, OH, 1948. 12 1. MICROFILM 85/8433 (C) <MicRR>. [G1259].

SHEEHAN -- Sheehan, Thomas W. *The Sheehan (Sheehand) family [microform].* Cleveland, OH, 1969. iv, 93 leaves, genealogical table MICROFILM 85/8430(C) <MicRR>. [G1259].

SHEEHAN -- Sheehan, Thomas W. *The ancestry of the Sheehan brothers and sisters [microform].* Cleveland, OH, viii, 230 leaves. MICROFILM 86/8651 (C) <MicRR>. [G1259].

SHUPE -- Hamel, Claude Charles. *Genealogy of the Shupe family [microform]: early settlers in Amherst, Lorain County, Ohio.* Amherst, OH, 1948. 7 leaves.
MICROFILM 86/5715 (C) <MicRR>. [G1262].

SIMON -- Hudson, Roland Vernon. *My Simon ascendants [microform].* Tiffin, OH, R.V. Hudson, 1975. 61 leaves.
MICROFILM 86/5975 (C) <MicRR>. [G1262].

SMITH -- Hays, Hugh Howard. *The chronicles of the descendants of Ephraim Smith [microform].* Cleveland, OH, 1942. 176p., 3 leaves of plates.
MICROFILM 85/8438 (C) <MicRR>. [G1266].

SMITH -- Smith, Jesse Lowe. *Smith genealogy (Absalom Smith) Sept. 1933 [microform].* Newark, OH, 1964. 21 leaves.
MICROFILM 85/8440 (C) <MicRR>. [G1266].

SOUTHWORTH -- Southworth, George C. S. *Descendants of Constant Southworth [microform] 2nd ed.* Salem, OH, Harris & Co., 1897. 32p.
MICROFILM 85/5025 (C) <MicRR>. [G1267].

SPOONER -- Spooner, Thomas. *Records of William Spooner, of Phymouth, Mass., and his descendants [microform].* Cincinnati, OH, Press of F.W. Freeman, 1883. 694p.
MICROFILM 8687 (C). [G1268].

SQUIER -- Hamel, Claude Charles. *Genealogy of a branch of the Squire(?) family that settled in Erie Co., Ohio, and married into the Baatz family of that county [microform].* (Amherst, OH,) 1948. 8 leaves. (Name may be SQUIER). MICROFILM 84/695 (C). [G1268].

STAHL -- Stahl, Jacob Peter. *The Stahl family history [microform].* Dayton, OH, 1924 (Alliance, OH, Bradshaw Print. Co.) 140p.
MICROFILM 85/7949 (C). [G1268].

STAVELY -- Stavely, Frederick W. *The Stavely family of Frederick W. Stavely* *[microform]: the early Stavelys, the Staveleys of Ireland, the Stavelys of America.* Akron, OH, 1969. 175p. MICROFILM 86/5267 (C) <MicRR>. [G1270].

STEEN -- Steen, Moses D. A. *The Steen family in Europe and America [microform]: a genealogical, historical, and biographical record of nearly three hundred years: extending from the seventeenth to the twenieth century.* Cincinnati, OH, Monfort & Co., 1900. 562p MICROFILM 84/8360 (C). [G1271].

STEINHAUER -- Steinhauer, Karl Frederick. *Some genealogical notes on the Steinhauer family, of St. Louis and Denver [microform]: originally from the Pfalz, or Palatinate, of Germany.* Springfield, OH, Weber and Harrison, 1931. 4p., 1 leaf of plates, geneal. table. MICROFILM 86/6106 (C) <MicRR>. [G1271].

STILES -- Smith, Sarah Augusta Prior. *Abram Stiles (Styls and Styles), John Milliken (Milligan and Milligin) [microform].* Columbus, OH, 1920. 35 leaves. Cover title: The Milliken and Milligan family of Pennsylvania and Ohio. A collection of data needed to obtain membership in the Daughters and Sons of Revolution societies, for the descendats of Abram Stiles and John Milliken, especially for descendants of John Prior and wife Patience Milliken, consisting of manuscript leaves with mounted photographs fastened together in binder. MICROFILM 85/7951 (C). [G1272].

STEWART -- Stewart, Mrs. Sallie Giesy, et al. *The Stewarts of Coitsville [microform] a history of Robert and Sarah Stewart, of Adams County, Pa., and their descendants with a part of their ancestors.* Youngstown, OH, T. Kerr & Son, 1899. 190, 8p. 9 leaves of plates. MICROFILM 83/5929 (C) <MicRR>. [G1274].

STEWART -- Stewart, W.B. *A Stewart family and some others [microform]* Cleveland, OH, Gates Press, 1947. 199p., 10 leaves of plates. 1 genealogical table folded in pocket. MICROFILM 86/6787 (C) <MicRR>. [G1274].

STEWART -- Hamel, Claude Charles. *Genealogy of John Stewart, brother of Walter Stwart, of Londonderry, N.H., Boxford, Hopkinton, and Blandford, Mass., and Suffield Conn.* [microform] Amherst, OH, 1951. 5 leaves. MICROFILM 86/6825 (C) <MicRR>. [G1274].

SULLIVAN -- Sullivan, Oscar Matthias. *Jeremiah Sullivan of Summit County, Ohio* [microform]: *his descendants and collateral lines.* St. Paul, MN, 1942. 17, 6 leaves MICROFILM 86/6826 (C) <MicRR>. [G1274].

SWANGO -- NAS. *A History of the Swango family* [microform] Eaton, OH, 1959. 132p. MICROFILM 85/8480 (C) <MicRR>. [G1275].

SWASEY -- Swasey, Benjamin Franklin. *Genealogy of the Swasey family* [microform]: *which includes the descendants of the Swezey families of Southhold, Long Island, New York and the descendants of the Swayze families of Roxbury, now Chester, New Jersey.* Cleveland, OH, Priv. print for A. Swasey, 1910. MICROFILM 85/7873 (C) <MicRR>. [G1275].

T

TOPE -- Tope, Melancthon. *History of the Tope family* [microform]: *setting forth a full account of the trials, sucesses, pecular characteristics, ocupations &c., of this race of people in this country down to date.* Bowertown, OH, Patriot Office, 1896. 78p. MICROFILM 84/8296 (C) <MicRR>. [G1282].

TORRENCE -- Stewart, Harriet Rebecca Torrence. *Chart of the Torrence, Findlay, Brownson, Paull, Irwin, McDowell and Smith families of Pennsylvania* [microform]: *published as a memorial to Hon. John Findlay*

Torrence of Cincinnati by his sister (author).
Cincinnati, OH, Henderson-Achert-Krebs Lith.
Co., 1894. 1 sheet geneal. table.
MICROFILM 86/5215 (C) <MicRR>. [G1282].

TOWNSEND -- Cummings, Marian Sill. *William
Townsend of Tyringham, Massachusetts
[microform]: his ancestors and descendants
with allied Tolman, Sill, Skinner, Hitchcock,
Bennett, and Hiller.* East Cleveland, OH, M.S.
Cummings, 1932. 42, 8p., 1 coat of arms.
MICROFILM 84/3209 (C). [G1283].

TRUESDELL -- Truesdell, Wesley E. *Twelve
generations from the colonial immigrant to the
present time [microform].* NP, 1938. 11p.
Cover title: Turesdell family record:
Massachusetts, Connecticut, New York, Vermont,
Ohio. MICROFILM 85/3258 (C). [G1285].

UV

VANDERCOOK -- Neikirk, Floyd Edwin. *Some
descendants of Isaac Vandercook, b. 1682, d.
1750 [microform]: through Michael Vandercook,
member of the Committee of Safety, soldier of
the Revolution, Albany Militia.* Clyde, OH,
1953. 54 leaves. Typescripts (typewritten).
MICROFILM 85/8483 (C) <MicRR>. [G1287].

Van ETTEN -- Scott, Eva Alice. *Jacobus
Jansen van Etten [microform]: some ten
generations in America of Jacobus Jansen Van
Etter, immigrant from Etten, North Brabant,
Holland to Kingston, New York, about 1663.*
Youngstown, OH, Edwards Bros., 1950. xx, 164,
17p. MICROFILM 86/8235 (C) <MicRR>. [G1287].

W

WADSWORTH -- Baldwin, C. C. *Wadsworth
[microform].* Cleveland, OH, Leader Print Co.,
1882. p. 205-215. From the author's Candee
genealogy. Cleveland, 1882.
MICROFILM 85/5186 (C) <MicRR>. [G1289].

WAGNER -- Kintner, Nannie Wagner. *History of the Wagner family [microform].* Carrollton, OH, Carroll chronicle press, 1917. 12p. MICROFILM 85/8555 (C) <MicRR>. [G1289].

WARD -- Ward, Henry Parker. *A memorial of Hudson Champlin Ward (1830-1897) [microform]: setting forth a manner so personal that it will interest his most immediate friends only... and a chapter memorial of his deceased eldest son, William Vines Ward.* Columbus, OH, 1899. 163p. Limited edition: 50 copies (signed). MICROFILM 85/5491 (C) <MicRR>. [G1291].

WARD -- Ward, Henry Parker. *The life of Dr. Isaac Blowers Ward (1800-1843) and of his wife Anna Vines (1803-1852) [microform]: together with some accounts of their near relatives...: also the complete genealogy of Dr. Ward's descendants to A.D. 1900.* Columbus, OH, 1900. 251p. Limited ed. of 35 copies. MICROFILM 37385 (C). [G1291].

WATERS -- Waters, Wilson. *Ancestry of the Waters family of Marietta, Ohio [microform].* Marietta, OH, 1882. 31p. MICROFILM 74463 (C). [G1294].

WATERS -- Sisson, Eliza Paddock Waters. *Reminiscences of the Bradford and Waters families [microform].* Marietta, OH, J. Mueller & Son, 1885. 16p. MICROFILM 85/5199 (C). [G1294].

WEBB -- Hamel, Claude Charles. *Genealogy of a branch of the Webb family [microform]: which came to Amherst Township, Lorain County, Ohio in 1814 or 1815.* Amherst, OH, 1948. 4 leaves. MICROFILM 86/6833 (C) <MicRR>. [G1295].

WEBER -- Hamel, Claude Charles. *Genealogy of the Weber family of Elyria, Lorain County, Ohio, which married into the Hamel family of Amherst, Ohio [microform].* Amherst, OH, 1948. 4 leaves. MICROFILM 86/5256 (C) <MicRR>. [G1295].

WEEKS -- Weeks, Frank Edgar. *Genealogy of Francis Weekes, of Providence, R.I., Gravesend, Hempstead and Oyster Bay, L.I. and collateral lines, Bowne, Burrowes, Carpenter, Cooke, Cornell, Davenport, De Forest Emery, Feake, Fones, Freeman, Goodwin, Fowler, Hoag, Ireland, Jansen, Kierstede, Kip, Montagne, Mosher, Paddy, Reddocke, Sands, Stevenson, Sutton, Taber, Thorn, Warren, Winthrop [microform].* Kipton, OH, 1938. ca. 750p. MICROFILM 85/8775 (C) <MicRR>. [G1295].

WEITKAMP -- Weitkamp, Arthur Robert. *The genealogy of the Weitkamps [microform].* Cincinnati, OH, 1941. 51 leaves. MICROFILM 85/8761 (C) <MicRR>. [G1296].

WELLS -- Roe, Mary Josephine. *Genealogy of Gen. James Wells and descendants, 1883-1892 (sic) [microform].* Cincinnati, OH, Webb Stationery & Print Co., 1892. 142p. MICROFILM 12366 (C). [G1296].

WIANT -- Prather, Rena Wiant. *Waint family genealogy, 1782-1970 [microform].* Springfield, OH, Quality Letter Shop, 1970. 40, vi leaves. MICROFILM 82/683 (C) <MicRR>. [G1297].

WINTERMUTE -- Wintermute, J. P. *The Wintermute family history [microform].* Delaware, OH, 1900. 335p. MICROFILM 85/9502 (C) <MicRR>. [G1303].

WOGAMAN -- Kuhns, Ezra McFall. *Wogaman, Burkett, Holdery [microform].* Dayton, OH, 1948. 11p. MICROFILM 86/6835 (C) <MicRR>. [G1304].

WOODWORTH -- Monson, Marie. *A genealogy of Richard Woodworth, 1758 Ireland - 1843 Ohio, Revolutionary War, his wife Sarah Ann Robinson and collateral families [microform].* North Bend, OR, Monson, iv, 79 leaves. MICROFILM 85/8460 (C) <MicRR>. [G1306].

WRIGHT -- Wright, Edman Wait. *Wright family history [microform]*. Elyria, OH, 1961. 58p. MICROFILM 85/8109 (C) <MicRR>. [G1307].

XYZ

ZEHE -- Sheehan, Thomas W. *The Zehe family history [microform]* Cleveland, OH, 1972. iv, 62 leaves. MICROFILM 85/8463 (C) <MicRR>. [G1309].

ZORBAUGH -- Zorbaugh, Chalres Louis. *Ancestral trails [microform]: history of the Zorbaugh family, the Evans family, the McClure family, the Harvey family, the Clapp family.* Wooster, OH, Collier Print Co., 1941. 267p., 1 leaf of plates. "Limited edition of 100 copies". MICROFILM 87/6324 (C) <MicRR>. [G1309].

360

BIBLIOGRAPHIC SOURCES

GRUNDSET, Eric B. & Bebe, Metz. Library Catalog, Volume Three Centennial Supplement: Acquisitions 1985-1991. Washington, DC, NATIONAL SOCIETY of the DAUGHTERS of the AMERICAN REVOLUTION, 1992.

KAMINKOW, Marion J. Genealogies In The Library of Congress. Baltimore, 1972. 2. v. A-J and L-Z.

KAMINKOW, Marion J. Genealogies In The Library of Congress, Supplement 1972 - 1976. Baltimore: Magna Carta Book Company, 1976.

KAMINKOW, Marion J. Genealogies In The Library of Congress, Second Supplement 1976 - 1986. Baltimore: Magna Carta Book Company, 1987.

KAMINKOW, Marion J. A Complement To Genealogies In The Library of Congress. Baltimore: Magna Carta Book Company, 1981.

LIB. OF CONGRESS STAFF Genealogies Cataloged in the Library of Congress Since 1986. Washington, DC, Cataloging Distribution Service, Library of Congress, 1991.

LIB. OF CONGRESS STAFF Local History & Genealogy, Reference Collection, Author/Title Index & Shelflist. Washington, DC, March 16, 1993.

NGS LIBRARY STAFF National Genealogical Society, Library Book List, 5th Edition. Arlington, Virginia, National Genealogical Society. 1988.

NGS LIBRARY STAFF National Genealogical Society, Library Book List, 5th Edition Supplement. Arlington, Virginia, National Genealogical Society. 1989.

MICHAELS, Carolyn Leopold and Kathryn S. Scott. Library Catalog, Volume One, Second Revised Edition, Family Histories and Genealogies. Washington, DC, National Society of the Daughters of the American Revolution, 1983.

MICHAELS, Carolyn Leopold and Kathryn S. Scott. Library Catalog, Volume One - Supplement - Family Histories and Genealogies. Washington, DC, National Society of the Daughters of the American Revolution, 1984.

VIRDIN, Donald O. Virginia Genealogies and Family Histories. Bowie, Maryland, Heritage Books, Inc., 1990.

VIRDIN, Donald O. Pennsylvania Genealogies and Family Histories. Bowie, Maryland, Heritage Books, Inc., 1992.

SUPPLEMENTAL OHIO FAMILY
HISTORY & GENEALOGY SOURCES

The following is a list of Library of Congress reference material, with the Library's call numbers, related to Ohio. Material cited is from the Library of Congress History & Genealogy Section Reference Collection, Author/Title Index & Shelflist, dated March 16, 1993. Similar or identical material is often available from historical society and major genealogical libraries in Ohio and, occasionally, in other major collections.

Ohio.   Adjutant general's dept.
The official roster of the soldiers of the American revolution buried in the state of Ohio. Dailey, Jane Frances (Dowd).
E255 .038 LH&G.

Ohio.   Roster commission.
Official roster of the soldiers of the state of Ohio in the war of the rebellion., 1861-1866...
E525.3 .038 LH&G.

Ohio.   Adjutants general's dept.
Roster of Ohio soldiers in the War of 1812.
E359.5.02 03 1968 LH&G.

Ohio.   Auditor of State
A short history of Ohio land grants.
E495 .028 1955 LH&G.

Ohio.   State Library, Columbus
County by county in Ohio genealogy.
Z1323 .044 1977 LH&G.

Ohio 1810 tax duplicate: Petty, Gerald McKinney.
F490 .P44 LH&G.

Ohio 1820 census index. Jackson, Ronald Vern.
Teeples, Gary Ronald, joint author. United States. Census Office, 4th census, 1820.
F490 .J32 LH&G.

Ohio 1825 tax duplicate.
   Index of the 1825 tax duplicate.
   F490   .P43 LH&G.

Ohio 1830 census index.   Jackson, Ronald Vern.
   Teeples, Gary Ronald, joint author. United
   States. Census Office, 5th census, 1830.
   F490 .J325 LH&G.

Ohio 1840 census index.   Jackson, Ronald Vern.
   Teeples, Gary Ronald, joint author. United
   States. Census Office, 6th census, 1840.
   F490 .J33 LH&G.

Ohio authors and their books;
   Coyle, William, ed.
   Z1323 .C6 LH&G.

Ohio biographies,   portraits,   and   histories
   index /
   Jackson, Ronald Vern.
   Z1323 .J3 1982 LH&G.

Ohio cemeteries /
   Smith, Maxine Hartmann.   Ohio Genealogical
   Society.
   F490 .03618 1978 LH&G.

Ohio cemeteries.
   Klaiber, Teresa Lynn Martin,
   1949 - Ohio Genealogical Society
   F490 .03618 1978 Suppl LH&G.

Ohio cemetery records
   Bentley, Elizabeth Petty
   F490 .0362 1984 LH&G.

Ohio city & county directories
   Z1323 .P49 1986 LH&G.

Ohio city & county directories
   Phillips, W. Louis
   Z1323 .P49 1986 LH&G.

Ohio county area key /
   Flavell, Carol Willsey. Clint, Florence, joint
   author. Area key. Z1323 .F57 LH&G.

Ohio Family Historians.
1830 Federal population census, Ohio: Index.
Ohio Library Foundation, Columbus.
F490 .O363 LH&G.

Ohio Family Historians
Index to the 1850 Federal population census of
Ohio. United States. Census Office. 7th
census, 1850.
F495 .O35 LH&G.

Ohio genealogical guide /
Bell, Carol Willsey.
F490 .B45 1984 LH&G.

Ohio genealogical periodical index:
Bell, Carol Willsey.
Z1323 .F58 1983 LH&G.

Ohio Genealogical Society.
First families of Ohio.
F490 .F49 1982 LH&G.

Index to official roster of Ohio soldiers in the
war with Spain, 1898-1899.
E725.8 .B76 1991 LH&G.

Ohio, the cross road of our nation, records and
pioneer families.
Ohio Genealogical Society.
F490 .O39 LH&G.

Ohio Genealogical Society. Erie County Chapter.
Ohio Veteran's Home death records.
F490 .O4 1984 LH&G.

The Ohio Guide,
Writers' program. Ohio.
F496 .W96 LH&G.

Ohio guide to genealogical sources /
Bell, Carol Willsey
Z1323 .B453 1988 LH&G.

Ohio handbook of the Civil War.
Harper, Robert S.
E525 .H3 LH&G.

Ohio Historical Society
Central Ohio local government records at the
Ohio Historical Society / Matusoff, Karen L.
Z1323 .O45 1978 LH&G.

Ohio Historical Society. Archives Library
Guide to the Ohio county and municipal records
for urban research.
CD3447 .A1 Y66 LH&G.

Ohio in the war;
Reid, Whitelaw, 1837-1912.
E525 .R34 LH&G.

Ohio Lands:
Bell, Carol Willsey
F490 .B452 1983 LH&G.

Burke, Thomas Acquinas
HD243.O3 B87 1989 LH&G.

Ohio lands and their history /
Peter, William E. (Edwards), 1857-1952.
HD243.O3 P4 1979 LH&G.

Ohio lands, Chillicothe Land Office
Clark, Marie Taylor
F490 .C55 1984 LH&G.

Ohio lands south of the Indian boundary line /
Clark, Marie Taylor
F490 .C55 1984 LH&G.

Ohio Library Foundation, Columbus
1820 Federal populations census, Ohio: Index.
United States. Census Office, 4th census.
F490 .O367 LH&G.

Ohio local and family history sources in print.
Z1323 .A3 1984 LH&G.

Ohio marriages
Smith, Marjorie Corrine, 1910-
F490 .S53 1980 LH&G.

The Ohio Open Records Law and Genealogy.
Fenley, Ann
F490 .F36 1989 LH&G.

Ohio place names:
   Overman, William Daniel, 1901-
   F492 .O8 LH&G.

Ohio resources for genealogists.
   Douthitt, Ruth Long.
   Some references for genealogical searching in
   Ohio. 1971.
   F490 .D68 1971 LH&G.

The   Ohio   Society,   Sons   of   the   American
   Revolution.
   Sons of the Revolution.   Ohio Society
   E202.4. O3 A6 1988 LH&G.

Ohio source records from the Ohio Genealogical
   Quarterly.   Genealogical Publishing Co.
   F490 .O385 1986 LH&G.

Ohio towns names.
   Overman, William Daniel, 1901-
   F489 .O8 LH&G.

Ohio Valley genealogies, relating chiefly to
   families in Harrison, Belmont and Jefferson
   Counties   in   Ohio,   and   Washington,
   Westmoreland,   and   Fayette   Counties   in
   Pennsylvania.
   Hanna, Augustus, 1863-1950
   F516 .H24 1968 LH&G.

Ohio Valley History, West Point to Lewisport.
   Bolin, Daniel Lynn
   Z1251.O4 B64 LH&G.

Ohio wills and estates to 1850
   Bell, Carol Willsey
   F478 .B44 LH&G.

Ohio's Western Reserve
   Lindsey, David
   F497.W5 15 LH&G.

CROSS-REFERENCE TABLE OF FAMILY NAMES

This cross-reference table lists family names given in titles and accompanying descriptive statements recorded in this bibliography. Note that hyphenated names, such as FOX-JONES are, almost always, listed separately, e.g. under FOX and under JONES.